CURRENT ISSUES OF

Current Issues of UK Asylum Law and Policy

Edited by
FRANCES NICHOLSON
PATRICK TWOMEY
Human Rights Law Centre
University of Nottingham

Routledge
Taylor & Francis Group
LONDON AND NEW YORK

First published 1998 by Dartmouth and Ashgate Publishing

Reissued 2018 by Routledge
2 Park Square, Milton Park, Abingdon, Oxon, OX14 4RN
711 Third Avenue, New York, NY 10017

Routledge is an imprint of the Taylor & Francis Group, an informa business

A Library of Congress record exists under LC control number: 98071961

ISBN 13: 978-1-138-61341-6 (hbk)
ISBN 13: 978-1-138-61342-3 (pbk)
ISBN 13: 978-0-429-46370-9 (ebk)

Contents

List of Tables

Abbreviations

AIA 1996	Asylum and Immigration Act 1996
AIAA 1993	Asylum and Immigration Appeals Act 1993
ARC	Asylum Rights Campaign
CA	Court of Appeal
CAHAR	Ad Hoc Committee on the Legal Aspects of Territorial Asylum, Refugees and Stateless Persons
CIREA	Centre for Information, Discussion and Exchange on Asylum
CIREFI	Centre for Information, Discussion and Exchange on the Crossing of Borders and Immigration
EC	European Community/ies
ECHR	European Convention for the Protection of Human Rights and Fundamental Freedoms
ECtHR	European Court of Human Rights
ECRE	European Council on Refugee and Exiles
ELR	Exceptional leave to remain
EU	European Union
EXCOM	Executive Committee (of UNHCR)
FCA	Federal Court of Appeal (Canada)
HC	House of Commons
HL	House of Lords
IAA	Immigration Appellate Authority
IAT	Immigration Appeal Tribunal
ICCPR	International Covenant on Civil and Political Rights
ILPA	Immigration Law Practitioners' Association
IND	Immigration and Nationality Directorate
JCWI	Joint Council for the Welfare of Immigrants
JHA	Justice and Home Affairs
KB	King's Bench
LAG	Legal Action Group
LBC	London Borough Council
LJ	Lord Justice

MP	Member of Parliament
NGO	Non-governmental organisation
NHS	National Health Service
QBD	Queen's Bench Division
SSHD	Secretary of State for the Home Department
SI	Statutory Instrument
TEU	Treaty on European Union
UN	United Nations
UNGA	United Nations General Assembly
UNHCR	United Nations High Commissioner for Refugees

Journals and Law Reports

All E.R.	All England Law Reports
A.L.R.	Australian Law Reports
B.H.R.C.	Butterworths Human Rights Reports
B.Y.I.L.	British Yearbook of International Law
C.L.P.	Current Legal Problems
C.M.L.Rev.	Common Market Law Review
Columbia	Columbia Human
H.R.L.R.	Rights Law Review
Corn.Int.L.J.	Cornell International Law Journal
D.L.R.	Dominion Law Reports
Eur.P.L.	European Public Law
E.H.R.R.	European Human Rights Reports
F.C.	Federal Court Reports (Canada)
Georgetown Imm.L.J.	Georgetown Immigration Law Journal
Harvard H.R.J.	Harvard Human Rights Journal
H.L.R.	Housing Law Reports
H.M.S.O.	Her Majesty's Stationery Office
I.C.L.Q.	International and Comparative Law Quarterly
I.H.R.R.	International Human Rights Reports
I.J.Ref.L.	International Journal of Refugee Law
I.L.M.	International Legal Materials
Imm. A.R.	Immigration Appeals
I.N.L.P.	Immigration and Nationality Law and Practice
J.C.M.S.	Journal of Common Market Studies
J.R.S.	Journal of Refugee Studies

N.L.J.	New Law Journal
P.L.	Public Law
R.C.S.	Canadian Supreme Court Reports/Recueil des arrêts de la Cour suprême du Canada
T.L.R.	Times Law Report
U.C.L.A. Law Review	University of California Los Angeles Law Review
U.N.T.S.	United Nations Treaty Series
U.Pitt.L.Rev.	University of Pittsburgh Law Review
W.A.	Written Answer (in Hansard)
W.L.R.	Weekly Law Reports

Reported Case Law

United Kingdom

Adan and Nooh v. Secretary of State for the Home Department, CA, [1997] 1 W.L.R. 1107; [1997] 2 All E.R. 723; Imm. A.R. 251, **101, 118, 119, 120, 121, 138, 139, 159, 180, 236, 241, 250, 254**

Anandanadarajah v. Immigration Appeal Tribunal, CA, [1996] Imm. A.R. 514, **105, 108, 115, 180**

Atif Adli Drrias v. Secretary of State for the Home Department, CA, [1997] Imm. A.R. 346, **189–90**

Baljit Singh v. Secretary of State for the Home Department [1994] Imm. A.R. 42, **148**

Bugdaycay and Others v. Secretary of State for the Home Department [1987] 1 A.C. 514; [1987] 1 All E.R. 940; [1987] Imm. A.R. 250, **73, 170, 181**

Canbolat v. Secretary of State for the Home Department, CA, [1997] Imm. A.R. 442, **78, 160**

Conteh v. Secretary of State for the Home Department [1992] Imm. A.R. 594, **242**

Fothergill v. Monarch Airlines Ltd [1981] AC 250, **112**

Gashi and Nikshiqi v. Secretary of State for the Home Department, IAT, [1997] I.N.L.P. 96, **127, 149, 159, 179**

Gilgham v. Immigration Appeal Tribunal, CA, [1995] Imm. A.R. 129, **171**

Gogo Mustafaraj v. Secretary of State for the Home Department [1994] Imm. A.R. 78, **160**

Hersi and Others v. Secretary of State for the Home Department [1996] Imm. A.R. 569, **255**

Ikhlaq and Ikhlaq v. Secretary of State for the Home Department, CA, [1997] Imm. A.R. 404, **101, 110, 116, 118**

Imad Ali El-Tanoukhi v. Secretary of State for the Home Department, CA, [1993] Imm. A.R. 71, **104, 114**

James v. Eastleigh Borough Council [1990] 2 AC 751, **245**

Kingori v. Secretary of State for the Home Department, CA, [1994] Imm. A.R. 539, **180, 183, 190**

European Court of Human Rights

UN Committee against Torture

Other Jurisdictions

UK-Based Organisations Working on Refugee and Asylum Issues

African Churches Council for Immigration and Social Justice (ACCIS), Unit 6–7, 321 Essex Road, London N1 3PS; tel./fax 0171 704 2331.

AIRE Centre (Advice on Individual Rights in Europe), 74 Eurolink Business Centre, 49 Effra Road, London SW2 1BZ; tel. 0171 924 0927; fax 0171 733 6786.

Amnesty International UK, 99–119 Roseberry Avenue, London EC1R 4RE; tel. 0171 814 6200; fax 0171 833 1510.

Anglo-Philippines Association for Real Togetherness (APART), c/o Ken Strudwick, 46 Hayley Road, Lancing, West Sussex; tel. 01903 763949.

Association of Visitors to Immigration Detainees, c/o Mrs A. Atter, 53 Western Road, Winchester, Hants S022 5AH; tel. 01962 863 317.

Asylum Aid, 244A Upper Street, London N1 1RU; tel. 0171 359 4026; fax 0171 354 9187.

Asylum Medical Care, Psychological and Medical Services, The Surgery, 29 Willoughby Road, London N8 OIE; tel. 0181 967 7010; fax 0181 349 2407.

Asylum Rights Campaign, 46 Francis Street, London SW1P 1QN; tel. 0171 798 9008; fax 0171 798 9010.

British Agencies for Adoption and Fostering (BAAF), Skyline House, 200 Union Street, London SE1 0LY; tel. 0171 593 2000; fax 0171 593 2001.

Campaign to Close Campsfield, c/o 111 Magdalen Road, Oxford OX4 1RQ; tel. 01865 724452/ 726804.

Children's Legal Centre, University of Essex, Wivenhoe Park, Colchester CO4 3SQ; tel. 01206 873820/872466; fax 01206 874026.

Christian Action for Justice in Immigration Law, c/o Iona Community, Pearce Institute, Govan, Glasgow G51 3UU.

Commission for Racial Equality, Elliot House, 10–12 Allington Street, London SW1E 5EH; tel. 0171 828 7022; fax 0171 630 7605.

Detention Advice Service, 244a Upper Street, London N1 1RU; tel. 0171 704 8954; fax 0171 354 9187.

Educational Grants Advisory Service, 501–505 Kingsland Road, London E8 2DY.

Electronic Immigration Network, c/o Rochdale REC, tel. 01706 352374; fax 01798 711259; e-mail ein-admin@mcr1.poptel.org.uk

Evelyn Oldfield Unit, 356 Holloway Road, London.

Free Representation Unit, Room 140, 1st floor, 49–51 Bedford Row, London WC1R 4LR; tel. 0171 831 0692.

Greater Manchester Immigration Aid Unit, 400 Cheetham Hill Road, Manchester M8 7El; tel. 0161 740 7722; fax 0161 740 5172.

Human Rights Watch, 2nd Floor, 33 Islington High Street, London N1 9LH; tel. 0171 713 1995; fax 0171 713 1800; e-mail hrwatchuk@gn.apc.org

Immigration Advisory Service, County House, 190 Great Dover Street, London SE1 4YB; tel. 0171 357 6917; fax 0171 378 0665.

Immigration Law Practitioners' Association (ILPA), Lindsey House, 40/42 Charterhouse St., London EC1M 6JH; tel. 0171 251 8383; fax 0171 251 8384; e-mail ilpa@mcr1.poptel.org.uk

Independent Immigration Support Agency, 3rd Floor, Ladywell House, Hurst Street, Birmingham B5 4BN; tel. 0121 622 7353.

Institute of Race Relations, 2–6 Leeke Street, King's Cross Road, London WC1X 9HS; tel. 0171 837 0041; fax 0171 278 0623.

Interights, Lancaster House, 33 Islington High Street, London N1 9LH; tel. 0171 278 3230; fax 0171 278 4334.

International Refugee Trust, 4 Chiswick Lane North, London W4 2JF; tel. 0181 994 9120; fax 0181 742 0315.

International Social Services in the UK, Cranmer House, 39 Brixton Road, London SW9 6DD; tel. 0171 735 8941; fax 0171 582 0696.

Joint Council for the Welfare of Immigrants (J.C.W.I.), 115 Old Street, London EC1V 9JR; tel. 0171 251 8706/8708; fax 0171 251 8707.

JUSTICE, 59 Carter Lane, London EC4V SAQ; tel. 0171 329 5100; fax 0171 329 5055; e-mail justice@gn.apc.org

Law Centres Federation, Duchess House, 18–19 Warren Street, London W10 5DB; tel. 0171 387 8570; fax 0171 387 8368.

Legal Action Group, 242–244 Pentonville Road, London N1 9UN; tel. 0171 833 2931; fax 0171 837 6094.

Liberty (NCCL), 21 Tabard Street, London SE1 4LA; tel. 0171 403 3888; fax 0171 407 5354.

London Interpreting Project, The Print House, Ashwin Street, London E8 3DL; tel. 0171 923 3437.

Medical Foundation for the Care of Victims of Torture, 96–98 Grafton Road, London NW5 3EJ; tel. 0171 813 7777; fax 0171 813 0011.

Merseyside Immigration Advice Unit, 34 Princes Road, Liverpool L8 1TH; tel. 0151 709 8360; fax 0151 709 4996.

Nafsiyat Intercultural Therapy Centre, 278 Seven Sisters Road, London N4 2HY.

National Association of Citizens' Advice Bureaux, Myddleton House, 115–123 Pentonville Road, London N1 9LZ; tel. 0171 833 2181; fax 0171 833 4371.

National Coalition of Anti-Deportation Campaigns, 22 Berners Street, Brimingham B19 2DR; tel. 0121 554 6947; fax 0121 507 1567.

North Birmingham Mental Health NHS Trust, 71 Fentham Road, Erdington, Birmingham B23 6AL.

North of England Refugee Service, 1st Floor, 19 Bigg Market, Newcastle-upon-Tyne NE1 1UN; tel. 0191 222 0406; fax 0191 222 0239.

Northern Refugee Centre, Jew Lane, off Fitzalan Square, Sheffield S1 2BE; tel. 0114 270 1429.

Praxis, Pott Street, London E2 0EF; tel. 0171 729 7985.

Refugee Arrivals Project, Room 2005, 2nd Floor, Queen's Building, Heathrow Airport, Hounslow, Middlesex TW6 1DL; tel. 0181 759 5740; fax 0181 759 7058.

Refugee Council, Bondway House 3–9, Bondway, London SW8 1SJ; tel. 0171 582 6922; fax 0171 582 9929. Unaccompanied child asylum-seekers panel; tel. 0171 582 4947. RASU (Refugee Advisers' support Unit) tel. 0171 582 9927.

Refuge Legal Centre, Sussex House, 39–45 Bermondsey Street, London SE1 3XF; tel. 0171 827 9090 (administration); tel. 0171 378 6242 (advice); tel. 0171 378 6243 (detention); tel. 0831 598 057 (emergencies); fax 0171 378 1979.

Refugee Legal Group, c/o North Islington Law Centre, 161 Hornsey Road, London N7 6DU; tel. 0171 607 2461; fax 0171 700 0072.

Royal College of Nursing, Immigration Advisory Service, 107 Harley Street, London W1N 1DA; tel. 0171 637 1828; fax 0171 636 8789.

Runnymede Trust, 133 Aldersgate Street, London EC1A 4JA; tel. 0171 600 9666; fax 0171 600 8529.

Scottish Refugee Council, 43 Broughton Street, Edinburgh EH1 3JU; tel. 0131 557 8083/4; fax 0131 556 7617.

Scottish Refugee Council, 98 West George Street, Glasgow G2 1PJ; tel. 0141 333 1850; fax 0141 333 1860.

Southall Black Sisters, 52 Norwood Road, Southall, Middlesex UB2 4DW; tel. 0181 571 9595; fax 0181 574 6781.

Stonewall Immigration Group, 16 Clerkenwell Close, London EC1R 0AA; tel. 0171 336 8860; tel. 0171 336 0620 (immigration); fax. 0171 336 8864; http://www.stonewall.org.uk

UKCOSA, the Council for International Education, 9–17 St Alban's Place, London N1 ONX; tel. 0171 226 3762; fax 0171 226 3373.

UNHCR, Office of the Representative for the UK and Ireland, 21st floor Millbank Tower, 21–24 Millbank, London SW1P 4QP; tel. 0171 828 9191; fax 0171 630 5349.

World University Service, 20 Dufferin Street, London EC1Y 8PD; tel. 0171 426 5800; fax 0171 251 1314.

Contributors' Biographical Details

Peter Billings, Research Student, Faculty of Law, University of Southampton.
Peter Billings LLB, graduated in 1995 from the University of Southampton, where he is currently completing his doctoral studies on comparative asylum determination procedures. He also tutors public law and civil liberties at the university.

Nicholas Blake QC, 2 Garden Court Chambers, London.
Nicholas Blake has practised immigration and asylum law for some 20 years. He is co-author of Macdonald and Blake *Immigration Law and Practice in the UK* (Butterworths, 4th edition, 1995) and was chair of the Immigration Law Practitioners' Association in 1994–98. He has appeared in many of the leading cases in the UK and Europe, including *T., Chahal, Savchenko, Onibiyo,* and *ex parte J.C.W.I.*

Geoffrey Care, Deputy Chief Adjudicator (retd), London; President of the International Association of Refugee Law Judges.
Geoffrey Care was admitted as a solicitor in 1953 and moved to Zambia in 1956, where he became an advocate, then took silk and served as a High Court Judge. He was later admitted as an attorney in Botswana and worked as head of the law school at Jos University, Nigeria. On his return to the UK in 1979, he became an immigration adjudicator, and from 1993 was chairman of the Immigration Appeals Tribunal. He served as deputy chief adjudicator from 1988 until 1996 and is currently president of the International Association of Refugee Law Judges which was set up in September 1997.

Richard Dunstan, Policy Executive at the Law Society and Secretary to the Law Society's Immigration Law Subcommittee.
Richard Dunstan was refugee officer at Amnesty International UK from 1986 until 1997. He is author of the AIUK reports *Prisoners with a voice: asylum seekers detained in the United Kingdom* (1994), *Playing human pinball: Home Office practice in "safe third country" asylum cases* (1995), *Slamming the door: the demolition of the right of asylum in the United Kingdom* (1996),

and *Cell culture: the detention and imprisonment of asylum-seekers in the United Kingdom* (1996).

Dr Maknun Gamaledin-Ashami, Policy and Monitoring Officer, City Parochial Foundation, London.
Dr Maknun Gamaledin-Ashami has worked since 1990 as policy and monitoring officer for two London-based charitable trusts, the City Parochial Foundation and the Trust for London. Recent refugee-related studies include research on refugee community organisations in London and issues of identity, the role of mother-tongue schools, and homelessness in London among young people from the Horn of Africa. He gained a PhD in social and political science at the University of Cambridge in 1985, after which he worked at the Refugee Studies Programme, Oxford, as a senior research officer and manager of the Refugee Participation Network.

Madeline Garlick, Researcher, JUSTICE, London.
In 1996–97 Madeline Garlick worked as a researcher with JUSTICE, the British section of the International Commission of Jurists, on the JUSTICE/ILPA/ARC project on refugee law reform issues in the UK. She practised as a lawyer in the refugee law and general litigation area in Melbourne, Australia, until 1995. A year later she completed an LLM at the University of Cambridge, before moving to work for a year at JUSTICE. In 1997 she moved to Sarajevo, Bosnia-Herzegovina, to work as legal advisor to the Commission for Real Property Claims of Refugees and Displaced Persons (CRPC), set up under the Dayton Peace Agreement.

Selina Goulbourne, Head of Law, University of Coventry.
Selina Goulbourne is principal lecturer in law at the School of International Studies and Law, Coventry University. She has researched and published on race and the legal profession in England and on access to legal education and the legal profession in Jamaica. Her current research interests include immigration and human rights in Eastern Europe and she is also editor of *Law and Migration* (vol. 6, International Library of Studies on Migration, Edward Elgar, 1998).

Alison Harker, Senior Field Officer, City Parochial Foundation, London.
Alison Harker studied social administration at the London School of Economics and Political Science. She was trained as a social worker at Newcastle University. She has been working in the field of social and

community work for the past 14 years. At present she is the senior field officer for two London based charitable trusts, the City Parochial Foundation and the Trust for London, and has a special interest in refugee issues. Alison Harker is the author of *The Study of the Factors which Influence People to become Refugees and the Forces which Affect their Decision to Return Home or Remain in a Host Country* (1994).

Alison Harvey, Appeal Caseworker, Refugee Legal Centre, London.
Alison Harvey is a barrister and holds degrees in French and Philosophy and Human Rights Law. In addition to her work at the Refugee Legal Centre, she has worked for Asylum Aid and the Asylum Rights Campaign, and with both Amnesty International and JUSTICE. Current areas of research include quality control of representatives in asylum appeals (for the Asylum Rights Campaign).

Dr Colin Harvey, Lecturer, Faculty and School of Law, Queen's University Belfast.
Colin Harvey gained his LLB in law from Lancaster University in 1992 and went on to research his doctoral thesis on refugee and asylum law in the European Union and the UK at the University of Nottingham. On completion of his doctorate he became a lecturer in law at the University of Wales, Aberystwyth and in 1997 was appointed a lecturer at the Faculty and School of Law at Queen's University Belfast.

Caroline Hunter, Barrister and Lecturer, Department of Law, University of Nottingham.
Caroline Hunter is a barrister and lecturer in law at the University of Nottingham. She has written extensively on housing law and is deputy general editor of the *Encyclopedia of Housing Law and Practice* and the *Housing Law Reports,* and joint author of "Homelessness and Allocations" (LAG).

David Jobbins, Refugee Outreach Team Leader, Lambeth, Southwark and Lewisham Health Authority.
In 1995–97 David Jobbins was the specialist health access adviser in the National Development and Policy Team of the British Refugee Council. In this post he worked with the NHS, regional refugee councils and other refugee organisations around the country with the objective of improving the access to and appropriateness of NHS services for refugee communities. Before that he worked for a number of Health Authorities in London over a period of seven years in a variety of roles covering service and capital development

issues. He sits on the London Division Child Placement Panel of Barnados.

Dr Tom Lam, Research Fellow and Administrative Head of the Centre for Chinese Studies, University of the South Bank, London.
Tom Lam arrived in the UK in 1979 as a refugee. He studied geography at Reading and the London School of Economics and has worked for a Greenwich health project on the Vietnamese and primary health care.

Anne Owers, Director, JUSTICE, London.
Anne Owers has been director of JUSTICE, the British section of the International Commission of Jurists, since 1992, and as such co-directed the JUSTICE/ILPA/ARC project on refugee law reform issues in the UK. Her other positions include membership of the Lord Chancellor's Advisory Committee on Legal Education and Conduct, and chair of the trustees of the Refugee Legal Centre. Before her appointment to JUSTICE she was general secretary of the Joint Council for the Welfare of Immigrants (JCWI) in 1986–92.

Dr Michael Peel, Senior Medical Examiner, Medical Foundation for the Care of Victims of Torture, London.
Dr Michael Peel qualified from St Mary's Hospital, London, in 1978. He has specialist qualifications in both general practice and occupational medicine and is currently a senior lecturer and honorary consultant at the United Medical and Dental Schools of Guy's and St Thomas's Hospitals. He has been seeing patients regularly at the Medical Foundation for the Care of Victims of Torture for the purpose of writing medical reports since January 1993. In the last five years, he has spent short periods working in Afghanistan, Mozambique and Angola. Papers by him based on his experiences of helping Zaïrean asylum seekers, and a follow-up study of Algerians have been published in the British Medical Journal.

Simon Russell, Refugee Officer, Amnesty International UK, London.
Simon Russell graduated in politics and Russian in 1989 and then worked as a counsellor at the Hebrew Immigrant Aid Society in Rome for a year. He moved to work in Israel and the former Soviet Union until 1992 when he returned to the UK to work at the Refugee Legal Centre. He took up his current post as a refugee officer for the UK section of Amnesty International in October 1997.

Dallal Stevens, Lecturer in Law, School of Law, University of Warwick.
Dallal Stevens qualified as a solicitor in 1990 and in the same year was appointed as a lecturer in law at the University of Warwick. She is involved in teaching common law and competition law at undergraduate and postgraduate level. Her research interests include competition law and asylum law and policy, on which she has written widely.

Dr Hugo Storey, Immigration Appellate Authority adjudicator; Honorary Research Fellow, University of Leeds.
Hugo Storey was a Council of Europe human rights research fellow, before becoming a lecturer and now an honorary research fellow in the Department of Law at the University of Leeds. He is co-editor of *Butterworths Immigration Law Service* and of the recent publication *Asylum Law*. He is a full-time adjudicator with the UK Immigration Appellate Authority and also a member of the Council of the International Association of Refugee Law Judges. The views expressed in this paper are the personal views of the author only.

Dr Rachel Trost, Lecturer in Law, Faculty of Law, University of Southampton.
Rachel Trost, LLB, Dr. en droit, has been involved in teaching at the University of Southampton for a number of years, and has taught subjects including human rights and immigration law. She was associate professor at the universities of Paris I and II in 1988–89.

Dr Charles Watters, Lecturer in Mental Health, Tizard Centre, University of Kent.
Dr Charles Watters has experience in both mental health services research and in health services management. In 1987–90 he was responsible for evaluating a project in inner city Bristol aimed at improving mental health services for black and ethnic minorities. He then worked for Bristol and District Health Authority where he had responsibility for developing and negotiating mental health contracts. His research centres on the areas of "race", culture and mental health. He is currently working on a book with Dr Suman Fernando on *Race Culture and Mental Health in Europe*, which includes material on the problems faced by refugees and asylum seekers.

Dr Craig Young, Senior Lecturer, Department of Environmental and Geographical Sciences, Manchester Metropolitan University.
Dr Craig Young is senior lecturer in geography at the Department of Environmental and Geographical Sciences at Manchester Metropolitan

University. He gained his BSc and PhD in geography from Edinburgh University. His research interests lie in the area of human geography, including the role of representations of geography and place in social, economic political and cultural processes.

The Editors

Frances Nicholson, Airey Neave Research Fellow, Department of Law, University of Nottingham.
As Airey Neave research fellow in 1996–97, Frances Nicholson researched aspects of UK asylum law and policy, organised a conference on "Refugee Rights and Realities" and is co-editor with Patrick Twomey of two edited collections of papers from the conference, of which this is one. Formerly deputy editor of *Keesing's Record of World Events*, she completed an MPhil in International Relations at Cambridge in 1994. She is now continuing her research into UK and European asylum and refugee policy on a freelance basis.

Patrick Twomey, Lecturer in law, Human Rights Law Centre, University of Nottingham.
Patrick Twomey specialises in human rights law with particular emphasis on refugees. He has taught human rights at summer schools and courses at the College of Europe Bruges, Belgium, and the Aabo Akademi, Finland, the University of Malta, the University of Veliko Turnovo, Bulgaria, and in Estonia for the EC PHARE Democracy Project. He directed the Airey Neave-funded asylum project at Nottingham where he teaches an LLM course on the international protection of refugees. He is co-editor with Frances Nicholson of *Refugee Rights and Realities: Evolving International Concepts and Regimes* (CUP, forthcoming, 1998).

Introduction

> I asked myself with anxiety which flag would the ship sail – Norwegian, German, English? And then I saw floating above the stern the Union Jack, the flag under which so many refugees, Italian, French, Hungarian and of all nations have found asylum. I greeted the flag from the depth of my heart (1876).[1]

Peter Kropotkin's appreciation for the sanctuary offered to him by the United Kingdom ought to be tempered by the fact that as soon as it became possible for foreigners, and particularly the underprivileged, to reach these shores in any significant numbers, the liberalism of late 19th century policy of admission for political activists was replaced by one of restriction and exclusion. The time between the Aliens Act 1905 and the Asylum and Immigration Act 1996 has been marked by legislation and regulations which breach the spirit and letter of the UK's international legal obligations. It has also been characterised by the political stoking of prejudice and fear amongst the putative host population, whether with regard to the "identity" of the nation or to its economic well-being.

> Many asylum-seekers already experience a "climate of fear" ... with even young schoolchildren talking about them as "bogus, welfare scroungers, beggars, dirty and disgusting". There is ready encouragement all around, from Lord Tebbit's repeated rejection of multi-cultural Britain, to the Sun's claim that 3,000 gypsies are heading for Britain "to milk the benefits system" (1997).[2]

Although the Labour government elected in May 1997 announced a review of asylum procedures and policy it remains unclear at the time of writing what reforms, if any, will actually be introduced. Mindful of this, the chapters in this book combine to make a forceful case for a comprehensive review with the goal of a structured policy on asylum seekers which upholds the UK's international human rights obligations to provide protection from

1 Kropotkin, P., *Memoirs of a Revolutionary* (London, 1899) p. 37, quoted in Dummett, A. and Nicol, A., *Subjects, Citizens, Aliens and Others: Nationality and Immigration Law* (Wiedenfeld and Nicolson, 1990) at p. 93.

2 "Britain's Little Refugee Problem", *Guardian*, 22 Oct. 1997.

persecution. The collection is offered as one contribution to a wide and ongoing debate on the need for fair and effective procedures to replace the piecemeal reactive policies of recent years.

The book brings together 18 essays by a cross-section of authors working on refugee and asylum law and policy and related areas from academic, legal practice, non-governmental, medical and community spheres. Each chapter examines an issue of contemporary interest and originated as one of some 50 papers presented at a conference on *Refugee Rights and Realities* at the University of Nottingham on 30 November 1996. Other papers, more international in focus, which were presented at the conference will be published later in 1998 by Cambridge University Press under the title *Refugee Rights and Realities: Evolving International Concepts and Regimes*. Organised by the Nottingham Human Rights Law Centre, the conference was attended by some 200 delegates, drawn from the government, academia, legal practice and the voluntary sector, from over a dozen countries and was part of an asylum research project funded by the Airey Neave Trust conducted in the Centre. While the conference format comprised nine workshops on distinct themes, the essays included in this collection are organised into two sections.

The First Section

The first section focuses on issues of legal process and policy and covers questions ranging from the development of asylum law and policy in the UK to the country's obligations under international law. Special emphasis is placed on events leading up to the approval of the Asylum and Immigration Act 1996 and on the prospects for reform under the Labour government elected in May 1997.

The first three chapters in this section provide a background to recent developments. Dallal Stevens identifies fundamental flaws in the UK's historical treatment of asylum seekers, flaws that are a recurrent aspect of more recent legislation.

Chapter two by Craig Young examines the inter-relationship between law and geography raised at the time of the debate on the 1996 Act. The representation of space is shown as carrying a political charge, as the Conservative government sought to portray asylum seekers as deviants whose increase in numbers amounted to a potentially uncontrollable threat that required a strong state response.

The third chapter by Richard Dunstan shows how the various Resolutions and Conclusions adopted in 1992–95 by European Union Justice and Home Affairs Council shaped the provisions of the 1996 Act. It argues that, in order both to conceal the Act's links with the obscure and undemocratic process of EU harmonisation and in order to deny the serious failings of previous policy and legal changes, ministers resorted to "bogus" arguments, distorted or partial statistics, and outright untruths.

Chapters four to seven examine procedural and substantive issues of current relevance. Chapter four by Rachel Trost and Peter Billings assesses the impact of the 1996 Act's removal of full appeal rights for unsuccessful asylum seekers from so-called "safe countries of origin". It explores the arguments for a depoliticisation of the process, for refocussing on the individual rather than on numbers and nationalities and for considering comparative experience which has used independent bodies to provide greater openness, objectivity and expertise.

The fifth chapter, by Asylum Adjudicator Hugo Storey, tracks the development of the internal flight alternative (IFA) test as part of the refugee definition in English law from its origins to the July 1997 decision in *ex parte Robinson*.

Chapter six, by Amnesty International Refugee Officer Simon Russell, takes the example of claims based on sexual orientation to investigate the treatment of the concept of "membership of a particular social group" as defined in Article 1A of the 1951 Convention. It examines recent English case law in the light of Canadian and US jurisprudence. While remaining optimistic, it highlights how narrow legalistic, definitional analysis can distract from, indeed bedevil, the provision of protection from persecution.

In chapter seven, Dr Michael Peel of the Medical Foundation for the Care of Victims of Torture briefly outlines some of the problems faced by doctors writing medical reports for asylum seekers.

Chapter eight, by the former Deputy Chief Adjudicator and current President of the International Association of Refugee Law Judges Geoffrey Care, provides an insider's perspective of defects of the 1993 asylum legislation, which have resulted in a system that is both costly and inefficient. He argues that the 1996 Act entrenches those aspects of the 1993 Act which gave rise to bottlenecks in the system.

Chapter nine by Alison Harvey is based on a Refugee Legal Centre research project which comprised statistical and qualitative analyses of some 600 decisions of Special Adjudicators. It looks at the practical and methodological problems of statistical analysis of legal decisions, examines factors affecting the outcome of asylum appeals and emerging trends, and highlights the importance of empirical research in enlarging and refining the terms of the asylum debate.

Chapter 10 by Anne Owers and Madeline Garlick of JUSTICE draws on research undertaken for a 1997 report entitled *Providing Protection: Towards Fair and Effective Asylum Procedures* which identified basic principles that should underlie a fair asylum process. They argue for a full, independent and costed review of the present legislative and procedural structure in order to establish a more coherent and coordinated system which is more transparent and less adversarial in nature and which focuses on the obligation to provide protection to those who need it.

The last two chapters in the first section concentrate on the wider human rights implications of recent UK policy changes and argue for a more human rights based approach. Chapter 11 by Colin Harvey stresses the humanitarian imperative of protection in the interpretation and application of law and policy and the need to explore other aspects of international human rights law applicable to refugees.

In the same vein chapter 12 by Nicholas Blake QC, former Chair of the Immigration Law Practioners' Association, considers the UK asylum regime against the backdrop of the UK's international legal obligations governing admission and expulsion. Examining recent case law in the UK and the European Court of Human Rights, it argues that UK policy should derive from a liberal construction of human rights entitlements afforded by international law instead of the narrow reliance of the 1993 and 1996 Acts on the 1951 Convention: a narrowness of construction that risks consigning the Convention to "desiccation and irrelevance".

The Second Section

The second section of the book is concerned with issues beyond those involved in the quest for refugee status and provides a detailed examination of various social, health and welfare issues of particular concern to refugees and asylum seekers. The subject matter of these chapters ranges from access to health care, housing rights, the education of refugees, and questions of language to employment and race relations, with the contributors reflecting the wide range of disciplines concerned with the day-to-day experience, needs and rights of asylum seekers and refugees in the UK.

The health problems faced by refugees and asylum seekers are the focus of chapters 13 and 14 by David Jobbins and Charles Watters respectively.

The former describes moves by the Department of Health to improve the information provided to newly-arrived asylum seekers on health screening and access to the National Health Service and steps being taken to establish appropriate and effective follow-up health-screening arrangements in certain London health authorities. The latter chapter outlines the implications of recent developments for the mental health of refugees and asylum seekers and the response of local authorities. It identifies refugees' mental health care needs, looking also at the perspectives of refugees themselves. Finally, it considers some theoretical and methodological issues in undertaking research on refugees and suggests that lessons can be learnt from studies of settled minority communities.

Educational issues are the subject of chapters 15 and 16. The former, by Alison Harker and Maknun Gamaledin-Ashami of the City Parochial Foundation, is based on a 1995 study, updated to include information on the current situation, regarding access to education for refugees and asylum seekers. It examines the experience of young male refugees in London and the serious constraints, both educational and social, which they encounter. The next chapter by Tom Lam assesses the language problems faced by the long-established Vietnamese refugee community in London. It reports that the mother-tongue competency of the younger generation of Vietnamese is diminishing with the result that elderly Vietnamese are now alienated, not only from the host population, but also their younger relatives, highlighting the need for a more positive attitude towards the provision of mother-tongue education for minority children in the UK.

Chapter 17 by Selina Goulbourne examines the provisions of the 1996 Act which impose criminal sanctions on employers illegally employing individuals subject to immigration control. It outlines the fears expressed by many groups, including employers' organisations, about the resulting negative impact on race relations and calls for the repeal this section of the Act.

The final chapter by Caroline Hunter describes the government's withdrawal of asylum seekers' rights to housing over the last four years and the practical consequences of these policies. It details the courts' response to these developments, effectively reviving the Poor Law, and the limitations inherent in this response. It represents an appropriate conclusion to this collection for several reasons. Firstly, it highlights how the fear and uncertainty inherent in negotiating the asylum process are compounded by fear and uncertainty regarding access to the basics for survival let alone dignity, thus mirroring the trend of asylum determination in requiring abjectness or destitution before help is forthcoming. It highlights the dehumanisation of the asylum seeker, who is perceived as part of a threatening "flood" when outside the jurisdiction and as an economic burden to be "shipped" between local authorities if they manage to gain entry. Finally, it concludes with a note of expectation, that, as called for elsewhere in this collection, a new government might somehow see change.

This year marks the 50th anniversary of the Universal Declaration of Human Rights, which proclaims in Article 14(1): "Everyone has the right to seek and to enjoy in other countries asylum from persecution". Even at that time a draft article which provided a right to "to seek and to be *granted* asylum" failed to gain sufficient state support to be included in the Declaration. Over the intervening 50 years the level of commitment to the institution of asylum by developed states has plummetted. The UK has followed, and sometimes led, this trend. Whether through harmonisation of standards or delegation of responsibility, UK asylum law and policy of recent years cannot honestly be viewed as being other than an incremental erection of hurdles that undermine individuals' opportunity to seek and to enjoy that which is theirs as of right: asylum from persecution. Overall, this collection examines some of the pitfalls and opportunities before the current government as it faces the task of reforming the asylum regime in the UK. It makes an urgent case for a clearer commitment to principles of rights protection and a more humane regime which complies with the UK's freely undertaken international law obligations.

The Human Rights Law Centre wishes gratefully to acknowledge the financial support of the Airey Neave Trust for the research project in the Centre. It support enabled the Centre to host the 1996 conference which gave rise to this publication. The editors would like to thank the contributors for their original papers which made the conference such a success and for their various revisions made during the editorial stage. We would also like to thank all those who contributed to the smooth running of the conference, including members of the Nottingham Student Human Rights Law Centre, Pat FitzGerald who typeset the book, and Leysa Day, in particular, whose secretarial support was invaluable throughout the research project.

Frances Nicholson and Patrick Twomey
Human Rights Law Centre
University of Nottingham
February 1998

SECTION I

LAW, POLICY AND THE DETERMINATION PROCESS

1 The Case of UK Asylum Law and Policy: Lessons from History?

DALLAL STEVENS

> This country has a proud and consistent record in its treatment of refugees. We will take no lectures from anyone about our willingness to protect those people in real danger of persecution. Our humanitarian record is second to none.[1]

In the United Kingdom, the 1990s have witnessed unprecedented legislative activity in the asylum field. The emergence of two statutes in three years in an area which, until recently, remained remarkably untouched by legislative interference reflects a major change in attitude towards asylum seekers.

Throughout the parliamentary debates on both the Asylum and Immigration Appeals Act 1993 and the Asylum and Immigration Act 1996, government and opposition spokespeople were at pains to proclaim the UK's long-standing humanitarian record in relation to asylum seekers and refugees. This chapter considers the accuracy of such claims, and seeks to place the current debate on asylum law and policy in an historical context. It briefly charts the development of UK asylum policy and anticipates some contemporary issues which have proved particularly problematic.

Historical Background

13th to 18th Century

There is evidence to suggest that England was acting as a country of refuge from as early as the 13th century. Until the late 18th century, however, the word "refugee" had not become a generic term; rather, individuals fleeing

1 Charles Wardle, House of Commons, H.C. Hansard, Vol. 240, Col. 1077, 31 March 1994.

from persecution or oppression were viewed, alongside other foreigners, as "aliens", with nothing to distinguish the normal migrant from those with cause to escape their countries of origin. Between the 13th and 16th centuries, this latter group consisted in the main of victims of religious intolerance. Historically, the large-scale movement of peoples on the basis of religion did not reach its peak until the 16th century and the break with Rome. For England, one of the largest of these religious refugee groups were the Protestant Huguenots who began arriving on English soil from 1559, following the death of Henry II of France and the outbreak of 30 years of civil war.[2] The Spanish rule in the Netherlands under the infamous Duke of Alva also gave rise to a wave of Protestant exiles; but perhaps the best known example of oppression of the Protestant minorities on the continent which led to a flow of asylum seekers to England was the St Bartholomew's Day massacre in Paris in 1572.[3]

English generosity towards religious "asylum seekers" did, however, have its limits. For example, it is recorded that in excess of 15,000 Jews were expelled from England in 1290.[4] Even in the case of Protestants, where it was politically expedient for England to welcome any person claiming to suffer at the hands of Catholic rulers, occasional expulsions were not unknown. Extremism was regarded with great suspicion. In 1561, Queen Elizabeth ordered the Anabaptists to leave the country within 20 days or face imprisonment and confiscation of their belongings.[5]

From the 16th to the 18th century, England saw significant increases in its alien population. While many were "refugees" or "asylum seekers", many were not. The arrival of aliens was tolerated particularly where, as in the case of the Huguenots, it was considered that they brought with them useful skills which could be passed on to the indigenous population. While the ruling classes may have been satisfied with the advantages which migrants brought, the latter's superior skills or their failure to assimilate did occasion some resentment within the local population, particularly amongst artisans who viewed the new arrivals as a threat to their livelihood. Any suggestion of widespread tolerance in this period therefore has to be cautiously advanced.

In the 17th century, one of the more significant events in terms of its impact on the flow of asylum seekers was the revocation of the Edict of Nantes

---

2 Smiles, S., *The Huguenots* (John Murray, London, 1868, 6th edn).

3 Holmes, C., *John Bull's Island: Immigration and British Society, 1871–1971* (Macmillan, 1988), p. 6.

4 Cunningham, *Alien Immigrants to England* (Sonnenschein, 1897), p. 70.

5 Dummett, A., and Nicol, A., *Subjects, Citizens, Aliens and Others* (Weidenfeld and Nicolson, 1990), p. 57.

in 1685 by Louis XIV and the subsequent expulsion of the Huguenots from France. Once more Calvinists were forced to seek refuge with their neighbours across the water, and once more they were apparently welcomed. It was, in fact, the arrival of these new-style migrants which occasioned the first usage of the term "refugee", a word which remained reserved solely for the Huguenots until the end of the 18th century. Not until 1796 did usage of the term "refugee" extend to include "all such as leave their country in times of distress".[6]

Despite the occasional order expelling a particular group once they were established in England, little was done by way of legislation to prevent the initial entry of aliens. With the onset of the French Revolution in 1789 and the wars with France from 1793 to 1815, some limited regulations were introduced. In 1793, an Act was implemented "for establishing regulations respecting aliens arriving in this kingdom, or resident therein, in certain cases".[7] The preamble to the Act is telling:

> Whereas a great and unusual number of persons, not being natural-born subjects of his Majesty ... have lately resorted to this kingdom: and whereas, under the present circumstances, much danger may arise to the publick tranquillity from the resort and residence of aliens, unless due provisions be made in respect thereof.

The importance of this early Act arises not only from the fact that it was the first major enactment of legislation concerning aliens, but also from its anticipation of a number of provisions which would be implemented in the 20th century: the power to refuse "aliens of any description" permission to land; registration of personal details with the Chief Magistrate by all aliens; the possibility of bail for any person who was "not within the description limited by [the] act in the different cases ... mentioned";[8] and a right of appeal within six days.[9] One of the main aims of the law was to ensure that aliens arriving after 10 January 1793 gave to the port officer a written declaration of their names, rank, or occupation as well as details of their place of residence while in the country. Failure to give such a declaration, or giving a false declaration, could lead to expulsion from the realm, transportation for life, or

6 Marrus, M.R., *The Unwanted: European Refugees in the Twentieth Century* (Oxford, 1985), p. 8, citing the *Encyclopaedia Britannica*, 1796.

7 33 Geo. 3, c.4.

8 Para. XXIII.

9 Paras XXXIX and XL.

death if found within the realm after being sentenced to transportation.[10] Masters of vessels were also required to declare on arrival the numbers, names and occupations of any "foreigners" on board their vessels. If they neglected to do so, they could be fined £10.[11] Such a provision, which placed the onus on the ship's captain to police passengers, may be rightly described as a forerunner of the current carriers' liability legislation. The Act went on to empower the King to direct by proclamation or by order in council that "aliens of any description" be refused permission to land if it were "necessary for the safety or tranquillity of the kingdom".[12] Furthermore, regulations were introduced whereby restrictions could be placed on the movements of aliens around the country.[13] As described, provision was made for various penalties for infringement, ranging from fines to capital punishment.[14]

The one issue which received no direct mention was that of asylum or refuge. It fell to later Acts, introduced to continue and amend the 1793 statute which had a life-span of only one year, to indicate whether any special treatment was to be extended to asylum seekers. The 1798 Act, for example, noted in its rather lengthy preamble:

> [W]hereas the refuge and asylum which on grounds of humanity and justice, have been granted to persons flying from the oppression and tyranny exercised in France, and in countries invaded by the armies of France, ... may ... be abused by persons coming to this kingdom for purposes dangerous to the interests and safety thereof; ... it is therefore necessary to make further provisions for the safety of this kingdom with respect to aliens, and particularly to the end that a just distinction may be made between persons who either really seek refuge and asylum from oppression and tyranny, ... and persons who, pretending to claim the benefit of such refuge and asylum ... have or shall come to ... this kingdom with hostile purposes.[15]

Despite this preamble, no further clauses were specifically aimed at refugees. It is interesting to note that in 1798 legislators were already beginning to talk of "abuse" of the asylum process, a term now widely used to justify the

10 Paras III and XXXVIII.

11 Para. II.

12 Para. VII.

13 Para. VIII.

14 For an interesting discussion of the 1793 Act and comparisons with immigration provisions in the 20th century, see Roche, T., *The Key in the Lock* (John Murray, 1969).

15 38 Geo. III, c. 50.

implementation of restrictive asylum laws.

The 19th Century: A Period of Liberalism?

Though the measures introduced towards the end of the 18th century were of some value while the UK was at war with France, their use diminished after 1815, and the expulsion provisions were not generally enforced, despite repeated repeal and reintroduction in amended form until 1826. Thus, between 1793 and 1800, 436 aliens were removed from the kingdom, but in 1801–15 only 218 were removed, and in 1816–23 the figure was down to 17.[16] In 1826, an Act for the Registration of Aliens appeared on the statute book (containing some similar provisions to the 1793 Act),[17] to be repealed and replaced by an Aliens Registration Act of 1836.[18] The main feature of the 1836 Act was its durability: unlike most other acts of its kind, it had no limitation of duration clause, and remained on the statute book until repeal in 1905.[19] It provided for compulsory registration by aliens on arrival, and repeated the obligation contained in the Act of 1793 to declare known aliens on board ship.[20]

Both the 1826 and 1836 Acts contained milder penalties (fines or prison sentences) than preceding statutes and did not permit expulsion for failure to register. In 1848, a further law was enacted granting the government power to expel "when and so often as One of Her Majesty's Principal Secretaries ... [had] Reason to believe ... that for the Preservation of the Peace and Tranquillity of any Part of this Realm it [was] expedient to remove therefrom any Alien".[21] The 1848 Act lasted only one year.[22] In the period 1850 to 1905, no further

---

16 Return of Number of Resident Aliens 1793–1816; Return of Number of Persons sent out of UK under Alien Act, 1816–19; Return of Number of Aliens directed to depart Realm, 1850. Note: the statistics conflict for some years. In 1803, it was reported that the King made a proclamation ordering 1,700 French aliens to quit the country but not being permitted to land on the continent, they returned and were allowed to remain.

17 7 Geo. IV, c. 54.

18 6 and 7 William IV, c. 11.

19 Aliens Act 1905, section 10(2).

20 Paras II and III.

21 11 and 12 Vict., c. 20: "An Act to authorise for One Year, and to the End of the next session of Parliament, the Removal of Aliens from the Realm", preamble.

22 It was re-enacted for Ireland alone in 1882 for three years: Prevention of Crime (Ireland) Act 1882, sections 15, 45 and 46 Vict., c. 25.

aliens' legislation of any significance was implemented.[23]

This apparent reluctance in the latter part of the 19th century to add to the statute book lends support to the view that the much lauded liberalism of the 19th century extended to asylum and refugee policies. One historian notes that the British authorities from 1823 to the end of the century did not expel a single refugee from Britain.[24] While eminent politicians of the day openly supported a liberal policy, the *Times* newspaper carried occasional self-congratulatory articles on British asylum policy:

> Every civilised people on the face of the earth must be fully aware that this country is the asylum of nations, and that it will defend the asylum to the last ounce of its treasure, and the last drop of its blood. There is no point on which we are prouder or more resolute. ... We are a nation of refugees.[25]

Unlike its European neighbours, Britain opened its doors to any refugee who wished to enter; there was no bar. Despite considerable external pressure, and accusations that England was harbouring unsavoury political activists, a "swarm of intriguers" and "heroes of barricades",[26] the British government held true to its open-door policy. This somewhat surprising approach is perhaps best considered as a reflection of the fact that England's experience of refugees, French Huguenots in the main, had been on balance very positive. Far from becoming a burden upon the host nation's purse, many exiles were an asset, bringing with them new skills and wealth. Here, once again, it is important to distinguish the views of the ruling classes from those of the masses. The indigenous population often voiced anti-immigrant sentiments or organised protests,[27] and of course it mattered little to them whether the "alien" was a refugee or immigrant. In addition, certain groups, such as the Irish, were treated particularly harshly by both the governing classes and the people.

Researchers have found it difficult to explain the unusual liberalism of 19th century asylum policy;[28] the issue is undoubtedly complex and no one explanation satisfactory, particularly as it is clear from the conflicting evidence

23 Porter, B., *The Refugee Question in mid-Victorian Politics* (Cambridge University Press, 1979), p. 3; the most that aliens were asked to do from the late 1850s onwards was to show their passports at the ports. *Ibid.*, p. 206.

24 *Ibid.*, p. 1.

25 *Times*, 28 Feb. 1853.

26 From Correspondence respecting Foreign Refugees in London, Parliamentary Papers, 1852.

27 Dummett and Nicol, *op. cit. supra* n. 5, p. 52.

28 See e.g., Porter, *op. cit. supra* n. 23, ch. 7.

provided by articles in the *Times*, parliamentary speeches and the views of refugees themselves that 19th century Britain did face difficult questions over the refugee issue. It, too, had to wrestle with two competing forces: the ideal of humanitarianism and the reality of xenophobia. It is remarkable that the former does, on the whole, seem to have prevailed – at least until the 1870s and 1880s, when the British economy entered a period of decline and the new (Russian and Jewish) refugees were deemed less acceptable than their predecessors.

The Shifting Policies of the 20th Century

1890–1905: The Arrival of a New Act

Signs in the 1870s of declining confidence in the open-door asylum policy developed into outright anxiety by the turn of the century. The large-scale migration of peoples, particularly East European and Russian Jews, stoked this anxiety at a time of economic uncertainty and international tension in the years preceding the First World War. It is estimated that approximately 2.5 million Jews emigrated from Eastern Europe and Russia to Western Europe between 1880 and 1914.[29] Though some commentators have cautioned against labelling the Jewish emigrants as "refugees",[30] there is no doubt that a large number did choose to leave their homelands as a direct result of an increase in anti-Semitic activities, as well as for economic reasons.[31] The numbers who reached the UK fluctuated between 1880 and 1914. One estimate stands at 120,000 East European Jews;[32] another suggests that net immigration in 1881–83 was about 5,000 to 6,000 per year, falling to 2,000–3,000 in 1884–86, and that the numbers remained low until 1890, when expulsion orders were introduced in Eastern Europe.[33] This did not prevent the House of Commons Select Committee on Emigration and Immigration (Foreigners) 1888–89 from noting that the 1836 Aliens Registration Act had, "to a very great extent, been allowed to fall into desuetude,"[34] and from recommending that measures

29 Marrus, *op. cit. supra* n. 6, p. 27.

30 *Ibid.*

31 Note that there is a view that East European and Russian Jews were refugees: e.g. Gainer, B., *The Alien Invasion* (Heinemann, 1972), preface.

32 Marrus, *op. cit. supra* n. 6, pp. 36–37.

33 Gainer, *op. cit. supra* n. 31, p. 3.

34 1889 (311) x, p. iv.

(similar to those contained in the 1836 Act) should be adopted to record the arrival of alien passengers and their details,[35] a recommendation which was promptly implemented.[36] Thus ships' captains were once more required to declare to customs officers at the port of arrival the numbers, names and occupations of known foreigners on board their vessels.

From 1890, it appears that the numbers arriving varied between 3,000 and 7,000 per annum.[37] Though this "wave" of immigrants was much exaggerated, an impression was created both in policy-making circles and amongst members of the public that there was an immigration crisis. This despite the fact that many amongst the Jewish community, who were seen as the greatest threat, were only passing through the UK on their way to the United States. Inaccurate statistical reporting, the decline of British industrial power, worsening economic conditions and an increase in unemployment all had some part to play in a hardening of public attitude towards immigrants and refugees. The worst affected area was the East End of London, which suffered greater economic deprivation and overcrowding than most other quarters of the capital. It was often to this area that impoverished aliens were drawn and it was this area which voiced the loudest anti-immigrant and anti-Semitic sentiments. By the turn of the century, there was a ground-swell of opinion calling for legislation. Jewish resistance to such calls did not gather pace until it was too late.

The politicisation of the alien issue had begun with the report of the Select Committee on Emigration and Immigration in 1889.[38] Though political interest was weak at first, the anti-alien lobby gradually began to exert pressure on the government to implement restrictive legislation. In 1903, the Royal Commission on Alien Immigration was asked to report on the alien question.[39] After hearing extensive evidence, mainly about the poverty, hygiene, overcrowding and miserable condition of many of the immigrants, the Commission recommended the repeal of the 1836 Act and the implementation of new legislation which would give powers to a new Immigration Department to examine all immigrants on arrival to establish whether they were "undesirable" or not. Undesirables were defined as "criminals, prostitutes,

---

35 1889 (311) x, p. xi.

36 1888 (305) xi; 1889 (311) x, and see Garrard, J.A., *The English and Immigration* (Oxford, 1971), p. 28.

37 *Ibid.*

38 1888 (305) xi; 1889 (311) x.

39 Cds 1741 and 1742.

idiots, lunatics, persons of notoriously bad character, or likely to become a charge on public funds".[40] It was also recommended that a Court of Summary Jurisdiction should determine any proceedings taken before it.[41] No mention was made of the particular plight of the asylum seeker or refugee.

The government adopted the Commission's recommendations and introduced the Aliens Bill 1904.[42] This Bill failed to survive parliamentary scrutiny, but was replaced in the next session by a new version: the Aliens Bill 1905.[43] The second Bill included an important variation to the Commission's suggestions in the form of an exemption for refugees from prosecution for political offences. This failed to satisfy the Liberal Party which took up the cause of Jewish and alien rights and vigorously opposed the new proposals. Liberal efforts both in the House of Commons debates and in Committee were to little avail. The single amendment of note to the 1905 Bill was that not only would refugees be exempted from prosecution for political offences, but also refugees fleeing punishment on the grounds of religion or "persecution, involving danger of imprisonment or danger to life and limb, on account of religious belief".[44] With this vital concession won at the last hurdle, the Act received Royal Assent on 11 August 1905.

The Aliens Act granted significant powers to the Secretary of State and put into place an independent administrative regime. The main administrative power was vested in immigration officers, medical inspectors and port Immigration Boards. It was the function of the immigration officer, alongside a medical inspector, to assess whether an immigrant was "undesirable" within the meaning of the Act and should be refused permission to land.[45]

Any immigrant who could prove that he or she was seeking admission to the UK on grounds of religious or political persecution was exempt from the Act's ambit:[46]

> [I]n the case of an immigrant who proves that he is seeking admission to this country solely to avoid persecution or punishment on religious or political grounds or for an offence of a political character, or persecution, involving danger of imprisonment or danger to life or limb, on account of religious belief,

40 *Ibid.*, p. 41, Recommendation 4(c).

41 *Ibid.*, Recommendation 4(d).

42 Aliens Bill 1904, No. 147.

43 Aliens Bill 1905, No. 187.

44 Gainer, *op. cit. supra* n. 31, p.196; Aliens Act 1905, section 1(3).

45 See Aliens Act 1905, section 1(3) for definition of an undesirable immigrant.

46 See Aliens Act 1905, section 1(2).

> leave to land shall not be refused on the ground merely of want of means, or the probability of his becoming a charge on the rates.[47]

For the first time, a refugee was now required to *prove* his or her status, a radical departure from the *laissez-faire* notions of the 19th century.[48]

The power to expel an alien, contingent on specified conditions, was vested in the hands of the Secretary of State, subject to a court recommendation.[49] Aliens subject to expulsion were criminals convicted of imprisonable offences or prostitutes, who had been found wandering without ostensible means of support, or were living in unsanitary conditions due to overcrowding, or those who had entered the UK having committed a non-political offence and who could be extradited.[50] The exclusion from expulsion for individuals who had committed crimes of a political nature was an important concession and offered some security for political refugees. By contrast, persecution on political or religious grounds would not prevent possible expulsion if a refugee fell within one of the expulsion categories of section 3(1) of the Act (cited above).

The Home Secretary was also directly involved in appointments to the appellate bodies, the Immigration Boards for every port, which each comprised three members "having magisterial, business, or administrative experience".[51] It was the role of the Immigration Boards to hear appeals against the decisions of the immigration officers. Basic questions raised on appeal could be decided independently by the Immigration Boards and were binding on the Home Secretary, but more problematic issues – relating to whether a ship was an "immigrant ship", whether an individual was an "immigrant", whether a crime was an extradition crime, or whether an offence was of a political character – had to be referred to the Secretary of State, whose decision was binding on the Boards.[52] The Home Secretary, Herbert Gladstone, was keen to exert as much power as he could to ensure that they approached their duties humanely.[53] In March 1906, he wrote to the Boards in the following terms:

---

47 Aliens Act 1905, section 1(2).

48 Marrus, *op. cit. supra* n. 6, p. 37.

49 Aliens Act 1905, section 3(1)(a).

50 *Ibid.*, section 3(1)(a) and (b).

51 *Ibid.*, section 2. The Secretary of State approved the lists from which the appointments were made.

52 *Ibid.*, section 8(4).

53 Gainer, *op. cit. supra* n. 31, p. 203.

> that, having regard to the present disturbed condition of certain parts of the Continent, the benefit of doubt, where any doubt exists, may be given in favour of any immigrants who allege that they are flying from religious or political persecution in disturbed districts, and that in such cases leave to land may be given.[54]

These directions of the Home Office gave rise to the criticism that Gladstone's enforcement of the Act was lax and to renewed calls for more restrictive legislation. Yet there is evidence to suggest that the Act was applied conscientiously.[55] It was not until the 1910 Annual Report on the Aliens Act that the Inspector provided any statistics on the application of the legislation to refugees.[56] In that report he commented:

> The right of asylum for political and religious refugees is preserved by the Act, which provides that "in the case of an immigrant who proves that he is seeking admission to this country solely to avoid persecution or punishment on religious or political grounds or for an offence of a political character, or persecution, involving danger of imprisonment or danger to life or limb, on account of religious belief, leave to land shall not be refused on the ground merely of want of means, or the probability of his becoming a charge on the rates". It is sometimes assumed, though I have never seen any evidence produced in its support, that under the cloak of this provision crowds of undesirable aliens – violent criminals of every sort and anarchists – have passed into this country without let or hindrance. This assumption is not supported by the facts. The number of immigrants admitted on the sole ground that they were political or religious refugees during the five years was 603, of whom 505 were admitted in 1906 (the year of very disturbed conditions in Russia), 43 in 1907, 20 in 1908, 30 in 1909, and 5 in 1910.[57]

It would seem, therefore, that very few refugees were admitted, despite Gladstone's "benefit of the doubt" plea. The same was not, it appears, true of the "normal" immigrant. Statistics recording the numbers of *immigrants* (as opposed to refugees) rejected in first instance under the Act indicate a relatively low rate of rejection: 935 out of 27,639 aliens subject to inspection in 1906;

54 Letter, addressed by the Secretary of State for the Home Department to Members of the Immigration Boards, 9 March 1906, in Regulations Made by the Secretary of State for the Home Department with Regard to the Administration of the Aliens Act 1905, Cd. 2879.

55 See, for example, the Annual Reports for the Aliens Act 1905, 1906–14.

56 Annual Report for the Aliens Act 1905 for 1910, Cd. 5789.

57 *Ibid.*, p. 36.

975 out of 17,982 in 1907; 724 out of 13,050 in 1908; 1,066 out of 35,755 in 1910.[58] Many of those rejected appealed to the Immigration Boards and were successful.[59]

While the impact of the Aliens Act 1905 on alien admissions may not have been as great as anticipated, it introduced into British policy-making the concept of immigration and refugee control, a concept that was soon to become entrenched. Between 1909 and 1914, a spate of serious offences by criminal aliens combined with mounting international tension led to new legislation.[60]

War Legislation: 1914–20

The Aliens Restriction Act of 1914[61] gave power to the King, through Orders in Council, to impose any restrictions on aliens which appeared necessary. The range of possible restrictions was set out in section 1 of the Act and included prohibitions on landing and embarking, residence restrictions, registration conditions, powers to search, detain and arrest, and powers of deportation.[62] Several Orders were issued as a result of the 1914 Act granting sweeping powers to the Home Secretary. No mention was made of individuals fleeing from persecution but, as the Aliens Act 1905 was still in force, theoretically it could still be applied. However, as HM Inspector noted in his Annual Report for 1914, "[t]he two Acts are based on such widely different principles that there is no similarity in their operation and no continuity in their effects".[63] He therefore considered it pointless to issue a detailed report on the 1905 Act for the year 1914.

The difficulty of applying two quite different statutes may have been felt by those seeking asylum in the UK. There is evidence to suggest that Belgian, Russian and Polish refugees were all subjected to the full force of the

---

58 Annual Reports for the Aliens Act 1905 for the years 1906, 1907 and 1908 (Cds 3473; 4102; 4683). (Garrard, *op. cit. supra* n. 36, p. 107, cites slightly different figures, 931 in 1906; 974 in 1907; 720 in 1908, apparently compiled from the Annual Reports of Her Majesty's Inspectors under the Aliens Act.)

59 In 1906, 796 appealed and 442 were successful; in 1907, 601 appealed and 173 were successful; in 1908, 321 appealed and 112 were successful. Annual Reports for the Aliens Act 1905 for the years 1906, 1907 and 1908 (Cds 3473; 4102; 4683).

60 See Gainer, *op. cit. supra* n. 31, pp. 206–07 for discussion of these events.

61 4 and 5 Geo. 5, c. 12.

62 Aliens Restriction Act 1914, section 1.

63 Annual Report of the Aliens Act 1905 for 1914, Cd. 7969, p. 21.

restrictions issued under the 1914 Act.[64] Case-law of the time also referred to the peculiar problems of admission faced by refugees. In *Rex v. Home Secretary, ex parte Duke of Château Thierry*,[65] the court, in considering the power of the Home Secretary to deport an alien under the Aliens Restriction Act 1914 and the Aliens Restriction (Consolidation) Order 1916, confirmed that protection from expulsion was to be afforded political refugees, but not others, and established clearly that the Secretary of State had vast discretionary power in such matters. It is clear that the judiciary considered that decisions on refugees should be made by the Home Secretary alone without interference by the courts. Investment of such wide discretion in the Home Secretary has continued since then to be a fundamental, and at times worrying, aspect of asylum policy. More recently, there has been a preparedness by some contemporary judges to question ministerial discretion, giving rise to occasional conflict between the executive and judiciary.[66]

An issue of arguably greater concern was the decision, in 1919, to extend the provisions of the Aliens Restriction Act.[67] Despite the recognition that the powers introduced by the 1914 Act were emergency provisions, it was seen fit to extend them for one year and to exercise them "not only in [emergency situations], *but at any time*" (emphasis added). No provision was made for refugees under the new Act and, in its repeal of the Aliens Act 1905, English law lost the statutory protection previously afforded to this vulnerable group.[68] Once the Aliens Order of 1920 came into being, it was evident that the Executive was keen to hold on to the sweeping powers it had been granted during the war. Following the *Duke of Château Thierry* case in 1917, the courts were prepared to accept that such power extended to the definition of a refugee as well as deportation of refugees, and the 1920 Order did nothing to contradict such an assumption. In fact, the Order, while reproducing the same

64 Cesarani, D., "An Alien Concept? The Continuity of Anti-Alienism in British Society before 1940" in *The Internment of Aliens in Twentieth Century Britain*, Cesarani, D., and Kushner, T., eds (Cass, 1993), p. 36; Saunders, D., "Aliens in Britain and the Empire During the First World War", (1985) *Immigrants and Minorities*, Vol. 4, No. 1, pp. 5–27, at 8.

65 *Rex v. Home Secretary, ex p. Duke of Château Thierry* [1917] 1 K.B. 922.

66 See, e.g., *Secretary of State for the Home Department v. Abdi and Gawe* CA [1994] Imm. A.R. 402; *R. v. Secretary of State for the Home Department ex p. Adbi and Gawe* HL 1 W.L.R. 298; [1996] 1 All E.R. 641. See also chapter 11 of this book by Colin Harvey.

67 Aliens Restriction (Amendment) Act 1919, 9 and 10 Geo. 5, c. 92.

68 Aliens Restriction (Amendment) Act 1919, section 16(2).

conditions giving rise to expulsion as contained in the 1905 Act, pointedly omitted the exception for political refugees which had previously existed.[69] This omission was partially mitigated by the Extradition Act 1870, which still applied and which protected against extradition of anyone who had committed a political offence.[70]

The 1914 and 1919 Acts, together with the Aliens Order of 1920, made no provision for appeal to an independent immigration board, as had been partially provided for under the 1905 Act. This lacuna in the legislation was questioned in 1930 by the Jewish Board of Deputies, but while the Home Secretary of the day was sympathetic to the concerns of the Board, he did not consider that the introduction of an immigration board to deal with refusals of leave to land was necessary. Instead, he offered an assurance "that applications for leave to land by persons seeking refuge from persecution will continue to receive sympathetic consideration both at the Home Office and the ports".[71] Interestingly, the question of an appeal in the case of deportation proceedings received more support, and the Home Office agreed, in 1931, to set up an advisory appeal committee in deportation cases, the first occasion in which some checks were placed upon the Home Secretary's discretion. Though the committee only considered 33 cases in four years, the Home Secretary accepted the committee's advice in every case, and it seemed that the committee did not consider itself bound to follow Home Office policy.[72]

The Aliens Order of 1920 permitted the Secretary of State to detain aliens who were in contravention of the Order as well as those who had been refused leave to land.[73] Again, in line with the broad discretion granted to the Home Secretary under the legislation, he could direct an alien to be detained in any manner (where an alien had contravened the Order) or give his approval to places of detention to which aliens refused permission to land could be sent on the direction of an immigration officer. Since the legislation made no exception for refugees or asylum seekers, it was open to an immigration officer or the Secretary of State to detain individuals escaping persecution, if leave to land had been refused. Though the Aliens Order has been severely criticised for the severity and all-embracing nature of its measures, the detention provisions have continued to find favour with contemporary governments.

69 Aliens Order 1920, section 12.

70 Extradition Act 1870, section 3 (1).

71 *Times*, 17 March 1930, p. 22.

72 Report of the Committee on Immigration Appeals ("Wilson Report"), 1967, Cmnd. 3387, pp. 74–5.

73 Aliens Order 1920, section 3(3) and (4).

The Build-up to the Second World War

The continuance of the 1914 and 1919 Acts and subsequent Orders ensured that, prior to the Second World War, Britain had sufficiently restrictive legislation in place to deal with increasing numbers of refugees from Germany. While refugees had to comply with the "means test" and passport requirements included in the provisions,[74] the UK continued the policy of imposing visa restrictions, which had been started during the First World War, although these restrictions were relaxed against most Western European countries. Whereas the legislation earlier in the century had recognised that refugees required special treatment, if not a special regime, the government persisted in the interwar period in applying general immigration laws to refugees. Its view of asylum was uncompromising and unwavering: "We do not ... admit that there is a "right of asylum", but when we have to decide whether a particular political refugee is to be given admission to this country, we have to base our decision ... on whether it is in the public interest that he be admitted".[75] Thus refugees would only be admitted on giving assurances that they would not become a charge on the public funds, that refuge would be temporary, and that employment would be restricted so as not to displace British labour.[76]

Despite the continuity of its own restrictive laws, the UK participated in international discussions on the refugee question. In 1922, Nansen, the High Commissioner for Russian refugees, gained the agreement of over 50 countries to adopt a system of identity documents for refugees, known as the Nansen certificate.[77] Under the auspices of the League of Nations, three Conventions were signed conferring certain basic rights on refugees. The first, the Convention relating to the International Status of Refugees, was agreed in October 1933 and provided basic rights to "Russian, Armenian and assimilated refugees".[78] The UK accepted the Convention subject to certain reservations. The first, and most important, was its insistence that the Convention was "applicable only to Russian, Armenian and assimilated refugees who at the date of the ... accession no longer enjoy the protection of their country of

74 Aliens Order 1920, sections 1(3)(a) and 6C(1)(b). The abolition of the Aliens Act 1905 resulted in the means test exception for refugees being removed.

75 Quoted in Sherman, A., *Island Refuge: Britain and Refugees from the Third Reich 1933–39* (London Elek, 1973), p. 49.

76 See Aliens Order 1920, section 1(3)(b) which required that an alien produce a written permit from his employer issued by the Minister of Labour.

77 13 League of Nations Treaty Series 237.

78 UK Treaty Series No. 4 (1937), Cmd. 5347, Art. 1.

origin". Through this time limitation, the UK carefully ensured that there was no risk of a refugee problem arising in the future. The second Convention, which dealt specifically with the Status of Refugees from Germany, again provided the refugees with some basic civil rights.[79] As this was only a provisional treaty, it was felt necessary to conclude a new convention to consolidate the work which had been carried out by the League of Nations on refugees. The Convention concerning the Status of Refugees coming from Germany was duly signed by seven European countries. Once more, the UK ratified the Convention subject to certain reservations. It narrowed the definition of refugees coming from Germany, contained in Article 1, to those "who at the date of ratification no longer enjoy the protection of the German Government", thereby limiting its responsibilities to those who had proved that they had lost Germany's protection by 26 September 1938, the date of the UK's ratification. This restriction was, at the time, condemned as a loophole by which the government could evade its responsibilities under the Convention.[80]

In 1938, the "crisis year" for refugees, the government decided to impose a visa requirement for German and Austrian passport holders. The main reason cited was the need to control the flow of (Jewish) refugees. In the same year, Britain attended an international conference on the refugee problem held in Evian which had been proposed by the United States government. For some, the Conference achieved little other than the establishment of a permanent Intergovernmental Committee with headquarters in London whose function was to assist refugees and liaise with the League of Nations.[81] In the discussions, the UK delegation emphasised its "traditional policy" of giving shelter to persons who were compelled to leave their own country due to persecution for their political and religious beliefs or racial origins, but pointed out that it was not a country of immigration for demographic and economic reasons. Having provided this background to UK policy, the government representative conceded that Britain was prepared "on the grounds of humanity to adopt an even more liberal policy".[82] Signs of this new liberal policy did not become apparent until November 1938, after *Kristallnacht* in Germany. Though the existing domestic legislation remained intact, the introduction of voluntary committees to supervise lists of asylum seekers, the use of block

79 UK Treaty Series No. 33 (1936), Cmd. 5338.

80 See, e.g., Lafitte, F., *The Internment of Aliens* (Penguin, 1940), p. 222.

81 Marrus, *op. cit. supra* n. 6, pp. 170–72.

82 Contribution which His Majesty's Government in the United Kingdom is able to make to the Problem of Emigration from Germany and Austria, Intergovernmental Committee, Evian, France, 11 July 1938.

visas, and the supply of public funds helped increase the flow of refugees to Britain.[83] While some commentators are critical of British asylum policy in this period, others maintain that the record was "an honourable one".[84] Notwithstanding such differences in perspective, almost all are in agreement that the subsequent internment policy during the war was a disgrace.[85]

By persisting in treating immigrants and refugees alike, regardless of questions of persecution, the Home Office maintained complete control over entry. Even at a time when the needs of the asylum seekers were acknowledged by the international community to be pressing, the UK government still viewed the issue in terms of numbers and "quality" of entrants and was particularly concerned about the impact on employment which an influx of refugees might have. Newspaper reports of the time are redolent of the scaremongering often employed today (witness the *Daily Mail*'s report in 1938, "Aliens Pouring into Britain").[86] Comparisons can be made with recent headlines of the tabloid press, reporting a "tidal wave" of immigrants and "bogus" asylum seekers.[87]

Post Second World War: the Creation of a Modern Asylum Policy

Following the war, a new Order, the Aliens Order 1953, replaced the 1920 Order in immigration matters, and provided the main regulations regarding entry of aliens until it was repealed by the Immigration Act 1971. The appearance of a new Order did little to alter the legacy of the 1914 and 1919 Acts and the Aliens Order 1920. No special regime existed to deal with asylum applications. There was no right of appeal. The Home Secretary still maintained total discretion in refugee cases. As late as 1962, the courts were still of the opinion that, in deportation cases, the question of political asylum was a matter for the Home Secretary alone.

---

83 For a broader discussion of the change in policy, see London, L., "British Immigration Control Procedures and Jewish Refugees 1933–1939" in *Second Chance: Two Centuries of German-speaking Jews in the United Kingdom*, Mosse, W.E., ed. (Mohr, 1991), pp. 485–517.

84 Stent, R., *A Bespattered Page? The Internment of His Majesty's "most loyal aliens"* (Andre Deutsch, 1980), p. 21; and see Sherman, *op. cit. supra* n. 75, p. 267.

85 See Lafitte; Cesarani and Kushner eds; Stent, *op. cit. supra* notes 80, 64, 84.

86 Quoted in Sharf, A., *The British Press and the Jews under Nazi Rule* (Oxford University Press, 1964), pp. 155–74.

87 See, e.g., *Daily Express*, 26 Oct. 1991 and also chapter 2 of this book by Craig Young.

In the postwar period, the UK also signed the 1951 Geneva Convention on the Status of Refugees (but did not incorporate it into English law).[88] Despite this accession to international law, the practice adopted by the UK after 1951 was quite ill-defined. One had to turn to parliamentary statements for information on Home Office policy.[89]

Although the somewhat rudimentary asylum regime managed to cope for a decade-and-a-half after the war, changes to legislation on Commonwealth citizens in 1962 altered the position. In the UNHCR's view, many such citizens who sought asylum in the UK after 1962, and who were refugees, were admitted but were not granted asylum and were consequently denied the treatment to which they were entitled under the Convention.[90] A further problem in the postwar structure, which began to receive greater attention, was the lack of a right of appeal for both immigrants and asylum applicants. This again reflected the system established after 1914, with the exception of the Aliens Deportation Advisory Committee which existed from 1932 to 1936 and which had a minimal impact. Criticisms of the status quo led the government, in 1967, to set up a committee (the "Wilson Committee") to report on whether a right of appeal should be made available to aliens.[91]

Although very little time was spent in consideration of refugee rights, there was agreement that claims to political asylum "could be suitably dealt with under the appeal system" proposed.[92] The Committee recommended further that special arrangements needed to be made to expedite the hearing of appeals where the appellant was seeking political asylum, and that some such appeals would need to be heard in private. It was also accepted that where an appellant claimed to be a refugee within the competence of the UNHCR, the UK Representative of the High Commissioner should be given notice of the proceedings and have an opportunity to make his or her views known.[93] In line with the recommendation of the Wilson Committee, an immigration appeals system was established.

---

88 Convention Relating to the Status of Refugees, 1951, Cmd. 8465, ratified by the UK on 11 March 1954..

89 See, e.g., H.C. Hansard, Vol. 529, Col. 1508, 1 July 1954.

90 Select Committee on Race Relations and Immigration, Session 1977–78, "The Effect of the UK's Membership of the EEC on Race Relations and Immigration", (410–ix), Minutes of Evidence, 6 July 1978, p. 169, paras 14 and 15.

91 Report of the Committee on Immigration Appeals ("Wilson Report"), 1967, Cmnd. 3387.

92 *Ibid.*, para. 145.

93 *Ibid.*, recommendation (16), p. 66.

In 1971, immigration law was completely overhauled by the Immigration Act 1971 and the Aliens Order 1953 was repealed. The Act itself made no mention of refugees and one had to turn to the immigration rules or to the rules on appeal to discover the underlying policy. The recommendation that the UNHCR be advised of appeals by asylum applicants was adopted and the UNHCR was given permission to be treated as a party to an appeal where a person claimed to be a refugee under the Convention.[94] Though this may have seemed an important improvement, the value of the UNHCR's presence in such appeals was questioned soon after its implementation. A working party on appeals against refusals of asylum in the UK, set up by an umbrella organisation of refugee agencies,[95] expressed its concern in evidence to a Select Committee "that the participation of the Office of the UNHCR apparently made little difference to the outcome of an appeal".[96]

New immigration rules, the real core of immigration policy, were also drafted to control the entry of Commonwealth citizens. However, the draft rules omitted any mention of refugees. As a result, the Office of the UNHCR proposed some refugee provisions, but the final version limited the reference to asylum and refugees to three brief clauses (in the Rules for Control after Entry).[97] In 1978, the UK Representative of the UNHCR commented that these rules had been grafted onto the main text of the immigration rules at a late stage in the proceedings and, as a result, were "restrictive", "somewhat vague" and appeared as "exceptions of a residual or 'last resort' character, rather than principles of normal practice".[98] A major regret of the UNHCR was that the UK had failed to incorporate the Convention and the 1967 Protocol into its domestic law and, further, that it had not established a formal procedure for the determination of refugee status by an independent body (in line with the recommendations of the UNHCR's Executive Committee).[99] With reference to the second of these issues, the UK Representative of the UNHCR

94 Immigration Appeals (Procedure) Rules 1972, SI 1972. No. 1684, para. 7(3).

95 The Standing Conference on Refugees, which consisted of 30 agencies helping refugees in the UK and overseas, had established the working party in May 1977 following a review of appeals against asylum refusals by the Home Office.

96 Select Committee on Race Relations and Immigration, *op. cit. supra* n. 90, p. 254, para. 4.

97 See Statement of Immigration Rules for Control After Entry – Commonwealth Citizens (HC 80), paras 30, 49, and 50.

98 Select Committee on Race Relations and Immigration, *op. cit. supra* n.90, p. 168, para. 11.

99 See Conclusions of the Executive Committee, 1977, No. 8 (XXVII)(d).

noted that

> the fact that ... persons seeking asylum are treated in and under the Immigration Rules as just another sort of immigrant has led, first in the minds of officials administering the Rules, then among professionals discussing the immigration rules and policies, and finally in the minds of a considerable portion of the general public, to a complete blurring of the distinction between immigrant and refugee.[100]

Asylum Policy in the 1980s and 1990s

There had therefore been little progress made since the 18th and 19th centuries, when all categories of migrants were described as "aliens" and warranted identical treatment under the policy and legislation. It will be noted from the above rules that "asylum" was treated as a separate status from "refugee" for those cases which the Home Office did not think warranted refugee status but where protection was justified. Although the description of asylum was in the same terms as the definition of a refugee under the Convention, and the above distinction seemed illogical, asylum without refugee status was retained as a separate status until July 1984.[101] It is probable that the UK wanted to maintain the distinction in order to argue that the granting of asylum was a purely domestic act and therefore at the discretion of the state.

The 1980s proved an important period in the development of asylum policy in the UK. Though some improvements were made, many gaps still existed in refugee determination, and many new problems emerged as the government sought ways to contend with the increase in asylum claims. It is worth remembering that the first specific mention of the Convention only occurred in the 1980 immigration rules, although the Convention's terminology had been previously used.[102] Nor was any procedure for establishing refugee status set out in the rules. Immigration officers were granted broad discretion in deciding if cases involved refugee issues and ought to be referred to the Home Office.[103] The burden of proving a case rested on the shoulders of the applicant and the standard of proof was on a "balance of probabilities".

---

100 Select Committee on Race Relations and Immigration, *op. cit. supra* n. 90, pp. 168–69, para. 11.

101 Home Affairs Committee – Race Relations and Immigration Sub-Committee, "Refugees", Session 1984–85, Minutes of Evidence, 17 Dec. 1984, p. 68, para. 5.

102 Statement of Changes in Immigration Rules (HC 394), para. 16.

103 *Ibid.*, para. 64.

The use of administrative detention, with all its associated problems, began to increase in line with the rise in applications.[104] Carriers' liability legislation appeared on the statute book in 1987, and the government began to impose visa restrictions with growing regularity, normally against a country which was producing asylum seekers. Despite the Wilson Committee's recommendations in the 1960s regarding appeal rights for asylum applicants, no in-country right of appeal existed for port applicants who had not been granted entry clearance for another purpose.[105] In relation to the lack of an in-country right of appeal, the Home Office acknowledged that there was "some force in the argument that a right of appeal after removal is of no benefit to someone who maintains that he will be in danger of persecution in the country to which he is being returned".[106] Nevertheless, it was still the Government's position that it would be undesirable to introduce an in-country right of appeal "because it would be likely to stimulate a large number of unfounded applications made only with the aim of securing a right of appeal in this country and thus gaining entry for those not otherwise qualified for it".[107]

Although one of the main concerns surrounding the asylum debate in the mid-1980s was this lack of appeal rights for all cases, considered a fundamental lacuna in the law, the Home Affairs Committee examining the issue of asylum and refugees in 1984–85 suggested that there was general satisfaction with the asylum arrangements:

> Most of those from whom we received evidence regard Britain's general record on asylum as satisfactory. UKIAS states that "the Home Office cannot be criticised for its general asylum policy", and the BRC regards the government's record as "generally good". Criticism has instead been directed at particular aspects of the asylum procedures.[108]

This is a somewhat surprising conclusion, particularly by UKIAS (United Kingdom Immigrants Advisory Service) and the British Refugee Council. First, it is unclear what is meant by the Home Office's "general asylum policy",

---

104 See for a wider discussion of detention Amnesty International, *Prisoners without a Voice: Asylum Seekers detained in the UK* (Amnesty International, 1994).

105 Immigration Act 1971, section 13(3).

106 Home Affairs Committee – Race Relations and Immigration Sub-Committee, *op. cit. supra* n. 101, p. 76, para. 40.

107 *Ibid.*, para. 40.

108 Home Affairs Committee, "Asylum and Refugees with Special Reference to the Vietnamese", Session 1984–85, p.xxxvi, para. 94.

or the judgment of its record as "generally good". Secondly, and more importantly, many of the criticisms which had been raised in earlier reports still persisted, such as the non-implementation of the Convention and Protocol, the wide discretionary powers of the Home Office and immigration officers, the lack of a universal in-country right of appeal, the administrative nature of the procedures, the slowness of the refugee determination process, and the growing use of detention. In addition, refugee support groups were reporting with concern the emergence of the "refugee in orbit" phenomenon and the use of the safe third country "rule".[109]

The culmination of the development of asylum policy in recent years has been the arrival of the first specific legislation on asylum: the Asylum and Immigration Appeals Act 1993 and the Asylum and Immigration Act 1996. The importance of the 1993 Act lay in the fact that it was the first *statute* since the Aliens Act 1905 to attempt to deal with the issue of asylum and that it extended an in-country right of appeal to all categories of claimants (in certain cases, to the higher courts). To this extent, it could be argued that the UK had finally recognised the importance of asylum and refugee law and was putting into effect its much vaunted claim of traditional generosity. Closer examination of the statute raises a number of matters of concern.[110] Though a right of appeal was incorporated, the implementation of a "fast-track" appeals system significantly limited the value of the extended appeal rights; cases deemed to be without foundation (mainly "safe third country" cases) could not be appealed beyond the special adjudicator if he or she agreed with the decision of the Home Secretary to remove a claimant. Despite government claims that detention is used only as a last resort, the Act did nothing to allay fears about the excessive use of detention for asylum applicants and the situation remained very much as it had been prior to the Act. For many critics of the UK's asylum policy, the 1993 Act was regarded as an exercise in reducing numbers of applications rather than a genuine attempt to protect the rights of refugees.[111]

109 See also chapter 4 of this book by Rachel Trost and Peter Billings.

110 On the background to the Asylum and Immigration Appeals Act 1993, see Macdonald, I., and Blake, N., *Macdonald's Immigration Law and Practice,* (4th edn, Butterworths, London, Edinburgh 1995); Stevens, D., "Race Relations and the Changing Face of United Kingdom Asylum Policy", (1992) *Patterns of Prejudice*, Vol. 26, Nos 1 and 2, pp. 96–102; Stevens, D., "The Re-introduction of the United Kingdom Asylum Bill", (1993) 5 I.J.Ref.L., pp. 91–100.

111 See, particularly in relation to children, Stevens, D., "Refugee Law and the Rights of the Child" in *Families Across Frontiers*, Lowe and Douglas eds (Kluwer, 1996), pp. 449–464.

Some support for this opinion was found when, in October 1995, the government announced its decision to enact new legislation on asylum. The system introduced by the 1993 Act was not as effective in reducing the backlog and speeding up the process as had been hoped. The proposed measures, and those finally incorporated in the Asylum and Immigration Act 1996, may rightly be regarded as having one objective: deterrence. The removal of social security benefits for those who do not claim asylum immediately on arrival and for appellants, the withdrawal of an in-country right of appeal in certain "safe third country" cases, and the "white listing" of countries for which there would be a presumption that asylum applications were not well-founded are difficult to justify in terms other than that of deterrence. Ministerial sound-bites such as "Britain should be a safe haven, not a soft touch"[112] and Britain must be "a haven, not a honeypot"[113] do little to assuage fears about the new restrictive legislation of the 1990s. The impression gained is of a government which has concentrated unduly on avoiding being seen as a "soft touch" at the expense of being a "safe haven" for genuine refugees.

Conclusion

In 1991, Roy Hattersley, the then deputy leader of the Labour Party, spoke of "the reputation that Britain has enjoyed for 500 years as a country that accepts refugees as a moral duty".[114] Any examination of the history of asylum policy must question the grounds for such a contention. Parliamentarians have adopted a nostalgic view of UK asylum policy which appears to be based largely on a short period in the mid-19th century when restrictions were not imposed and Britain irritated its European neighbours by accepting a number of political activists. There does not seem sufficient evidence to support the notion that the UK has exhibited a deeply-rooted belief in the right to asylum. Rather, the evidence points to the opposite conclusion, that the UK has always adopted an asylum policy based on expediency for itself rather than on any humanitarian principles. There have been two periods in which this has been starkly revealed: the first was that preceding the second world war; the second is the current period. At both these stages in asylum history, the UK government demonstrated its suspicion of asylum applicants, its inability to cope with the numbers

112 "Lilley to curb benefits for asylum seekers", *Independent*, 12 Oct. 1995.

113 H.C. Hansard, Vol. 268, Col. 700, 11 Dec. 1995.

114 H.C. Hansard, Vol. 198, Col. 373, 5 Nov. 1991.

seeking entry, and its preference for a potentially harsh system of selectivity. The result at present is a municipal law which is unable to differentiate between the "genuine" refugee and the "bogus" and which therefore tacitly accepts that some refugees will fail to be granted asylum. The reality of current UK asylum policy is that humanitarian protection is not deemed to be as great a priority as tight border controls and the deterrence of asylum seekers.

Bibliography

Amnesty International, *Prisoners Without a Voice: Asylum Seekers Detained in the UK* (Amnesty International, 1994).

Amnesty International, *Playing Human Pinball: Home Office Practice in "Safe Third Country" Asylum Cases* (Amnesty International, 1995).

Cesarani, D., "An Alien Concept? The Continuity of Anti-Alienism in British Society before 1940" in *The Internment of Aliens in Twentieth Century Britain*, Cesarani, D. and Kushner, T., eds (Cass, 1993).

Cohen, S., *Still Resisting After all these Years* (Greater Manchester Immigration Aid Unit, 1995).

Correspondence respecting Foreign Refugees in London, Parliamentary Papers, 1852.

Cunningham, *Alien Immigrants to England* (Sonnenschein, 1897).

Dicey, *Lectures on the Relation between Law and Public Opinion in England during the 19th century* (Macmillan, 1926 edition).

Dummett, A., and Nicol, A., *Subjects, Citizens, Aliens and Others* (Weidenfeld and Nicolson, 1990).

Gainer, B. ,*The Alien Invasion* (Heinemann, 1972).

Garrard, J.A., *The English and Immigration* (Oxford University Press, 1971).

Holmes, C., *John Bull's Island: Immigration and British Society, 1871–1971* (Macmillan, 1988).

Lafitte, F., *The Internment of Aliens* (Penguin, 1940).

London, L., "British Immigration Control Procedures and Jewish Refugees 1933–1939" in *Second Chance: Two Centuries of German-speaking Jews in the United Kingdom*, Mosse, W.E. ed. (Mohr, 1991).

Marrus, M.R., *The Unwanted: European Refugees in the Twentieth Century* (Oxford University Press, 1985).

Porter, B., *The Refugee Question in mid-Victorian Politics* (Cambridge University Press, 1979).

Roche, T., *The Key in the Lock* (John Murray, 1969).

Saunders, D., "Aliens in Britain and the Empire During the First World War", (1985) *Immigrants and Minorities*, Vol. 4, No. 1, pp. 5–27.

Sharf, A., *The British Press and the Jews under Nazi Rule* (Oxford University Press, 1964).

Sherman, A., *Island Refuge: Britain and Refugees from the Third Reich 1933–39* (London Elek, 1973).

Smiles, S., *The Huguenots* (John Murray, London, 1868, 6th edition).

Stent, R., *A Bespattered Page? The Internment of His Majesty's "most loyal aliens"* (Andre Deutsch, 1980).

Stevens, D., "Race Relations and the Changing Face of United Kingdom Asylum Policy", (1992) *Patterns of Prejudice*, Vol. 26, Nos 1 and 2, pp. 96–102.

Stevens, D., "The Re-introduction of the United Kingdom Asylum Bill", (1993) 5 I.J.Ref.L., pp. 91–100.

Stevens, D., "Refugee Law and the Rights of the Child" in *Families Across Frontiers*, Lowe and Douglas eds (Kluwer, 1996), pp. 449–64.

2 Political Representations of Geography and Place in the Introduction of the UK Asylum and Immigration Act (1996)[1]

CRAIG YOUNG

As the end of the 20th century draws near, individual nation states find themselves in a very different context of asylum seeking from that of the middle years of the century, when important international conventions and agreements on asylum were developed. Probably the most important of these is the 1951 Geneva Convention, under which the United Kingdom government has a legal obligation to protect refugees. In the early 1950s the main image held of asylum seekers was of white Europeans emerging from the destruction of the Second World War. Today, there are rising numbers of refugees and asylum seekers across the globe. In 1994 there were 27,000,000 refugees globally, and 496,200 asylum applications to Western Europe and North America alone.[2] Since the 1950s, improvements in global communications, and changes in geopolitical circumstances, have led to a rise in asylum applications from around the world (the "new asylum seekers" from Asia, the Middle East and Africa). In general, the response of the developed world has been to tighten asylum procedures in order to reduce the number of successful

1 An earlier version of this paper appeared as Young, C., "Political Representations of Geography and Place in the UK Asylum and Immigration Bill (1995)" (1997) *Urban Geography,* 18, 62–73. Reproduced with the permission of V.H. Winston and Son, Inc.

2 Sheridan, M., "War and Terror Make 27 Million Homeless", *Independent,* 16 Nov. 1995.

claims.[3]

Immigration and asylum are high profile political issues throughout Western Europe. Asylum applications rose rapidly after 1989 (principally due to the break up of Eastern and Central Europe) at a time when governments were under considerable pressure due to economic recession. Immigrant communities throughout Western Europe, often the products of labour migration in the 1960s, have become the targets for resurgent right wing nationalism using ethnic minorities as "scapegoats". The rising number of asylum applications and the perceived threat of a new wave of immigration from East and Central European countries have fuelled public and governmental concern. One result has been cooperation at the European level to establish a new control regime, even if this cooperation is not always explicitly acknowledged.[4]

In addition, individual European Union (EU) governments have sought to establish even tighter controls.[5] While all EU countries face similar problems, concern about asylum also relates to a particular state's historical context and the domestic political situation. The actions of the UK Conservative government mirrored this European trend until it lost power in May 1997. In 1993 the Asylum and Immigration Appeals Act was passed. This Act established new rights of appeal, but also introduced stricter criteria for granting asylum and established a "fast-track" system for certain appeals.[6] In 1995 the Conservative government introduced a new Asylum and Immigration Bill, which received royal assent in July 1996 as the Asylum and Immigration Act (AIA). The Act is seen as an attempt to bring the UK into line with tougher

3 On recent trends in asylum seeking see Crawley, H., "The Refugee Crisis Facing Western Europe" (1993) *University of Sussex Research Papers in Geography*, 11; Kliot, N., "Global Migration and Ethnicity: Contemporary Case-Studies" in *Geographies of Global Change*, Johnston, R.J., Taylor P.J. and Watts M.J., eds (Blackwell, 1995), pp. 175–90; Collinson, S., "Visa Requirements, Carrier Sanctions, 'Safe Third Countries' and 'Readmission': The Development of an Asylum 'Buffer Zone' in Europe" (1996) *Transactions of the Institute of British Geographers*, NS 21, 76–90; Hovy, B., "Asylum Migration in Europe: Patterns, Determinants and the Role of East-West Movements" in *The New Geography of European Migrations*, King, R., ed. (Belhaven Press, 1993), pp. 207–27; King, R., ed. *Mass Migration in Europe: The Legacy and the Future* (Wiley, 1993); Tuitt, P., *False Images: The Law's Construction of the Refugee* (Pluto, 1996).

4 See section entitled "A 'Home Grown' Policy" in chapter 3 of this book by Richard Dunstan.

5 Collinson, *op. cit. supra* n.3.

6 See chapter 1 of this book by Dallal Stevens.

immigration and asylum controls which have been imposed throughout the EU. It extends the "fast-track" procedure, first introduced in 1993, to include applicants coming from so-called "white list" countries where "there is in general no serious risk of persecution", restricts applicants' entitlement to benefits, and makes it an offence to employ an illegal immigrant.[7]

The introduction of this Act needs to be interpreted in the context of the "new right" ideology of the then Conservative government. Fyfe notes that this fused concepts from neo-liberalism (the individual, freedom of choice, a market society) with neo-conservatism (strong government and a disciplined society) into an ideology in which "the preservation of a free society and a free economy is guaranteed by ... the authority of a strong state".[8] The implications of this ideology for law and order legislation were policies which placed more emphasis on personal responsibility (e.g. Neighbourhood Watch) and, conversely, on increased penetration of civil society by the state (e.g. tougher laws and policing). The 1996 Act illustrates both these points. It attempted to place responsibility for the employment of illegal immigrants firmly on individual employers. At the same time, the government of the time portrayed the Bill as a tough response by the state to "bogus" asylum seekers, which would control immigration and thus maintain good race relations.[9]

The Bill provoked widespread debate about the need for, and the nature of, the legislation. Ministers of the then Conservative government portrayed it as an attempt to tackle the rising number of applications and the potential for racial tension due to increased illegal immigration. Opponents condemned it as an attempt to play a "race card" to attract voters, and as persecution of society's most marginal groups in order to achieve public sector savings. The implications of the Act are that asylum seekers have to engage with much stricter asylum procedures. It is feared that the result will be that refugees may face return to their countries of origin and possible torture and death in contravention of the UK's obligations under international human rights law.[10]

One reading of the debates surrounding the introduction and passage of the Bill through parliament is that they raise complex issues regarding the

7 H.C. Hansard, Vol. 268, Col. 699, 11 Dec. 1995.

8 Fyfe, N.R., "Law and Order Policy and the Spaces of Citizenship in Contemporary Britain" (1995) *Political Geography* 14, 177–89.

9 For the implications of the employment measures under the 1996 Act for race relations see chapter 17 of this book by Selina Goulbourne.

10 See chapter 11 of this book by C.J. Harvey.

interrelationships between law and geography.[11] Given the numbers of refugees and asylum seekers, the social and spatial impacts of this kind of legislation are considerable. However, this is more than a case of law impacting on space. The introduction of this Bill involved a series of discourses about legal process, race, citizenship, human rights and geopolitics. Another aspect of the political discourse focused on the geographical context of asylum seeking. Geographical images, geographical knowledge, and geographical concepts were used to legitimise and challenge the need for, and the nature of, this legislation.

Geographers have stressed that if we accept law as socially constructed, then we must also see socially held ideas about geography and space as central to the construction and interpretation of law.[12] Socially (and politically) held ideas about space and place have influenced the making of UK legislation in parliamentary debates.[13] In these cases political discourse deployed particular understandings or portrayals of space and place to justify the need for legislation or to defend its form. In the debates at the time of the passage of the Criminal Justice and Public Order Act (1994), for example, the arguments for its introduction rested partly on the construction of "the countryside" as a "purified rural space" in which "traditional" country pursuits were in danger of being destroyed by "urban invaders" (notably hunt saboteurs, "ravers", and "new age travellers") who were linked with criminal activity.[14] Similarly, in parliamentary debates on the Police and Criminal Evidence Act (1984) the notions of "public" and "private" space were debated with regard to the definition of the jurisdiction of new powers of policing.[15]

---

11 In this context see also Kobayashi, A., "Racism and Law in Canada: A Geographical Perspective" (1990) *Urban Geography,* 11, 447–73; Kobayashi, A., "If Kant were a Refugee ...: Recent Challenges to Concepts of Space and Citizenship in Refugee Law" (1996). Paper presented at the Law and Society Annual Conference, "The Law of Space and Place" session, University of Strathclyde, Glasgow.

12 See Blomley, N.K., *Law, Space and the Geographies of Power* (Guilford Press, 1994); Blomley, N.K. and Clark, G.L., "Law, Theory and Geography" (1990) *Urban Geography* 11, 433–46; Herbert, S., "The Trials of Laurence Powell: Law, Space, and a 'Big Time Use of Force'" (1995) *Environment and Planning D: Society and Space* 13, 185–99.

13 Sibley, D., "The Sin of Transgression" (1994) *Area,* 26, 300–3; Sibley, D., *Geographies of Exclusion* (Routledge, 1995); Smith, S.J., *The Politics of 'Race' and Residence* (Polity Press, 1989); Fyfe, *op. cit. supra* n. 8.

14 Sibley, *ibid.*

15 Fyfe, *op. cit. supra* n. 8.

The way in which space is represented thus carries a political charge, and law "draws upon a complex range of geographies and spatial understandings".[16] These representations can be decisive because law making is largely carried out by a very small, but powerful, minority. In the debates on the Asylum and Immigration Bill political actors portrayed, or represented, geographical processes, places and people in places in particular ways. They constructed representations of asylum seeking and asylum seekers, of the UK as a potential destination for asylum seekers, and of the countries of origin of asylum seekers. In this chapter each of these socially-held ideas about the geography of asylum seeking is analysed to demonstrate its influence on the legitimation and construction of this legislation (whilst acknowledging that other discourses are also involved).

Asylum Seekers and Asylum Seeking

In the government's rhetoric surrounding the introduction of the Bill representations of the geographical process of asylum seeking, and of asylum seekers, were central in legitimising the new legislation. Asylum seeking and asylum seekers were represented as a "problem".[17] Asylum seekers were often portrayed as being "merely" economic migrants. Asylum seeking was conflated with illegal immigration and linked to abuse of the asylum system and illegal activities. A statement by Ann Widdecombe, the then Home Office Minister of State, began:

> The Bill deals with four areas – asylum, illegal employment, immigration racketeering, and entitlement to housing and child benefit. All of those raise pressing problems. What gives *the asylum problem* particular urgency is the growing scale of the abuse of the system .... By abusing [asylum] people from abroad with no legitimate claim to be here can fend off removal and secure a prolonged stay, during which they can work in the black economy and take advantage of a range of public services and benefits.[18]

This association of asylum seekers with illegality was also emphasised in media representation. An article in the *Daily Telegraph* started with the title "Asylum seekers", and then proceeded with the sub-title "Dutch stem the

---

16 Blomley, *op. cit. supra* n. 12, p. xi.

17 See also Jackson, P., *Maps of Meaning* (Routledge, 1989).

18 H.C. Hansard, Standing Committee D, Col. 3, 19 Dec. 1995 (emphasis added).

flood of *illegal immigrants*".[19] It continued:

> The number of applications for political asylum are generally accepted as a reliable indicator of the size of a country's illegal immigrant problem .... 70 per cent [of asylum seekers] make their claim only after they have entered the country, disappeared into obscurity and have subsequently ... either committed a crime or been detected in some other way.[20]

Several Opposition MPs challenged this representation of asylum seekers, noting that "[o]ur Asian and black constituents are being talked about as potential invaders of our country, and as potential bogus applicants for housing benefit and social security benefit", and that "[t]he constant reiteration of the idea that every immigrant is a problem or a threat is bad for race relations".[21]

The scale of asylum seeking was also represented as a growing problem. According to Michael Howard (then Home Secretary) "the scale of the problem is alarming" to the extent that "we have a real problem in this country".[22] Government ministers and the media referred to an "upsurge in applications", a "rising tide of bogus asylum applications", and suggested that unless the UK took action, "the flood gates will be blown asunder".[23] The imagery of tides, floods and the UK being "swamped" by immigrants echoed UK Conservative rhetoric from the 1960s onwards.[24]

In the early 1990s, as shown in Table 2.1, the UK had a fairly high number of, proportion of, and rate of increase in, applications relative to other EU countries (although in 1996 this trend was reversed). As Table 2.2 shows, however, in the context of this period there was nothing remarkable about the absolute numbers of applicants in the UK. Numbers of applications in the UK rose dramatically from the end of the 1980s (some of the fluctuation from year to year reflects the fact that totals include numbers of dependants which varies between cases). This was due to the break up of the former Soviet bloc

---

19 Greaves, W. and Smit, B., "Asylum-seekers: Dutch Stem the Flood of Illegal Immigrants", *Daily Telegraph,* 27 Oct. 1995 (emphasis added).

20 *Ibid.*

21 H.C. Hansard, Vol. 268, Cols 746, 728, 11 Dec. 1995.

22 Mills, H. and Davies, P.W., "Howard's Asylum Clampdown Moves Closer", *Independent,* 21 Oct. 1995; Travis, A. and Carvel, J., "Howard Admits 'White List' Intentions Amid Accusation of Playing Race Card", *Guardian,* 26 Oct. 1995.

23 Nirj Deva MP (Con.) in Deva, N., "Fair and Firm on Immigration", *Independent,* 22 Oct. 1995; Michael Howard MP (Con.) in Travis, A., "2m Face Job Checks on UK Status", *Guardian,* 21 Nov. 1995; Greaves, W. and Smit, B., *supra* n. 19.

24 Jackson, *op. cit. supra* n. 17; Tuitt, *op. cit. supra* n. 3.

Table 2.1 Asylum statistics for selected European countries 1993–96

Country of application	Asylum applications				% of total applications			
	1993	1994	1995	1996	1993	1994	1995	1996
Austria	4,400	N/A	N/A	N/A	0.7	–	–	–
Belgium	26,900	14,300	11,400	12,200	4.1	3.9	3.5	4.3
Denmark	14,400	6,700	5,100	5,900	2.2	1.8	1.6	2.1
Finland	2,000	800	900	700	0.3	0.2	0.3	0.2
France[1]	29,300	28,600	24,200	20,600	4.5	7.9	7.4	7.3
Germany[1]	419,400	165,400	166,300	151,300	64.2	45.5	50.6	53.9
Italy	1,600	1,800	1,800	600 [2]	0.2	0.5	0.5	0.0
Netherlands	35,400	52,600	29,300	22,900	5.4	14.5	8.9	8.2
Norway	12,900	3,400	1,500	1,800	2.0	0.9	0.5	0.6
Spain[1]	16,400	13,300	7,400	6,100	2.5	3.7	2.2	2.2
Sweden	37,600	18,600	9,000	5,800	5.8	5.1	2.7	2.1
Switzerland	24,700	16,100	17,000	18,100	3.8	4.4	5.2	6.4
UK	28,000	42,200	55,000	34,800	4.3	11.6	16.7	12.4
Total	653,000	363,800	328,900	280,800	100	100	100.1 [3]	99.7 [3]

1 Figures based on data from Intergovernmental Consultations on Asylum, Geneva, but adjusted to include an estimated number of dependants.
2 Includes an estimate of the number of applications lodged in Dec. Date for full year not available at time of publication.
3 Percentages do not add exactly due to rounding.

Sources: Home Office Statistical Bulletin, *Asylum Statistics United Kingdom 1996*, Issue 15/97, 22 May 1997, Table 2.5; Amnesty International, *A Briefing on the Government's Proposed Changes to the Arrangements for Dealing with Applications for Asylum in the UK* (Amnesty International United Kingdom, 1995).

in Eastern Europe, the rise of the so-called "new asylum seekers" from Asia, the Middle East and Africa linked to improved access to international travel, and the tightening of asylum procedures since 1992 in other EU countries.[25] Some of this increase can be attributed specifically to the deterioration of the human rights situation in Algeria, Nigeria, Somalia, Sudan and former Yugoslavia.[26]

Again, government rhetoric linked this increase to the willingness of

25 Collinson, *op. cit. supra* n. 3; Tuitt, *op. cit. supra* n. 3; Amnesty International, *A Briefing on the Government's Proposed Changes to the Arrangements for Dealing with Applications for Asylum in the UK* (London, 1995).
26 Amnesty International, *ibid.*

Table 2.2 Asylum statistics for the United Kingdom

Number of applicants (including dependants) 1988–96

1988	5,700
1989	16,800
1990	38,200
1991	73,400
1992	32,300
1993	28,000
1994	42,200
1995	55,000
1996	34,800

Decisions made (% of applications) 1986–96

	1986–90 (average)	**1992–93**	**1994**	**1995**	**1996**
Granted asylum	20	6	4	5	6
Granted "exceptional leave to remain"	62	43	17	16	13
Refused asylum	18	51	79	79	81

Number of decisions made 1994–96

	1994	**1995**	**1996**
Number of decisions	20,900	27,005	38,960
Granted asylum	825	1,295	2,240
Granted "exceptional leave to remain"	3,660	4,410	5,055

Sources: Home Office Statistical Bulletin, *Asylum Statistics United Kingdom 1996*, Issue 15/97, 22 May 1997; Amnesty International, *A Briefing on the Government's Proposed Changes to the Arrangements for Dealing with Applications for Asylum in the UK* (London, 1995); H.C. Hansard, Standing Committee D, Cols 186–87, 18 Jan. 1996.

refugees to abuse the system. Conservative MP Nicholas Baker stated that the increase in applicants "is not the measure of a world that is breaking up now – the world had plenty of troubled areas in 1988". He went on to write: "It reflects the increase in number of those trying to get round our immigration controls and enter Britain by applying for asylum."[27] Both Conservative and

27 Baker, N., "Why We Need Asylum Curbs", *Independent*, 27 Oct. 1995.

Opposition MPs challenged this interpretation of geopolitics and its relationship with asylum seeking noting that there were still many areas of political instability.[28] More significantly, the proportion of applicants actually gaining asylum or "exceptional leave to remain" fell suddenly, from an average of over 80 per cent in 1986–90 to around 20 per cent in 1994 (Table 2.2). This dramatic shift has been attributed largely to the impact of the 1993 Act, though the government was also accused of operating a quota of around 20 per cent since 1993.[29] It is also symptomatic of the government's "strong state" approach to asylum seeking.

The justification for this new legislation thus relied upon a combination of "new right" ideology and of particular constructions of the geography of asylum seeking. In these constructions it is the irresponsibility of those individuals who are prepared to abuse the asylum system and of those prepared to profit by employing illegal immigrants, which is to blame for the increase in applications, not geopolitical reality. Asylum seekers were constructed as a "problem". This construction relied on linking asylum seekers to "abuse" of asylum and to illegal activities. It also relied heavily on the fact that they are "out of place".[30] Not only are they linked to "scrounging" or illegal activities, but they are "foreigners" doing it in "our" country. The irresponsibility of the individual is linked to the portrayal of the increase in applications as a force potentially beyond the control of the state (hence the imagery of floods and tides). The response which was thus required was that of a strong state prepared to make tough decisions to regulate these social and geographical processes.

The United Kingdom as a Host Country

Ideas about the geographical context of asylum seeking were also mobilised to legitimise the introduction of this legislation by employing a particular portrayal of the UK as a destination for asylum seekers. The government portrayed the UK as a country with a good record on accepting asylum seekers.[31] The impression given was that the UK had previously been "soft" on asylum seekers, and that this legislation was a fair response to international

28 For example, H.C. Hansard, Vol. 268, Cols 717, 769, 11 Dec. 1995.
29 Amnesty International, *op. cit. supra* n. 25.
30 Cresswell, T., *In Place/Out of Place* (University of Minnesota Press, 1996).
31 For historical analysis of the UK's record on accepting asylum seekers see chapter 1 of this book by Dallal Stevens.

circumstances and the increasingly hard line stance of the UK's "tough" European neighbours on the issue. This line of representation was started at the 1995 Conservative Party Conference when Peter Lilley stated that "Britain should be a safe haven, not a soft touch" for asylum seekers.[32] It was continued in several "sound bites", such as Michael Howard's statement that he had "borne in mind ... the importance of doing nothing to imperil this country's honourable tradition of offering sanctuary to genuine refugees – that we should be a haven, not a honeypot".[33] In particular, the UK was portrayed as having a "proud record of giving refuge to those fleeing genuine persecution".[34]

The UK was portrayed as a country with a particular appeal for "bogus" asylum seekers. As Michael Howard suggested: "For far too many people across the world, this country is far too attractive a destination for bogus asylum seekers and other illegal immigrants. The reason is simple: it is far easier to obtain access to jobs and benefits here than almost anywhere else."[35] The UK was thus portrayed as being perceived as "soft" on asylum seekers, as a "haven" and "attractive" to "bogus" applicants. Its asylum procedures were abused because as a "proud" and "honourable" country the UK was a "soft touch" compared to its tough European neighbours.

Though it is true that the increase in applications to the UK was in part due to the fact that other EU countries had tightened up asylum procedures, this representation of the UK as a relatively "soft touch" was contested by human rights and refugee groups. The United Nations (UN) Human Rights Committee considered that the UK government's treatment of illegal immigrants, asylum seekers and those ordered to be deported gave "cause for concern".[36] Refugee groups claimed that procedures were already so tight that "there is a real risk that genuine refugees could be sent back to persecution, torture or even death".[37] The 1996 Act was seen as even more serious. Amnesty International believed that "these measures amount to an effective demolition

32 Editorial, "The Wrong Card. It is Asylum Procedures, not Refugees, which should be Targeted", *Times*, 26 Oct. 1995.

33 Mills, H. and Davies, P.W., *supra* n. 22: for other examples see H.C. Hansard, Vol. 268, Col. 755, 11 Dec. 1995; *ibid.*, 12 Dec. 1995.

34 H.C. Hansard, Vol. 268, Col. 699, 11 Dec. 1995, Michael Howard (Con.).

35 Kirkbride, J., "Bogus Marriage Racketeers Face Seven Years' Jail", *Daily Telegraph*, 21 Nov. 1995.

36 *Times* editorial *supra* n. 32; UN Human Rights Committee, CCPR/C/79/Add.55, 27 July 1994, para. 15.

37 Mills, H., "Curbs on Asylum-seekers 'Already Too Tight'", *Independent*, 26 Oct. 1995.

of the existing asylum process".[38] Others held that the proposals would "effectively wipe out asylum in this country".[39]

The view of the UK as a "soft option" for asylum seekers was also contested in the media. As an editorial in the *Guardian* suggested: "Britain is not a "magnet" for the rootless and wretched of the world, as even the most cursory study of European ... responses to such movements of population would prove beyond doubt." Even the *Times* dismissed such a view as "populist, and xenophobic nonsense" and declared that "Britain is anything but a "soft touch" for would-be refugees".[40]

Again, the then Conservative government fused the "new right" ideology of the strong state with a particular construction of the geographical aspects of asylum seeking to legitimise this new legislation. By portraying the UK as a "soft touch" and linking this to the way that the UK is supposedly perceived as a place by asylum seekers, particularly "bogus" applicants and those involved in illegal immigration, the justification was made for increased intervention by the strong state. This not only enabled the government to regulate asylum seeking more tightly, it also changed the image of the UK as a place, making it less attractive for "bogus" asylum seekers. Since the introduction of the Act numbers of asylum applications have indeed decreased from 43,965 in 1995 to 27,930 in 1996, a fall of over 36 per cent.[41]

The Countries of Origin

The construction of this legislation in parliamentary debates involved the deployment of politically constructed ideas about how countries can be categorised and about the geography of human rights. The form of this legislation thus rested in part on the deployment of geographical knowledge regarding ways of classifying countries and the realities of specific countries.[42] This was most clearly seen in the debates surrounding Clause 1 of the Bill, the extension of special appeals procedures. The main feature of this clause

38 Amnesty International, *op. cit. supra* n. 25, p. 1.

39 Mills, H., *supra* n. 37.

40 Editorial, "The Politics of Red Meat", *Guardian,* 25 Oct. 1995; *Times* editorial *supra* n. 32.

41 H.C. Hansard, Vol. 290, Col. 1030, Oral Answer.

42 See, for example, H.C. Hansard, Standing Committee D, Cols 16–18, 22, 26–28, 9 Jan. 1996; *ibid.*, Cols 73–75, 11 Jan. 1996; *ibid.*, Cols 197–202, 210–12, 18 Jan. 1996; H.C. Hansard, Vol. 272, Cols 433–34, 21 Feb. 1996.

was the introduction of a "white list" of designated countries. These countries are to be regarded as "safe" in that there is a presumption that "there is in general no serious risk of persecution" there and that claims from such countries are therefore not well founded. Applications from these countries are considered, but the burden of proof rests on the applicant. Applicants who are refused no longer have the right of appeal to the Immigration Appeal Tribunal (although they do have the right to appeal to the next stage, i.e. to an independent adjudicator). This procedure is designed to accelerate and reduce the cost of processing asylum claims.[43]

The problem with designating countries as "safe" is that it relies on an evaluation of sociopolitical conditions in the countries of origin of asylum seekers. Designation hinges on the categorisation of countries and on the role of this categorisation in the definition of refugee status. The then government categorised certain countries as "safe" so that claims from those countries face the presumption that they are not well founded. Guidelines issued by the UN High Commissioner for Refugees stress that the primary factor to be considered is the specific evaluation of the applicant's statement, that they have a "well founded fear of persecution", rather than a judgment on the situation prevailing in his or her country of origin.[44] The Conservative government was thus accused of making its evaluation of a country's sociopolitical status a key part of determining refugee status. The political representation and categorisation of countries is thus a central part of the operation of this legislation. The problem with this is summarised by Amnesty International's statement:

> The determination of whether persons would be at risk of persecution in their own country is a difficult and complex process relying heavily on an evaluation of statements and claims that are not always susceptible to proof, and on an objective assessment of the political and human rights situation in countries that are often undergoing complex and rapid change. Only a careful examination of each asylum-seeker's individual circumstances can exclude the possibility that he or she would be at risk on or after return.[45]

At the time the government denied that designation of countries would negatively affect consideration of applications from those countries.

43 *Ibid.*, Vol. 268, Cols 701–02, 11 Dec. 1995.

44 UNHCR, Handbook on Procedures and Criteria for Determining Refugee Status, Geneva, 1992, para. 37.

45 Amnesty International, *op. cit. supra* n. 25, pp. 12–13.

Designation of a country is carried out with respect to certain criteria. These are that for each country: (i) "there is in general no serious risk of persecution"; (ii) "they generate significant numbers of asylum claims in the UK", and (iii) "a very high proportion of claims proves to be unfounded".[46] The phrase "in general no serious risk of persecution" was a contentious one. According to the UN guidelines "countries where there is any risk of persecution or other threats to life or freedom, should not be considered 'safe'".[47] However, the government's designation of countries did not mean that they were considered universally safe, as the Home Secretary made clear when he stated that

> [designation] will not amount to a declaration that we necessarily consider countries to be universally safe, or to have political and judicial institutions that function to western standards ... What we will be saying is that a country has functioning institutions, and stability and pluralism in sufficient measure to support an assessment that, in general, people living there are not at risk.[48]

Several criteria were advanced to determine if there was "in general no serious risk of persecution" in a country. These are the stability of the country; the state's adherence to international human rights instruments; presence of democratic institutions, elections and political pluralism; freedom of expression for individuals and the media; and the availability and effectiveness of legal avenues for protection.[49] Designation of a country thus relied on an assessment of the "reality" of its sociopolitical characteristics, and it is in this deployment of geographical knowledge that problems arose.

Designation is problematic because it involves generalising about a country. This potentially ignores the problems of minority groups. In the debates surrounding Clause 1 of the bill, the examples of Christians and Ahmadis in Pakistan, the Roma people in Romania and Bulgaria, Greek Catholics in Romania, and homosexuals in a number of the "white listed" countries were deployed. These examples were used to illustrate that, though these countries may be safe "in general", for some social groups there are very real risks of persecution. However, people in those social groups will potentially be categorised along with the majority in those countries.

Designation also involves the danger of masking the geography of human

46 H.C. Hansard, Vol. 268, Col. 703, 11 Dec. 1995.

47 As cited in H.C. Hansard, Standing Committee D, Col. 31, 9 Jan. 1996.

48 *Ibid.*, Vol. 268, Col. 703, 11 Dec. 1995.

49 H.C. Hansard, Standing Committee D, Col. 65, 11 Jan. 1996.

rights within a country. Regional variations in persecution related to the geography of ethnicity or political and religious affiliation may be obscured. Designation of parts of countries is not possible under this Act. The government of the time considered that those fearing persecution by other citizens in particular regions of countries could move within that country or appeal to the State. For the Opposition this approach was unrealistic. Diane Abbott stated:

> As a result of ... colonialism many countries have borders that bear no relation to the ethnic, cultural or demographic realities that underlie them. ... The Government ... know that many countries are arbitrary amalgamations of tribes, created by some colonial mapmaker ... so their use of the phrase "in general" shows that they are refusing to be ... sensitive to the realities of politics in many countries.[50]

Again, arguments about the "reality" of the sociopolitical geography of countries were important in defining the form of this legislation.

Debate also focused on the designation of specific countries. The designated countries are Bulgaria, Cyprus, India, Ghana, Pakistan, Poland and Romania.[51] In the period January to November 1995, 7,980 applications were received from these countries, of which 30 from India, 25 from Pakistan, 15 from Ghana and 15 from Romania were granted either refugee status or "exceptional leave to remain". The proposition that these are "safe" countries was challenged by human rights groups. Amnesty International's response was: "It is absolutely ridiculous to assume that those countries have a clean bill of health on human rights. We have serious concerns about all the countries on the list."[52] India was reported to have thousands of political prisoners, subject to torture, ill-treatment, "disappearance" and execution without trial. Pakistan was alleged to torture prisoners (some to death) and had high levels of political killings according to the Home Office. Poland and Romania had "prisoners of conscience", and the latter was accused of torture and ill-treatment, as well as restrictions on freedom of expression. In Ghana inter-tribal conflict led to 1,000 deaths and 150,000 displaced persons in 1994, and "prisoners of conscience" were also reported there.[53]

---

50 *Ibid.*, Col. 37, 9 Jan. 1996.

51 H.C. Hansard, Vol. 268, Col. 703, 11 Dec. 1995 and Vol. 282, Cols 691–718, 15 Oct. 1996.

52 Travis, A., "Howard's Asylum List Draws Fire", *Guardian*, 12 Dec. 1995.

53 Penman, D., "The Seven Countries on Howard's 'White List'", *Independent,* 26 Oct. 1995.

The selection of a country for designation was the focus of Opposition amendments in Select Committee which stressed the need for transparency in the designation process. One amendment proposed that designation could not take place without the country in question being debated in parliament.[54] Pakistan was raised as one example, on the grounds that it should not be designated due to the existence of different forms of slavery there affecting "millions" of people. Lady Olga Maitland challenged this view saying that Pakistan had clear laws against slavery and that there was no evidence for its existence on this scale. The Chairman of the Select Committee swiftly intervened to prevent the debate of specific instances. However, David Alton responded that this example demonstrated that "the practice in a number of states is the issue that would be addressed if we had to consider such orders [in] the House".[55] Examples of persecution in both India and Pakistan were described by Max Madden to support his view that "any dispassionate assessment of the political reality there ... would exclude those countries from a designated list".[56]

Another amendment sought to oblige the government to consult human rights groups before designating countries. Again, the politically constructed nature of the portrayal of countries was a central point here, and it was argued in Committee that "we must rely on NGOs, which are often more dispassionate and objective".[57] The unsuccessful nature of these amendments effectively left the designation of countries in the hands of the then Home Secretary, Michael Howard, as designation could only be challenged by using the "negative procedure" in the House of Commons. This is a little used, time consuming and difficult to implement procedure which the Opposition predicted would have little success in stopping the designation of countries as "safe".

This issue is of considerable importance as it is possible to designate further countries in future. Nigeria was highlighted as one country which it was feared could have been designated under a Conservative government, as it fitted the criteria of high numbers of applicants to the UK and low acceptance rates. Nigeria had already been included in a pilot fast-track scheme in 1995, and it was suggested that only the "murder" of the Ogoni activist Ken Saro-Wiwa

---

54 H.C. Hansard, Standing Committee D, Cols 29 and 33, 9 Jan. 1996; *ibid.*, Cols 145–50, 151–59, 16 Jan. 1996.

55 *Ibid.*, Cols 156–57, 16 Jan. 1996; *ibid.*, Cols 200–01, 18 Jan. 1996.

56 *Ibid.*, Col. 212, 18 Jan. 1996.

57 H.C. Hansard, Standing Committee D, Col. 75, 11 Jan. 1996 David Alton (Lab.).

in November 1995 prevented its designation as "safe". Earlier that year a British official sought to present Nigeria as "free from political persecution" to EU asylum officials, claiming that the Home Office felt that only opposition leaders were at risk. A Home Office guidance document which was operational during most of 1995 stated that there was no danger to student and political activists, trade union members, and no evidence of persecution of the Ogoni people.[58]

EU officials "thought the British analysis severely defective", with pro-democracy campaigners, ethnic minorities, and human rights campaigners possibly having a legitimate claim to being persecuted.[59] The Refugee Council described the government's view as "an acutely distorted picture of political and human rights conditions".[60] Opposition MPs argued in Select Committee that "this country assessment ... is an example of gross incompetence on the part of the Home Office" and declared that "the case of Nigeria raises profound questions about the objectivity of the Home Office in the compilation of the designated list".[61] By November 1995 the Home Office had only granted asylum to one individual from Nigeria out of 2,032 applications made in that year (and only four since 1993), prompting the Refugee Council to comment:

> What this proves is that ... there is an informal "white list" already in operation. This is an example of a country in which it is quite clear human rights abuses are going on a massive scale and yet when they seek asylum in the UK more than 99 per cent are refused. It is simply not credible that less than one per cent of these people are genuine refugees.[62]

The then Conservative government was criticised, for example, by Amnesty International[63] for proposing to use low rates of successful applications from a country as a reason for designating it as "safe", when those low rates were largely held to be the product of its own legislation which itself was criticised for the stringency of its application.

58 Amnesty International, *op. cit. supra* n. 25, Carvel, J., "EU Dismisses British View of Nigerians' Risk of Persecution", *Guardian*, 26 Oct. 1995; H.C. Hansard, Standing Committee D, Col. 33, 9 Jan. 1996.

59 Carvel, J., *ibid.*

60 Travis, A., "Tory MPs Told how to Answer Awkward Questions on Racism", *Guardian*, 25 Oct. 1995.

61 H.C. Hansard, Standing Committee D, Col. 33, 9 Jan. 1996 Keith Hill MP (Lab.).

62 Travis, A., "'White List' Already in Effect, Claim Refugee Organisations", *Guardian*, 21 Nov. 1995.

63 Amnesty International, *op. cit supra* n. 25, p. 11.

Conclusion

With the change to a Labour government in May 1997 the future of asylum law in the UK is uncertain. In Opposition the Labour Party was strongly opposed to the Asylum and Immigration Act. The then shadow Home Secretary, Jack Straw, was alleged to have hinted that a new Labour government would scrap this "racist legislation".[64] Whatever the future holds, the introduction of the 1996 Act represented the last stage of the then Conservative government in redefining the UK as an asylum space. Politically, the Act was an example of the ideology of the neo-Conservative "strong state" in action. Asylum seekers, linked to illegal activities, were portrayed as a deviant "other". Increases in the numbers of applications were represented as potentially beyond the control of the state. The response required was thus one of a strong state to regulate the "threat" that asylum seeking apparently posed.

The political debates which legitimised and challenged the introduction of this legislation, and which influenced its construction, included a number of discourses some of which have not been considered explicitly here, notably those on race, citizenship and international relations. However, exploring the key geographical ideas which have been deployed has highlighted their importance in legitimising legislation and in constructing law. In particular, the designation of "white list" countries is of central importance in attempts to redefine the refugee as a legal subject and thus for the future of asylum seeking in the UK. In its wider context the 1996 Act is but one part of attempts to redraw the world map of asylum spaces, as individual nations and supra-national organisations (notably the EU) in the developed world seek to create a new, stricter asylum regime.

64 Travis, A., "Straw Vows to Scrap 'Racialist Asylum Laws'", *Guardian*, 27 Oct. 1995.

Bibliography

Amnesty International, *A Briefing on the Government's Proposed Changes to the Arrangements for Dealing with Applications for Asylum in the UK* (London, 1995).

Blomley, N.K., *Law, Space and the Geographies of Power* (Guilford Press, 1994).

Collinson, S., "Visa Requirements, Carrier Sanctions, 'Safe Third Countries' and 'Readmission': the Development of an Asylum "Buffer Zone" in Europe" (1996) NS 21, *Transactions of the Institute of British Geographers*, 76–90.

Crawley, H., "The Refugee Crisis Facing Western Europe" (1993) *University of Sussex Research Papers in Geography*, 11.

Hovy, B., "Asylum Migration in Europe: Patterns, Determinants and the Role of East-West Movements" in *The New Geography of European Migrations*, R. King, ed. (Belhaven Press, 1993), pp. 207–27.

King, R., ed., *Mass Migration in Europe: The Legacy and the Future* (Wiley, 1993).

Kliot, N., "Global Migration and Ethnicity: Contemporary Case-Studies" in *Geographies of Global Change*, R.J. Johnston, P.J. Taylor and M.J. Watts, eds (Blackwell, 1995), pp. 175–90.

Kobayashi, A., "Racism and Law in Canada: A Geographical Perspective" (1990) 11 *Urban Geography*, 447–73.

Tuitt, P., *False Images: The Law's Construction of the Refugee* (Pluto, 1996).

Young, C., "Political Representations of Geography and Place in the UK Asylum and Immigration Bill (1995)" (1997) 18 *Urban Geography*, 62–73.

3 A Case of Ministers Behaving Badly: The Asylum and Immigration Act 1996

RICHARD DUNSTAN

The Asylum and Immigration Act 1996, which became law on 24 July 1996, represents the nadir of a process – begun in the mid-1980s – aimed at distancing the United Kingdom from its obligations under international law to admit and protect refugees.

From 1985, the Conservative government steadily introduced a range of measures clearly intended to prevent or deter new arrivals of asylum seekers, or to induce those already here to abandon their asylum claim. The imposition of visa requirements on nationals of all significant refugee-producing countries, and their enforcement by the imposition of financial penalties on airlines and shipping companies bringing asylum seekers without the necessary visa or papers, has made it almost impossible for would-be refugees to travel to the United Kingdom – other than by the use of forged travel documents and unorthodox means of travel, often involving clandestine entry to and enforced stop overs of varying duration in one or more transit countries.

The creation, under the Asylum and Immigration Appeals Act 1993, of special "fast-track" procedures for certain cases enabled the Home Office to "pass the buck" by returning such asylum seekers to a country they transitted through before reaching the United Kingdom – and where, it is held, they should have sought asylum – without examining the merits of their asylum claim and without any guarantee that the authorities of the transit (or "third") country are willing to do so. Furthermore, the growth of a "culture of disbelief" among Home Office caseworkers, compounded by a tendentious assessment of the human rights situation in some refugee-producing countries, has led to a growing number of wrongful refusals. Since July 1993, despite there being no appreciable change in the nature or quality of asylum claims, the proportion of *successful* applications has fallen substantially (and to surprisingly uniform levels). In addition, the level of means tested social security benefits available to asylum seekers has been reduced, and increasing numbers of asylum seekers have been arbitrarily detained, from the time of application, in immigration detention centres and criminal prisons.

The 1996 Act, however, has taken this process to the point where the right to seek asylum itself is in grave peril. Not only does the Act provide for the effective abolition of all appeal rights in most "safe third country" cases and an extension of the scope of the "fast-track" appeal procedures to a broad range of cases (including those where the applicant is from one of a "white list" of supposedly "safe" countries), but it removes most asylum seekers' entitlement to means tested social security benefits during the (often lengthy) period that their asylum claim is under consideration. In this writer's view, the procedural provisions of the 1996 Act have substantially reduced the effectiveness of legal safeguards in the asylum process, thereby militating even further against the fair and just resolution of individual asylum claims. However, it is the social security provisions of the 1996 Act, including the denial of social security benefits to *all* those exercising their statutory right to appeal against a refusal of asylum, that most threaten the right of asylum. These are so arbitrary and extreme that, for some asylum seekers, the existence of legal safeguards has become somewhat meaningless.

While waxing lyrical about the United Kingdom's "honourable record" of granting asylum to "genuine refugees" and the government's "commitment" to the 1951 UN Convention on Refugees,[1] Conservative ministers repeatedly sought to justify the provisions of the 1996 Act by placing a heavy emphasis on the evident misuse of the asylum process by persons merely seeking to circumvent the UK's general immigration controls or avoid deportation. From the time the new provisions were first announced, in October 1995, hardly a single ministerial speech or statement on the subject has failed to condemn and deplore, sometimes in the most florid language, the "abuse" of the asylum process by "bogus refugees" and, in particular, the "abuse" of the asylum appeals mechanism by "bogus appellants". Not surprisingly, these pejorative terms have also cropped up time and time again in a seemingly orchestrated series of highly partisan and alarmist articles in pro-Conservative newspapers, most notably the *Daily Mail* and *Daily Express*.[2]

The irony is that, in seeking to defend the new measures in parliament and in public, Conservative ministers resorted to a tissue of "bogus" arguments, distorted or partial statistics, and outright untruths. Paradoxically, this extensive

---

1 For analysis of this record see chapter 1 of this book by Dallal Stevens.

2 See also chapter 2 of this book by Craig Young.

ministerial dissimulation has been necessary not only to deflect the (entirely well-founded) criticism of the 1996 Act's principal provisions by an impressive range of commentators and actors in the asylum field, but also to conceal the provenance of many of the provisions and, perhaps most disturbingly, to gloss over the patent failure (in public policy terms) of previous initiatives against asylum seekers, including the Asylum and Immigration Appeals Act 1993 itself. For the principal point to be made about this dissimulation is that it has tended to obstruct constructive analysis of the (not inconsiderable) problems associated with the current pattern of asylum seeking and, accordingly, the development of radical proposals for a truly functional asylum regime.

This chapter examines just four aspects of this dissimulation: (i) the former Conservative government's defence of the 1996 Act's provisions in respect of social security benefits (Section 11 of the Act); (ii) its justification for the effective abolition of appeal rights in most "safe third country" cases (Sections 2 and 3 of the Act); (iii) its denial of the relationship between much of the 1996 Act and a series of resolutions adopted by the Justice and Home Affairs Council of the European Union; and (iv) its refusal to accept responsibility for the manifest failings and inefficiencies of the existing asylum regime.

The Social Security Provisions

Section 11 of the 1996 Act removes completely the entitlement to means tested social security benefits (Income Support, Housing Benefit and Council Tax Benefit) of those who apply for asylum *after* entering (legally or otherwise) the United Kingdom. Those persons who apply for asylum immediately upon arrival at an airport or seaport retain an entitlement to such benefits while awaiting an *initial* decision on their asylum claim by the Home Office. However, Section 11 also provides for the cessation of such port applicants' entitlement to benefits from the point at which they receive a negative decision from the Home Office. In other words, means tested welfare support is no longer available to rejected asylum seekers during any appeal to the Immigration Appellate Authority (IAA). These provisions came into force on 24 July 1996, the day the Act became law, but were in fact first enacted, by means of ministerial regulations, in February 1996.[3] The Regulations were subsequently withdrawn after being declared unlawful by the courts, and their

3 The Social Security (Persons from Abroad) Miscellaneous Amendment Regulations 1996, S.I. 1996 No. 30.

chequered history is worthy of close examination for the light it throws on Conservative ministers' overall approach to the fulfilment of what are, after all, international obligations voluntarily assumed.

The Regulations were first announced by the then Secretary of State for Social Security, Peter Lilley, during the Conservative Party Conference on 11 October 1995, and were first published (in draft form) by the Department of Social Security (DSS) the following day. On the same day, the government appointed Social Security Advisory Committee (SSAC), which examines all draft Social Security regulations and is empowered to make recommendations to the Secretary of State, invited comments on the draft Regulations by interested organisations and individuals.

At that time, the draft Regulations were set to come into force on 8 January 1996, a remarkably tight timetable that did not allow for them to be debated, and voted on, by Parliament. However, in late December, following his receipt of a highly critical report on the draft Regulations by the SSAC and under pressure from Liberal Democrat MPs, Lilley conceded a delay in enactment in order to allow for debates in Parliament.

In submissions to the SSAC, an impressive range of organisations argued that, in flagrant disregard of the government's obligations under international law, the Regulations would unjustly deny access to the welfare benefits system by those individuals who, for legitimate and wholly understandable reasons, apply for asylum *after* entering the United Kingdom, rather than immediately upon arrival. They maintained that the draft Regulations made inadequate provision for those individuals who become trapped in the United Kingdom due to a major change of circumstances (such as a coup) in their own country, and that they would unjustly deny all those seeking to appeal against a refusal of their asylum claim access to the welfare benefits system, thereby seriously undermining the universal right of appeal established as recently as July 1993 under the Asylum and Immigration Appeals Act 1993. The UN High Commissioner for Refugees, for example, argued that legal safeguards in the asylum process "may be rendered ineffective if individual asylum seekers are unable to sustain themselves physically during the sometimes lengthy period in which their status is determined. ... Within the humanitarian spirit of the [1951 UN] Convention lies a State's obligations to ensure that asylum seekers enjoy basic subsistence support to sustain them in dignity during this waiting period".[4]

The SSAC report on the draft Regulations, published on 11 January 1996

4 *Representations to the Social Security Advisory Committee by the United Kingdom Branch Office of UNHCR*, Oct. 1995.

(the same day that the Regulations were laid before parliament), agreed that "by penalising all but a minority of asylum seekers, without regard to the strength or validity of their claim", the draft Regulations were "arbitrary and unjust" and would have "drastic and unwelcome consequences" for "some of the most vulnerable and defenceless in our society". The SSAC report also noted that "apart from the extreme hardship that would be caused for so many, the proposed Regulations would also be operationally very cumbersome and raise many practical difficulties" and "would entail considerable administrative costs as well as substantial charges to local authority and other budgets outside Social Security". In particular, the SSAC noted the difficulties likely to be associated with serving notice of an interview or appeal hearing on asylum seekers "without an address or funds". Concluding that "a more equitable and satisfactory approach ... would be to ensure faster and more efficient asylum procedures" the SSAC recommended that the draft Regulations be abandoned.[5]

However, the government refused to accept the recommendation of the SSAC – or even to make amendments to the Regulations as originally drafted – and made only one concession to the SSAC's forthright criticisms. It abandoned retrospective transitional arrangements that would have resulted in at least 13,000 asylum seekers already in the system losing their existing benefit entitlement on the day that the Regulations came into force. Following a short, late night debate in the House of Commons, the Regulations came into force on 5 February 1996.

In April 1996 the Regulations were severely criticised by the Glidewell Panel, an independent panel established by refugee groups to examine the new measures and chaired by Sir Iain Glidewell, a recently retired Appeal Court judge.[6] Concluding that the Regulations would render many asylum seekers homeless and destitute, the Panel called in vain upon the government to reflect on the, by then only too real, consequences of the new policy. Then, on 21 June 1996, following a legal challenge on behalf of a young Zaïrean

---

5 *Report by the Social Security Advisory Committee under Section 174(1) of the Social Security Administration Act 1992*, Cm 3062, Jan. 1996. Apart from UNHCR, the SSAC received submissions from over 200 concerned organisations and individuals, including the Refugee Council, Amnesty International, and the Commission for Racial Equality.

6 Glidewell Panel, *Report from an Independent Enquiry into the Implications and Effects of the Asylum and Immigration Bill 1995 and Related Social Security Measures* (16 April 1996).

woman (Ms B) who had applied for asylum a matter of hours after entering the United Kingdom on 8 February using a forged Greek passport, the Regulations were declared *ultra vires* by the Court of Appeal. Condemning the Regulations as "uncompromisingly draconian" and intolerable in "a civilised nation", the Court ruled that "Parliament cannot have intended a significant number of genuine asylum seekers to be impaled on the horns of so intolerable a dilemma – the need to abandon their claims to refugee status or alternatively to maintain them as best they can but in a state of utter destitution". In particular, and in language redolent of many submissions to the SSAC, the Court held it "unlawful to alter the benefit regime so drastically as must inevitably not merely prejudice, but on occasion defeat, the statutory right of asylum seekers to claim refugee status".[7]

However, within days the government moved to evade this legal ruling by introducing a new clause (with provisions almost identical to those of the discredited Regulations) into the Asylum and Immigration Bill, then almost at the end of its passage through the House of Lords. An amendment by opposition peers to mitigate the effect of the new clause by allowing "after entry" applicants three days grace to make their claim before losing benefit entitlement was then twice overturned by the government, first in the House of Commons (despite the abstention of a number of Conservative MPs) and then, with the support of dozens of Conservative hereditary peers who did not even attend the debate in the House of Lords. Accordingly, the Regulations' provisions became incorporated as Section 11 of the Asylum and Immigration Act 1996, and re-entered into force on 24 July 1996.

On 8 October 1996, however, the government suffered further embarrassment when the High Court ruled that, under Section 21 of the National Assistance Act 1948, local authorities have a duty to provide food, warmth and shelter to asylum seekers who would otherwise be left homeless and destitute by the social security and housing provisions of the 1996 Act. Finding it "impossible to believe that Parliament intended that an asylum seeker, who was lawfully here and who could not lawfully be removed from the country, should be left destitute, starving and at risk of grave illness and even death because he could find no one to provide him with the bare necessities of life", the Court also concluded that such an intention would in any case amount to a breach of both the 1950 European Convention on Human

7 *R. v. Secretary of State for Social Security, ex p. B. and the Joint Council for the Welfare of Immigrants*; C.A. [1996] 4 All E.R. 385; [1997] 1 W.L.R. 275.

Rights and the 1951 UN Convention on Refugees.[8] On 17 February 1997, the local authorities' appeal against this ruling was rejected by the Court of Appeal.[9]

In seeking to justify these provisions' distinction between "port" and "after entry" applicants, Lilley and other ministers have relied heavily upon their contention that "after entry" asylum applications are inherently of less merit than "port" asylum applications, and that therefore "after entry" applicants are less deserving of welfare benefits. In his formal response to the SSAC's report, and also in the subsequent Commons debates on both the Regulations and the hastily added clauses to the Asylum and Immigration Bill, Lilley claimed that the proportion of those granted asylum is "lower for in-country [that is, after entry] applicants".

In fact, the Home Office's own figures show this claim to be groundless. Between January 1992 and September 1996, a total of 4,630 "after entry" applicants were granted asylum, compared with a total of 1,770 "port" applicants. In other words, of the total of 6,400 individuals granted asylum in this period, the vast majority (72.3 per cent) were "after entry" applicants. It seems reasonable to conclude that each and every one of these 4,630 genuine refugees had good reasons for applying for asylum *after* entering the United Kingdom, rather than immediately upon arrival. As the Home Office's own research has also demonstrated, the overwhelming majority of those granted asylum in recent years were *not* financially independent at the time of application, and were therefore reliant upon welfare benefits to meet their needs for food, warmth and shelter during the often lengthy waiting period.[10]

Moreover, in each of the past five years the recognition rate (that is, the proportion of substantively determined cases in which asylum was granted) among "after entry" applicants was actually *higher* than that among "port" applicants. In 1992, the recognition rate among "after entry" applicants was 6.6 per cent, while that among "port" applicants was 4.9 per cent; in 1993, the

---

8 *R. v. Hammersmith and Fulham London Borough Council ex p. M., R. v. Lambeth London Borough Council ex p. P., R. v. Westminster City Council ex p. A., and R. v. Lambeth London Borough Council ex p. X.*, CA, Justice Collins, 8 Oct. 1996, *Times* Law Report 10 Oct. 1996.

9 *R. v. Hammersmith and Fulham London Borough Council ex p. M., R. v. Lambeth London Borough Council ex p. P., R. v. Westminster City Council ex p. A., and R. v. Lambeth London Borough Council ex p. X.* CA, 17 Feb. 1997, *Times* Law Report 19 Feb. 1997.

10 Home Office Research Study No. 141, *The Settlement of Refugees in Britain*, 1995.

figures were 12.8 per cent and 4.3 per cent respectively; and in 1994, the figures were 4.9 per cent and 4.7 per cent. Overall, during the three year period 1992–94 the total proportion of "after entry" applicants granted asylum after full consideration of their asylum claim (7.96 per cent) was almost twice that of "port" applicants (4.65 per cent).[11] Similarly, in 1995, not only did the vast majority (73.3 per cent) of the 1,295 individuals granted asylum by the Home Office apply after entry, but the recognition rate among "after entry" applicants was 6.57 per cent, and that among "port" applicants was 3.85 per cent.[12] Again, in the first nine months of 1996, not only did the vast majority (75.7 per cent) of the 1,185 individuals who were granted asylum apply after entry, but the recognition rate among "after entry" applicants was 6.02 per cent, and that among "port" applicants was 4.03 per cent.[13]

Finding themselves contradicted by their own statistics, ministers then adopted a new line, contending that all those who apply for asylum after entering the UK would previously have had to demonstrate (to an immigration officer) that they can support themselves financially during their stay in the United Kingdom. In rejecting the SSAC's criticisms and recommendations, for example, Lilley claimed that "on arrival in this country all those from the main [refugee-producing] countries will have been interviewed by the immigration authorities, questioned about their intentions in visiting the United Kingdom and *asked to confirm that they have the means to support themselves without recourse to public funds*".[14] It was largely on the basis of this claim that ministers later resisted the opposition parties' call for the insertion of a three day period of grace into the Bill's provisions. Indeed, as late as October 1996, the then Home Office minister Ann Widdecombe claimed that *all* those "after entry" applicants granted asylum in recent years entered the country *only* after giving an undertaking to support themselves without recourse to public funds.[15] However, these glib claims ignore both the valid reasons why many genuine refugees seek to make their asylum application only *after* entry, rather than immediately upon arrival, and the real life circumstances in which

11 Source for all 1992–94 figures: Home Office Statistical Bulletin 15/95, Tables 4.1, 4.2 and 4.3.

12 Source for 1995 figures: Home Office Statistical Bulletin 9/96, Tables 4.4a and 4.4b.

13 Source for 1996 figures: H.C. Hansard, Vol. 284, Col. 209, 31 Oct. 1996.

14 Para. 17 of the government's formal response to the SSAC report on the Regulations, Cm 3062.

15 In response to questioning by this writer at a fringe meeting, organised by the Refugee Council, during the Conservative Party Conference, 8 Oct. 1996.

such applications are made.

As noted above, since January 1992 the Home Office has granted asylum to more than 4,600 "after entry" applicants. Of course, in *some* of these cases the individual will – as ministers claim – have been legally resident in the United Kingdom (for instance, as a student or visitor) at the time of application, and will have applied for asylum due to a significant change of circumstances in his or her country. However, in many – almost certainly most – of these cases the individual will have applied for asylum shortly after entering the country – legally or otherwise – *with the specific intention of seeking asylum.*

The reasons for this are well-documented. As the SSAC concluded: "lack of knowledge of the procedures, arriving in a confused and frightened state, language difficulties or fear of officialdom may all be insuperable barriers to making any kind of approach to the authorities at [the] port of entry". Moreover, as described above, the blanket imposition of visa regimes on refugee-producing countries and their enforcement by carrier sanctions has forced many would-be refugees to resort to the use of forged travel documents and unorthodox means of travel to the UK. Accordingly, in some "after entry" cases, these unorthodox means of travel will have included clandestine entry to the UK (for instance, in the back of a lorry), thereby bypassing any examination by an immigration officer. In other cases, and for the reasons identified by the SSAC, the individual will have given evasive or misleading answers to any questions posed during examination by an immigration officer, and these will have been accepted. In a great many cases, the individual will anyway have travelled to and entered the United Kingdom using a false European Union Member State passport, thereby bypassing any examination by an immigration officer.

Indeed, it was in this manner that Ms B – the subject of the June 1996 ruling by the Court of Appeal – entered the UK on 8 February 1996, using a forged Greek passport. As an apparent European Union national, Ms B was waved through immigration control without any formal examination. It is evident that this is now a favoured practice among the criminal agents who offer and arrange such unorthodox means of travel. Furthermore, it is evident that such agents often advise their "customers" to enter the UK first rather than apply for asylum on arrival, even travelling with the individual in order to reclaim the forged travel document after entry (presumably for reuse).

Having disingenuously contended that all those "after entry" applicants granted asylum in recent years entered the country *only* after giving an undertaking to support themselves without recourse to public funds, ministers have also relied heavily on the existence of a supposed "safeguard" in the

1996 Act, covering those who find themselves trapped in the United Kingdom due to serious upheaval in their country. This "safeguard" provides for an exemption to the denial of benefit entitlement in those "after entry" cases where the asylum claim is made "within three months" of a declaration by the Secretary of State that the country in question has undergone "a fundamental change in circumstances". However, ministers consistently failed to mention that, since 5 February 1996, not one such declaration has been made – not even in respect of Liberia or Afghanistan – and that, accordingly, this "safeguard" has no value whatsoever.

Somewhat surprisingly, given their repeated humiliation in the courts, ministers of the previous government rushed to declare the curtailment of most asylum seekers' benefit entitlement "a success", on the basis of the "sharp decline" in the number of asylum applications after February 1996.[16] Indeed, there has been a significant fall in the number of applications, particularly "after entry" applications. In September 1996, for example, new applications were down 50 per cent on the same month in 1995, and for the first time in years there were more "port" applicants (1,205) than "after entry" applicants (805).

However, even if one discounts the immense hardship of homelessness and destitution caused to as many as 10,000 vulnerable men and women since February 1996, this is not quite the whole picture. In early 1996, ministers repeatedly claimed that the curtailment of asylum seekers' entitlement to benefits would save as much as £200 million per year, and opponents of the measures were castigated as irresponsible and profligate with taxpayers' money. However, it was always apparent that ministers had made no allowance for the inevitable increase in public expenditure arising from the shifting of the burden of care onto local authorities. In March 1996, faced with the threat of legal action from three local authorities, the government was forced to confirm that it would provide 80 per cent relief of the additional costs that local authorities incurred as the result of their continuing obligations to the children of asylum seekers under the Children Act 1989. The government later confirmed that the Department of Health has earmarked £25 million to cover such relief to local authorities.[17] Furthermore, following the October 1996 ruling of the High Court in respect of local authorities' obligations under the National Assistance Act 1948, the Association of Directors of Social Services estimated that in London alone local authorities would face associated

16 For example, H.L. Hansard, Vol. 574, Col. 192, 5 Oct. 1996.

17 H.L. Hansard, Vol. 574, Col. 181, 15 Oct. 1996.

costs of at least £190 million in the next financial year.[18] Subsequently, the government confirmed that it would provide financial relief of £165 per week per person to local authorities in respect of costs incurred while meeting their obligations under the 1948 Act. It will be noted that the SSAC, among others, warned of such additional costs in January 1996. Furthermore, there is growing evidence of the "practical difficulties" warned of by the SSAC. In October 1996, for example, the *Guardian* newspaper reported the case of a homeless (and presumably destitute) asylum seeker who could not be traced by his solicitor to be informed of his successful appeal and grant of asylum.[19]

Appeal Rights in "Safe Third Country" Cases

Sections 2 and 3 of the 1996 Act abolish the right to appeal, *prior to expulsion*, against a refusal of asylum on "safe third country" grounds, in those cases where the "third country" in question is the United States, Canada, Switzerland, Norway or an EU Member State. These provisions, which came into force on 1 September 1996, effectively permit the Home Office *summarily* to expel those arriving at the UK's borders via one or more of these countries, without examining the merit of their asylum claims and without any guarantee that the authorities of the "third" country will do so.

One of the most striking aspects of these provisions is that they abolish a legal safeguard that – notwithstanding its obvious shortcomings – has proven to be extremely valuable in practice. For it is clear that, between its creation in July 1993 and its abolition on 1 September 1996, the appeal mechanism in "safe third country" cases provided vital protection to a large proportion of those refused on "safe third country" grounds by the Home Office.

For example, a study of 60 asylum seekers (selected at random) refused on "safe third country" grounds in the period 1 September 1994–31 March 1995, carried out by this writer for Amnesty International and published in June 1995, revealed a 43 per cent success rate at appeal.[20] Subsequently, an analysis of 419 "safe third country" appeals determined in the period 1 January–11 October 1995, undertaken by the London office of UNHCR, demonstrated a 42 per cent success rate, and comparable studies by the Immigration Law Practitioners' Association (ILPA) and the Refugee Legal Centre produced

18 "Asylum costs keep old in hospital", *Guardian*, 17 Oct. 1996.

19 "Asylum Lunacy", Letters, *Guardian*, 22 Oct. 1996.

20 Dunstan, R., *Playing Human Pinball: Home Office Practice in "Safe Third Country" Asylum Cases*, (Amnesty International UK, 1995).

almost identical figures. Of course, such a high proportion of successful appeals not only underscores the considerable value of this legal safeguard, but casts serious doubt on the integrity of the Home Office's initial decision-making in such cases.

In seeking to justify the provisions of Sections 2 and 3, Conservative ministers repeatedly argued that a right of appeal *prior to expulsion* is unnecessary in such cases because "it is reasonable to assume that our European neighbours are safe countries".[21] However, this argument overlooks the cardinal rule of refugee protection: that each and every case must be examined on an *individual* basis, in order to take account of the particular circumstances leading to the making of the asylum application. The issue in dispute at "safe third country" appeals is not so much that of whether France, or Germany or Canada is, in general terms, "unsafe" for all asylum seekers (although, in the case of *some* countries, this may well be the issue). Rather, the issue in dispute is that of whether the country in question is "safe" *for the individual concerned*, in that he or she will be readmitted to that country *and* will have there an effective opportunity to seek and, if appropriate, obtain asylum.

Moreover, in seeking to justify the provisions of Sections 2 and 3, Conservative ministers went to great lengths to obscure the true value of the now defunct right of appeal in such "safe third country" cases. During the first major debate on the Asylum and Immigration Bill in the House of Commons, on 11 December 1995, the then Home Secretary, Michael Howard, sought to sweep objections aside by falsely claiming that the success rate among such "safe third country" appeals is a mere "four per cent".[22] This attempt to diminish the value of the now defunct appeal mechanism was subsequently repeated by Howard's junior ministers, Ann Widdecombe and Timothy Kirkhope, during sessions of the House of Commons Standing Committee on the Bill. Despite being pressed to do so, no minister has since explained, or apologised for, this misleading of parliament.

A "Home Grown" Policy?

Possibly the biggest fiction perpetuated by Conservative ministers over the past two years is their contention that the provisions of the 1996 Act are entirely

21 H.C. Hansard (Standing Committee D on the Asylum and Immigration Bill), Col. 339, 25 Jan. 1996 (Timothy Kirkhope, MP).

22 H.C. Hansard, Vol. 268, Col. 705, 11 Dec. 1995.

"home grown". In October 1995, Michael Howard, delighted delegates at the Conservative Party Conference with his boast that "immigration policy will be decided here in Britain, and not in Brussels". At the Conservative Party Conference in October 1996, an audacious Howard repeated this conceit by proclaiming – again to loud cheers – that "immigration policy belongs in Britain, not in Brussels, and that's where it's going to stay!" However, the simple fact of the matter is that the asylum provisions of the 1996 Act form part of a secretive, and therefore undemocratic, process of harmonising asylum policy within the European Union (EU) – in other words, the creation of a *common* EU asylum policy. For, notwithstanding Howard's jingoistic boasting, the two main procedural elements of the Act – the creation of the so-called "white list" mechanism (Section 1) and the effective abolition of the right to appeal in "safe third country" cases (Sections 2 and 3) – are drawn directly from EU agreements, drafted by an obscure group of EU home affairs officials and signed by Howard or his predecessor at meetings of the EU Justice and Home Affairs (JHA) Council.[23]

The creation of the controversial "white list" mechanism, for example, is specifically provided for in the EU "Resolution on manifestly unfounded applications for asylum" and the EU "Conclusions on countries in which there is generally no serious risk of persecution",[24] both signed by the then Home Secretary, Kenneth Clarke, and his EU counterparts at the December 1992 meeting of the JHA Council in London. Indeed, some of the wording of Section 1 of the 1996 Act has been lifted directly from the December 1992 Resolution and Conclusions.

Similarly, the effective abolition of appeal rights in "safe third country" cases is a key provision of the EU "Resolution on minimum guarantees for

23 For further discussion of the implications of the October 1997 signing of the Amsterdam Treaty, under which legislative and judicial powers over key areas of asylum law and policy, have been transferred from Member States to Community competence see Nicholson, F., and Twomey, P. (eds), *Refugee Rights and Realities: Evolving International Concepts and Regimes* (Cambridge University Press, 1998 forthcoming).

24 Council of (Immigration) Ministers, Resolution on Manifestly Unfounded Applications for Asylum" and "Conclusions on countries in which there is generally no serious risk of persecution", London, 30 Nov./1 Dec. 1992. For text see General Secretariat of the Council, "Compilation of Texts on European Practice with respect to Asylum" (March 1996 update), 4464/1/95 REV1, and Plender, R., *Basic Documents on International Migration Law* (2nd edn, Kluwer, 1997) Part VIII.

asylum procedures",[25] signed by Howard and his EU counterparts at the June 1995 meeting of the JHA Council in Luxembourg. This Resolution also provides (in Paragraph 31) that "Member States will take account of [the principles set out in this Resolution] in the case of all proposals for changes to their national legislation [and] will strive to bring their national legislation into line with these principles by 1 January 1996". As ministers have since openly conceded when it suits them (the need to obscure the link having largely evaporated with the passing of the 1996 Act), a number of EU Member States (for example, Denmark, Finland, France, Germany and the Netherlands) have already done so, while others are in the process of doing so.

These EU resolutions and conclusions were drawn up in near secrecy by a group of EU home affairs officials, known as the Ad Hoc Group on Immigration from the time of its formation in October 1986 until the implementation of the Maastricht Treaty on European Union in November 1993, and more latterly as Steering Group 1 (Asylum and Immigration) of the K4 Committee of senior officials.[26] This committee performs a coordinating role with regard to activities in the area of Justice and Home Affairs, the so-called "third pillar" of intergovernmental cooperation under the Maastricht Treaty.

None of these documents has been properly scrutinised and debated – let alone approved – by the UK parliament. Indeed, it is apparent that until the latter part of 1995 most MPs – including front bench Labour opposition MPs – were quite unaware of the documents' existence. In fact, the process is so obscure that in July 1992, some four months after taking office, the then Home Secretary, Kenneth Clarke, publicly professed his ignorance of it.[27] Yet there can be no question that the process that has produced these documents is intended to produce a common EU asylum policy. As Clarke candidly conceded in July 1992: "I'm amazed that British ministers have been allowed to get away with it for so long."

The principal significance of this harmonisation process is that, to date, it has resulted in the adoption of unsatisfactory common standards which fall

25 Council of JHA Ministers, "Resolution on Minimum Guarantees for Asylum Procedures", 20 June 1995, (1996) O.J. C274/13.

26 In turn, a number of specific working groups report to the Steering Group, and in general it is in these working groups that the work of drafting such Resolutions, Conclusions and Joint Actions is undertaken. However, the writer understands that under the Irish Presidency of the EU there was a proposal for a two-tier structure, with meetings of the working groups and the K4 Committee itself only.

27 "Secrecy over Immigration Stuns Clarke", *Guardian*, 2 July 1992.

short of international norms. Most EU governments seem increasingly preoccupied with reducing the number of refugees and asylum seekers allowed to enter their territory, rather than with ensuring respect for the fundamental principles of refugee protection, and this has resulted in the creation of various "screening out" procedures and the setting up of separate, accelerated mechanisms for specific categories of asylum claims – such as "manifestly unfounded" or "safe third country" cases – deemed not to merit full examination.

In nearly every instance these new procedures lack certain essential safeguards and, accordingly, they provide greatly reduced levels of protection to genuine refugees. Individual EU governments have then pressed for these standards to be reflected, as part of the harmonisation process, in the resolutions and conclusions drawn up by the K4 Committee and adopted by the JHA Council. As described above, these EU resolutions and conclusions, although technically not legally binding, have then shaped new national legislation (or changes to existing legislation and practice) in other EU Member States. In short, the harmonisation process has resulted in an erosion of the standard of refugee protection *to the lowest common level.*

Of course, if relatively wealthy and powerful governments (which receive only a relatively small proportion of the total number of refugees in the world) take it upon themselves to erode the standards of refugee protection, there is a real risk that other countries will feel inclined to follow that example. Indeed, many Central and Eastern European states, which have less well-established procedures and experience, increasingly find themselves the recipients of asylum seekers returned under the "safe third country" concept and as a result of readmission agreements concluded with western European States, with the result that refugees run the risk that they may eventually be *refouled* to persecution in contravention of states' obligations under international law.[28]

To date, the UK government has generally followed the pace setters in this process, adopting new restrictive measures provided for in the JHA Council documents and already adopted by a number of its EU partners. However, since at least August 1995 the K4 Committee structure has been working on a draft JHA Council "joint action" (similar to a resolution) on minimum standards for the reception conditions of asylum seekers. By June 1996, however, a new draft of this joint action provided that all asylum seekers should, according

28 See e.g. Collinson, S., "Visa Requirements, Carrier Sanctions, 'Safe Third Countries' and 'Readmission': The Development of an Asylum 'Buffer Zone'" in *Europe* (1996) NS21:1 *Transactions of the British Inst. of Geographers* 76.

to need, "receive adequate means of subsistence to enable them to live decently" during the waiting period, either by being housed in "centres and lodgings" or by receiving "benefit sufficient to cover board and lodging". Such wording appears to reflect the view of UNHCR, among others, that states are obliged to provide "basic subsistence support" to needy asylum seekers during the often lengthy waiting period.

However, when the matter of this draft JHA joint action was raised by opposition peers during the final debates on the social security provisions of the then Asylum and Immigration Bill in July 1996, ministers made it clear that the government "shall not be agreeing to anything which is not compatible with this country's arrangements, and that includes our benefit arrangements in relation to asylum seekers".[29] Sure enough, a subsequent draft text of the joint action contains a markedly different, and somewhat ambiguous, provision: that "asylum-seekers who do not have sufficient means of support should *in accordance with national provisions* receive adequate means of subsistence". In short, it would appear that the Conservative government has been pressing for the final text of this joint action to reflect the (extremely low) standard of the 1996 Act. Of course, in the fullness of time this may lead to other governments (including non-EU governments) following down the same path – indeed, the writer understands that the Australian and New Zealand governments have recently proposed new social security provisions not dissimilar to those of Section 11 of the 1996 Act.

Glossing Over Past Failures

As already noted, throughout the two year period preceding the May 1997 general election Conservative ministers placed a heavy emphasis on the increase in the number of asylum applications since the late 1980s, and on the extent of misuse of the asylum process by those merely seeking to circumvent general immigration controls. Moreover, ministers have deliberately linked these two issues in order to create the impression of an asylum regime overwhelmed by a wave of "bogus refugees". Not only does this simplistic and emotive reasoning fail to take proper account of the ever present causes of refugee flows, but it glosses over the manifest failings of the previous asylum regime – a regime substantially remodelled as recently as July 1993. Yet responsibility for this failure lies squarely with the then Conservative

29 H.L. Hansard, Vol. 574, Col. 1203, 22 July 1996 (Lord Mackay of Ardbrecknish).

government itself.

In 1992 and 1993, Home Office ministers and officials repeatedly claimed that the new procedures established by the Asylum and Immigration Appeals Act 1993 would remove the growing delays in the asylum process, by providing for "prompt and fair" decisions. Indeed, during its passage through Parliament, ministers confidently predicted that the 1993 Act would result in initial decisions being made within a *maximum* of one month from the time of application, and in asylum cases being fully resolved (that is, including any subsequent appeal to the Immigration Appellate Authority (IAA)) within a *maximum* of three months. In fact, decision times on new applications have lengthened since July 1993. By August 1996, the Home Office was taking an average of 11.6 months to make an initial decision (on cases submitted post-July 1993). In short, on average initial decisions (on new applications) are currently taking almost 12 times longer than the *maximum* period predicted by ministers in 1992–93.[30] Furthermore, appeals to the IAA are currently taking an average of some 10 months to be determined, with the result that, on average, the full resolution of new asylum cases is taking some 21 months, that is, about seven times as long as the *maximum* time scale predicted by ministers in 1992–93 and, indeed, provided for in the legislation.[31]

There are clearly a number of factors contributing to this failure to meet the targets set out in 1992–93. These include the minimal use of computer technology and the retention of outdated and highly inefficient working practices within the Home Office, a serious under-resourcing of the asylum appeals mechanism (with insufficient numbers of IAA adjudicators), the excessively legalistic and adversarial culture of the appeals mechanism, and the inherent unfairness of the process as a whole (leading to an inordinate number of time-consuming challenges in the courts by way of judicial review). However, perhaps the most significant consequence of this failure is the enduring incentive the current system provides for those simply seeking to circumvent the UK's general immigration controls by making unfounded asylum applications. This incentive is compounded by the Home Office's comprehensive failure to effect the expulsion of unsuccessful asylum applicants. Statistically, the chances of an unsuccessful applicant being

30 New applications are given priority over those outstanding applications made before July 1993; as of August 1996, initial decisions on these applications were taking 44.8 months, on average. On the basis of these official figures, the writer estimates that, across the board, the Home Office is currently taking an average of some 27 months to reach an initial decision on an asylum application.

31 Source for all figures: H.C. Hansard, Vol. 284, Col. 208, 31 Oct. 1996.

removed (that is, expelled) from the United Kingdom at the end of the process are relatively small. Between January 1992 and September 1996, a total of 90,350 asylum seekers were refused by the Home Office and approximately 80 per cent of all subsequent appeals to the IAA were dismissed. In other words, over this period some 72,000 rejected asylum applicants reached the end of the asylum process and, having exhausted all appeal rights, became liable to removal. Yet, during the same period, only 10,888 rejected asylum seekers were actually removed or made a voluntary departure from the United Kingdom.[32]

Clearly, with the full resolution of asylum cases taking almost two years, on average, and with the chances of an ultimately unsuccessful asylum applicant being expelled from the UK being as little as one in seven, the incentive for those seeking only to circumvent UK immigration controls to make an unfounded asylum claim is strong. In short, the manifest failure of the asylum regime constructed in July 1993, for which the Conservative government alone was culpable, is leading directly to costly and destructive misuse of the asylum regime. Moreover, the problems associated with such misuse of the asylum process will not be remedied until this failure is addressed.

Conclusions

It is a commonly held view that in 1996, unlike in 1992–93, the Conservative government lost the argument about asylum seekers and lost it badly. In the face of credible, consistent and effective criticism from a wide range of organisations representing or concerned with the interests of refugees, ministers not only failed to make the case for yet another pre-election overhaul of the asylum regime, but the inherent injustice of their draconian cocktail of procedural and administrative changes was identified and condemned by those previously unheralded champions of refugee rights, the *Economist* and the *Times*. Having arrogantly swept aside the principled objections of its own Social Security Advisory Committee and having ignored the protestations of the UN High Commissioner for Refugees, no less, the government has since found itself humbled in the courts. And a spirited resistance in the House of Lords was finally put down only by the undemocratic, and constitutionally controversial, wielding of the hereditary vote.

---

32 Source for refusal/removal figures: Home Office Statistical Bulletin 9/96; and H.C. Hansard, Vol. 284, Col. 209, 31 Oct. 1996.

However, the hollowness of this moral victory is all too evident. Ministers themselves have not been moved by this substantial criticism, and their original proposals have been implemented almost to the letter. There are some who argue that this failure can be explained solely in terms of the markedly different paradigms of ministers and refugee agencies. As one proponent of this view told the writer in October 1996: "they see a different set of people to us – we see cases of refugees, they see cheats and fraudsters".

While there is no doubt a great deal of truth in this last remark, the writer begs to differ. From the latter part of 1995 through to the early months of 1997, senior and junior ministers in two major departments have consistently met reasoned argument with a tissue of spurious argument, distorted or partial statistics, false premises, and plain mendacity. Ministers have not been willing to recognise – let alone learn from – the mistakes of their predecessors, and have steadfastly refused to question past orthodoxies. Moreover, the standard policy cycle of problem definition, options analysis, implementation, evaluation and review has been broken. Given the consistency of this dissimulation over a prolonged period, it seems naive to believe that ministers have not known what they were doing. Indeed, Conservative ministers' casual dismissal of the many harrowing examples of hardship that have emerged in recent months suggests to this writer that they have no more shame than they do integrity.

Yet, there is hope. After a decade of policy failure (preceded by years of policy neglect), the new Labour government creates an opportunity to develop a truly fair and efficient asylum regime, that is, one in which decisions are taken and effected as expeditiously as is consistent with the need to identify all those who merit protection. Given the complex and problematic nature of asylum determination, and the grave consequences of error, it is essential that such a regime includes proper safeguards, as well as adequate welfare support during the waiting period. There are many challenges to be met: greater fairness (and, indeed, efficiency) will require a more *consensual* approach on the part of the relevant authorities (with greater involvement of refugee agencies in the decision-making process), as well as greater cooperation with other EU Member States (particularly with regard to "safe third country" cases). Similarly, greater efficiency (and, indeed, fairness) will require a much less legalistic and adversarial appeal mechanism, the exclusion of "cowboy" legal representatives from the asylum process (which will in turn require an extension of legal aid to cover representation at the appeal stage), and more effective enforcement of negative decisions (including more constructive use of Immigration Act detention).

The creation of such a regime is unlikely to win approving headlines in the *Daily Mail* and the *Daily Express*. But under a truly functional asylum regime, those who qualify for protection would be promptly identified and those who do not so qualify would be fairly and expeditiously removed, thereby minimising the incentive for costly – and ultimately destructive – misuse of the asylum regime by those merely seeking to circumvent general immigration controls.

Possibly the two most important issues to be addressed are the asylum appeals mechanism, and – perhaps the thorniest issue of all – the expulsion of unsuccessful applicants. The effectiveness of the appeal mechanism is crucial to the efficiency of the procedure as a whole, not least because it can impose standards and consistency on the Home Office's initial decision-making, while any gains in efficiency through reform of the procedures will be rendered meaningless by a continuing failure to *implement* decisions through the removal of unsuccessful applicants.

In the opinion of this writer, the quasi-judicial and inordinately adversarial nature of the existing IAA appeal mechanism is simply not conducive to the fair and expeditious determination of large numbers of asylum appeals, and an administrative form of appeal would be more appropriate. Under an administrative appeal model, costly and time consuming appeal "hearings" would be eliminated. Rather, appeals against a refusal of asylum would be examined and determined by appeal caseworkers, located in an independent appeal body and drawing on their own sources of information about the human rights situation in countries of origin. Appellants would be able to submit to the appeal body their response and counter-argument to the Home Office's reasons for refusal, and appeal caseworkers would be able to test credibility by means of face-to-face interviews. In this way, the refusal and the appellant's response would be subjected to independent scrutiny, without the need for a time consuming reworking of the refusal by the Home Office (to meet the inappropriate but testing demands of a quasi-judicial hearing), and the grossly inefficient court-like practices of the IAA (including the listing of several hearings for the same date and time) would be obviated. Moreover, the distortions and resultant inefficiencies associated with an inordinately legalistic and adversarial appeal hearing would be avoided. Whilst the logistics of such a radical reform are not to be underestimated, this writer believes that a functional administrative appeals mechanism could be established within existing budgetary restraints, through a radical reallocation of resources.

Bibliography

Collinson, S., "Visa Requirements, Carrier Sanctions, 'Safe Third Countries' and 'Readmission': The Development of an Asylum 'Buffer Zone' in *Europe* (1996) NS21:1 Transactions of the British Inst. of Geographers 76.

Dunstan, R., *Playing Human Pinball: Home Office Practice in "Safe Third Country" Asylum Cases*, (Amnesty International UK, 1995).

Glidewell Panel, *Report from an Independent Enquiry into the Implications and Effects of the Asylum and Immigration Bill 1995 and Related Social Security Measures* (16 April 1996).

Home Office Research Study No. 141, *The Settlement of Refugees in Britain*, 1995.

4 The Designation of "Safe" Countries and Individual Assessment of Asylum Claims

RACHEL TROST AND PETER BILLINGS

One of the most significant features of recent asylum policy changes in the United Kingdom has been the introduction and subsequent expansion of abbreviated procedures for the determination of asylum applications and appeals. These measures have involved a "safe third country" policy which was brought within an accelerated procedure for unfounded claims in 1993 and given legislative form in 1996,[1] the Short Procedure introduced as a practical measure in 1995,[2] and the authorisation of a system of designating

1 Asylum and Immigration Act (AIA) 1996 s. 2(2), relating to s. 6 of the Asylum and Immigration Appeals Act (AIAA) 1993, provides conditions for the removal of an asylum claimant to a safe third country, namely "(a) that the person is not a national or citizen of the country or territory to which he is to be sent; (b) that his life and liberty would not be threatened in that country by reason of his race, religion, nationality, membership of a particular social group, or political opinion; and (c) that the government of that country or territory would not send him to another country (...) otherwise than in accordance with the [1951 Geneva] Convention". Previously the concept of safe country was formulated in case law (*Bugdaycay and Others v. Secretary of State for the Home Department, Re Musisi* [1987] A.C. 514; *R. v. Secretary of State for Home Department, ex p. Akyol* [1990] Imm. A.R. 571), in the Statement of Changes in Immigration Rules HC 725 para. 180K (1993) and HC 395 para. 345) and brought within the AIAA 1993 Sch.2 para. 5(3)(a); see *R. v. Secretary of State for the Home Department, ex p. Mehari* [1994] Imm. A.R. 151.

2 The Short Procedure Pilot scheme was introduced by the Home Office on 15 May 1995 for nationals of eight countries. It was an internal policy change, there was no debate in parliament nor was it based on either primary or secondary legislation. It is currently employed for the majority of asylum applicants who apply at the Home Office and those who apply at Gatwick, and Heathrow Terminals 2 and 3. Applicants are interviewed by an Immigration Officer (IO) either on the day they applied for asylum or shortly thereafter. See Jagmohan, J.,

countries of origin as safe under the Asylum and Immigration Act 1996.[3] Speedy and efficient disposal of asylum applications, with appropriate safeguards, is undoubtedly to the benefit of all concerned. However, the government's resolve to introduce stronger measures to curb illegal "economic" immigration,[4] as expressed in the Asylum and Immigration Bill 1995, met with considerable opposition and serious criticism both inside and outside parliament.[5]

The value of expeditious procedures together with the gravity of the consequences of such decisions and the need for procedural guarantees were highlighted by the Executive Committee of the United Nations High Commissioner for Refugees (UNHCR)[6] well before these recent developments. European measures have provided the framework for accelerated procedures to be applied to manifestly unfounded claims[7] and for cases falling within both the safe country and the host third country concept

---

The Short Procedure: An Analysis of the Home Office Scheme for Rapid Initial Decisions in Asylum Cases pp. 1–2 (Asylum Rights Campaign, 1996).

3 AIA 1996 s. 1(2), amending Sch. 2 para. 5 to the 1993 Act, extends the "fast-track" special appeals procedure to asylum applicants "if the country or territory to which the appellant is to be sent is designated in an order made by the Secretary of State by statutory instrument as a country [...] in which it appears to him that there is in general no serious risk of persecution".

4 *New Curbs On Illegal Immigration*, Home Office News Release, 18/7/95.

5 H.C. Hansard, Vol. 281, Col. 813, 15 Jul. 1996 (Jack Straw); Amnesty International, *Slamming the Door: The Demolition of the Right to Asylum in the UK* (1996); *The Asylum and Immigration Bill 1995: The Report of the Glidewell Panel* (1996). Chaired by the recently retired Lord Justice of Appeal Sir Iain Glidewell, the panel was established in January 1996 by voluntary organisations and charitable trusts working in the fields of race relations and the protection of refugees. In the absence of a Special Standing Committee, it was the only independent forum for receiving evidence on the merits of the Bill. The panel found that in most cases the Bill would not achieve the government's stated intentions, and would damage race relations in the UK and increase racial discrimination. Despite these criticisms, the Bill, with only minor amendments, received the Royal Assent on 24 July 1996.

6 UNHCR Executive Committee Conclusions No.30 (XXXIV) *The Problem of Manifestly Unfounded or Abusive Applications for Refugee Status or Asylum* (1983).

7 "Resolution on Manifestly Unfounded Applications for Asylum" (1992) para. 2 (SN 4822/92 WGI 1282 AS 146).

to be considered under those procedures.[8] The Council of Ministers of the European Union (EU) has also repeatedly reaffirmed its determination to guarantee protection to refugees in accordance with the 1951 Geneva Convention.[9] It is the delicate balancing of these principles, which are on the one hand humanitarian, focusing on protection of the individual, and on the other political and practical, focusing on the need to reduce the perceived excessive pressure on the asylum determination process, that each state authority seeks to address. The competing priorities resulting from the combination of these principles were identified in *ex parte Abdi*, in which the House of Lords gave support to the legislative priorities of speed and efficiency, to the detriment of certain human rights concerns.[10] They were also identified by the Glidewell Panel.[11]

A recurrent and trenchant criticism of these procedures is that they may in effect categorise an individual by virtue of the country from which s/he has come, resulting in a failure to consider each application individually on its merits, as required by the UN Convention. This was raised as a fundamental objection to the principle and practice of the "white list" system.[12] It may similarly be applied to the Short Procedure, which may be described as the procedural precursor to a white list, and also to the safe third country ground for removal of an asylum claimant, without substantive consideration of the application.

The requirement that individual consideration be given to each applicant derives from the Geneva Convention and has been confirmed by the EU

---

8 "Conclusions on Countries in which there is Generally No Serious Risk of Persecution" (1992) (SN 4821/92 WGI 1281 AS 145) para. 3; "Resolution on a Harmonised Approach to Questions concerning Host Third Countries" (1992) (SN 4823/92 WGI 1283 AS 147) para. 1, agreed by Ministers of the Member States of the European Communities responsible for Immigration, London, 30 Nov.–1 Dec. 1992.

9 EU "Resolution on Minimum Guarantees for Asylum Procedures", (O.J. 1996 C274/13 adopted 20 June 1995, Brussels) para. 1 and EU Resolutions, *supra* notes 7 and 8, referring to the 1951 Geneva Convention relating to the Status of Refugees (189 U.N.T.S. 137), as amended by the 1967 New York Protocol (606 U.N.T.S. 267).

10 *R. v. Secretary of State for the Home Department, ex p. Abdi and Gawe* [1996] 1 W.L.R. 298, per Lord Slynn (dissenting), at 305 and 307, see *infra* n. 27.

11 *The Glidewell Report, op. cit. supra* n. 5, particularly at 38, Conclusion ii, as to the consistency of the legislation with the UK's obligations under international law.

12 H.C. Hansard, Vol. 281, Col. 809, 15 July 1996 (Jack Straw).

Council of Ministers. The essentially individual definition of a refugee, which forms the basis of the protection provided by the Geneva Convention, is strengthened by the requirement of nondiscrimination "as to race, religion or country of origin".[13] The Resolution on Minimum Guarantees for Asylum Procedures, approved by the Justice and Home Affairs (JHA) Council of Ministers affirms that "all asylum applications will be examined and decided upon individually, objectively and impartially".[14] The emphasis on individual determination is further confirmed by the Joint Position defined by the JHA Council of Ministers in 1996 in that "[E]ach application for asylum is examined on the basis of the facts and circumstances put forward *in each individual case* and taking account of the objective situation prevailing in the country of origin".[15] Collective determination is envisaged only in the positive sense of a situation in which "a whole group of people are exposed to persecution".[16] Examination of each application individually may then be limited to identifying whether the individual is a member of the group.[17] There is no provision for exclusion from the expectation that each application will be dealt with individually, nor, in particular, for that exclusion to be justified on the negative basis that a person belongs to a country or a group not subject to persecution. Yet this humanitarian approach as regards the substantive aspects of determination of refugee status may be rendered nugatory by procedures which allow for rejection of a claim on the basis of the safety of the country from which the person comes, thus precluding any substantive consideration of the merits of the individual claim.

Safe country policies, whether relating to countries of origin or to countries

---

13 1951 Refugee Convention, Arts. 1 and 3. The principle of the declaratory nature of recognition as a refugee requires an asylum claimant to be treated as a potential refugee unless and until not so recognised. See Macdonald, I. and Blake, N., *Macdonald's Immigration Law and Practice* (Butterworths, 4th edn, 1995), para. 12.6; UNHCR *Handbook on Procedures and Criteria for Determining Refugee Status* (1988), para. 28.

14 EU "Resolution on Minimum Guarantees for Asylum Procedures", *supra* n. 9, para. 4 and *cf.* para. 20.

15 (Emphasis added). "Joint Position of 4 March 1996 defined by the Council on the basis of Article K.3 of the Treaty on European Union on the harmonised application of the definition of the term 'refugee' in Article 1 of the Geneva Convention of 29 July 1951 relating to the status of refugees", 96/196/JHA (1996) O.J. L63/2. The Joint Position provides guidelines which do not bind the legislative or judicial authorities of member states.

16 *Ibid.*, para. 2.

17 *Ibid.*

of asylum, encapsulate an acute and poignant form of the tension, which is present in asylum procedures in general, between the competing perspectives of immigration control and humanitarian concern. If the country is indeed safe for the individual, the protection of the 1951 Convention may not be necessary or appropriate.[18] If, however, the safety proves illusory, the individual asylum seeker may be removed and possibly subjected to *refoulement* without the normal safeguards appropriate to an asylum application. The process of designation of third countries or countries of origin as safe, the objectivity and openness of this process, the reliability of the information used, the ability of relevant officials to make consistent use of this information and their overall training are vital issues if wrong decisions are to be avoided and the protection of the 1951 Convention is to be guaranteed effectively. This chapter will examine ways of ensuring fairness and objectivity in the application of the restrictive legislation whilst working towards a policy which takes fuller account of the human rights standards to which the UK is committed.

Certification of a Third Country as "Safe"

The notion of a manifestly unfounded or inadmissible claim, employed by almost all of the EU member states,[19] is most frequently used as the basis for applying an accelerated procedure or to justify immediate removal of the asylum seeker to a "safe third country" (sometimes also known as a "first country of asylum"), possibly with a non-suspensive right of appeal.[20] The crucial determination that a country is "safe" may be left to the decision of the authority responsible for dealing with an asylum application. In the UK it is the Secretary of State who must certify that, "in his opinion, the conditions ... are fulfilled".[21] Despite the recommendation of the UNHCR that the consent of the receiving state be obtained and despite Opposition amendments designed to ensure that people who are sent back to a "safe" third country "are not left

18 *Glidewell Report*, *op. cit. supra* n. 5, para. 6.3.4. This does not remove the obligation of *non-refoulement*. See also UNHCR, *Fair and Expeditious Asylum Procedures* (Geneva, 1994) para. 5.

19 An exception being Luxembourg. See Care, G., *Guide to Asylum Law and Practice in the European Union*, (Immigration Law Practitioners' Association, London, 1996) 77.

20 *Ibid.*

21 AIA 1996 s. 2(1)(a); *cf.* AIAA 1993, Sch. 2 para. 5(1) as amended by s. 1 of the 1996 Act.

entirely without an opportunity to claim asylum",[22] the position remains that the Secretary of State is under no obligation to consult the authorities of the receiving country.[23] The uncertainties concerning the safety even of countries such as Belgium and France, due to the possibility of *refoulement*, the inadequacy of procedures or time limits for access to those procedures, have been highlighted by both the courts and commentators.[24] An asylum seeker's vulnerability to such uncertainties may be accentuated by the implementation of the increasing number of bilateral readmission agreements, including ones between EU and central or eastern European countries in which effective protection from *refoulement* cannot be guaranteed.[25]

The certificate of the Secretary of State may be challenged on appeal to a Special Adjudicator on the ground that the conditions relating to the safety of the country were not fulfilled or have ceased to be fulfilled.[26] For the safety of a country to be effectively verified by the adjudicator, it is essential that the objectivity of the decision of the Secretary of State and the reliability of the information on which his decision is based may be properly assessed. The adjudicator's power to request documents may in practice ensure that relevant material is available to all involved in an appeal. It does not, however, meet the arguments of unfairness raised against the judgment that, in law, the Secretary of State is under no obligation to disclose all material on which his certificate is based, and that only documentation which supports the Secretary

---

22 Standing Committee D, Col. 221 at Col. 224, 23 Jan. 1996, (Bernie Grant).

23 Immigration Rules HC 395 para. 345, as amended by HC 31 (1996).

24 *R. v. Special Adjudicator, ex p. Turus; R v. Immigration Appeal Tribunal, ex p. Bostem* [1996] Imm. A.R. 388; *R. v. Secretary of State for the Home Department, ex p. Martinas* [1995] Imm. A.R. 190; *R. v. Secretary of State for the Home Department, ex p. Kanapathypillai* [1996] Imm. A.R. 116. However, see also *Canbolat v. Secretary of State for the Home Department* CA [1997] Imm. A.R. 442, Times Law Report, 9 May 1997. Relevant articles include Shah, P., "Refugees and Safe Third Countries: United Kingdom, European and International Aspects" (1995) Eur.P.L.259; European Council for Refugees and Exiles (ECRE), *"Safe Third Countries": Myths and Realities* (1995); Amnesty International, *Playing Human Pinball: Home Office Practice in "Safe Third Country" Asylum Cases* (1995); Symes, M., *The Law relating to "Without Foundation' Asylum Claims* (Refugee Legal Centre, 1996). See also chapter 8 of this book by Geoffrey Care.

25 ECRE, *ibid.* para. 21 and appendix D; UNHCR, *Certain Comments by the United Nations High Commissioner for Refugees on the Asylum and Immigration Bill 1995* (UNHCR, London, 1996), pp. 8–9; Acherman, A. and Gattiker, M., "Safe Third Countries: European Developments", (1995) 7 I.J.Ref.L. 19 at 23–24.

26 AIA 1996 s. 3(1)(a).

of State's decision is to be provided, by law, to the adjudicator at the hearing.[27] In addition to openness and equality, there is an obvious need for reliable information and documentation systems in this context (see below).

Legislation in some countries makes the notion of a "safe third country" more specific by designating, or providing authority for designating particular states as safe. Commonly this is applied to countries within a common travel area[28] or within the European Union. An important example of this approach is found in Germany where the Basic Law (constitution) has since 1993 identified all EU Member states as "safe".[29] Other countries may be designated as safe on the basis that the authorities are obliged by law to apply both the 1951 Refugee Convention and the 1950 European Convention for the protection of Human Rights and Fundamental Freedoms (ECHR), criteria which, interestingly, are not even fulfilled in at least one EU member state, notably the UK, although the 1997 change of Government has finally resulted in a commitment to incorporate the 1950 Convention into UK law. This designation has been implemented in relation to a number of countries including, controversially, all those bordering Germany.[30] In a significant decision on 14 May 1996, the Federal German Constitutional Court interpreted these measures as creating a non-rebuttable presumption of safety, affirming

27 *R. v. Secretary of State for the Home Department, ex p. Abdi and Gawe* [1996] 1 W.L.R. 298 at 307. "The current procedure is not such as to enable the special adjudicators fully to perform their task and is calculated to produce unfairness," per Lord Slynn (dissenting), agreeing with Steyn LJ (CA). The sufficiency of the Home Secretary's statement and the lack of an obligation to disclose all material "in the very special context of this abbreviated procedure" were confirmed by the House of Lords, see per Lord Mustill, *ibid.* at 300.

28 E.g. the Nordic travel area under the Convention between Denmark, Finland, Norway and Sweden concerning the Waiver of Passport Control at the Internal-Nordic Borders (no. 29 12/07/1958 C); see ECRE, *Asylum in Europe* (1994) Volume II, p. 61.

29 Basic Law (Grundgesetz) Art. 16a, para. 2.

30 Basic Law, Art. 16a para. 2; Asylum Procedure Act, Annex I to Section 26a Asylverfahrensgesetz, as discussed in Marx, R., and Lumpp, K., "The German Constitutional Court's Decision of 14 May 1996 on the Concept of 'Safe Third Countries' – A Basis for Burden-Sharing in Europe?" (1996) 8 I.J.Ref.L. 419. See also Blay, S. and Zimmermann, A., "Recent Changes in German Refugee Law: a Critical Assessment", (1994) A.J.I.L. 88, 361–78; Wisskirchen, C., "Germany: Assault on the Constitutional Right to Asylum" (1994) 8 I.N.L.P. 87 and 136 at 137–39; Noll, G., "The Non-Admission and Return of Protection Seekers in Germany" (1997) 9 I.J.Ref.L. 415.

the legislator's competence both to "establish by law the certainty that the third country is "safe" for refugees" and "to choose the information on which the assessment ... is to be based".[31] This provides a sombre but potentially influential example. Assessment of the safety of a country for the individual asylum seeker is excluded from the asylum determination process in all but the most exceptional circumstances.

In the UK, the provision of an in-country right of appeal, a key feature of the 1993 legislation, has been partially reversed by the AIA 1996. The Bill would have excluded appeal from within the UK against a certificate of the Secretary of State that any third country was safe.[32] However, following a government amendment, certain countries are designated, having the effect of limiting the circumstances in which appeal is only exercisable from outside the UK. Where an applicant faces deportation to one of the countries named, s/he cannot appeal while still in the UK. The 1996 Act mentions "member states", understood to be member states of the EU, and those designated by statutory instrument, subsequently identified as Canada, Norway, Switzerland and the United States.[33] Some limited democratic controls are provided by the legislation in the form of the requirement of an affirmative resolution procedure for the initial order but subsequently only the minimal negative resolution procedure will apply.[34]

Involvement of Independent Bodies in the Determination Process

In the light of the many unresolved criticisms of the asylum determination process, the next section of this chapter looks at ways in which the objectivity of the asylum determination process can be strengthened and at how public confidence can be increased. One such reform involves an increased role for the UNHCR, as the main independent body having some involvement in domestic asylum procedures, as it is argued that the refugee determination process might thereby be improved and a less adversarial approach fostered.[35]

31 Marx and Lumpp, *ibid.*, at 419 and 424.

32 Asylum and Immigration Bill, clauses 2 and 3 (29 Nov. 1995).

33 AIA 1996, s.2(3); Standing Committee D, Col. 257, 23 Jan. 1996 (Timothy Kirkhope); Asylum (Designated Countries of Destination and Designated Safe Third Countries) Order 1996, (SI 1996 No.2671).

34 AIA 1996 s. 2(4) and (5).

35 Glidewell Report, *op. cit.* n. 5, at 17 (proposal by Joint Council for the Welfare of Immigrants) and 18 (Asylum Aid proposal).

The role of the UNHCR, the functions of which include supervision of the application of the 1951 Convention,[36] differs in each of the countries of the EU depending on domestic legislation and practice. Whereas in several countries its role does not extend beyond general consultation and advice, in some countries the UNHCR will be consulted before an asylum decision is reached or, as in the UK, may be a party to an appeal.[37] France is noteworthy in that a representative of the UNHCR may be a member both of the body determining refugee status and of the appellate body.[38] A more significant role is exercised by the UNHCR in Switzerland in the decision as to entry to the territory, which in turn gives access to the asylum procedure. An applicant at the Swiss border or particularly at an airport will not be sent back to his or her country of origin if the UNHCR disagrees with the decision of the Federal Office of Refugees as to the safety of the country for the applicant.[39]

It is unusual for the UNHCR or any other independent body to have a decisive role in the procedures, as happens most notably, in Denmark. The Danish Refugee Council (DRC),[40] in the absence of an UNHCR office in Denmark, has a prominent role in the nomination to the Refugee Appeals Board of one or two members who, in conjunction with the Bar's nominees, may constitute a majority of the "full" board.[41] This is a significant role in ensuring impartiality, which in other systems may be provided by the establishment of an independent appellate authority, as in the UK where, since 1987, adjudicators are no longer appointed by the Home Office but by the Lord Chancellor.[42]

The DRC also has a decisive role in the special procedure for applications

36 Goodwin-Gill, G., *The Refugee in International Law* (Oxford University Press, 2nd edn, 1996), 33.

37 Asylum Appeals Procedure Rules, 1996, para. 8(2) and 15(2); e.g. *R. v. Secretary of State for the Home Department, ex p. Sivakumaran* [1988] A.C. 958 (HL) per Lord Keith at 995.

38 Loi No. 52–893 du 25 juillet 1952 portant création d'un office français de protection des réfugiés et apatrides, art.3; Décret No. 80–683 du 3 sept. 1980 modifiant le décret No.53–377 du 2 mai 1953 relatif à l'office français de protection des réfugiés et apatrides, art.15; see Lambert, H., *Seeking Asylum* (Martinus Nijhoff, 1995) 43; see also Guimezanes, N., *Le droit des étrangers* (Armand Colin, 1987) 35.

39 Lambert, H., *ibid.*, at 46.

40 Consists of 18 voluntary agencies and is the principal agency involved in the reception and integration of refugees in Denmark.

41 Aliens Act, 1983, art. 53(2); see ECRE, *Asylum in Europe* pp. 51–102 at 70.

42 Transfer of Functions (Immigration Appeals) Order 1987 (SI 1987/465).

which are considered by the Directorate for Immigration to be manifestly unfounded. These include applications with no prospect of success according to the Board's case law on the grounds of asylum being possible in a third country. Such an application must be referred to the DRC, which can require that the case be dealt with under the normal procedures if it does not agree that the application is manifestly unfounded.[43] If, however, the DRC agrees with the proposal of the Directorate, the asylum seeker is required to leave the country without any appeal. This procedure may be compared to the power of a Special Adjudicator under the AIAA 1993 to refer an application certified as "without foundation" back to the Home Secretary for reconsideration or, alternatively, to confirm a negative decision.[44] One positive effect of the cooperation between the Danish Immigration Service and the DRC has been that, as the DRC itself has noted, "[h]aving a non-governmental-organisation (such) as the DRC participating in the procedure broadens the public confidence in the procedure".[45]

A body such as the DRC may provide objectivity in checking the initial decision made by the relevant authority. It does not, however, go as far as ensuring objectivity in the initial decision-making itself. François Julien-Laferrière, in a paper on the role of decision-making bodies[46] considers two possible approaches. According to the first, decisions as to refugee status are part of national asylum and immigration policy, the decision-makers being subject to political pressures and constraints in line with the need to control the numbers of migrants seeking to enter the territory. An alternative approach focuses on the individual in need of protection and under this scenario respect for human rights is ensured by making decision-makers independent of government. The system advocated is one in which the initial decision is taken by an independent administrative body, with the possibility of an appeal to a judicial body. Examples of decision-making bodies with some measure of independence from the government may be found in a number of EU countries.[47] In contrast, in the UK, the Home Office, as the body responsible

43 Danish Aliens Act 1983, art. 33(2).

44 AIAA 1993, Sch. 2, para. 5(6). The power of referral was not re-enacted in 1996.

45 L. Juelskjaer, Asylum Department, Danish Refugee Council. Letter to the authors 20 Sept. 1996.

46 Julien-Laferrière, F., "Le rôle des instances de décision" in *Europe and Refugees: A Challenge?*, Carlier, J.-Y. and Vanheule, D., eds (Kluwer, 1997), pp. 107–23.

47 For example, Belgium (Commissariat général aux réfugiés et apatrides), France (Office français de protection des réfugiés et apatrides, OFPRA) and Germany (Bundesamt für die Anerkennung ausländischer Flüchtlinge). Julien-Laferrière,

for decisions on refugee status, clearly considers asylum within an immigration policy context to such an extent that a revival of the alternative human rights perspective has become an urgent concern. The independence of the decision-making body could offer the best guarantee of objectivity and prevent effective protection of refugees from being subsumed under considerations of domestic and international politics.

"White List" Designation and Accelerated Procedures

The concept of safe countries of origin, or the "white list", now contained in section one of the 1996 Act, has its origin in EU agreements drafted in secret meetings and subsequently signed by the Home Secretary without any consultation and debate in parliament.[48] During debate on the Bill, the government agreed to a House of Lords amendment that the initial list of countries on the white list should be subject to the affirmative procedure,

F., *ibid.*, n. 5, See also Lambert, H., *op. cit. supra* n. 38, pp. 21–30. In both Belgium and France an applicant's access to the asylum procedure depends on permission to enter the territory, the latter decision being under the authority of a government minister.

48 The creation of the "white list" was specifically provided for in the "Resolution on Manifestly Unfounded Applications for Asylum" para. 8, and the "Conclusions on Countries in which there is Generally No Serious Risk of Persecution" para. 1, *supra* nn. 7 and 8. These were signed by the then Home Secretary, Kenneth Clarke, in Dec. 1992 at a meeting of the European Justice and Home Affairs Council of Ministers in London. See also European parliament, Directorate General for Research, *Asylum in the European Union: The "Safe Country of Origin" Principle*, People's Europe Series, W–7 (Feb. 1997). More recently, EU Member States declared, in a "Protocol on asylum for nationals of Member states of the European Union" signed along with the Amsterdam Treaty in October 1997, that "given the level of protection of fundamental rights and freedoms by the Member States of the European Union, Member states shall be regarded as constituting safe countries of origin in respect of each other for all legal and practical purposes in relation to asylum matters" (Treaty of Amsterdam (1997) O.J. C340/01 (10 Nov. 1997). Under Arts. 73i and 73k of the Treaty itself significant asylum and immigration issues are brought within the area of Community competence, although the UK, Denmark and Ireland have negotiated protocols under which they remain outside these common provisions with an option to opt in in respect of individual measures. For further details see Nicholson, F., and Twomey, P. (eds), *Refugee Rights and Realities: Evolving International Concepts and Regimes*, part four (Cambridge University Press, forthcoming 1998).

later amendments being subject only to the negative procedure.[49] As such parliament will have the choice of simply accepting or rejecting a new list of countries and will not have the option of accepting some while rejecting others.

Stronger safeguards are needed to control executive power to designate countries for inclusion on the list, because it is questionable whether the Executive may be depended upon to make objective designations.[50] The Home Secretary stated that all relevant information about conditions in the country concerned would be taken into account in designating countries.[51] At present, what constitutes "all relevant information" appears to be largely determined on the basis of information provided by diplomatic missions of EU member states, and produced by the Centre for Information, Discussion and Exchange on Asylum (CIREA).[52] "These reports form the basis of secret "joint assessments" of situations in countries of origin ...",[53] therefore, it is unclear to what extent there is adequate consideration of, among others, the US State Department *Country Reports on Human Rights Practices*, the *World Report* of Human Rights Watch and Amnesty International's *Annual Report*, which "are the very minimum required to make an assessment of human rights in countries of origin".[54]

---

49 S.1(8) and (9) 1996 Act and the Asylum (Designated Countries of Destination and Designated Safe Third Countries) Order 1996, S.I. 1996 No. 2671.

50 For example, the presence of foreign policy considerations was clearly evident from the manner in which the then Home Secretary, Michael Howard attempted to deport the Saudi dissident Mohammad al-Mas'ari to Dominica in January 1996. Preservation of good foreign trade and diplomatic relations with Saudi Arabia apparently took precedence over human rights considerations (*Guardian*, 6 March 1996).

51 H.C. Hansard, Vol. 268, Col. 702, 11 Dec. 1995 (Michael Howard, then Secretary of State for the Home Department).

52 Set up by EU Immigration Ministers in Lisbon in 1992. Its objectives are to "gather, exchange and disseminate information and compile documentation on all matters relating to asylum" in order to develop greater informal consultation and thus facilitate harmonisation of asylum practice and policy. See *Decision Establishing the Clearing House*, Council of Ministers, 30 Nov. 1992 [SN 2836/93 WGI 1505], S.II.

53 Reilly, R., *Closing the Door: The Concept of Safe Countries of Origin in European Countries* (Refugee Council, July 1996) at 1.

54 Fletcher, T., "A Comment on Documentary Problems involved in Countering 'Safe Country of Origin' Proposals", (Refugee Legal Centre), contained in *Safe Countries of Origin and Safe Third Countries*, Immigration Law Practitioners' Association conference materials, (8 July 1996). Baroness Blatch in the House

The following three criteria were applied in relation to the designation of countries as generally safe: firstly, there must be no serious risk of persecution;[55] secondly the country must be one which generates a large number of asylum applicants; and thirdly, a high proportion of the asylum applications which are generated from that state are unfounded.[56] Conspicuously absent was any mention of an assessment of the human rights situation,[57] or whether the refugee agencies are to be involved in the designation process. The participation of the latter is arguably a prerequisite to a thorough and balanced assessment of whether a country is "safe". In Denmark the Danish Immigration Service determines which countries will be placed on the list of safe countries. Crucially, however, "if the DRC disagree strongly with the inclusion of certain countries on the list, they do have the right to veto and can present their concerns to the Immigration Service. It is likely that [in such circumstances] ... a country would be removed from the list".[58]

---

of Lords spoke of independent evidence available to ministers upon which to base country assessments, stating: "[I]n addition to reports from the Foreign and Commonwealth Office we take *account* of the views of other western governments, independent press reporting and reports from organisations such as Amnesty. ... I mention just three independent sources of advice: the US State Department; the Carter Centre; and Amnesty International." (H.L. Hansard, Vol. 571, Cols 1086 and 1088, 23 April 1996). However, there is no legal prescription in either the 1996 Act or any of the accompanying secondary legislation imposing a duty upon Home Office officials to consult such documents.

55 Which is in itself more onerous than the requirement in the 1951 UN Convention which requires the applicant to have "a well founded fear of persecution". The inadequacies in the usage of the phrase "in general no serious risk ..." were explained by Lord McIntosh of Haringey in the House of Lords. (H.L. Hansard, Vol. 571, Cols 1061–62, 23 April 1996).

56 Michael Howard, *supra* n. 51.

57 UNHCR has suggested alternative criteria for deciding when a country is "generally safe": its respect for human rights and the rule of law; its record of not producing refugees; its ratification and compliance with human rights instruments; and its accessibility to independent national and international organisations for the purpose of verifying and supervising respect for human rights. ("Certain Comments by the UNHCR on the Asylum and Immigration Bill", written submissions to the Glidewell Panel, at 14).

58 Provision for the safe country concept is not included in Danish legislation but in explanatory notes accompanying the 1994 amendment to the Danish Aliens Act. Louise Juelskjaer letter to the authors 20 Sept. 1996.

The "White List", Accelerated Procedures and Their Impact on Individual Assessment of Asylum Applications

Applicants on the list of designated countries encounter three additional hurdles in making their asylum claim. First, they must overcome the onerous burden of proof[59] and a presumption that claims from designated countries were not well founded.[60] "Evidence of the risk of such a mentality developing [was] provided by a leaked Foreign Office memorandum on the "white list" which state[d] that asylum claims by nationals of countries on the list are 'likely to be refused'".[61] Little comfort may be drawn from declarations of intent from the Immigration and Nationality Directorate (IND) stating that "asylum applicants from a "designated" country will be given a full opportunity to put forward details of the claim in the same way as asylum seekers from any other country".[62] Having the opportunity to put forward details of the claim is one thing, having those details assessed fairly and objectively may be quite another.[63]

The second obstacle is the so-called "short procedure" (SP) scheme, which the Home Office announced on 20 March 1996 would apply to the "great majority of claims".[64] Placing asylum applicants, particularly port applicants, in the SP puts them at a severe disadvantage.[65] For applicants faced with a presumption that there is "generally no serious risk of persecution" in their country of origin, the position is even more precarious. The withdrawal of the

59 "[A] double burden of proof will be placed on applicants originating from these countries". Jack Straw, *supra* n. 12.

60 Michael Howard, *supra* n. 51.

61 Amnesty International, "Submission to the Glidewell Panel in respect of the Asylum and Immigration Bill and related measures", written submissions to the Glidewell Panel, *supra*, n. 5.

62 IND letter to authors, 23 Sept. 1996.

63 The examiner "must apply the [Convention] criteria in a spirit of justice and understanding and his judgement should not, of course, be influenced by the personal consideration that the applicant may be an 'undeserving case'". *UNHCR Handbook on Procedures and Criteria for Determining Refugee Status*, para. 202.

64 H.C. Hansard, Vol. 282, Cols 159–60, 23 Jul. 1996 (Timothy Kirkhope, written answer). In the period May 1995 to June 1996, just three applicants (0.05 per cent) considered under this procedure were accepted as refugees, 5,735 applicants were refused and 996 were still under consideration. Figures relate to initial decisions taken by the Home Office.

65 For a comprehensive exposition of the vulnerability of port applicants see Jagmohan, J., *op. cit. supra* n. 2 at 15.

self-completion questionnaires (SCQ), removed a vital preparatory tool which can be seen as essential for "designated" asylum applicants in their efforts to rebut the strong presumption that their country of origin is generally safe. Consultation with a legal representative at the very least, and with medical practitioners and social workers over a period of four weeks,[66] is a necessary prerequisite to any asylum applicant having the "fullest opportunity" to disclose all the relevant information in an asylum claim. To submit, as the Home Office do, that the SP procedure does not inhibit an applicant's ability to present their case appears untenable when one considers that only 0.05 per cent of applicants were accepted under the SP between May 1995 and June 1996,[67] and contrast it with the 2,200 (6 per cent) applicants who were, after the initial decision, granted refugee status in 1996.[68]

Immigration Officers can no longer be considered as mere gatekeepers following the introduction of the SP, their role is now crucial in shaping the flow of information passed onto the caseworkers, which can materially affect the outcome of an application. It would be beneficial to all parties concerned if Immigration Officers were assigned to deal with cases from specific geographical areas, as this would give them enhanced familiarity with conditions, events, political parties, social, religious and ethnic groups in those areas. The genuine asylum seeker would have a better opportunity to disclose fully the facts surrounding their subjective evidence and objective situation. With greater expertise in relation to specific regions, Immigration Officers would also be better placed to probe applicants and reveal weaknesses and inconsistencies with greater speed and certainty. [69]

---

66 This period of time equates with that which was afforded to asylum applicants who were given SCQs to complete, which prior to the SP was the standard practice for in-country applicants, and to port applicants following completion of the pro forma interview. SCQs are still issued to those applicants arriving from certain countries specifically exempted from the SP scheme (Iraq, Iran, Libya, Somalia, Liberia, Rwanda, Afghanistan, Palestine, the Gulf states (except Kuwait), Bosnia, Croatia and the Federal Republic of Yugoslavia), and in relation to those ports of entry not yet employing the SP. *Ibid.* at 2.

67 *Supra* n. 64.

68 Home Office Statistical Bulletin, *Control of Immigration: Statistics United Kingdom, Second Half and Year 1996* at 7.

69 "[E]xperience has shown that [...] interviewing officers do not always have specialist knowledge and have often asked extremely basic questions and have shown that they are not up to date with political events and developments in other countries, let alone issues affecting minorities and regional politics." Jagmohan, J., *op. cit. supra* n. 2 at 28.

Since one of a number of criteria in the guidelines issued to the immigration service governing detention is the likelihood of a negative decision by the Asylum Screening Unit (ASU),[70] it is reasonable to surmise that for "white list" applicants, there is an increased likelihood of being subject to detention, given that the SP was clearly the precursor to the "white list", and the SP has resulted in minute recognition rates.[71] For a "white list" applicant the implications of being detained are acute, because whilst asylum seekers exempt from the SP have on average eight months awaiting a decision, and therefore that length of time to advance additional supporting evidence, those who are detained have just five days.[72] Such a short time in which to adduce supporting evidence is clearly grossly inadequate for several reasons. Personal access to legal representation is restricted whilst in detention because it is dictated by prison appointment times, and furthermore the arduous task of obtaining additional supporting evidence is exacerbated by being inside the confines of a detention centre or prison.

The third obstacle concerns the special appeals procedure established in the 1993 Act, which has been extended to cover the appeal rights of those listed as arriving from "safe" countries. The Procedural Rules for all "fast-track" appeals, in force since 1 September 1996, provide that an appeal must be lodged not later than *two* working days where, inter alia, the appeal relates to a certified claim.[73] Abbreviated time constraints severely hamper the ability

70 "... factors to be taken into account in assessing the need to detain will include ... the expectation of removal within a reasonable period of time" (*Immigration Service Instructions to Staff on Detention* issued 3 Dec. 1991, at 1). However, it is also stated in the Operational Instructions (p. 2) that "the aim should be to free detention space for those who have shown a real disregard for the immigration laws *and* who are able to be removed within a realistic timescale". White list applicants cannot be deemed to have "real disregard for immigration laws" merely by virtue of their country of origin. Therefore if one element of this requirement is not satisfied, legitimate questions could be asked of any Home Office policy or practice which detains "white list" applicants as a matter of course.

71 However, "in many instances detention would appear to be quite arbitrary, dependent on the availability of detention spaces". Witherow, R., "Detention of Asylum Seekers: A Continuing Cause for Concern" (1995) 9(2) I.N.L.P. 59 at 60.

72 As do applicants who apply for asylum from within the UK. Those port applicants who are not detained have 30 days to make further representations. Prior to the Home Office announcement on 20 March 1996 the time limit was 10 days. Jagmohan, J., *op. cit. supra* n. 2 at 2.

73 The Asylum Appeals (Procedure) Rules 1996 SI 2070, Rule 5(1). A Special Adjudicator must decide the appeal not later than 42 days after receiving notice

of all appellants to lodge a successful appeal, but this is especially acute in relation to applicants from "white list" countries, since representatives may often be seeking to verify the existence of human rights abuse or civil unrest in countries such as Ghana, India or Pakistan, a process which may prove both problematic and time consuming. The substantive issue of whether the applicant suffered from a well-founded fear of persecution also has to be established within this narrow time frame, whereas the fast-track appeals procedure originally established under the 1993 Act concerned applications which had been summarily refused on "safe third country grounds",[74] for which a substantive examination of the application's merits, was not necessary. Applicants on the list of designated safe countries of origin not only face truncated appeals procedures, but the opportunity to appeal to the Immigration Appeal Tribunal is also denied.[75]

Instead of achieving the government's stated aim of reducing the backlog of cases awaiting a decision, paradoxically it is likely to clog up the determination system further as applicants turn to the High Court and judicial review. Judge David Pearl in oral evidence to the Glidewell Panel agreed with representations made by the Refugee Legal Centre (RLC) to the effect that the 1996 Act would result in the Special Adjudicators prioritising "fast-track" cases because of the anticipated increase in numbers to be dealt with under the accelerated procedures. This would result in consideration of the substantive cases being put back further, "and waiting lists could well increase beyond what they are at the present time".[76]

The Conservative government which took the AIA 1996 through parliament placed great faith in the extension of the special appeals procedures as the mechanism which would effectively sift through the "manifestly unfounded" claims so that the "genuine" claims could be dealt with expeditiously. However, for asylum seekers who emanate from designated "safe countries of origin", the ramifications are serious because of the special appeals procedure which restricts appeal rights, both in terms of the strict deadlines imposed and the removal of the right of appeal to the Immigration Appeal Tribunal. Furthermore, the Home Office practice of subjecting applicants to the Short Procedure has placed those applicants from designated

---

of the appeal or within 10 days where the appeal relates to a certified claim. *Ibid.*, Rules 9(1) and 9(2).

74 Or because it was considered "frivolous or vexatious", AIAA 1993, Sch. 2, 5(3)b.

75 AIA 1996 s. 1(7), amending sch. 2(5) to the 1993 Act.

76 Judge David Pearl in oral evidence to the Glidewell Panel. *Glidewell Report, op. cit. supra* n. 5 at 13.

countries in a particularly vulnerable position. Notwithstanding the possible abolition of the "white list" in the future,[77] there remains a need for a critical examination of the legal and administrative methods adopted to tackle the rise in asylum applications, to address the backlog of claims awaiting a final decision and to remove fraudulent claims expeditiously.[78] Any such examination must, however, keep in mind that compassion and control must be the twin goals of any asylum policy.

Lessons from Experience in North America

Turning to the situation in the United States, experience has shown that attaining these goals met with a very different, arguably more balanced response at the start of the 1990s. There was by 1989 a consensus among refugee commentators that the system was not working.[79] It was criticised for having too few officials assigned to asylum adjudication, for their low level of qualification and for the fact that adjudicators reported to Immigration and Naturalisation Service (INS) district offices, and were therefore often perceived as having an "enforcement perspective".[80] The asylum regulation promulgated on 27 July 1990,[81] mandated the creation of a corps of

77 Bennetto, J., "Straw to abandon Tory asylum laws", *Independent*, 29 May 1997. Within a month of forming the new Labour government, there were signs of a new approach to immigration, with the announcement that all asylum procedures were to be reviewed. The abolition of the "white list" was indicated as being one of the proposed reforms.

78 The figure stood at 69,650 at the end of 1995, a year in which the Home Office made 27,010 decisions. Cited by Harvey, A., *The Risks of Getting it Wrong: The Asylum and Immigration Session 1995/96 and the Determination of Special Adjudicators* (Asylum Rights Campaign, 1996) at 16. In 1996 the number of initial decisions reached by the Home Office had risen to 39,000, "the highest number of decisions made in a single year and can be mostly attributed to the expansion of the Asylum Directorate's short procedure" (*supra* n. 68).

79 Helton, A., "The INS is the one that's Abusing Political Asylum", *Houston Chronicle*, 22 Feb. 1989, at 3. Cited by Beyer, G., "Establishing the United States Asylum Corps" (1992) 4(4) I.J.Ref.L. 455 at 466.

80 In much the same way, as the immigration officials in the UK are currently viewed by academics, immigration practitioners and indeed the Home Office itself as having a "primary function" of "maintaining immigration control at ports of entry". IND letter to the authors, 23 Sept. 1996.

81 55 Fed. Reg. 30,674 (1990), codified in the Code of Federal Regulations at 8 CFR s. 208.

professional Asylum Officers (AOs) trained in international relations and international law.[82] In addition to the increased training asylum officers were to receive, asylum adjudication functions and enforcement responsibilities were separated. The rule also established the Resource Information Centre, designed to collect, produce and disseminate information gathered from a variety of sources about human rights conditions around the world.[83] The four week training programme for AOs, included three weeks of specialised asylum training which covered a variety of topics, including: (i) the policy context and the political and legal challenges which the new programme sought to address; (ii) international human rights and international refugee law; (iii) a review of US asylum law, regulations and policies; (iv) asylum procedures and operations instructions; (v) conditions in asylum applicant countries of origin; (vi) interviewing techniques and role playing (including sessions devoted to "confronting one's baggage of preconceptions and presumptions regarding eligibility for asylum"); (vii) cross cultural interviewing and sensitivity; and (viii) assessments of each AO's interviewing techniques, analytical abilities and writing skills.[84]

One could point to the fact that AOs are equipped with the power to grant asylum,[85] whereas Immigration Officers (IOs) in the UK are not, as a justification for a difference in training. However, given recent legislative and policy developments and the crucial role now allocated to IOs, enhancing their training and support is fundamental to ensuring the impartiality and the sensitivity required for what is an arduous and important task.[86]

All new Immigration Officers in the UK attend a five week induction

---

82 8 CFR s. 208.1 (b) (1990), as amended (1995).

83 The asylum rule also sought to reaffirm the neutral refugee definition and diminish the role of the State Department in deciding domestic asylum claims. See below for discussion of the advantages of a resource centre for *all* actors in the determination system.

84 Asylum case analysis and decision-writing, supervision and quality control and stress management and burnout prevention were also covered. Beyer, G., *op. cit. supra* n. 79 at 472.

85 8 CFR s. 208.2 (1990), as amended (1995): "An application that is complete ... shall be either adjudicated or referred by Asylum Officer's under this part in accordance with s.208.14"; s. 208.14(1)(b) (1990), as amended (1995) provides: "An Asylum Officer may grant asylum in the exercise of discretion to an applicant who qualifies as a refugee under s.101(a)(42) of the Act, 8 U.S.C. 1101 (a)(42)."

86 Comprising the need to verify foreign conditions, and avoid evidentiary lacunae, cross-cultural and linguistic misunderstandings.

training course followed by four weeks at their post where for the first three of these weeks they are mentored by an experienced IO. Following this they return to formal training for one final week. There is no specialised asylum training. Asylum applications are examined along with all other categories of immigrants, visitors, business people and students. The training programme in the UK is comparable with that in the USA insofar as it covers immigration policy, procedures, and the relevant Acts and regulations. Furthermore, IOs receive instruction on "attitudes and awareness, cross cultural and disability awareness, interview skills and techniques and language study".[87] Other "key areas" identified in the programme are technical skills, effective office practices and management.[88] What is lacking from the programme is any reference to international human rights law, international refugee law and, following the advent of the designated safe country of origin list, there is crucially no mention of training about conditions prevailing in asylum applicant countries of origin. There is no indication that interviewing officers receive training in order to deal with traumatised applicants who may be suffering the effects of torture or other forms of persecution, nor do they indicate whether staff are equipped to recognise when applicants are suffering from other psychological or physical problems. Furthermore, as recognised in UNHCR's Training Module, "the interview process could in itself trigger off anxiety symptoms", while "the need for medical intervention should be understood in order to assist the applicant with his or her mental state before any further interviewing can take place".[89]

Additionally, in order to maintain a high level of quality and consistency in decision-making in the USA, a Quality Assurance Unit was established within the Asylum Division and given responsibility for monitoring the regulations. Moreover, reflecting the importance of keeping abreast of developments in conditions in countries of origin, AOs are required to spend at least four hours a week in continuing education activities. Within the UK the supervisory role at ports of entry is provided by a Chief Immigration Officer (CIO) and there is no reference made to a continuing education requirement, only that "training is given an *ad hoc* basis when needs are

87 IND letter to the authors, 23 Sept. 1996.

88 *Ibid.*

89 UNHCR, *Training Module on Interviewing Applicants for Refugee Status*, (1995) at 33. In the case of individuals who have suffered from sexually related torture, abuse or other forms of gender related persecution it may be appropriate to allow applicants to provide the details of their account in writing thereby avoiding the need to recount traumatic events in front of strangers, *ibid.* at 45.

identified".[90] Such a requirement would appear to be a necessity, particularly given the impact which designation of a country as "safe" can have on an applicant's case.

Equally consequential for asylum applicants in the USA were the changes in relation to the procedures governing the asylum interview. The asylum regulation of 27 July 1990 directs the AO to take an active role in the interview process, in an effort to "elicit all relevant and useful information bearing on the applicant's eligibility for ... [asylum]".[91] Conditions are fostered so that the applicant has the best possible opportunity for giving a comprehensive account of all the important elements of the claim. Such an approach is clearly distinguishable from the sterile questioning and the "culture of disbelief" which pervades the interviewing process by immigration officials in the UK, despite UNHCR guidelines.[92]

These elements are the subject of considerable attention during Asylum Officer training in the USA. In its training syllabus, *The Context and the Challenge: Improving [Refugee and] Asylum Adjudication under the 1990 Final Rule*, the INS states that "to the extent possible, we want to ensure that our decisions are made on the basis of objective legal considerations, and not on the basis of the personal opinion of the adjudicator".[93] In Canada, before

90 IND letter to the authors, 23 Sept. 1996.

91 8 CFR s. 208.9(b) (1990), revised (1995).

92 Para. 196 of the *UNHCR Handbook on Procedures and Criteria for Determining Refugee Status* provides that during an asylum interview "the duty to ascertain and evaluate all the relevant facts is shared between the applicant and the examiner. Indeed, in some cases, it may be for the examiner to use all the means at his disposal to produce the necessary evidence in support of the application". Applicants under the "short procedure" are simply informed: "You have asked for asylum in the United Kingdom and I will now ask you questions and ask you to tell me why you need asylum in the United Kingdom." Following the completion of travel and family details the interviewer will simply ask: "What particular event caused you to leave your own country?" This is inadequate as a means of eliciting all relevant information from an asylum applicant who is unlikely to be aware of what the Home Office considers "material factors" (Statement of Changes in Immigration Rules, HC 395 paras. 340–4) and who may in the light of the simplistic question merely respond with an account of the last persecutory event rather than relating the whole series of events to which they were subjected. Jagmohan, J., *op. cit. supra* n. 2 at 46.

93 Ruppel, J., "The Need for a Benefit of the Doubt Standard in Credibility Evaluations of Asylum Applicants" (1991–92) 23(1) Columbia H.R.L.R. 1 at 17 n. 60, citing the INS, which, while using the term "adjudicator", is referring to AOs.

reforms in 1989 swept away the adversarial mode of assessing claims "the government was expected to fight every application, and refugee claimants were left to their own devices to marshal sufficient evidence to rebut *de facto* assumptions of non-genuineness".[94] Almost a decade later, the position facing asylum applicants in the UK is chillingly similar to this description of the Canadian determination system, save that the situation is exacerbated in the UK by a truncated and limited appeals procedure.

Adopting an adversarial posture in the interviewing room panders to the perceived "enforcement" or "control" function which IOs are presently trained to discharge. IOs should now more than ever be regarded as vital for analysing key issues at the preparatory stage and as such as a vital support system for case workers in the Asylum Division of the Home Office. Training developed to develop skills more tailored towards conducting a harmonious investigation would augment the productivity of the meeting for both parties.

Human Rights Information Databases

In order to ease the onerous task facing legal practitioners in gathering human rights reports from regions in a designated safe country, within the restricted time frame imposed by the fast-track appeals procedure, important lessons may also be learned from North American models. A human rights information database should be established analogous to the Resource Information Centre (RIC) in the USA[95] and the Immigration and Refugee Board Documentation Centre (IRBDC) established in Canada in 1988. These centres are charged with collating and issuing digests of information on conditions on countries of origin.

---

94 Hathaway, J. and MacMillan, L., *Rebuilding Trust: Report of the Review of Fundamental Justice in Information Gathering and Dissemination at the Immigration and Refugee Board* (Osgoode Hall Law School, York University, Dec. 1993) at 7.

95 The RIC is the entity in the central office of the INS. Information collected on country conditions is made available to AOs and information gathered from sources such as Amnesty International and Human Rights Watch is directly available on the database to each officer. Contrast this position with that of IOs at ports in the UK who have no direct access to databases and who may in theory consult the Home Office country reports but in practice are unlikely to have the time to do so. (Information from Eileen Bye (Joint Council for the Welfare of Immigrants)).

In Canada, for instance, country profiles include relevant historical material, a chronology of significant events, current information on political, ethnic and religious groups, on law and practice and an extensive bibliography.[96] IRBDC human rights reports have their basis in identifiable, publicly available and verifiable sources, and the reports are accessible, thus allowing for challenge comment and verification.[97]

The advantages of such a resource centre are twofold. First, it allows fairer decisions based on credible sources of information to be made. This is because, procedurally, the likelihood of an imbalance in the information available between parties should be reduced, and also because the time taken to gather all the relevant evidence on behalf of the applicant lessened.[98] Second, such a resource centre speeds up the adjudicatory system. Documentary evidence may benefit the applicant by corroborating their narrative, but it may also aid those processing the claim in identifying contradictions and inconsistencies in accounts of persecution. This should facilitate the quicker identification of meritorious applicants and prevent undeserving claimants from deceiving officials and clogging up the system.[99]

Both Asylum Officers and Refugee Hearing Officers[100] have direct access

---

96 Rusu, S., "The Development of Canada's Immigration and Refugee Board Documentation Centre" (1989) 1(3) I.J.Ref.L. at 319.

97 IRBDC holdings include reports, articles, analyses, periodicals and monographs from traditional human rights monitors, including media accounts, Amnesty International Reports, US State Department reports, reports of the UN organs and regional human rights rapporteurs, and analyses by NGOs such as the Minority Rights Group, the Netherlands Institute for Human Rights, the Danish Centre of Human Rights, the Norwegian Institute of Human Rights and the Lawyers' Committee for Human Rights. *Ibid.* at 324.

98 This presupposes that the information resource centres allow the dissemination of materials publicly. Even where this is not the case, those participating in the process may have increased faith in the decision-makers' capacity to reach the correct decision, whether positive or negative, if the evidence on which they base that decision is drawn from a resource centre which contains materials drawn from a range of sources.

99 In Canada, where documentary evidence is employed to demonstrate that the applicant is not truthful, the evidence serves "as a rebuttable presumption in [the] determination process", Hathaway, J., *The Law of Refugee Status* (Butterworths, 1991), p. 83.

100 Although Refugee Hearing Officers (RHO) in Canada do not have the power to grant asylum in the same manner as AOs in the USA, prior to any full asylum hearing to determine the merits of the applicant's case, the RHO will check all

to their respective information databases. This is in stark contrast to the availability of information produced by the Centre for Information, Discussion and Exchange on Asylum (CIREA), the EU database.[101] CIREA information is only disseminated to EU ministers, national authorities participating in the work of the clearing house and the European Commission. Section IV of the Decision Establishing the Clearing House ambiguously states that, "ministers shall determine the framework and conditions for the clearing house to disseminate information to international organisations, non-governmental organisations, universities and the media in particular". It states that joint reports on third countries drawn up on the basis of the information gathered may, "depending on national procedures, ... be made available to the parties involved in a dispute when there is an *appeal* against a decision by the authorities responsible for matters concerning asylum".[102]

Such partiality in the balance of resources available to the various agents in the determination process is inequitable. Unfortunately, however, the decision in *ex parte Abdi*, legitimised such inequalities in the asylum adjudicatory system in the UK.[103] The existence and availability of a database would prevent such inequalities since, if there is strong evidence supporting the appellant's contention that a given country is not safe, such evidence is more likely to be available to both them and their counsel and it will also be available to the adjudicators. If there is convincing evidence in favour of an asylum applicant's case, then the wish of the Home Office to give quick refusals to unmeritorious applications "cannot override the importance of giving due consideration to those applications for asylum which are or may be genuine and well founded".[104]

---

the applicant's personal information and interview the applicant. The RHO presents the facts at issue before the hearing over which two members of the Immigration and Refugee Board preside.

101 *Supra* n. 52.

102 (Authors' emphasis.) Annex III.4 *Circulation and Confidentiality of Joint Reports on the Situation in Certain Third Countries*, adopted by the European Council 20 June 1994. This is annexed to the *Decision Establishing the Clearing House*, *supra* n. 52.

103 *Supra* n. 27.

104 *Ibid.*, per Lord Slynn (dissenting) at 306.

Conclusions

Full and fair consideration of an individual asylum applicant's case will inevitably be coloured both by the perspective of those framing the legislation and by the personnel, training and resources invested in the administration of the system. It is questionable whether the IND, imbued as it is with a control ethos, would be receptive to a reformulation of its role as a facilitator, rather than a regulator, of the determination system.

The authors ideally advocate the establishment of a wholly separate body, free from historical and policy commitments to a regulatory mandate. Greater involvement of an independent body could also bring increased objectivity and confidence to the decision-making stage. A reformed training programme at the very least would reflect the pivotal role fulfilled by Immigration Officers.[105] Geographical specialisation, coupled with relevant language skills, knowledge of cultural and political systems, and interviewing techniques designed to assist the applicant rather than confront them is imperative to prevent more applicants being subject to *refoulement*. Furthermore, geographical specialisation and improved training for Immigration Officers would reduce the likelihood of an erroneous determination by the Asylum Division, and obviate the need for time consuming and costly appeals. If the hazards that accompany dangerous assumptions about certain countries of origin are to be avoided, then gathering together publicly available and verifiable sources from traditional human rights monitors and analyses by NGOs will be fundamental to safeguarding a meaningful right to petition for asylum. Natural justice and international human rights law dictate that the UK must adjudicate asylum applications fairly, in good faith, without bias, affording sufficient time to present a case adequately, and with equal access to all relevant information for all involved in the process. Without such guarantees the United Kingdom's commitment to the 1951 Geneva Refugee Convention loses much of its meaning and credibility.[106]

---

105 Indeed the UNHCR have stated that in order to ensure the quality of decisions is maintained within the time constraints imposed by the current legislation, "the system should receive more resources, especially trained personnel at both the initial and appeals level", UNHCR written submissions to the Glidewell Panel, *op. cit. supra* n. 5, at 2.

106 See also chapters 11 and 12 of this book by C.J. Harvey and Nicholas Blake respectively.

Bibliography

Amnesty International, *Playing Human Pinball: Home Office Practice in "Safe Third Country" Asylum Cases* (Amnesty International British Section, London, 1995).

Amnesty International, *Slamming the Door: The Demolition of the Right to Asylum in the UK* (Amnesty International United Kingdom, London, 1996).

Anker, D., "Determining Asylum Claims in the United States, Summary Report of an Empirical Study of the Adjudication of Asylum Claims before the Immigration Court" (1990) 2(2) I.J.Ref.L. 252.

Anker, D. et al., *The Law of Asylum in the United States: A Guide to Administrative Practice and Case Law* (American Immigration Lawyers' Association, 1991).

Beyer, G., "Establishing the United States Asylum Corps" (1992) 4(4) I.J.Ref.L.455.

Byrne, R. and Shacknove, A., "The Safe Country Notion in European Asylum Law" (1996) 9 Harvard H.R.J. 185.

Care, G., *A Guide to Asylum Law and Practice in the European Union* (ILPA, London, 1996).

European Council for Refugees and Exiles, *Asylum in Europe* (ECRE, London, 1994).

Glidewell Panel, *The Asylum and Immigration Bill 1995: The Report of the Glidewell Panel* (1996).

Goodwin-Gill, G., *The Refugee in International Law*, (Clarendon, Oxford, 2nd edn, 1996).

Guimezanes, N., *Le droit des étrangers* (Armand Colin, Paris, 1987).

Hailbronner, K., "The Concept of 'Safe Country' and Expeditious Asylum Procedures: A Western Perspective" (1993) 5(1) I.J.Ref.L. 31.

Harvey, A., *The Risks of Getting it Wrong: The Asylum and Immigration Session 1995/96 and the Determination of Special Adjudicators* (Asylum Rights Campaign, London, 1996).

Hathaway, J. and MacMillan, L., *Rebuilding Trust: Report of the Review of Fundamental Justice in Information Gathering and Dissemination at the Immigration and Refugee Board*, (Osgoode Hall Law School, York University, 1993).

Jagmohan, J., *The Short Procedure: An Analysis of the Home Office Scheme for Rapid Initial Decisions in Asylum Cases*, (Asylum Rights Campaign, 1996).

Lambert. H., *Seeking Asylum: Comparative Law and Practice in Selected European Countries* (Martinus Nijhoff, Dordrecht, 1995).

Marx, R., and Lumpp, K., "The German Constitutional Court's Decision of 14 May 1996 on the Concept of 'Safe Third Countries' – A Basis for Burden-Sharing in Europe?" (1996) 8 I.J.Ref.L. 419.

Noll, G., "The Non-Admission and Return of Protection Seekers in Germany" (1997) 9 I.J.Ref.L. 415.

Reilly, R., *Closing The Door: The Concept of Safe Countries of Origin in European Countries* (Refugee Council, London, 1996).

Ruppel, J., "The Need for a Benefit of the Doubt Standard in Credibility Evaluations of Asylum Applicants" (1991–92) 23(1) Columbia H.R.L.J. 1.

Rusu, S., "The Development of Canada's Immigration and Refugee Board Documentation Centre" (1989) 1(3) I.J.Ref.L. 319.

Shah, P., "Refugees and Safe Third Countries" (1995) Eur.P.L. 259.

Symes, M., *The Law relating to "Without Foundation" Asylum Claims* (Refugee Legal Centre, 1996).

Tuitt, P., *False Images: The Law's Construction of the Refugee* (Pluto Press, London, 1996).

UNHCR, *Fair and Expeditious Asylum Procedures* (Geneva, 1994).

UNHCR, *Handbook on Procedures and Criteria for Determining Refugee Status* (Geneva, 1988).
UNHCR, *Training Module on interviewing Applicants for Refugee Status* (Geneva, 1995).
Witherow, R., "Detention of Asylum Seekers: A Continuing Cause for Concern" (1995) 9(2) I.N.L.P. 59.

5 The "Internal Flight Alternative" (IFA) Test and the Concept of Protection

HUGO STOREY

The "internal flight alternative" or "IFA" is an integral part of the definition of refugee as contained in Article 1A(2) of the 1951 Convention on the Status of Refugees. Recognition of its status as such has been an established feature of the international jurisprudence on the IFA.[1] In the United Kingdom case law, however, it has had a chequered history. Indeed it is fair to say that it was only in the very recent full judgment of the Court of Appeal in the case of *ex parte Robinson*,[2] that we now have a leading case which ranks alongside earlier flagship cases commonly identified in the international jurisprudence on asylum law.

In the international jurisprudence the IFA test has always been seen to raise awkward problems. These include not only problems of textual interpretation but also of the ongoing ability of the 1951 Convention to afford effective protection to asylum seekers. There has been a constant concern about the potential rigours of the test, its uncertain implications for asylum seekers, and the scope it offers decision-makers to raise the test as an extra hurdle at any point in the processing of a claim. At the same time the judicial exploration of the concept appears to have been a driving force in seeking to widen the scope of Convention protection so as to bring it more in line with contemporary human rights law and to view the Convention itself as just one

1 For detailed treatment of international jurisprudence, see Storey, H., "The Internal Flight Alternative: A Re-examination of the International Jurisprudence" I.J.Ref.L. (forthcoming).

2 *R. v. Secretary of State for the Home Department ex p. Robinson*, CA 11 July 1997, [1997] 3 W.L.R. 1162; [1997] 4 All E.R. 210, Lord Woolf MR, Potter LJJ. The Court of Appeal had dealt with the same case in an earlier judgment, 11 Oct. 1996 (FC3 96/6129/D). At Divisional Court level it came before Popplewell J (QBD) 10 May 1996 (CO/1495/96).

vital part of a broader legal framework of protection established by major international human rights treaties. Despite UK case law being slow in dealing authoritatively with IFA issues, it is argued in this article that in *Robinson* and two other recent Court of Appeal judgments, that of *Adan*[3] and that of *Ikhlaq and Ikhlaq*,[4] there are signs that the UK courts are now far more committed to playing a full role internationally and nationally in achieving a coherent and contemporary judicial framework of understanding of the IFA and indeed other major aspects of refugee law.

The relatively undeveloped state of the UK case law is somewhat curious, in that the international jurisprudence on the IFA regularly cites certain UK decisions as key historical reference points, with the biblical-sounding case of *ex parte Jonah*[5] being seen as one of the first of several cases to establish basic IFA principles. One equally curious fact returned to in the concluding part of this chapter is that in one respect *Jonah* appears to embody an approach only now coming to the fore.

This chapter examines the parameters now set for IFA in the case of *ex parte Robinson* and assesses the longer term implications of *Adan*, with particular focus on Simon Brown LJ's deployment of the concept of protection. It then turns briefly to compare and contrast UK case law with international jurisprudence. It is hoped that by forming a clearer picture of the now distinct features of the former, more attention can be given to areas in which UK courts might learn from international jurisprudence and also possibly contribute to the development of a more consistent and coherent international interpretation of the Convention.

Treatment by the Courts before 1996

The 1985 case *ex parte Jonah* concerned a claim by a former trade union leader who feared persecution upon return to Ghana. Nolan J rejected as "going much too far" the proposition that "if a person has to refrain from political activity in order to avoid persecution he has to qualify for political asylum". This case also essayed a working definition of persecution and further stated

3 *Adan and Nooh v. Secretary of State for the Home Department* [1997] 1 W.L.R. 1107; [1997] 2 All E.R. 723; Imm. A.R. 251.

4 *Ikhlaq and Ikhlaq v. Secretary of State for the Home Department*, CA [1997] Imm. A.R. 404.

5 *R. v. Immigration Appeal Tribunal (IAT) ex p. Daniel Boahim Jonah* QBD [1985] Imm. A.R. 7.

that the issue of persecution was "one of fact and degree", a maxim which all subsequent case law has reiterated. Notwithstanding the strict terms in which he had dealt with the general issue of a person's political activity, Nolan J went on to make a favourable finding on the particular case before him. Despite there being no material risk to Jonah if he were to live in a remote village, he would there be separated from his wife and unable also to pursue his employment as a trade union official which he had carried out for some 30 years. The likely consequence of his removal from the UK, concluded Nolan J, would be that Jonah would be persecuted. If, up to the present, it has been the simple maxim set out in *Jonah* that has been seen as authoritative whereas the actual decision has been seen as somewhat eccentric, there are signs that recent case law may attach more significance to the latter.

Leaving aside cursory references to IFA issues, for example by Lord Goff in *Sivakumaran*,[6] the next case of note was *Yurekli*.[7] Therein, Otton J endorsed the approach enjoined in *ex parte Jonah* of seeing the issue as hinging essentially on the issue of persecution being one of fact and degree in every particular case. *Yurekli* concerned a Turkish Alevi Kurd who had been persecuted in his home village and had subsequently lived peacefully, albeit not without difficulties, in Istanbul. In reviewing the Secretary of State's decision refusing his claim to refugee status, Otton J stated that:

> The basis of the [the Home Secretary's] decision was the fact that he was able and had been shown to be able to live in his country for a period of two years a substantial period of time in a part where he was not persecuted in the way that he was when he was living at home. It is true that this meant that he lived away from the family and that he was unable to obtain regular employment when he was discovered to be a Kurd.[8]

However, he concluded, the latter was a factor which the Home Secretary was entitled to take account of, without that causing him to fall into error in concluding he was not in fear of persecution. The Court of Appeal upheld this judgment, although Neil LJ did state initially that "this aspect of the matter troubled me".[9]

6 *R. v. Secretary of State for the Home Department, ex p. Sivakumaran* [1988] 1 A.C. 958 at 1001. (This case went on to the European Court of Human Rights as that of *Vilvarajah and others v. UK*, 1991, Series A, No.215.)

7 *R. v. Secretary of State for the Home Department ex p. Celal Yurekli* [1990] Imm. A.R. 334.

8 *Yurekli, ibid.* at 339–400.

9 *Yurekli v. Secretary of State for the Home Department* CA [1991] Imm. A.R. 153 at 153.

The 1991 case of *ex parte Gunes*[10] gave approval to paragraph 91 of the UNHCR's *Handbook on Procedures and Criteria for Determining Refugee Status* as a helpful guide in operating the test. Paragraph 91 states that:

> The fear of being persecuted need not always extend to the *whole* territory of the refugee's country of nationality. Thus in ethnic clashes or in cases of grave disturbances involving civil war conditions, persecution of a specific ethnic or national group may occur in only one part of the country. In such situations, a person will not be excluded from refugee status merely because he could have sought refuge in another part of the same country, if under all the circumstances it would not have been reasonable to expect him to do so.[11]

In this case Simon Brown J (as he then was) was faced with another case involving an asylum claim by a Turkish Kurd in which the Secretary of State had concluded that the applicant could live in safety in Turkey *anywhere* save only in his original village. Approving *ex parte Jonah*, Simon Brown J resoundingly rejected the contention of the applicant that proof of a localised fear of persecution was sufficient to entitle him to refugee status. However, in the course of his short disposal of this contention, Simon Brown J sought support from the text of paragraph 91 of the *Handbook* in the following terms:

> Implicit in that final clause is this. If in all the circumstances it would be reasonable to expect someone to return to another part of his country of nationality then that is a matter that can properly found an adverse decision on a claim to refugee status.[12]

This comment reflected a readiness to treat *reasonableness* as a test of safety elsewhere, without the need for much analysis of the meaning of the term.[13]

In a 1992 Divisional Court judgment concerning *Vigna*,[14] the same approach was taken, although no authorities were cited. Roch J was unreceptive to the further argument adduced by Counsel which relied on guidance given by the UNHCR in a confidential memorandum sent to governments to the

---

10 *R. v. Secretary of State for the Home Department ex p. Gunes* QBD [1991] Imm. A.R. 278.

11 UNHCR, *Handbook on Procedures and Criteria for Determining Refuge Status* (Geneva, 1979, re-edited 1992) hereafter the *Handbook*.

12 *Ex p. Gunes, supra* n.10 at 282.

13 Contrast the post 1996 position discussed below at notes 37 and 38.

14 *R. v. Secretary of State for the Home Department ex p. David Siril Vigna* QBD [1993] Imm. A.R. 93.

effect that

> although the Colombo area is not an area generally affected by armed conflict, a person could not be expected to return there in safety and dignity unless that person had close relatives living there or, alternatively, had lived there himself for some time prior to leaving Sri Lanka or had worked in that area for some time prior to leaving Sri Lanka.[15]

In the 1993 case of *El-Tanoukhi*[16] the Court of Appeal again confirmed and applied the *ex parte Gunes* approach to the case of a Lebanese citizen whose original claim rested on a fear of return to Israeli-occupied parts of southern Lebanon. It rejected an argument that this approach misconstrued Article 1A(2) read in the light of Articles 1C(4) and 33 which (so ran the argument) treated "territories" and "country" as indivisible concepts. Such an argument would entail, the Court of Appeal noted, upholding a claim to refugee status on the strength of well-founded fear of persecution "in any part of the country in question, no matter how small". The Court of Appeal could not accept that construction. Lloyd LJ also emphasised the importance in analysing an IFA of examining the general situation in a country, noting that "the Home Secretary is ... entitled to take into account conditions in the country as a whole in deciding whether it is safe to return the applicant to the Lebanon under Article 33". He added that that "would be entirely consistent with paragraph 91 of the *Handbook*".[17]

Confirmation that the courts continued to adhere closely to the IFA test as contained within the Convention so as to afford no general relaxation of the requirement of proving fear country-wide was given by the Court of Appeal in another Sri Lankan Tamil case concerning *Niyaz*.[18] Its stance was that it would not automatically bring into play paragraph 91 of the *Handbook* just because the country of origin had a civil war going on. In concluding that there was a reasonable guarantee of safety for the claimant concerned in the south and the west of Sri Lanka both in 1993 and now, Henry LJ added that:

> It is complained on behalf of the applicant that the internal alternative was not highlighted sufficiently at the [adjudicator] hearing. The onus in these matters

15 *Vigna, ibid.* at 94.

16 *Imad Ali El-Tanoukhi v. Secretary of State for the Home Department* CA [1993] Imm. A.R. 71.

17 *Ibid.* at 74.

18 *R. v. Secretary of State for the Home Department ex p. Niyaz*, CA, judgment of 30 Nov. 1995 (FC3 95/7419/D).

> is on the applicant. The internal flight alternative is always present when effectively there is a civil war going on, but that civil war is only in certain parts of the country.

Whilst this analysis would appear correctly to describe the general position under the law of the Convention, it did not appear to show much, if any, concern to ensure judicial harmony with the approach set out at paragraph 91 of the *Handbook*.

Summing up, despite seeing the IFA as an essential element of the Convention schema, there was little sign until 1996 that UK judges either welcomed, or saw the necessity for, decision-makers analysing or applying the IFA to do so within a clear or settled framework of analysis.

The 1996 Turning-point

A telling sign that the IFA cried out for fuller treatment was posted in a March 1996 judgment of the Court of Appeal, in the course of which Hobhouse LJ cited with approval the observation of Tuckey J in the Divisional Court that "the question is how far and wide the concept of reasonableness goes. That may be a matter which these courts have to consider".[19]

In *Probakaran* in the Divisional Court, Jowitt J did not tackle the IFA in depth, but he did enunciate what appears to be a highly coherent and succinct statement of the IFA test as an integral Convention requirement:

> It seems to me that if there is a safe place, from a Convention point of view, to which a person can be returned within his own country, it may in a number of cases be unimportant whether he would be at risk of persecution for a Convention reason in the part of that country from which he had come. The only relevance of whether there might be a risk of persecution for a Convention reason would be whether that risk established the question of whether it was shown to be unreasonable to require that the asylum seeker go back to the safe part of his country.[20]

In the same case Jowitt J tackled a related procedural question, as to whether a judicial decision-maker has a duty to apply a test of reasonableness, even when it has not been raised previously. In *ex parte Probakaran* Jowitt J

19 *Anandanadarajah v. Immigration Appeal Tribunal* CA [1996] Imm. A.R. 514.

20 *R. v. Immigration Appeal Tribunal ex p. Probakaran* QBD [1996] Imm. A.R. 603 at 604.

concluded that the issue of reasonableness could properly be raised even when, as in this instance, it had not been raised until after grounds for leave to apply for judicial review had been settled. That clashed with the position taken in the first of three court treatments of *ex parte Robinson*, by Popplewell J in his May 1996 judgment. Albeit recognising that "the questions of safety and reasonableness are ... two separate matters", the latter concluded:

> The fact that [an alternative place] is safe does not necessarily mean that it is reasonable. On the other hand, if the only matter which the applicant puts forward is that it will not be safe to go to a place A but there is no suggestion on *his* behalf that it would be otherwise unreasonable to go to place A, it is not incumbent upon the Adjudicator to go out of his way to consider the question of reasonableness if the only question that is being put by him is one of safety.[21]

In the October 1996 judgment on *Robinson*[22] by the Court of Appel, which was to prove the first of two treatments by it of this case, the Court clarified but did not resolve this issue in the following terms. Saville LJ saw the issue as one which had to be considered in the context of a broader technical issue of whether there was a duty on the Immigration Appeal Tribunal (IAT), irrespective of the grounds advanced for the grant of leave [to appeal to the Tribunal], to consider whether there were any grounds upon which leave should be granted. His worry was that any duty to investigate whether there were any arguable points

> would ... if adopted, not only impose an additional burden on the Tribunal and indeed the courts, but would also encourage what the Master of the Rolls has recently described as "satellite litigation", that is to say litigation not for the purpose of resolving the substantive point in issue – in the present case whether the applicant should be granted asylum – but some other peripheral point altogether. The encouragement of such "satellite litigation" is not, in my judgment, in the interests of justice.

One difficulty, however, with the prudent warning about "satellite litigation" in general, was that to make it here seemed at odds with his own assertion earlier that the context of whether to grant asylum was one which was the very opposite of "satellite litigation".

Nevertheless Saville LJ did consider that the issue warranted the Court of Appeal giving leave to appeal. In one of two concurring judgments, Otton LJ

21 *Robinson*, *supra* n. 2, QBD ruling of 10 May 1996.

22 *Robinson*, *supra* n. 2, CA ruling of 11 Oct. 1996.

stressed that in asylum cases "the court may nevertheless consider the point provided that the point is of such cogency and so apparent from the papers and of such importance that it required the IAT to consider it before refusing leave or dismissing the applicant's appeal".[23]

Subsequently, in *Sureshkumar*,[24] the Court of Appeal noted that in *Robinson* the IFA had not been raised in terms either before the adjudicator or before the Tribunal. As in Sureshkumar's case it had been, however, the application before the Court which stood to be dismissed. If *Sureshkumar* was content to leave IFA issues to be further examined at a full hearing of *Robinson*, it did usefully note a difference between the terms of paragraph 91 of the *Handbook*, in which the IFA criterion is expressed in the *past* tense, and the terms of paragraph 343 of the Immigration Rules which state:

> If there is a part of the country from which the applicant claims to be a refugee in which he would not have a well-founded fear of persecution, and to which it would be reasonable to expect him to go, the application may be refused.[25]

This formulation, the Court noted, "looks to the future, after the person claiming refugee status has arrived in this country".

Thus, as to the overall position reached in the UK case law by the end of 1996, one could say as follows: there were signs of UK case law seeking to operate the reasonableness test with more finesse. There were some promising innovations urging more recourse to internationally known cases. However, neither the IAT nor the courts had succeeded in establishing any definite framework for analysis. Furthermore, both the IAT and the courts appeared to remain embroiled in IFA issues as they were seen to arise within the immigration rules. Attempting to resolve that problem was involving extra and inevitably forensic layers of interpretation. The need for judicial clarification had become critical.

The Issue of Paragraph 343

Just at the time that the courts had shown clear signs of a readiness to deal thoroughly with the IFA test, the Tribunal was entangling it with a broader jurisdictional issue relating to the status of immigration rules on asylum which

23 *Ibid.*

24 *R. v. IAT ex p. Sureshkumar*, CA, 19 Dec. 1996 (FC3 96/7459/D).

25 *Statement of Changes in Immigration Rules* (1993–94) HC 395, 23 May 1994.

are purely discretionary. In the IAT case of *Ahmed*,[26] Professor Jackson as chairman confirmed the view he had taken in the earlier case of *Dupovac*[27] that paragraph 343 of HC 395 represented a relaxation of the Convention IFA test to be applied as a matter of discretion by the original decision-maker. Controversially, however, he further found that this did *not* leave it open to the *appellate authorities* to relax the IFA test by reference to paragraph 343 discretion. In his view that route of interpretation had been cut off by the enactment of the Asylum and Immigration Appeals Act 1993. His reasoning was as follows:

> The problem which ensues on appeal, however, is that on any appeal under the 1993 Act it will not be open to an adjudicator to consider this exercise of discretion – the sole issue under that Act on appeal is whether removal would be contrary to the Refugee Convention (see section 8 [of the 1993 Act]). Just as discretion to consider an asylum application despite the existence of a third safe country is contained in the rules but is not a matter for consideration on appeal under the 1993 Act, so is the discretion under paragraph 343 of HC 395 excluded from consideration.[28]

Jackson cited in support the analysis given in *Mehari* by Laws J which concluded that "section 19(1)(a)(ii) [of the Immigration Act 1971] can have no application in a section 8 case".[29] However, there were clear difficulties over its acceptance in relation to the IFA and paragraph 343. For one thing the courts in *Anandanadarajah*[30] and the more recent *ex parte Probakaran,*[31] appeared to be proceeding on the opposite premise and to be considering paragraph 343 discretion as one which could be exercised by adjudicators and the Tribunal. Furthermore, in *Ikhlaq* (13679), a closely reasoned determination dated 15 July 1996 with Pearl J as chairman, the Tribunal dissented "reluctant[ly]" from the conclusions drawn in the differently constituted Tribunal chaired by Professor Jackson in the case of *Ahmed*

26 *Muhubo Aden Ahmed* (13371).

27 *Dupovac* (R 11846).

28 *Ahmed, supra* n. 26. See for the ambit of the 1993 Act appeal *R. v. Secretary of State ex parte Mehari* [1994] Imm. A.R. 151, *Munchula* (12986) and [1996] Imm. A.R. 344. Prof. Jackson reiterated the same view in a 6 Dec. 1996 determination, *Nirmalan* (14361).

29 *Mehari, ibid.* n. 28, at p.169.

30 *Anandanadarajah, supra* n. 19.

31 *Probakaran, supra* n. 20.

(13371). The reasons for not following the latter's conclusions were stated as follows:

> For our part, we cannot see how the discretion under paragraph 343 of HC 395 is excluded from consideration by an adjudicator and, on appeal, by the Tribunal. We do not see how *Mehari* ... supports the exclusion of jurisdiction; indeed the reverse, because Laws J [in *Mehari*] made it clear that the HC Rules are "... analogous to (though not identical with) that of a statutory instrument which may be prayed in aid to construe main legislation, where it is clear that the two are intended to form an overall code". [The Tribunal goes on to reject the analogy drawn with third country cases.]

In *Nirmalan*, Professor Jackson's Tribunal sought to answer these objections, conceding only:

> If we thought it possible to argue that the matter of reasonableness could come within the appellate jurisdiction we would be in favour of it doing so just as Laws J indicated in so doing [in the context of judicial review jurisdiction]. However, we cannot avoid the consequences of parliament's limitation on appellate jurisdiction.[32]

After 1996: the New Jurisprudence

By the end of 1996 the courts could no longer avoid resolving Tribunal conflicts over the IFA test or providing clearer guidance as to its effective criteria. Although the first case to demonstrate a new approach was that of *Adan*, there are good reasons for dealing first with the main case to confront directly the conflict of views between Judge Pearl and Professor Jackson at the IAT level. Definitive treatment came in the Court of Appeal's full hearing of *ex parte Robinson*, but by that time, of course, it had already ruled on the issue in the case of *Adan* and had also addressed some important aspects of it in *Ikhlaq and Ikhlaq*.

32 *Nirmalan, supra* n. 28.

Ikhlaq and Ikhlaq: from "IFA" to "IMO"

The key facts in *Ikhlaq and Ikhlaq*[33] concerned the question of whether a husband and wife who appeared to be able to show a well-founded fear of persecution on one part of Pakistan (Karachi) could fully satisfy the Convention definition in view of evidence indicating they had a viable alternative place (Rawalpindi) to live without unreasonable risk to themselves. The Court showed close awareness of key academic works and leading judgments on IFA made in other jurisdictions, that by the Canadian Federal Court in *Thirunavukkarasu*[34] in particular. In the best traditions of the English judiciary, however, it also showed a new readiness to tackle directly basic issues of the proper construction of the 1951 Convention, starting with the very topic of the test's name. Staughton LJ said that he would describe it "as an internal movement option [IMO], since anything resembling a flight will not necessarily be involved".

The IFA test constituted in his view the "second part of the definition of a refugee". A claimant could fulfil the first part of the definition once he had established that he was outside the country of his nationality owing to a well-founded fear of persecution for a Convention reason. For the purposes of this case Staughton LJ was prepared to assume that the Ikhlaqs met this part of the definition by virtue of their adverse experiences in Karachi. The second part of the definition required that "[t]hey have still to show that they are unable, or unwilling owing to such fear, to avail themselves of the protection of that country".

This approach to the Convention definition also helped situate, in his view, the proper context of paragraph 343. Having elsewhere described paragraph 343 as a rule "fathered" by the Convention and as representing a "quasi-legislative" provision designed to give effect to the Convention, he sought to be more precise, stating that paragraph 343 did "no more than describe one situation, possibly among many, where the second part of the definition of a refugee is not satisfied". Noting that he saw his conception of IFA as the same as that deployed by Hathaway[35] and Goodwin-Gill[36] and by the Canadian

33 *Ikhlaq and Ikhlaq, supra* n.4. See also *R. v. IAT ex parte Sivanetheran* 21 May 1997 (unreported) *per* Lord Bingham of Cornhill CJ at 7.

34 *Thirunavukkarasu v. Canada (Minister of Employment and Immigration)* Federal Court of Appeal [1994] 1 F.C. 589.

35 Hathaway, J., *The Law of Refugee Status* (Butterworths, 1991).

36 Goodwin-Gill, G., *The Refugee in International Law* (Clarendon, OUP, 2nd edn, 1996).

Federal Court, he then turned to consider the issue of the "reasonableness" of an IFA, by reference to paragraph 91 of the *Handbook*, as well as the use of that term in paragraph 343. He asked:

> Can one elucidate further the words "reasonable to expect him"? First one should note that the word "expect" does not here bear its primary meaning of regarding something as likely: it has nothing to do with prognosis. Rather it means something akin to require. That was not disputed before us.

Secondly, the enquiry was not as to what would be a reasonable course for the refugee to take. It was the decision-maker, that is, the person who was doing the expecting (or requiring) who had to be reasonable. So the question comes to this: would it be reasonable for the Secretary of State to expect (require) the Ikhlaqs to return to Rawalpindi, instead of claiming asylum in this country? The Court went on to conclude that in weighing up all the circumstances, including significant items relating to the medical health of the appellants, the Tribunal had duly weighed the subjective views of the couple and the objective evidence. Its decision that Rawalpindi qualified as a viable IFA (or rather IMO) for this couple was not, therefore, wrong in law.

The Court did not seek to resolve directly the vexed issue of the powers of a special adjudicator under section 8 of the 1993 Act as amended, which had been the cause of conflict at Tribunal level, but, by indicating that he would assume for the purposes of his treatment of the instant case that section 8 did not preclude the power of a special adjudicator to deal with reasonableness issues in their entirety, Staughton LJ signalled a preference for the view taken at Tribunal level by Judge Pearl.

The new readiness to expound the concept of reasonableness was also to the fore in a 15 January 1997 Divisional Court judgment by Latham J,[37] although its liberal rendering was to receive express disapproval by the Lord

37 Latham J in *R. v. IAT ex p. Kathiramalai Ganesh Vijendran* CO/2503/95 (unreported) on 15 Jan. 1997, on judicial review against a special adjudicator's decision that Colombo was safe for a Tamil Sri Lankan who had been coerced into providing medical attention to wounded separatist militants and had suffered arrest and beatings at the hands of government forces, stated that the Tribunal, in considering whether it was "reasonable" to expect the asylum seeker to stay in Colombo, had to show that it had specifically taken into account the following: (i) the extent of his connection to the area of proposed return; (ii) the effect on his quality of life, and (iii) whether as a result of being returned there he could have any satisfactory existence in that area.

Chief Justice, Lord Bingham in a 21 May 1997 judgment in a different case, *ex parte Sivanentheran.*[38]

Locus Classicus? The Court of Appeal's Full Judgment in *ex parte Robinson*[39]

Primarily prepared by Brooke LJ, the Court of Appeal judgment at a full hearing of this case dealt with several matters it saw to be of general importance, but the burden of the judgment represented a conscious attempt to deal authoritatively with the IFA test, in particular the scope of the IFA and the question of the jurisdiction of the appellate authorities to consider issues relating to the IFA. At its earlier stages, *Robinson*[40] had raised very squarely the issue of the correct approach to be followed when determining the option of the safety of a part of the country of origin and of the reasonableness of a claimant returning to that part, in this case Colombo, Sri Lanka.

The Court affirmed its view that the IFA was an essential element of the Convention definition of a refugee, notwithstanding the lack of any express reference to it in Article 1A(2) of the Convention. It relied in support on the international jurisprudence built up over the previous quarter of a century. It saw paragraph 91 of the *Handbook* as being instrumental in helping to elicit the correct IFA criteria by reason of the fact that it arose as part of the *Handbook* explanation of the phrase "is outside the country of his nationality" in Article 1A(2).

The vigour shown by the Court in tackling the IFA issue sprang from its clearly expressed intent to render an interpretation based on a "contemporary understanding" of the 1951 Convention, in accord with the basic tenets of international law principles on the interpretation of treaties, as recognised in classic English cases dealing with this subject.[41] According to such principles

38 In *R. v. Immigration Appeal Tribunal, ex parte Sivanentheran*, CA, 21 May 1997, the Lord Chief Justice, Lord Bingham, stated that in deciding upon the criterion of reasonableness it did not seem necessary "... to conduct a wide-ranging inquiry into the quality of life which a returning applicant for asylum might expect to enjoy in the part of his home country to which it was proposed to return him". It sufficed to "... address those features of conditions in the proposed destination which were said to render his return inappropriate or unreasonable".

39 *Robinson, supra* n. 2, judgment of 11 July 1997.

40 *Ibid.*, judgments of 10 May and 11 Oct. 1996.

41 In *Fothergill v. Monarch Airlines Ltd* [1981] AC 250 Lord Diplock said at 282D that this article in his view did no more than codify already existing public

it is legitimate, when interpreting a treaty, to take into account not only the context in which it was made but also any subsequent practice in the application of the treaty which established the agreement of the parties regarding its interpretation. Not for the first time, it saw the search for such a "contemporary understanding" as warranting close reference to leading overseas cases, including the Canadian cases of *Ward*[42] and *Thirunavukkarasu*[43] and the Australian case of *Randhawa*[44] in particular.

In turn, however, it saw the principles contained in these cases to be best reflected in an item of European Union intergovernmental policy, specifically paragraph 8 of the Joint Position of 4 March 1996 on the harmonised application of the definition of the term "refugee" in Article 1 of the Geneva Convention.[45] That the Court should have fixed its lodestar by the 1996 EU Joint Position text may prove to be a source of difficulties in future case law. This is especially so given criticism from various quarters that not all provisions of this text adequately accord with contemporary European or international understanding of Convention obligations.[46] In relation to the IFA, however, it appears to confirm the intention expressed more openly in *Adan* that a modern reading of the IFA test should make more decisive the concept of protection. That is so because the paragraph 8 drafting was carefully crafted so as to bring more to the fore the concept of "effective protection". The paragraph furthermore requires that such protection must be available in another part of the claimant's country "to which he may reasonably be expected to move".

Whether the possibly broader scope afforded by paragraph 8 has been fully endorsed was left in some doubt, however, by the Court's assumption

international law as set out in Art. 31(3)(b) of the 1969 Vienna Convention on the Law of Treaties.

42 *Canada (Attorney-General) v. Ward* [1993] 2 R.C.S. 689 and [1993] 4 D.L.R. 103.

43 *Thirunavukkarasu, supra* n. 34.

44 *Randhawa v. Minister for Immigration, Local Government and Ethnic Affairs*, Federal Court of Australia – General Division [1994] 124 A.L.R. 265.

45 O.J. L63/2. Para. 8 states: "*Relocation within the country of origin.* Where it appears that persecution is clearly confined to a specific part of a country's territory, it may be necessary, in order to check that the condition laid down in Article 1 A of the Geneva Convention has been fulfilled, namely that the person concerned 'is unable or, owing to such fear of persecution, is unwilling to avail himself of the protection of that country', to ascertain, whether the person concerned cannot find effective protection in another part of his own country, to which he may reasonably be expected to move."

46 See in particular para. 5.2, *Persecution by third parties*.

that this paragraph simply echoed the international jurisprudence, in particular the dictum of the majority of the Federal Court of Australia in the *Randhawa* that:

> If it is not reasonable in the circumstances to expect a person who has a well-founded fear of persecution in relation to the part of a country of nationality it may be said that, in the relevant sense, the person's fear of persecution in relation to the country as a whole is well-founded.[47]

How should a decision-maker go about determining whether it would not be reasonable in all the circumstances to expect the claimant to relocate internally? The Court saw the international jurisprudence to suggest four tests:

> For example, (a) if as a practical matter (whether for financial, logistical or other good reason) the "safe" part of the country is not reasonably accessible; (b) if the claimant is required to encounter great physical danger in travelling there or staying there; (c) if he or she is required to undergo undue hardship in travelling there or staying there; (d) the quality of the internal protection fails to meet basic norms of civil, political and socio-economic human rights.[48]

The Court went on to make very plain its preference for the "undue hardship" test outlined in (c). Correctly tracing its source to the Canadian jurisprudence, and the well-known statement of this "undue hardship" test by Linden JA in *Thirunavukkarasu*, the Court proceeded to remind itself of the key English cases on the IFA topic,[49] and then to set its stamp on what must now be considered the decisive rendering of this aspect of the IFA in UK law:

> Where it appears that persecution is confined to a specific part of a country's territory the decision-maker should ask: *can the claimant find effective protection in another part of his own territory to which he or she may reasonably be expected to move?* We have set out in paragraphs 18 and 19 of this judgment appropriate factors to be taken into account in deciding what is reasonable in this context. We consider the test suggested by Linden JA – would it be unduly harsh to expect this person to move to another less hostile part of the country – to be a particularly helpful one. *The use of the words "unduly harsh" fairly reflects that what is in issue is whether a person claiming asylum can reasonably be expected to move to a particular part of the country.*[50]

---

47 *Randhawa, supra* n. 44, Black CJ at 270 and Whitlam CJ at 280.
48 *Robinson, supra* n. 2, para. 18.
49 *Jonah, Yurekli, Gunes, El-Tanoukhi, supra* n. 5, 7 and 9, 10, and 16 respectively.
50 *Robinson, supra* n. 2, para. 29 (emphasis added).

On the procedural issue of whether the IFA issue could be raised against an appellant at any time in the decision process on his claim to be a refugee, the Court again found itself able to cut the Gordian knot in which earlier cases had become entangled by grounding itself squarely on clear public international law principles. It found that it was "the duty of the appellate authorities to apply their knowledge of Convention jurisprudence to the facts as established by them when they determine whether it would be a breach of the Convention to refuse an asylum seeker leave to enter as a refugee", and that "they are not limited in their consideration of the facts by the arguments actually advanced by the asylum seeker or his representative".[51] Dicta to the contrary in other cases were expressly disapproved.[52] The relevance of this general point to IFA was thus as set out two paragraphs earlier:

> The central issue in these appeals is whether this country would be in breach of its obligations under the Convention ... and we have shown in this judgment that a question of whether a particular part of the appellant's home country affords a safe haven or an internal flight alternative is one which may well have to be considered by a special adjudicator, whether the appellant raises it or not, when deciding pursuant to Rule 334(ii) whether the appellant is a refugee.[53]

The Court then proceeded to clarify the matter of the criteria the Tribunal should adopt in deciding to grant leave, especially when, as here, a new point was raised that was arguable but had no strong prospect of success.[54] In the case of *Robinson* the applicant's advisers had not been able to surmount these criteria. Their case had been based at a point in time when the situation in Colombo was at its most disrupted and the arguments they relied upon fell well short of showing "undue hardship" (those raised had been lack of secure accommodation for the applicants, lack of employment prospects and capacity for independent support and risk of repetition of detention). Thus, the Court concluded, the Tribunal had not erred in failing to recognise that the special

51 *Robinson, supra* n. 2, para. 37.

52 Specifically, Hobhouse LJ, *Anandanadarajah v. IAT* [1996] Imm. A.R. 514 at 519.

53 *Robinson, supra* n. 2, para. 35.

54 The appellate authorities were not required to engage in a search for new points, but did have to apply any readily discernible point in favour of the claimant. The Tribunal, in particular should grant leave to appeal where there was an obvious point of Convention law favourable to the asylum seeker,i.e. one which had a "strong prospect of success". Otherwise there would be a danger that "this country will be in breach of its obligations under the Convention" (para. 39).

adjudicator had not expressly dealt with the matter of lack of a safe haven or internal flight alternative in Colombo.

Robinson has finally put UK treatment of IFA on the map of international jurisprudence. That is not to say that it has resolved all key issues. Despite its close attention, for example, to the correct procedure to be followed where an IFA point *favourable* to a claimant has not been dealt with by a decision-maker, it did not tackle the thorny question of the correct criteria to be applied when the judicial stage of decision-making identifies for the first time an IFA point *unfavourable* to the claimant.[55]

The Court's delineation of the four suggested tests for an IFA as set out in paragraphs 18 and 19 of its judgment does not explain the basis on which this list is compiled. Nor does it clarify whether or when it sees any role for (a), (b) and (d).[56] In *Robinson* it particularly favoured the "undue hardship" test, but it did not expressly reject the other three. At paragraph 29 it described the four as "appropriate factors to be taken into account in deciding what is reasonable in this context". Even if the other three could now be said to have been put in the shade by the "undue hardship" test, their interrelationship with the "undue hardship" is likely to be the subject of closer treatment in future cases, especially the "human rights" test at (d).

On the other hand, the Court did confirm the strong indication it had already given in *Ikhlaq and Ikhlaq* that the test of reasonableness of an IFA was just as much part and parcel of the IFA test as was the issue of its safety. Thereby it has put an effective end to the recurrent confusion in both previous court and IAT treatments of IFA.

Paragraph 343

Has the *Robinson* judgment wholly solved the paragraph 343 issue? It certainly purported to lay to rest the section 8 argument which caused the difference of views at Tribunal level between Professor Jackson and Judge Pearl. The Court clearly agreed with Professor Jackson that the restriction on the grounds of appeal in asylum cases which is contained in Section 8 of the 1993 Act serves to limit the jurisdiction of a [special] adjudicator under Section 19(1) of the earlier Act in such cases to the single issue set out in Section 8 (para. 22 of its

55 As dealt with by the IAT in a case chaired by Geoffrey Care, in *Sulosan* (12543); see also *Ahmed* (13371), *supra* n. 26.

56 *Robinson, supra* n. 2.

judgment). Where Jackson had gone wrong, in the Court's view, was in believing that a complete IFA test incorporating reasonableness was not implicit in the Convention definition of a refugee, and that, it could only arise under UK law in purely discretionary rules contained within paragraph 343 of HC 395. Instead, the Court found it to be inherent in the definition and capable of being imported into the Convention by reference to paragraph 91 of the *Handbook* in any event.[57] That standpoint meant that even though the appellate authorities had to derive their powers to consider issues from the 1993 Act, section 8 could not create a restriction so as to exclude an IFA test, since the 1993 Act at sections 2 and 8(1) proscribed any criteria that were contrary to the UK's obligations under the 1951 Convention and its Protocol.

That still left, however, some explaining to do as to the remaining scope and utility of paragraph 343. Here it is hard to see that the Court took matters a great deal further. Paragraph 343, the Court noted, was one of a series of immigration rules designed to reflect the UK's Convention obligations and that, as such, it was:

> no more than the obverse side of the proposition that if there is no such safe haven then the claimant will be a refugee within the meaning of the Convention and this country will be bound to grant him asylum, as is made clear in paragraph 334.[58]

Paragraph 343 simply established, therefore, that when there did exist for a claimant a viable IFA (that is, one that was both safe and one to which he could reasonably be expected to go), then "he would not be *entitled* to have his claim to be a refugee accepted". Beyond that, however, the Court did not venture.

The Court's solution to the paragraph 343 issue has the virtue of simplicity. It does however create some difficulties. Its end result is that it involves reading a rule that embodies a discretion in an idiosyncratic fashion, by giving it a purely negative rendering. On what basis, one may still ask, should it not be given a positive rendering, i.e. so that it operates as a rule that potentially *relaxes* the IFA test? Could it not be relevant where, by virtue of having a viable IFA, a claimant falls outside the Convention definition of refugee and

57 *Robinson, supra* n. 2, paras 10–17 and 24.

58 *Ibid.* para. 27. One recent IAT determination, *Thurairajah* (14845), states that the effect of para. 343 is to give the Secretary of State a discretion to refuse a claim for asylum where requirements of this paragraph are fulfilled without the need to make any further findings on the merits of the claim.

the Convention's *non-refoulement* prohibition? Certainly the Court's effort to derive its rationale for a purely negative rendering of paragraph 343 from the *Convention* itself is not easy to square with Recommendation E of the Conference which established the Convention. This recommendation expressed the hope that the Convention "... will have value as an example exceeding its contractual scope and that all nations will be guided by it in granting so far as possible to persons in their territory as refugees and who would not be covered by the terms of the Convention, the treatment for which it provides".[59]

Voice of the Future? The Court of Appeal Judgment in *Adan*

The judgment of the Court in *Adan* preceded those made in *Ikhlaq and Ikhlaq* and in *Robinson*, but its greater sweep makes it appropriate to deal with last. The case concerned in fact four appellants, all of whom had been refused refugee status despite acceptance that they could not be returned to their respective countries of nationality. Their appeals arose as statutory appeals to the Court of Appeal from negative decisions by the IAT, not by way of judicial review. In the case of the two Somali applicants Adan and Nooh, this was because they had been granted exceptional leave to remain (ELR). In the case of the two Yugoslavs, Lazarevic and Radivojevic,[60] they were overstayers but it was accepted that, although they would be safe from persecution in Yugoslavia for draft evasion, the Yugoslav authorities at the time were refusing to accept their return until a bilateral agreement was signed by the UK.

In the case of the two Somalis it was accepted that they had a *past* or "historic" fear of persecution based on a Convention reason. It was further accepted that if returned they would currently faced a *generalised danger*. However, the Tribunal had not accepted that they had shown a current fear of persecution based on a Convention reason. In Adan's case this was because the risk he faced was on account of indiscriminate danger, not on account of his political beliefs or membership of a particular clan. In Nooh's case there was for the tribunal a second independent reason why she could not qualify:

---

59 See *1979 Handbook on Procedures and Criteria for Determining Refugee Status: Excerpt From the Final Act of the United Nations Conference of Plenipotentiaries on the Status of Refugees and Stateless Persons*, Annex 1, p. 56.

60 *Adan, supra* n. 3.

> if [Nooh] was to be able to travel to her traditional homelands, she would not suffer harassment and these areas can be regarded as "safe areas". We accept that [Nooh] might have to travel through "unsafe" areas to reach her homelands, but the fact remains that, having regard to the present situation in Somalia, [she] has been granted exceptional leave to remain in the United Kingdom.

Simon Brown viewed the four appeals as requiring resolution of two issues. The first was whether fear of persecution had always to be current or whether historic fear of persecution would suffice. The second arose only in relation to the Somali applicants and addressed the circumstances in which persecution for a Convention reason could properly be said to arise in the context of a civil war.

Bearing in mind that the interpretation of the Convention generally required a "broad brush approach", Simon Brown saw the four cases as requiring a fundamental enquiry into the proper construction of Article 1A(2) of the Convention definition of refugee. The latter he saw as best broken down into four clauses, two of them confined to persons not having a nationality. The first two he set out as follows:

> A refugee is someone who: (a) owing to well-founded fear of being persecuted for [a Convention reason] is outside the country of his nationality, and (b)(i) is unable to avail himself of the protection of that country, or (ii) owing to such fear, is unwilling to avail himself of the protection of that country.[61]

To satisfy (a), concluded Simon Brown, did not require that the fear remained current. It sufficed that a claimant be outside his country of nationality owing to past persecution and remain abroad on that account, in the sense that the causal link remains operative and has never been broken. Whilst he did not go as far as viewing past persecution as creating a *presumption* of present fear of persecution, he considered that one could expect the necessary causative link to remain so long as there had been no substantial delay between the two and there had been no obvious opportunity to return home.

Simon Brown accepted that to qualify as a refugee it was not enough to satisfy this first test. In addition he had to show he was "unable or ... unwilling to avail himself of the protection of that country". It was at this point that Simon Brown struck out in a novel direction. In both the previous UK jurisprudence and indeed most of the international jurisprudence, the "protection" limb of the test has been seen to require a claimant to show

61 *Adan, supra* n. 3, at 1114–15 and 258–59 respectively.

primarily an inability or unwillingness to avail oneself against *protection from persecution.* As such a person could not fall within the definition of refugee even if he was at risk of *generalised harm* falling short of persecution.

Simon Brown felt able to reject this reading unhesitatingly. From all the commentaries[62] and paragraph 91 of the *Handbook* it seemed clear to him that the concept of protection as used in Article 1A(2) had to be read as a *broader* concept than simple protection from persecution; it also embraced such aspects as denial of services by a claimant's country of origin, such as refusal of a national passport or denial of admission. The only proviso was that the fear or actuality of past persecution still played a causative part in his presence here.[63]

If up to this point Simon Brown's analysis was confined to an abstract level, he chose to single out the IFA context as a specific example of its practical implications. When considering paragraph 91 and reference therein to an IFA, he stated that "it exemplifies how refugee status may arise when there is an *overall failure to provide protection at home* giving rise to persecution in part of the country and ineffective internal protection from generalised danger in the rest". Furthermore, in the concluding part of his judgment setting out his findings on the appeal of each applicant, he made the following observation concerning the case of Ms Nooh, in which the Tribunal had based its refusal in part on an additional IFA ground:

> As to the Tribunal's conclusion that she would be safe in her homelands, they gave no reasons for ignoring the danger of her having to travel through unsafe areas to get there, and in any event appear to have overlooked the Special Adjudicator's finding that "she cannot look to find any greater safety anywhere else in Somalia".

Simon Brown's analysis, insofar as the IFA test is concerned, represents a major step towards a reading of the refugee definition which gives primacy to a *protection-based* definition over a *persecution-based* definition. In support of his approach it could further be said that both UNHCR and European

62 Simon Brown did not cite any sources, but in the course of dealing with the second issue Hutchison LJ noted a passage from Hathaway citing Andrew Shacknove's description of persecution as "but one manifestation of the broader phenomenon: the absence of State protection of the citizen's basic needs. It is this absence of State protection which constitutes the full and complete negation of society and the basis of refugeehood". *Adan, supra* n. 3 at 1126 and 271 respectively.

63 *Adan, supra* n. 3 at 1114 and 259 respectively.

interpretations of the refugee definition incline in this direction. Furthermore, his analysis of the concept of protection being wider than that of protection from persecution could also be said to be more in line with the flexibility of that concept in public international law. In the latter it can of course possess an external as well as an internal aspect. An example of the former arises in the context of the notion of diplomatic protection. As regards internal protection, it is recognised that protection from many forms of harm may engage the responsibility of the state. Assessment of this generally requires likewise an objective test in preference to a subjective test.[64] Ultimately, protection exists as an attribute of the sovereign state, part of what makes it able to meet one of the essential prerequisites of statehood – the ability to govern. If its origin resides in the classic duty of a state to defend its own citizenry, the growing corpus of international human rights law has undoubtedly required protection to be meaningful in terms of ensuring nationals are not put at risk of a denial of basic human rights safeguards within their own country.[65]

Simon Brown's forceful analysis is vulnerable to criticism on several counts. Firstly, his dismissal on textual grounds of a more limited reading of protection as deployed in Article 1A(2) was perhaps too closely related to his assessment of the particular arguments put to him by Treasury Counsel on that occasion. Secondly, throughout he appears automatically to have equated inability and unwillingness on the part of an *individual* – to avail himself of state protection – with the inability or unwillingness of a *state* or other source of established authority to protect an individual. In his treatment of Somalia, for example, his survey of protection was seen in terms of what various quasi-state sources of authority were able to offer by way of protection.[66] This equation risks divesting the concept of protection within Article 1A(2) of its link with individual action. Finally, there is the fact that it appears to be in advance of the broad body of international jurisprudence, which certainly in relation to the IFA requires the claimant to show continued exposure to country-wide persecution, in order for him to be able to satisfy the protection test, albeit moderated by a test of reasonableness in all the circumstances.[67]

64 See e.g. Shaw, M.N., *International Law*, (4th edn, CUP, 1997) 545.

65 See also chapter 12 of this book by Nicholas Blake. For recent IAT cases evincing a fuller appreciation of issues of access and of meaningful protection, see *Abdalla* (13933) and *Yousfi* (14779).

66 See, e.g., his comments on the role of President Egal and Gen. Aideed, *Adan*, *supra* n. 3 at 1122 and 267 respectively.

67 See *Randhawa*, *supra* n. 44.

Even if the Court of Appeal's bold stance in *Adan* fails to withstand House of Lords scrutiny, it is likely to be considered at the international level as a beacon for future development of asylum law and of the IFA concept in particular. An example of its practical implications for the IFA test was already supplied within the judgment itself, in the form of the conclusion it reached on the position of Ms Nooh. To prove that she satisfied this test it would suffice, the Court ruled, that she could show a risk in any prospective IFA of a generalised danger short of a fear of persecution. However, Simon Brown's very strong proviso to this new approach must be borne in mind. A claimant must continue to be able to demonstrate an *effective causal link* between past persecution and inability to return. Whilst this was a relatively straightforward matter for Ms Nooh to do, this proviso will prove a much harder task for many other claimants.

Contrast and Comparison between the International Jurisprudence and UK Case Law

Although it is outside the scope of this chapter to cover the international jurisprudence on the IFA as such, a brief overview of how the national case law converges or diverges is in order, in view of the growing concern within the UK to achieve a more unified international interpretation of the Convention. It has been shown that the UK jurisprudence on the IFA has had a chequered history, with relatively little close analysis of it attempted until quite recently. Nonetheless it is very clear that, since 1985 at least, the UK courts and tribunals have applied the IFA test robustly, even though for some considerable period they did not see any need to refer to it by name (IFA or otherwise) or to identify it expressly as a Convention "test".

In common with the international jurisprudence, UK courts and tribunals have, for example, adhered fairly strictly to the test as being one requiring the claimant to prove persecution country-wide. In line with established international case law, however, the Court of Appeal's new approach in the watershed case of *Robinson* reflects a concern to mitigate undue harshness the test can cause. In general UK jurisprudence has begun to demonstrate a much more international orientation, and to analyse relevant criteria much more by reference to contemporary English case law on the proper approach to construction of treaties incorporated into English law. As they have become more at ease with a more international approach, our courts and tribunals have become readier to attempt their own creative developments, in pursuit of what *Robinson* describes as a "contemporary understanding" of the 1951 Convention. Indeed in its earlier judgment in *Adan*, the Court of Appeal *per* Simon Brown LJ seeks to take the whole of asylum law into new territory, and to view the Convention as an instrument that primarily ensures a system of *effective protection*. As a result of the Court's singular attention to the IFA test in *Robinson*, UK jurisprudence now has a leading case that analyses the test in comparable depth to *Thirunavukkarasu* in Canada,[68] *Randhawa* in Australia,[69] *Re: RS* in New Zealand,[70] and the 1996 decision of the German Federal Constitutional Court[71] to name several leading international cases on the IFA test.

Approach to the Reasonableness Criterion

In contrast to some of the international jurisprudence (and one isolated IAT determination),[72] the courts had for a long time been content to treat paragraph 91 of the *Handbook* as helpful and unproblematic guidance on interpretation of the IFA test and to adopt wholesale its criterion of "reasonableness", without seeking to define that criterion more precisely. They have generally resisted, however, any interpretation of that criterion as an "override" such that a claimant can qualify as a refugee even when his fear of persecution for a Convention reason is localised only.[73] It is true that the Court of Appeal in *Adan* appeared ready, in claims based on lack of meaningful protection elsewhere, to accept criteria that require ongoing, country-wide fear of persecution to be shown only as a continuing background. The formula adopted by Simon Brown, LJ in *Adan* allows for a test based on a risk of generalised harm elsewhere to prove lack of an IFA, albeit this is only valid in cases where some effective causative link remains with a claimant's experience of past persecution or fear of it.

68 *Thirunavukkarasu, supra* n. 34.

69 *Randhawa, supra* n. 44.

70 *Re: RS* No. 523/92 (a decision of the New Zealand Refugee Status Appeals Authority, 17 March 1995).

71 Decision of Federal Administrative Court (Bundesverwaltungsgericht) referred to in (1996) 8 I.J.Ref.L. 207.

72 *Viz. Dupovac, supra* n. 27.

73 Thus, they have not taken the New Zealand road on this issue, as articulated in the leading case decided by the New Zealand Refugee Status Appeals Authority in *Re RS, supra* n. 70, at 29–32, although some IAT determinations have cited this decision approvingly.

Before 1996, both the courts and the Tribunal tended in many instances to assume a dichotomy between issues of "safety" and "reasonableness" and simply to presume that reasonableness was a criterion to be applied only when it was already established that there was a part of the country where a claimant could live without real risk of persecution for a Convention reason. These standpoints did not reflect the international jurisprudence which broadly sees reasonableness as a proper criterion for determining *both* whether an IFA is safe and whether it can be reached in safety. Neither did it fit with the traditional position taken by the UK courts. *Robinson* has resolved all that, although it should be noted that there remain a number of aspects relating to safety and reasonableness which still require clarification. In particular, these concern the invalidity or validity of comparative assessments of the risk of persecution in general, "normalcy" as an improper or proper bench mark for assessment of country levels of risk, both of which have been addressed very cogently in the New Zealand case *Re: RS*.[74] There also remains the vital matter of what should be common variables or indices of undue hardship which should be considered in each case.

The Court of Appeal's fresh treatment raises a question mark regarding one aspect of the reasonableness test. In *Ikhlaq and Ikhlaq* Staughton LJ found that, rather than the enquiry being into "what would be a reasonable course for the refugee to take, ... it is the decision-maker who is to be reasonable, the person who is doing the expecting (or requiring)". Whilst this view finds some support in the international jurisprudence, it clashes with that articulated by Rodger Haines in highly respected New Zealand decisions.[75]

The Point in Time at which the IFA Test is to be Applied

One point in the UK case law which previously lacked clear treatment concerns the proper point in time at which the IFA test is to be applied. The current edition of Macdonald's and Blake's *Immigration Law and Practice in the United Kingdom*, maintains that the discrete point in time for application of

74 *Re: RS, supra* n. 70.

75 See *Re RS, supra* n. 70, in which the focus is on the intentions and conduct of the individual actually involved. This judgment states: "The test is what is reasonable in the particular circumstances of the specific individual whose case is under consideration. The focus is not on the hypothetical reasonable person, but on what is reasonable in the particular (i.e. subjective) circumstances of the specific individual claimant."

the IFA test is when the claimant departs from his country of origin.[76] This argument has some underlying rationale, in that it may be thought harsh for a claimant who can show a well-founded fear at the time of departure from the country of origin to have to then go on to prove grounds for a continuing fear, since that would place additional burdens on him, in having in particular to furnish from abroad evidence of subsequent changes in his country of nationality. Furthermore, paragraph 91 of the *Handbook* appears to set the test in the past ("if ... it would not have been reasonable to expect him to do so"). However, this has not been the view taken in the bulk of the modern international jurisprudence, which has generally come to treat the crucial point in time as being the date of the hearing.

Nevertheless, one may say that in the UK case law the 1995 Court of Appeal judgment in *Ravichandran*[77] indirectly resolved this issue. In that case the distinct, but overlapping, issue of whether the test of a person qualifying as a refugee is at the date of (original) decision or at the date of hearing, was resolved by the Court deciding it is the latter. That plainly necessitated that *primary* focus at least be fixed squarely on the IFA test as being one relating to whether a claimant has an IFA at the date of the hearing. The reasons why a claimant did not seek an IFA prior to his date of departure remain, of course, relevant as part of his overall circumstances, past and present. They remain valid, as a secondary point of focus. This approach is able to embrace cases ranging from those where internal flight was left as a *hypothetical* option, through to those where it was *in fact attempted* by way of movement on to one or more other places inside the country of nationality (for example by Sri Lankan Tamils moving to Colombo). Nevertheless, the test essentially concerns the issue of whether a claimant could avoid real risk of persecution *upon return* and *now*, by relocating in one or more other parts of his country of nationality, away from his home locality or region.[78] This approach has now been directly endorsed by the Court of Appeal in *Robinson*, which found that "the relevant time at which to consider the position was when [the appellate authorities] came to make their decisions".[79]

76 Macdonald, I.A., and Blake, N., *Immigration Law and Practice in the United Kingdom* (4th edn, Butterworths, 1995) 388.

77 *Ravichandran v. Secretary of State for the Home Department* CA [1996] Imm. A.R. 97 (which came after publication of 4th edn of *Immigration Law and Practice in the United Kingdom*).

78 In *Vijendran, supra* n. 37, the court confirmed this approach.

79 *Robinson, supra* n. 2, para. 43.

The UK jurisprudence has rarely strayed from the approach of treating *both* personal and general country background factors as being essential in assessing a claimant's overall situation in relation to internal flight. In this respect it fully reflects the strong consensus in the international case law about the need for such a two dimensional approach.

Other Aspects

A general survey of UK asylum case law shows that it has gradually evolved a circumstantial, flexible, practical and realistic approach to the IFA test. There are also concrete signs of a change in the direction of engaging more with the international case law on IFA, particularly where UK jurisprudence is silent, tentative or equivocal. This reflects a more international approach to asylum law generally. More regular reference is being made in particular to diverse, well-researched sources of data about general country situations. Even though the very limited resources available to the UK Immigration Appellate Authority have not enabled it to ensure its own comprehensive IFA reports on countries where IFA is often a key issue, it is fast gaining expertise in how to obtain relevant reports and data, including by drawing on databases compiled by asylum appeal research departments in other countries.

From one point of view, these features are signs that the national jurisprudence is in good health and in accordance with leading overseas case principles. At the same time it has been equally apparent that viewed overall, the judicial decision-making on IFA has displayed an eclectic, *ad hoc* character. It has yet to be seen whether *Robinson* will end inconsistencies of approach at Tribunal level.[80] It is submitted that a higher level of consistency will not prove possible in the absence of the issuance of better guidelines, along the lines of those produced by the Canadian Immigration and Refugee Board. The latter would mean that decision-makers would need to show that their decisions on the IFA had been made within a systematic framework of analysis and by reference to a checklist of relevant factors. That would not end all criticism arising from different adjudicators or Tribunal panel members or judges reaching dissimilar conclusions about IFAs on cases concerning claimants from the same countries and in similar situations. It should, however,

80 For recent IAT cases dealing with IFA see *Singh* (14055), *Thurairajah* (14845), *Samantar* (14520). See also chapter 9 of this book by Alison Harvey and, for an adjudicator's view, chapter 8 of this book by Geoffrey Care.

reduce the frequency of such occurrences and make it more possible to defend dissimilar outcomes as a just and proper consequence of deciding each case on its particular circumstances, rather than according to some blanket approach to different categories or nationalities of claimants.

Human Rights Interlinking

As the UK approach has become decidedly more international, more linkages of IFA issues to international human rights norms are beginning to be attempted. The latter development goes wider, of course, than issues relating to IFA, but it is interesting to note that the same Tribunal chairman, Care, whose determination in *Gashi and Nikshiqi*[81] has raised general human rights issues under the Convention, saw fit in *Yang*[82] to link testing of IFA to the human rights provision of freedom of movement. These developments remain, however, extremely tentative. It must also be said that increased linking does not necessarily mean that the IFA test relies for its validity on a human rights underpinning. Although *Robinson* disclosed some hesitancy about a human rights test, it was significant that it did confirm the Court's acceptance that "the preamble to the Convention shows that the contracting parties were concerned to uphold the principle that human beings should enjoy fundamental rights and freedoms without discrimination".[83]

The Paragraph 343 Issue

This chapter has identified fixation on the paragraph 343 question as one of the main factors that led UK case law on the IFA to drift during the early and middle 1990s into an introspective and parochial phase. Sharpening conflicts at the Tribunal level and the eventual resolution in 1996/97, most notably in the case of *Robinson*, have hopefully put an end to that phase. There should not need to be any further equivocation, whether at primary decision-maker, adjudicator, Tribunal or court level, as to what powers the appellate authorities have in applying the full IFA test solely under the Convention schema.

---

81 *Gashi and Nikshiqi*, IAT *v. Secretary of State for the Home Department* [1997] I.N.L.P. 96.

82 *Yang*, *IAT* (13952) (unreported) 15 Oct. 1996.

83 *Robinson*, *supra* n. 2, para. 18.

However, applying it under the immigration rule schema (currently paragraph 343), which appears to authorise a discretion exercisable *within* the rules seems likely to give rise to further litigation.

Procedural Fairness

Robinson has stated in emphatic terms that the primary duty of decision-makers at all levels is to apply their knowledge of Convention jurisprudence to the facts as established by them, when they determine whether it would be a breach of the Convention to refuse to grant an asylum seeker refugee status, and that they are not limited in their consideration of the facts by the arguments actually advanced by the asylum seeker or his representative.[84] That decision casts much needed light both on the position in UK law and within existing international jurisprudence, in both of which there has been a degree of uncertainty. It clarifies the position with claimants who might not have had an IFA test applied *favourably* to their claim at earlier stages of determination of their asylum claims. It is now also clear that it will never be too late, so long as the IFA point is not merely arguable but has a "strong prospect of success".[85]

However, *Robinson* was silent about the situation of a claimant who finds an IFA point raised *against* him at a late stage in legal proceedings. In this regard, however, the IAT, drawing on a good understanding of international jurisprudence, has done useful groundwork which, if approved by the courts, would make the UK position very much in line with the "common sense" approach adopted in New Zealand, for example in the *Re: RS* No. 523/93 decision cited earlier. This forswears a heavily formal protection of natural justice safeguards as is required under Canadian law and practice. Yet, it does seek to ensure a claimant is not genuinely taken by surprise by the raising of an IFA issue at any stage of proceedings up until completion of a hearing. Such an approach seems more in line with international consensus.

In the European context, however, it is arguable that such an approach could prove inadequate to protect asylum claimants under the expanded "fast-track" provisions and related changes in procedural rules arising from the Asylum and Immigration Act 1996. Consider the issue, for example, of a person who is served with a direction to furnish fuller particulars of his evidence and to supply relevant case law and skeleton arguments; but who is not

84 *Ibid.* para. 37.

85 *Ibid.* para. 39.

informed at the same time that IFA may be a specific and central issue in his case. If his case eventually hinges on IFA, has procedural justice been fully respected?[86]

Substantive Fairness

Leading decisions in some other countries have recognised the ability of the IFA to operate as a first-hurdle or stand-alone test, eliminating the necessity for the national decision-maker to consider a claim to asylum on any other ground, before deciding to reject it.[87] On this issue the current UK position appears strongly to favour treating IFA as an issue to be addressed only after an appellant has made out his claim to localised persecution. Going by the position taken by the Court of Appeal in *Adan*, it is now imperative for this to happen in every case in which past persecution still operates as a factor causing current fear.

Cases in which it has been operated as a stand-alone or first hurdle test are still unusual. They tend to be confined to those in which the claimant himself admits or the evidence discloses the existence of a safe and accessible alternative internal location and no other good evidence suggests anything to the contrary, not even risk to the claimant for a non-Convention reason. Once again, it is far from certain, whether this stance will not alter in consequence of those provisions of the 1993 and 1996 legislation aimed at further speeding up the determination of appeals. Not only UK jurisprudence but guidelines agreed by EU ministers of the kind approved by the Court in *Robinson* may be under pressure to maintain international standards.

If the stance does alter, it may become more important for judicial decisions to relate assessment of IFAs to country data in a more systematic fashion.

---

86 This issue is of concern in other jurisdictions. Anxiety about it was openly expressed by UNHCR in "An Overview of Protection Issues in Western Europe: Legislative Trends and Positions Taken by UNHCR", (Sept. 1996) *1 European Series No. 3*, pp. 10–1, 30–2. The 1992 "London Resolution" of the Ministers of the Member States of the European Communities on manifestly unfounded applications for asylum (SN 2836/93 WGI 1505) at para. 7 clearly envisaged that claims in which there appeared to be an available IFA could be included within an accelerated procedure.

87 *Kanagaratnam Parameswary v. Canada (Minister of Employment and Immigration)* (Federal Court of Appeal, no. A–356–94), Strayer, Linden, McDonald, 17 Jan. 1996, p. 2.

This will entail attention to country-specific, background reports on IFAs, as well as to country-specific reports made under the supervision of major human rights treaty bodies which address state performance in relation to the right of *freedom of movement* internally as well as in relation to other human rights they guarantee which have relevance to IFA issues.

Another factor which is likely to cause UK jurisprudence to reappraise its current approaches to the IFA test is the emergence of a new source of international jurisprudence emanating not from the traditional amalgam of national case law, state practice, UNHCR standard-setting and academic authorities, but from international judicial bodies which supervise human rights treaties. It is beyond the scope of this chapter to dwell on the importance in this regard of the case law of the UN Committee against Torture (CAT) and of the organs of Council of Europe's European Convention on Human Rights in particular.[88] It is salient, however, to note that in both instances there are now leading cases in which the IFA issue has been central to the decisions reached.

For instance, in *Ismail Alan v. Switzerland*, the Committee against Torture, in reaching a finding of a violation by Switzerland of Article 3 noted, *inter alia*:

> The author already had to leave his native area, that Izmir did not prove secure for him either, and that, since there are indications that the police are looking for him, it is not likely that a "safe" area exists in Turkey. In the circumstances, the Committee finds that the author has sufficiently substantiated that he personally is at risk of being subjected to torture if returned to Turkey.[89]

Grounds for viewing the approach to the relocation test taken by the CAT in this case as being more liberal than that taken elsewhere in the international asylum jurisprudence have been strengthened by the similar approach taken by another international judicial body, the European Court of Human Rights, in its landmark judgment on the case of *Chahal*.[90] Much of the decision reached by the majority of the Court in this case turned crucially on the issue of whether the principal applicant, a Sikh militant who had become involved in the struggle for a separate Sikh homeland in Punjab, could avoid a real risk of torture or inhuman and degrading treatment contrary to Article 3 of the European Convention on Human Rights by living elsewhere in India. What is particularly

88 For further details see chapter 12 of this book by Nicholas Blake.

89 *Ismail Alan v. Switzerland*, Communication No.21/1995 (CAT/C/16/D/21/1996). See also (1996) 8 I.Ref.L.J. 440.

90 *Chahal v. UK* (70/1995/576/662) judgment of 15 Nov. 1996.

significant about the Court's careful and detailed treatment of this issue is the emphasis it placed on the need, when deciding whether safety could be found through relocation, for satisfactory evidence that the authorities of the state, in this case the Indian police force and security forces in particular, would be able to afford protection to its citizens throughout India in accordance with fundamental guarantees of civil and political human rights standards.[91] This judgment will obviously fuel arguments to the effect that no safe IFA can obtain unless the risk of persecution in an IFA is only avoidable if a claimant does not seek to enjoy or exercise fundamental human rights, such as the right to freedom of expression.

Arguably the approach to be adopted when assessing the degree of risk of persecution under 1951 Convention criteria should not be different in kind, simply because the fear being tested is not of inhuman and degrading treatment as such but a well-founded fear of persecution for a Convention reason. If more regular human rights linkages do become one of the features of UK jurisprudence on the IFA in the late 1990s, then in one way it might be seen to have come full circle from the first famous IFA decision in *ex parte Jonah*.[92] The decision of Nolan J (as he then was) not to consider that a viable IFA in a remote isolated village in Ghana would exist for a prominent trade unionist, may prove, in longer term historical perspective, more in tune with future judicial and executive rethinking.

Overall, however, the Court of Appeal has from 1996 shown that its late conversion to a more internationalist approach, both as regards the Convention generally and the IFA test in particular, will not prevent it playing a significant role in helping and perhaps synthesising some of the "interpretational divergencies" which still irk the international jurisprudence.

---

91 *Ibid.* paras 100, 102–04, 107.

92 *Ex p. Jonah, supra* n. 5.

Bibliography

Storey, H., "The Internal Flight Alternative: A Re-examination of the International Jurisprudence" I.J.Ref.L. (forthcoming).

Hathaway, J., *The Law of Refugee Status* (Butterworths, 1991).

Goodwin-Gill, G., *The Refugee in International Law* (Clarendon, 1996).

Shaw, M.N., *International Law*, (4th edn, CUP, 1997).

Macdonald, I.A., and Blake, N., *Immigration Law and Practice in the United Kingdom* (4th edn, Butterworths, 1995).

UNHCR, "An Overview of Protection Issues in Western Europe: Legislative Trends and Positions Taken by UNHCR", (Sept. 1996) *1 European Series No. 3.*

6 Sexual Orientation and Refugee Claims Based on "Membership of a Particular Social Group" Under the 1951 Refugee Convention

SIMON RUSSELL

This chapter examines the development of case law concerning the definition of a refugee under the 1951 Convention relating to the Status of Refugees (1951 Refugee Convention). Specifically, it investigates the treatment of the concept of "membership of a particular social group" and takes the example of claims based on sexual orientation. Recent developments in Canadian and United States courts are compared with those in the United Kingdom. It is outside the scope of this chapter to look at the types of harm specific to gay and lesbian claimants although, arguably, the biggest obstacle to recognition of such claimants in the UK is now in the definition of "persecution".[1]

Under the 1951 Refugee Convention a refugee is someone who "owing to well-founded fear of being persecuted for reasons of race, religion, nationality, membership of a particular social group or political opinion" is unable, or owing to such fear, is unwilling to return to his country of origin or former habitual residence.[2] In the UK, legislation does not set out specifically the definition of a refugee, unlike, for instance, the Irish Refugee Act 1996.[3]

1 See, e.g., *Belemet v. Secretary of State for the Home Department* Immigration Appeal Tribunal (IAT) (13958) (2 Oct. 1996, unreported) where the IAT found that when prosecution for consensual homosexual acts in private was being carried out "humanely" then this could not found a claim of persecution.

2 1951 Convention relating to the Status of Refugees, Art. 1 A(2). For context of UK asylum policy in international human rights law see chapters 11 and 12 of this book by C.J. Harvey and Nicholas Blake respectively.

3 Irish Refugee Act, No.17 of 1996.

Section 2 of the Asylum and Immigration Appeals Act 1993 provides for the primacy of the 1951 Refugee Convention and its 1967 Protocol over the Immigration Rules, which set down the practice and criteria to be followed in assessing asylum claims by the Secretary of State for the Home Department. Rule 334 of the current Immigration Rules[4] states that someone will be granted asylum in the United Kingdom if they meet the 1951 Refugee Convention definition of a refugee. The *Handbook* published by the United Nations High Commissioner for Refugees (UNHCR) to provide guidance as to the meaning of the 1951 Refugee Convention,[5] states:

> 77. A "particular social group" normally comprises persons of similar background, habits or social status. A claim to fear of persecution under this heading may frequently overlap with a claim to fear of persecution on other grounds, i.e. race, religion or nationality.
>
> 78. Membership of such a particular social group may be at the root of persecution because there is no confidence in the group's loyalty to the Government or because the political outlook, antecedents or economic activity of its members, or the very existence of the group as such, is held to be an obstacle to the Government's policies.

It is generally accepted that, although the *Handbook*'s guidance is not binding, it is persuasive authority.[6] The *Handbook* definition is interesting not only because of the breadth of its interpretation of the phrase "social group" but also because of the element of the persecutor's perception of the group, an aspect of the definition which some tribunals have failed to recognise. A fuller exposition of the meaning of "membership of a particular social group" can be found in various academic texts.[7] The texts differ between an "exclusive" approach, arguing that "social group" is not a category in itself but only refers to the other grounds in the definition, and an "inclusive" approach asserting that the drafters of the Convention meant to include all those claimants who could not fit into the other four grounds of the definition.

4 *Statement of Changes in Immigration Rules* (1993–94) HC 395.

5 UNHCR, *Handbook on Procedures and Criteria for Determining Refugee Status* (Geneva, re-edited 1992).

6 *Mendis v. Immigration Appeal Tribunal* [1989] Imm. A.R. 6.

7 Grahl-Madsen, A., *The Status of Refugees in International Law* (A.W. Sijthoff, 1966); Goodwin-Gill, G., *The Refugee in International Law* (2nd edn, OUP, 1996); Helton, A., "Persecution on Account of Membership in a Social Group as a Basis for Refugee Status" (1983) 15 Columbia H.R.L.R. 39.

One of the most authoritative texts[8] takes what has been called the middle way. In this text Professor Hathaway argues that the inclusion of the social group category in the 1951 Refugee Convention definition was not meant to be meaningless, but neither was it meant to be a catch-all category. The "middle way" is now the generally accepted approach to construing the definition of a particular social group and this will be discussed further below. With particular reference to homosexuals, Hathaway states that "homosexual and bisexual women and men constitute a second group defined by a fundamental, immutable characteristic".[9]

Developments in UK Law

According to the New Zealand Refugee Status Appeals Authority,[10] the English case law on whether homosexuals can constitute a "particular social group" is in disarray. Looking at the decided cases one must have some sympathy for this view. In *Binbasi*[11] Kennedy J assumed, without deciding, that homosexuals could constitute a social group, although the applicant failed on the grounds that since his sexual orientation would be expressed, if at all, in private it would not come to the attention of the authorities. The Immigration Appeal Tribunal (IAT) has considered the question a number of times, the two major occasions being in *Golchin*,[12] where the IAT found that homosexuals *per se* do not form a social group and in *Vraciu*,[13] where the IAT found that homosexuals in Romania did form a social group.[14] Interestingly, the IAT upheld *Golchin* only a day after the decision in *Vraciu* in a case involving a Jamaican gay man.[15]

8 Hathaway, J.C., *The Law of Refugee Status* (Butterworths, 1991).

9 *Ibid.*, p. 163.

10 *Re: GJ* (1312/93), unreported decision of the New Zealand Refugee Status Appeals Authority, 30 Aug. 1995.

11 *R. v. Secretary of State for the Home Department, ex p. Binbasi* [1989] Imm. A.R. 595.

12 *Golchin* IAT (7623) (1991, unreported).

13 *Vraciu* IAT (11559) (1994, unreported).

14 For detailed discussion of the case see, Bamforth, N., "Protected Social Groups, the Refugee Convention and Judicial Review: The *Vraciu* Case" (1995) Public Law 382.

15 *Jacques* IAT (11580) (1994, unreported). For difficulties in securing consistency within the IAT see chapters 8 and 9 of this book by Geoffrey Care and Alison Harvey respectively.

The "disarray" in the law has been deepened by two recent decisions of the IAT. In the case of *Secretary of State v. "S."*[16] a majority of the Tribunal (the legally qualified chair dissenting) found that the probable prosecution (and execution if convicted) of a gay man from Iran was a matter for the Iranian authorities and no question of persecution arose in the context of infringements of the law. (However, the Home Office conceded this case when leave to appeal was granted to the Court of Appeal.) By contrast, in *Stevanovich*[17] the IAT (the chair being the same person who had decided *Golchin*) accepted without argument that gay men could be members of a particular social group.

The confusion at the Tribunal level has been mirrored in first instance appeal decisions by special adjudicators. Several adjudicators have adopted and extended the reasoning in *Vraciu*. Others have dismissed appeals on bizarre credibility grounds (for example, when *Vraciu* came before a special adjudicator to decide the merits of his case, the adjudicator reasoned that most gay men were nice but that as the appellant was not nice, he could not be gay) or by equating homosexuals with paedophiles and stating that prohibition of consensual homosexual acts is justified. Adjudicators also appear to have some difficulty in accepting that prosecution for a consensual homosexual act is of itself persecution or that restrictions on gay and lesbian expression and association violate human rights and equality guarantees.

In a wider context, the IAT has considered the meaning of social group in *Otchere*.[18] The decision is notable for the advice which was given by the UNHCR representative on that occasion. This stated:

> [I]n the view of the High Commissioner there were a number of criteria which needed to be considered:
>
> 1. The group must be distinct as an identity within the broader society and definable by characteristics shared by its members.
>
> 2. Common characteristics or uniting factors could be various – ethnic, cultural or linguistic, or educational; they could include family background, economic activity, shared experiences, or shared values, outlook or aspirations.

---

16 *Secretary of State for the Home Department v. "S."* IAT (13124) (1995, unreported).

17 *Stevanovich* IAT (14773) (1996, unreported).

18 *Secretary of State for the Home Department v. Otchere and the UNHCR* [1988] Imm. A.R. 21.

> 3. The attitude of other members of society to the group.
>
> It was agreed that the characteristics must exist independently of the fact of persecution, but nevertheless the characteristics must play a significant role in the persecution. The persecution must be feared, or exist, on account of the characteristics. There must of course be evidence of persecution and simple membership of a group was not enough. The High Commissioner would consider that members of a group do not have to share all the characteristics mentioned above.[19]

The IAT implicitly approved UNHCR's guidance in this case. Whilst UNHCR has not produced a worldwide statement on whether homosexuals are members of a particular social group, the branch office in Washington, DC, has consistently stated that,

> [I]t is the opinion of the UNHCR, therefore, based on our interpretation of the refugee definition and on existing State practice, that lesbians and gay men who can show that they have a well-founded fear of persecution due to their sexual orientation fall within the refugee definition found in the 1951 Convention/ 1967 Protocol relating to the Status of Refugees.[20]

The Court of Appeal has considered the construction of "membership of a particular social group" several times recently. In *Savchenkov*[21] the Court of Appeal allowed the Secretary of State's appeal against the decision of the IAT that those who refused to engage in criminal activity in Russia could be considered members of a particular social group. It was common ground before the Court of Appeal that there was persuasive authority from the USA and Canada[22] and academic authority in the form of Hathaway's analysis that the definition of a particular social group was to be construed *ejusdem generis* with the other grounds of the 1951 Refugee Convention definition. In other words, membership of a particular social group denoted a civil or political status which is an immutable characteristic either beyond the power of the individual to change (akin to race) or so fundamental to one's identity or conscience that one should not be forced to change it (akin to religion or

19 *Ibid.*, pp. 26–7.

20 Letters to the Law Offices of Noemi E. Masliah of New York from Scott Busby, UNHCR branch office, Washington D.C., USA, 15 Sept. 1993, 27 July 1994, 2 March 1995.

21 *Secretary of State for the Home Department v. Savchenkov* [1996] Imm. A.R. 28.

22 See, especially *Canada (Attorney-General) v. Ward* [1993] 4 D.L.R. 103 at 1; [1993] 2 R.C.S. 689.

political opinion). This test was first propounded in a US Board of Immigration Appeals case in *Matter of Acosta*.[23] In *Ward*, the Canadian Supreme Court explicitly approved of this test and found:

> The meaning assigned to particular social group ... should take into account the general underlying themes of the defence of human rights and anti-discrimination that form the basis for the international refugee protection initiative. The tests ... identify three possible categories ...:
>
> (1) groups defined by an innate or unchangeable characteristic;
>
> (2) groups whose members voluntarily associate for reasons so fundamental to their human dignity that they should not be forced to forsake the association, and
>
> (3) groups associated by a former voluntary status, unalterable due to its historical permanence.
>
> The first category would embrace individuals fearing persecution on such bases as gender, linguistic background and sexual orientation, while the second would encompass, for example, human rights activists. The third branch is included more because of historical intentions, although it is also relevant to the anti-discrimination influences, in that one's past is an immutable part of the person.[24]

Although the Court of Appeal did not attempt, in *Savchenkov*, a comprehensive definition of a particular social group, in the way the Canadian Supreme Court had done in *Ward*, it is implicit in the judgment that the Canadian approach was accepted. Savchenkov failed to show he was a member of a particular social group, not because the *Ward* criteria were wrong, but because a citizen in a democracy had a duty to obey the law and it was, therefore, impermissible to say that performing this duty put one in a special social position, endowed with a civil or political status. The *ratio decidendi* of *Savchenkov* is, admittedly, somewhat obscure but recent guidance as to the true meaning of the judgment can be found in the Court of Appeal's decisions in *Quijano*[25] and *Lazarevic*.[26] In *Quijano* the Court held, *per* Thorpe LJ:

---

23 *Matter of Acosta*, US Board of Immigration Appeals, interim decision 2986, 1 March 1985.

24 *Ward supra* n. 22, pp. 33–4 and 739 respectively.

25 *Quijano v. Secretary of State for the Home Department* [1997] Imm. A.R. 227.

26 *Adan, Nooh, Lazarevic and Radivojevich v. Secretary of State for the Home Department* [1997] 1 W.L.R. 1107; [1997] 2 All E.R. 723; [1997] Imm. A.R. 251.

> [T]he application of the *Savchenkov* principles to the interpretation of particular social group results in a sensible construction of the article. ... Although it may not strictly be a product of the *ejusdem generis* rule it is in my judgment a sensible and necessary addition in order to determine whether a social group is particular for the purposes of article 1.[27]

Roch LJ added:

> I would subscribe to the third principle [the *ejusdem generis* rule] ... provided that it is accepted that there may be other "Convention reasons" in addition to race, religion, nationality and political opinion which can clothe a social group with a "civil or political status" which may emerge in the future by the application of the *ejusdem generis* rule.[28]

Interestingly, in view of several recent judgments, which are considered below, Morritt LJ disagreed that the application of the *ejusdem generis* rule formed part of the *ratio* of *Savchenkov* and was, therefore, not binding. He found that, although a particular social group will often have a political or civil status, this was not necessary in order for the group to be "particular". In *Lazarevic* the Court of Appeal, *per* Hutchison LJ, agreed with Hathaway's "middle ground" approach to the definition of the term "particular social group". He considered the decisions in *Savchenkov* and *Quijano* and concluded:

> I am prepared, for the purposes of the decision in the instant case, to treat *Savchenkov* as supporting a construction consistent with rather than more restricted than that favoured by Professor Hathaway based on *Acosta* and *Ward*. This accords with [the appellant's counsel's] submissions; he accepts that the words have to be construed *ejusdem generis* with the other four grounds but not in the restricted sense.[29]

It appeared that the approach of the US Board of Immigration Appeals in *Matter of Acosta* to the construction of a "particular social group" had been comprehensively approved by the Court of Appeal. The Court, in both cases, had considered the judgments of Laws J in *de Melo*[30] and Sedley J in *Shah*,[31]

27 *Quijano, supra* n. 25, p. 230.

28 *Ibid.*, p. 234.

29 *Lazarevic, supra* n. 26, p. 278.

30 *R. v. IAT ex p. de Melo and de Araujo* [1997] Imm. A.R. 43.

31 *R. v. IAT and Secretary of State for the Home Department ex p. Syeda Khatoon Shah*, QBD, *Times Law Report*, 12 Dec. 1996, [1997] Imm. A.R. 145. See also *infra* n. 36 for July 1997 appeal ruling and chapter 8 of this book by Geoffrey Care for further details on this case.

who doubted that the phrase "particular social group" must be interpreted *ejusdem generis* with the other 1951 Refugee Convention reasons. Sedley J, in particular, relied upon Goodwin-Gill's concerns about the value of the *Ward* decision[32] and that it may limit unduly the categories of people who could be included in the social group category. Sedley found:

> [I]t is not in my judgment necessary ... to situate the applicant within one of the *Ward* categories, though it would no doubt be valuable to be able to do so. These are aids to interpretation, not an exhaustive definition of the phrase "a particular social group" in the Convention. The dangers of a prescriptive approach will be apparent on any consideration of the shifting focus of systematic persecution in what has been a dreadful century for much of the human race. Take the street children of many South American cities, at constant risk of being killed by armed men beyond the control of the state. It might be difficult in the case of any one street child who reached a safe country to allocate him or her to a closely affiliated or cohesive social group except one defined by the fact that it is persecuted; yet it is hard to think that the framers of the 1951 Convention would have expected such a child to fall outside the protection which they were providing.[33]

Sedley J's finding here is a salutary reminder that the *ejusdem generis* rule approach to the construction of "social group" does not encompass wide groups of people at risk. It is submitted, however, that the restrictive interpretation of "social group" provided for by the *ejusdem generis* rule does not affect gay and lesbian claimants. Even if it were argued that sexual orientation is not an immutable characteristic, it is beyond doubt that it is a fundamental characteristic that no-one, whether homosexual or heterosexual, should be forced to change.[34] Goodwin-Gill argues for a social view of "social group" or, in other words, including in the 1951 Refugee Convention definition those "who in simple sociological terms, are *groups in society*, in the ordinary, everyday sense which describes the constitution or make-up of the community at large".[35] While Goodwin-Gill's analysis more closely accords with the guidance provided in the UNHCR *Handbook* it is submitted that on either of these two approaches to the phrase, gay men and lesbians can succeed in

32 Goodwin-Gill, *supra* n. 7, pp. 360–62.

33 *Shah supra* n. 31, pp. 151–52.

34 For a different view, see Park, J.S., "Pink Asylum", (1995) 42 U.C.L.A. Law Review 1115.

35 Goodwin-Gill, *supra* n. 7, p. 366 (emphasis in original).

being defined as members of a particular social group.

The cases of *Shah* and *Islam* came before the Court of Appeal in its recent decision of *R. v. Immigration Appeal Tribunal and Secretary of State for the Home Department, ex parte Syeda Khatoon Shah; Shahana Sadiq Islam v. Secretary of State for the Home Department.*[36] In these appeals it was common ground that the agreed principle in *Savchenkov* that "membership of a particular social group" should be construed *ejusdem generis* needed revision. Counsel for the appellants argued that the Court should adopt the reasoning of the Australian High Court in the recent case of *A. v. Minister for Immigration and Ethnic Affairs*[37] to the effect that the members of the group must share something which unites them, and which sets them apart from the rest of society and is recognised as such by society generally. The respondent's counsel argued that because the group must be "social" and "particular" there is a need for the group to be homogeneous and cohesive, with links between the members other than their fear of persecution, albeit that the group does not need to meet together in a social club. He argued that the adjective "social" refers to persons who are interdependent or cooperative and that the word does not refer to persons who simply have a shared characteristic. Counsel also argued that membership of the particular social group must be the causal factor behind the persecution feared. It was also agreed that the definition of "particular social group" had to be construed independently of the persecution feared.

Waite LJ, giving the leading judgment, approved the appellant's construction of the phrase "particular social group" and doubted that it was possible or desirable to make a more specific formulation other than the one referred to in the Australian High Court. However, Henry and Staughton LJJ took the opposite view. Staughton LJ, in particular, stated that "[the] expression does to my mind involve a number of people being joined together in a group with some degree of cohesiveness, co-operation or interdependence; the members must not be solitary individuals". Henry LJ qualified somewhat the definition promoted by the respondent's counsel by approving the dicta of Dawson J in *A. v. Minister for Immigration and Ethnic Affairs*[38] to the effect that a social group did not necessarily have to have a public front. Dawson J had said that:

36 Unreported, draft judgment handed down 23 July 1997. *Supra* n. 31 for earlier ruling in this case.

37 *A. v. Minister for Immigration and Ethnic Affairs* (24 Feb. 1997) [1997] 142 A.L.R. 331.

38 *Ibid.*

> A fundamental human right could only constitute a unifying characteristic if persons associated with each other on the basis of the right, or, it may be added, if society regarded those persons as a group because of their common wish to exercise the right.

Henry LJ went on to say that:

> ... there will exceptionally be those who though recognised by society as a social group lack any "cohesion" with their homogenous fellows and remain disparate individuals. From the examples to be found in the authorities, one could take the case of witches, of aristocrats lying low in the French Revolution, of Jews wholly assimilated into German life before the Nazis came to power, and hoping to escape detection. I therefore agree with Waite LJ that "cohesion" is not necessary in every case. In my judgment it is not necessary where the particular social group is recognised as such by the public, though it is not organised.

Henry LJ could have added homosexuals to this list. It is submitted that his recognition that external perceptions play a large part in the identification of a "particular social group" is vital to a finding that homosexuals can constitute such a group. The judgment of Staughton LJ that there must be an element of cohesion between members of the group, or interdependence, would have created a barrier to recognition of homosexuals. Despite the existence of a gay "subculture" which increasingly serves to connect people whose sole unifying factor is sexual orientation it is a truism to say that gay men and lesbians are disparate. To require an element of cohesion or interdependence would have narrowed the definition of "particular social group" by placing the emphasis upon what the members of the group do, rather than on who they are. It is submitted that such an approach is invalid and does not reflect historical realities. To take one of Henry LJ's examples from his list, it could not be argued that French aristocrats were persecuted for what they did, but rather because they were members of a certain class. Similarly, while persecution of gay men and lesbians can be identified as hatred of what they are perceived to do, it is more usual to characterise such persecution in terms of attacks upon who they are. For those reasons it is submitted that the Court of Appeal's decision does not overly restrict the social group definition so as to exclude gay and lesbian claimants. The Court of Appeal's judgment in these cases effectively opens a new chapter in the debate about the social group definition and, perhaps, marks a move away from the dominance of Hathaway's analysis of the phrase.

Returning to the conflicting IAT authorities in *Golchin* and *Vraciu*, it is clear that the latter case is more in line with *Savchenkov* and *Shah*. In *Golchin* the IAT did not accept that the drafters of the Convention would have had in their minds persecution suffered under the Nazis when adding "particular social group" to the definition, despite the obvious fact that the Convention was written to deal with the post-1945 refugee problem. This assertion ignored the comments of the Swedish delegate who introduced the social group category thus:

> [E]xperience had shown that certain refugees had been persecuted because they belonged to particular social groups. ... Such cases existed, and it would be as well to mention them explicitly.[39]

The position taken by the IAT also contradicted findings by the German Federal Administrative Court that, referring back to the internment of homosexuals in concentration camps, homosexuals could claim to be a persecuted group.[40] The US Department of State has also noted that the 1951 Refugee Convention was developed with a view to protecting those who had been persecuted by the Nazis.[41] However, in *Golchin* the IAT had found that consistency of interpretation of the Convention between signatory states was not necessary, arguing that it was up to each country to decide asylum policy in its own way.

Such an approach is unsatisfactory when considering any human rights instrument because it is inconsistent with the stated aims of the Universal Declaration of Human Rights to provide global minimum human rights which must be respected, irrespective of prevailing domestic norms[42] and the House of Lords has opined that it is desirable when construing an international convention that decisions in different jurisdictions should be kept in line with each other, as far as is possible.[43] It is submitted that it weakens the protection system to say that differences between countries can determine who is or who is not a refugee, and that the ultimate decision is a matter of discretion. If we take the IAT's decision to its logical extreme, a signatory state could claim that, for example, only Christians can claim religious persecution, or that only social democrats can claim political persecution.[44]

39 Quoted in Hathaway, *op. cit., supra* n. 8, p. 157.

40 Decision of the Bundesverwaltungsgericht, see (1989) 1 I.J.Ref.L. 110.

41 US Department of State memorandum of 7 Nov. 1980 re: *Case of Calvayea.*

42 Preamble to 1948 Universal Declaration of Human Rights.

43 *T. v. Secretary of State for the Home Department* [1996] AC 742.

44 For further discussion of the undesirability of disharmony in refugee determination, see Ramanathan, E.D., *Queer Cases: A Comparative Analysis* (forthcoming) Georgetown Imm.L.J.

This lack of consistency has also been overtaken by supra-national coordination in justice and home affairs policy in the European Union, particularly following the signing of the Maastricht Treaty on European Union (TEU) which provides for common immigration and asylum policies under the Treaty's intergovernmental "third pillar".[45] Although the former Conservative government in the UK resisted attempts to integrate these "third-pillar" policies within the main body of the Treaty, it did seek to develop common asylum policies on an intergovernmental level through the conclusion of resolutions such that on "manifestly unfounded applications for asylum"[46] and the Joint Position on a harmonised definition of "refugee".[47] Most recently the signing of the Amsterdam Treaty in October 1997 has taken such cooperation further by bringing asylum issues within the area of Community competence, although the UK, Denmark and Ireland have negotiated protocols under which they remain outside these common provisions with an option to opt in in respect of individual measures.

Notwithstanding UK caution at EU level, UK policy towards homosexual asylum seekers has been changing. From a policy of denial, the Home Office has appeared to accept the Canadian Supreme Court approach to the definition of social group and, in a letter to David Alton MP dated 31 January 1996, the then Home Office Minister of State Ann Widdecombe wrote:

> We interpret this provision in the Convention as follows:
>
> (i) the group is defined by some innate or unchangeable characteristic of its members analogous to race, religion, nationality or political opinion, for example their sex, linguistic background, tribe, family or class which the individual cannot change or should not be required to change; and

---

45 Treaty on European Union 1992, Art. K.1. See also chapter 3 of this book by Richard Dunstan.

46 Council of (Immigration) Ministers, "Resolution on Manifestly Unfounded Applications for Asylum", London, 30 Nov./1 Dec. 1992. For text see General Secretariat of the Council, *Compilation of Texts on European Practice with respect to Asylum* (March 1996 update), 4464/1/95 REV1, II.D., and Plender, R., *Basic Documents on International Migration Law* (2nd edn, Kluwer, 1997) p. 474.

47 EU Council of Justice and Home Affairs Ministers, "Joint Position of 4 March 1996 defined by the Council on the Basis of Article K.3 of the Treaty on European Union on the Harmonised Application of the Definition of the Term 'Refugee' in Article 1 of the Geneva Convention relating to the Status of Refugees" (1996) O.J. L63/2.

> (ii) there must be real risk of persecution by reason of the person's membership of the group.
>
> Whilst claims based on homosexuality might satisfy (i) within this definition, the requirements set out in (ii) would also have to be met in the individual case.

In other words, the Home Office accepts the *ejusdem generis* approach to the definition of social group which was adopted in *Ward* and approved in *Savchenkov*.

In *Golchin*, however, the IAT equated the meaning of social group with that of a minority group and then went on to exclude homosexuals from the definition. It ruled:

> [W]e think that there is a close approximation of "social group" to "minority group" as the term is used in the Convention. Both terms, we think, require characteristics of an historical and cultural nature which homosexuals as a class cannot claim.

It stated further:

> [L]ooking for some guidance to the definition of minority groups, there should be some historical element in a "social group" which predetermines membership of it "capable of affiliating succeeding generations": it is not enough, in our view, for association to arise by way of inclination.

These findings make assumptions about homosexuality which can not be objectively sustained. To say that "the class" of homosexuals has no history or culture is to disregard millennia of debate about the nature and place of homosexuals in society, from "the Symposium" to "Section 28"[48] and current interest in homosexual marriage.[49] Furthermore, the historical element leading to affiliation of successors is surely met by the fact that homosexuals have existed in all societies and all ages, making the "class" of homosexuals "self-generating by natural occurrence".[50] The IAT also failed to look behind the mere fact of what it termed "inclination" to ask what was the basis of the inclination. If sexual orientation is a matter of choice, then it is a political

48 The inclusion of this section in the Local Government Act 1988, which bans the "promotion of homosexuality" by local authorities, continues to generate much controversy and hostility.

49 See, e.g., Sullivan, A., *Virtually Normal* (Picador, 1996).

50 See Spencer, C., *Homosexuality: A History* (Fourth Estate, 1995).

decision and Golchin should have succeeded (pre-*Savchenkov*) on the grounds of suppression of a perceived or actual political opinion. If it is not a choice, but innate, then he would have come under the IAT's definition of a minority group.

It is arguable that *Golchin* was already inconsistent with the decided case law in that, while admittedly not bound to do so, it failed to follow the IAT decision in *Otchere*. It not only went against the advice of the UNHCR given in the latter case but also ignored the liberal and purposive attempt at construction therein. It led to the bizarre result that homosexuals could not be defined as members of a social group, whereas *Otchere* succeeded simply by being a past member of Military Intelligence in Ghana. In *Golchin* the IAT injected several extra elements into the Convention refugee definition in order to exclude homosexuals. The effect was to render the inclusion of the category "social group" nugatory, as it had no other meaning than that of race or nationality.

More importantly, in view of the judgment of the Court of Appeal in *Savchenkov,* the decision in *Golchin* can no longer be seen as good law. The approach in *Vraciu* is to be preferred as consistent with the principle of construing the definition *ejusdem generis* and in accord with the broad theme of the protection of human rights. In *Vraciu* the Tribunal accepted Hathaway's analysis of social group and looked, as the Canadian Supreme Court had done, at domestic law to decide whether homosexuals were afforded a civil or political status. The Tribunal declared:

> It would seem to us to be unarguable that in the society of the United Kingdom it has not been accepted that sexual orientation is recognised as identifying a person within a group having a meaning in society. Homosexuals are treated differently according to the criminal law, there is a great discussion as to the advisability of homosexuals in the armed forces. There is no doubt that there is both an internal and external recognition of those who are sexually orientated in such a way as to form a "group" so identified by that characteristic.[51]

The approach of the IAT in *Vraciu* is consistent also with the Court of Appeal's decision in *Shah*. The IAT pointed to the external recognition of homosexuals as a group as part of its identification, which echoes Henry LJ's judgment in *Shah*. The decision in *Vraciu* is in line with the case law of European, US and Commonwealth jurisdictions. In Ireland, sexual orientation is included as one

---

51 *Vraciu, supra* n. 13.

of the grounds of asylum in the Refugee Act 1996.[52] According to the International Gay and Lesbian Human Rights Commission in San Francisco, Belgium, Finland, France, Germany and the Netherlands have all recognised gay men and lesbians as refugees.[53] In the USA, Attorney-General Janet Reno declared precedent the case of *in re: Toboso-Alfonso*,[54] following representations by Congressman Barney Frank, which found a Cuban gay man to be a refugee because of his sexuality. In Canada the Immigration and Refugee Board has accepted that homosexuals come under the social group definition.[55] In New Zealand,[56] the appeals authority found an Iranian gay man to be a refugee on social group grounds and in Australia the Refugee Review Tribunal accepted the same in a series of three decisions in 1994.[57]

A Brief Word about Persecution

It is frequently the case that homosexuals are persecuted in their countries of origin in the form of prosecution for homosexual acts. Punishment for homosexual acts varies from a term of imprisonment (between one and five years in Romania, for a consensual act in private) to death by stoning (in Iran). In the UK some decision-makers find it difficult to accept that prosecution can be persecution. However, in *Vraciu* the IAT stated:

> Citing paragraph 57 of the *UNHCR Handbook on Refugees* Mr Jorro stressed that the prosecution of a particular social group may itself be persecution. So, said Mr Jorro, if the law provided for prosecution because of the practising of religion that could amount to persecution or it would amount to injurious action on a Convention ground in preventing the exercise of a fundamental human right. If therefore a particular social group was established it could be argued that prosecution of that social group would be discrimination amounting to persecution.
>
> We agree with Mr Jorro's general proposition in that prosecution may amount to persecution depending on the focus of the prosecution.

---

52 S. 1(1), Irish Refugee Act 1996.

53 International Gay and Lesbian Human Rights Commission and Lambda, *Asylum Based on Sexual Orientation: A Resource Guide* (1996).

54 *Re: Toboso-Alfonso*, Board of Immigration Appeals, 12 March 1990.

55 Case of *Jorge Alberto Inaudi*, Immigration and Refugee Board, 4 April 1992.

56 *Supra* n. 54.

57 N93/2240 21 Feb. 1994; N93/00846, 8 March 1994; N94/04178, 10 June 1994.

In the last line of that quotation it seems that the IAT is drawing a distinction between prosecution aimed at preventing consensual homosexual acts in private and prosecutions for other reasons, such as, for example, punishing non-consensual sexual acts. It is clearly established that fugitives from justice are not refugees.[58] This is the same distinction which was drawn by the European Court of Human Rights in *Dudgeon v. United Kingdom*,[59] where it was held that the blanket prohibition of consensual homosexual acts in private was not necessary in a democratic society for the protection of morals, public order, or the rights of others. It was left up to states, taking into account local conditions, to regulate sexual conduct, as long as there were not a total prohibition.[60] However, what is ostensibly prosecution could be persecutory if there is a discriminatory application of the law or if a punishment imposed is excessive for a Convention reason.[61] The leading case now on the meaning of persecution is that of the Court of Appeal in *Sandralingham and Ravichandran*,[62] *per* Simon Brown LJ:

> ... the question of whether someone is at risk of persecution for a Convention reason should be looked at in the round and all the relevant circumstances brought into account. I know of no authority inconsistent with such an approach and, to my mind, it clearly accords both with paragraph 51 of the UNHCR *Handbook* and with the spirit of the Convention.

In assessing whether the law relating to homosexual acts in the country from which an applicant has come is justifiable, it will be necessary to judge the law against international standards.[63] The UNHCR *Handbook* states:

> 59. In order to determine whether prosecution amounts to persecution, it will also be necessary to refer to the laws of the country concerned, for it is possible

58 *Cf. Handbook, supra* n. 5, para. 56; *Baljit Singh v. Secretary of State for the Home Department* [1994] Imm. A.R. 42, at 44; *Saidyban* IAT (12006) (unreported).

59 *Dudgeon v. United Kingdom,* Series A. No.59; (1982) 4 E.H.R.R. 149.

60 See Clements, L., *European Human Rights: Taking a Case under the Convention* (Sweet and Maxwell, 1994).

61 See, e.g., the dicta of Lord Reid in *R. v. Governor of Brixton, ex p. Schtraks* HL [1964] AC 556, at 584.

62 *Sandralingham and Ravichandran v. Secretary of State for the Home Department* [1996] Imm. A.R. 97 at 109.

63 For a comparative analysis of international standards see Wintemute, R., *Sexual Orientation and Human Rights* (Clarendon Press, 1995).

> for a law not to be in conformity with accepted human rights standards. More often, however, it may not be the law but its application that is discriminatory.
> ...
>
> 60. In such cases, due to the obvious difficulty involved in evaluating the laws of another country, national authorities may frequently have to take decisions by using their own national legislation as a yardstick. Moreover, recourse may usefully be had to the principles set out in the various international instruments relating to human rights. ...[64]

So, in assessing whether prosecution may amount to persecution, reference may be made to Article 8 of the 1950 European Convention on Human Rights[65] and the cases of homosexuals decided under it, particularly *Dudgeon*,[66] *Norris*[67] and *Modinos*[68] and to Article 17 of the 1966 International Covenant on Civil and Political Rights.[69] In all of these cases it was held that laws prohibiting consensual homosexual acts in private violated the right to private life. Looking at the current state of the case law on the meaning of "persecution", it is submitted that persecution will always arise from a breach of a non-derogable human right, a breach of a second category right not justified by a state of emergency, and discriminatory breaches of a third category right leading to consequences of a substantially prejudicial nature for the person concerned.[70] It is submitted that, even where a homosexual cannot show outright persecution but can show cumulative measures of discrimination, this should be sufficient, looking at the question of persecution in the round, for a claimant to succeed.[71]

---

64 *Supra* n. 5.

65 Art. 8(1) states: "Everyone has the right to respect for his private and family life, his home and his correspondence."

66 *Dudgeon, supra* n. 59.

67 *Norris v. Ireland*, Series A No.142; (1991) 13 E.H.R.R. 186.

68 *Modinos v. Cyprus*, Series A No.259; (1993) 16 E.H.R.R. 485.

69 Art. 17(1) states: "No one shall be subjected to arbitrary or unlawful interference with his privacy, family, home, correspondence, nor to unlawful attacks on his honour and reputation." See, for instance, *Toonen v. Australia* CCPR/C/50/D/488/1992, (1992) 1 I.H.R.R. 91.

70 *Gashi and Nikshiqi v. Secretary of State for the Home Department* IAT [1997] I.N.L.P. 96.

71 *Padhu* (12328) IAT (1995, unreported) or *Chiver* IAT (10758) (1994, unreported).

Conclusion

This chapter seeks to describe the law as it is of late 1997. The Court of Appeal's July 1997 decision in *Shah* contrasts with a line of cases approving the *ejusdem generis* principle of construing the phrase "membership of a particular social group" and makes it more difficult for lawyers to identify a common theme underlying attempts at a definition. It remains to be seen how the decision will be applied but, it is submitted, there is some cause for concern. If the *ratio* of the decision is taken to be that there must be an element of cohesion between members of the group it will become difficult for a group as diverse as gay men or lesbians to say that they belong to a group that is both "particular" and "social" within the meaning now given to those words by the Court of Appeal. However, there must remain some optimism that homosexuals will not be excluded by the effect of the judgment in the light of Henry LJ's findings and Waite LJ's judgment. What is certain is that there will be further litigation before the definition can be said to be settled. In passing, it may be significant that immigration rights for same-sex partners could be on the horizon. The Court of Appeal recently adjourned the appeal of *Dr Paolo Camara v. Secretary of State for the Home Department* against a decision of the Home Secretary not to allow him to remain in the UK with his male partner of many years. The Court had been informed that the Home Office is assessing its policy on this issue.[72] Such a policy would undoubtedly signal an end to official discrimination against gay men and lesbians in immigration policy and its impact on homosexual asylum seekers would be immeasurable.

72 "Immigration Rights for Gay Partners", *Independent*, 27 Aug. 1997; "Gay Foreigners Hopes Raised", *Guardian*, 27 Aug. 1997.

Bibliography

Goldberg, S.B., "Give Me Liberty or Give Me Death" (1993) 26 Corn.Int.L.J. 605.

Goodwin-Gill, G., *The Refugee in International Law* (OUP, 1996).

Grahl-Madsen, A., *The Status of Refugees in International Law* (A.W. Sijthoff, 1966).

Hathaway, J.C., *The Law of Refugee Status* (Butterworths, 1991).

Helton, A., "Persecution on Account of Membership in a Social Group as a Basis for Refugee Status" (1983) 15 Columbia H.R.L.R. 39.

Levy, S., (ed.), *Asylum Based on Sexual Orientation: A Resource Guide* (International Gay and Lesbian Human Rights Commission, 1996).

Park, J.S., "Pink Asylum" [1995] 42 U.C.L.A. Law Review 1115.

Ramanathan, E.D., *Queer Cases: A Comparative Analysis* (unpublished paper, 1997).

Spencer, C., *Homosexuality: A History* (Fourth Estate, 1995).

Sullivan, A., *Virtually Normal* (Picador, 1996).

Wintemute, R., *Sexual Orientation and Human Rights* (Clarendon Press, 1995).

7 Problems in Medical Report Writing for Asylum Seekers

MICHAEL PEEL[1]

This chapter outlines the particular problems in writing medical reports for asylum seekers. Amongst these are the fact that some forms of torture leave no scarring, and most leave scars that are nonspecific. The chapter argues that it is completely normal for accounts of ill-treatment to develop over a period of time, depending on the audience. Nevertheless, it explains that a doctor can be reasonably sure that the individual's story is likely to be true and be supported by physical findings, even though any individual scar could have a number of causes. It highlights the differing language used by doctors and lawyers in their work.

It is almost impossible to be certain whether or not an individual has been tortured.[2] There are a few specific exceptions, such as patterns of cigarette burns, but in general the doctor is always making a judgment. The absence of conclusive physical and psychological signs does not mean that the history of torture alleged did not happen.

Studies in Europe have suggested that between five per cent and 30 per cent of all refugees have been tortured.[3] Those from the United States suggest that 5–10 per cent of all foreign-born persons in large Health Maintenance Organisations have been tortured.[4]

As part of their basic training doctors are trained to ask questions about personal history, make an assessment of accuracy, and then conduct a physical examination. That is also what the doctors with expertise in this field do, and the American Medical Association agrees that these are the skills necessary

---

1 Senior Medical Examiner, Medical Foundation for the Care of Victims of Torture.

2 Montgomery, E. and Foldspang, A., "Criterion-related Validity of Screening for Exposure to Torture" (1994) 41 *Danish Medical Bulletin*, pp. 588–91.

3 *Ibid.*

4 American College of Physicians, "The Role of the Physician and the Medical Profession in the Prevention of International Torture and in the Treatment of its Survivors" (1995) 122 *Annals of Internal Medicine*, pp. 607–13.

to decide whether or not a person has been tortured.[5] Of course what matters more than that is experience, not only of the effects of torture generally, but also of the situation in specific countries. One of the areas of expertise of doctors from the Medical Foundation for the Care of Victims of Torture is that they will look into aspects that most other doctors ignore. Additionally, they try to specialise in a small number of countries, so that they have a clear understanding of the culture and political issues there, although their training enables them to write a report on an asylum seeker from any country.

Consultation

The environment of the Medical Foundation has been designed to be reassuring to its patients, and thought has been put into creating an atmosphere of calm. Having reassured the patient, and explained the purpose of the consultation, the doctor will take a careful history of those events relating to ill-treatment. Generally the doctor will be assisted by an interpreter experienced at putting an asylum seeker at ease, and understanding the specific issues involved in interpreting for this type of work.

This history will usually include the nature of the arrest, and physical ill-treatment at that time, if any. The circumstances of detention will be covered in detail, as these may relate both to physical and psychological symptoms. Any remembered incidents of specific ill-treatment will be recorded, especially if they relate to identifiable scars. The doctor will ask detailed questions, such as: "how big was the cell?", "was there any lighting?", "how could you go to the toilet?". People who have been there can answer these questions. It is possible, after interviewing a number of Zaïreans,[6] to know what conditions are like in Makala prison, or having reviewed the files of Algerians, to know how prison guards in Algeria usually behave.[7]

Doctors then ask about current medical symptoms, so as to determine the aches and pains attributable to ill-treatment in prison. Doctors have been trained to avoid loaded and leading questions. It has been shown that such questioning may lead to the compounding of a misunderstanding recorded by official

5 *Ibid.*

6 Peel, M.R., "Effects on Asylum Seekers of Ill Treatment in Zaïre" (1996) 312 *British Medical Journal*, pp. 293–94.

7 Peel, M.R., "Torture Continues in Algeria" (letter) (1996) 312 *British Medical Journal*, p. 1675.

interviewers.[8] The doctor will also ask about psychological symptoms. There is no way of proving that someone has difficulty getting to sleep, although sometimes we get incidental reports of neighbours complaining about people screaming in their sleep. It is impossible to be certain, but the way someone responds when describing experiences can be significant. However, the doctor must not project his or her cultural expectations onto the patient.

Examination

By this stage the doctor has a good idea of what to look for on examination, but that may be not much. The patient will be examined in detail, focusing particularly on those parts of the body where specific torture has been described. The whole body is examined because, from time to time, the doctor will find scars or other marks of which the patient is unaware. This may well be the first time the individual feels that his or her report of torture has been taken seriously. There are guidelines on physical examination published for doctors by the Medical Foundation,[9] and doctors follow these guidelines, but always take into consideration the specific circumstances of any case.

The doctor will then make a judgment about the patient, including his or her credibility. Occasionally a report cannot be produced, because the individual appears to be exaggerating. Usually the doctor believes what the individual has said. The doctor will then try to correlate the scars with the description of ill-treatment.

Each individual scar could be caused by a range of possible events, although a number of scars may corroborate each other. The doctor will make an assessment of whether the scarring is consistent with the patient's story. Where there are other events in the patient's history that could cause scarring, such as an accident, then the doctor will make a judgment about which of the possibilities is more likely to have caused each scar.

---

8 Gudjonsson, G.H., *The Psychology of Interrogations, Confessions and Testimony* (John Wiley, Chichester, 1992).

9 Forrest, D., "Guidelines for the Examination of Survivors of Torture" (Medical Foundation for the Care of Victims of Torture, London, 1995).

Opinion

Often there are discrepancies between the political asylum questionnaire (PAQ), which the asylum seeker must complete once they are given temporary admission to the UK, the legal representative's statement, and the medical report. Many aspects of memory affect this. First this may be a matter of focus, since the asylum seeker may stress different parts of the history, when questioned by people with different professional backgrounds. It is also true that people without a medical background are often unwilling and unqualified to ask the kind of direct questions about torture that are necessary to provide the relevant information. Secondly, even those who have not been through trauma find it very difficult to remember exact dates of events several years previously, and such errors are commonplace in general medical history taking. Furthermore, as an asylum seeker repeats the story, he or she remembers more of it, or is more willing to disclose more. Studies have shown that a degree of discrepancy would be probable if someone is telling the truth,[10] although a completely consistent series of reports would not necessarily suggest fabrication.

Electrical torture is relatively common in many countries, and that rarely shows scars. Very occasionally there is a small burn from a poorly applied electrode. More commonly the clips pull off with the muscular spasm, sometimes leaving scars around three millimetres across. These marks are not typical of any particular form of assault. In some countries, batons are wrapped with cloth, to avoid rough edges which can leave scars. This may be for internal political reasons, so that the judiciary can plead ignorance of torture, but it does not help the doctor.

Where there is an aspect of sexual abuse to the case, a patient will be particularly unwilling to go into detail until he or she is very comfortable with the person asking the questions.[11] This is very important because in sexual abuse cases in particular, there may well be no objective physical evidence of damage. Many of the women have had children before they are raped, and it is difficult to attribute damage to the genitalia, however violent the assault. Objects pushed through the anus do not usually cause recognisable damage several years after the event.

Psychological torture does not show physical scars either. Being insulted,

10 Mollica, R.F. and Caspi-Yavin, Y., "Measuring Torture and Torture-related Symptoms" (1991) 3 *Psychological Assessment*, pp. 581–87.

11 *Ibid.*

threatened, or left in the dark for long periods do not leave physical signs. Even fake executions may produce no physical symptoms. When describing their experiences, many people say that watching others being tortured is the most distressing. Many people will have seen close relatives and friends tortured, raped, humiliated and killed. In a number of counties this is a deliberate policy of the authorities. It is almost as upsetting for the individual to see total strangers tortured to death in front of them, and guards will often threaten that the same will happen to the individual if he or she does not cooperate. The memory of seeing someone screaming for help, yet being unable to do anything, lingers for many years. These memories return as nightmares, or they come when a person is trying to concentrate on something else. They can be very disruptive to normal social functioning, but there is no objective way of showing that they exist.

Language

When the report has been written, there are still a number of opportunities for misinterpretation of the report. Medical reports are written by doctors, who have a specific writing style that may not be understood by others. For example, a medical report will generally have a section entitled "history". A doctor will know that this is the patient's perception of what happened, if necessary elucidated by detailed cross-questioning. Those who do not understand this shorthand may assume that the history is an unquestioning acceptance or the patient's account, or assume that it is an independent description of what really happened. Additionally, doctors, like lawyers, use a specialised language, and use words like "depression" and "hysteria" with specific meanings which are different to those in lay use. It is easy to assume that the reader of the report will know what was meant, and that the writer's meaning is as it appears to the solicitor. It is necessary for each to understand the other's point of view and, if necessary, to check understanding.

Conclusion

Regularly, doctors hear that asylum seekers who have been seen for a report have had their claim for asylum turned down by the Home Office. Why might this be? Doctors experienced in this field are probably more open minded than the Immigration Service, because they do not believe that 95 per cent of the people we see are out to deceive us. The Medical Foundation seeks to ensure that the people who go there trust the staff, and so are more open. This should be helped by the nature and environment of the Medical Foundation. Minor discrepancies between stories are not a sign of dishonesty, although the Home Office seems to think that they are. Doctors know how to ask probing questions without appearing threatening. Also, it is clear to them what will happen if the government gets it wrong, and sends genuine refugees back the country they are fleeing.

Bibliography

American College of Physicians, "The Role of the Physician and the Medical Profession in the Prevention of International Torture and in the Treatment of its Survivors" (1995) 122 *Annals of Internal Medicine*, pp. 607–13.

Davies, G.M., "Contamination of Witness Memory in Theory and Practice" (1995) 35(2) *Medicine, Science and the Law*, pp. 95–101.

Forrest, D., "Guidelines for the Examination of Survivors of Torture" (Medical Foundation for the Care of Victims of Torture, London, 1995).

Gudjonsson, G.H., *The Psychology of Interrogations, Confessions and Testimony* (John Wiley, Chichester, 1992).

Mollica, R.F., Caspi-Yavin, Y., "Measuring Torture and Torture-related Symptoms" (1991) 3 *Psychological Assessment*, pp. 581–7.

Montgomery, E., Foldspang, A., "Criterion-related Validity of Screening for Exposure to Torture" (1994) 41 *Danish Medical Bulletin*, pp. 588–91.

Nice, D.S., et al. "Long-term Health Outcomes and Medical Effects of Torture Among US Navy Prisoners of War in Vietnam" (1996) 275(5) *Journal of the American Medical Association*, pp. 375–81.

Peel, M.R., "Effects on Asylum Seekers of Ill Treatment in Zaïre" (1996) 312 *British Medical Journal*, pp. 293–4.

Peel, M.R., "Torture Continues in Algeria" (letter) (1996) 312 *British Medical Journal*, p. 1675.

Weinstein, H.M., Dansky, L. and Iacopino, V., "Torture and War Trauma Survivors in Primary Care Practice" (1996) 165 *Western Journal of Medicine*, pp. 112–8.

8 Working With the Asylum Regime: an Adjudicator's Perspective

GEOFFREY CARE

The shift away from the enthusiasm which must have been present when the parties reached agreement on the text of the 1951 Geneva Refugee Convention is noticeable – and noted in policy conclusions in the Council of Ministers of the European Union (EU).[1] A less than ready application of the 1951 Convention is also discernible in the domestic laws of many countries outside the EU.

This chapter deals with some aspects of the implementation of the current legislation on asylum in the courts and tribunals in the United Kingdom, and the actual or potential fairness of the existing procedures. It also examines some realities concerning the independence of the judiciary and the internationalisation of this jurisdiction, its value, its reality and, above all, its relevance to the practicalities of what can, and should, be achieved.

The Legislation

Prior to the introduction of the Asylum and Immigration Appeals Act 1993 (AIAA 1993) there was no right of in-country appeal against a refusal of a claim "to asylum";[2] the only judicial remedy was by way of an application for judicial review. The 1993 Act introduced a right of appeal to the

1 See e.g. Joint Position of 4 March 1996 defined by the Council on the basis of Article K.3 of the Treaty on European Union on the harmonised application of the definition of the term "refugee" in Article 1 of the Geneva Convention of 25 July 1951 relating to the status of refugees, (1996) O.J. L63/2.

2 Art. 32 1951 Refugee Convention. See *R. v. Secretary of State for the Home Department ex p. Sivakumaran* [1988] 1 A.C. 958 and [1988] Imm. A.R. 147: *R. v. Immigration Appeal Tribunal ex p. Ashraf* 1988 Imm. A.R. 576.

Immigration Appellate Authority against all refusals of claims for recognition as a refugee (generally, and hereafter, referred to as an asylum claim). What the Act gave in fact was an appeal from any decision by the Secretary of State for the Home Department, which could lead to a serious possibility of a breach of Article 33 of the 1951 Refugee Convention, although it is in fact to Article 1A(2) of the Convention that we must look for a definition of a Convention refugee. In other words Article 1A(2) governs those who may not be *refouled* under Article 33.[3]

At the same time the Act also extended the use of the "safe third country" practice.[4] Whilst not a new concept,[5] the current legislation enables the Secretary of State to remove anyone arriving in the UK indirectly from the country in which he or she claims to have no protection for a Convention reason. Countries which apply the safe third country concept frequently do so on the basis that there is a norm of international law which states that an asylum seeker should make their claim in the first country they may safely do so, having crossed the boundaries of the country from which they have fled.[6] All that is required of the state, it is claimed, is that it be satisfied that the country of transit, to which it was proposed to remove the claimant, would receive and properly examine the claim and would not itself be likely to remove

3 *Gashi and Nikshiqi v. Secretary of State for the Home Department*, Immigration Appeal Tribunal (IAT), [1997] I.N.L.P. 96, establishes a definition or test for what amounts to persecution.

4 That is, the concept that a refugee should seek asylum in the first safe country he reaches. Sometimes known as the first safe country concept. See also chapter 4 of this book by Trost and Billings.

5 See e.g. *R. v. Secretary of State for the Home Department ex p. Akyol* [1990] Imm. A.R. 571; *R. v. Secretary of State for the Home Department ex p. Yassine and others* [1990] Imm. A.R. 354; *Adan, Nooh, Lazarevic and Radivojevic v. Secretary of State for the Home Department* CA 13 Feb. 1997 [1997] 1 W.L.R. 1107; [1997] 2 All E.R. 723; [1997] Imm. A.R. 251. See e.g. the laws of Austria, Canada, Denmark, France, Germany and the USA, all of which have over the past 10 years introduced such provisions.

6 It is difficult to understand why since generally the success of such a policy depends upon bilateral or multilateral accords or conventions, such as readmission agreements or the 1990 Dublin Convention determining the State Responsible for Examining Applications of Asylum Lodged in one of the Member States of the European Communities, 30 I.L.M. 425 (1991), which entered into force on 1 Sept. 1997. For a useful discussion of the issue see Byrne, R., and Shacknove, A., "The Safe Country Notion in European Asylum Law" (1996) 9 Harvard H.R.J. 185 at 200, 203.

him in breach of Article 33 to the country from which he sought international protection.[7]

The Act enabled the Secretary of State to issue a "certificate" in such cases. It was decided very early on that no actual identifiable piece of paper called a "certificate" was needed, it was enough for the papers to state that the Secretary of State so certified the claim.[8] Even during the discussion stages of the Bill it was never contemplated that there would be more than about 1,200 such cases each year. In fact, to date, out of anything up to 1,500 (and occasionally more than 2,000) appeals in a month, there were never more than 80–100 such appeals. Hearing certified appeals required relatively more time and effort than anticipated and led to more rejections of certificates than expected (in 1995 up to 42 per cent and in 1996 100 per cent of returns from Italy) and more judicial time, one suspects, than the drafters of the Act expected. Ultimately, at the time, Hidden J put the whole concept in further jeopardy by finding that Belgium was unsafe.[9] The adjudicators had already come to conclusions (admittedly not unanimously) that they were not satisfied that the procedures in a number of other countries prevented the UK from being in breach of Article 33 if the appellant was returned to them.[10] It was left to the courts on judicial review to try to reduce the disparity of adjudicators' opinions in this regard. However, since the Act gave the would-be refugee no right of further appeal to the Immigration Appeal Tribunal (IAT) the results were not consistent.

In pursuit of "harmonisation", EU ministers, have passed a number of Conclusions and Resolutions.[11] EU Member States have also signed up to

7 Schedule 6, AIAA 1993.

8 *Gogo Mustafaraj v. Secretary of State for the Home Department* [1994] Imm. A.R. 78, referred to with approval *Secretary of State for the Home Department v. Salah Ziar* IAT [1997] Imm. A.R. 456.

9 *R. v. Special Adjudicators ex p. Mehmet Turus, Adem Bostem, Awat Ammen, Adam Folly-Notsron, Selcuk Urugul* QBD [1996] Imm. A.R. 388, per Hidden J.

10 Other countries in Europe held to be unsafe have been; Austria, Bulgaria, France, Italy, Portugal and even Germany, Sweden and Switzerland. Note, however, the recent 1997 Court of Appeal ruling which found that the Home Secretary was entitled to find France safe for refugees. See *Canbolat v. Secretary of State for the Home Department* CA [1997] Imm. A.R. 442, *Times Law Report* 9 May 1997, and, for earlier QBD ruling, *R. v. Secretary of State for the Home Department and the Immigration Officer, Waterloo International Station ex p. Gulay Canbolat* [1997] Imm. A.R. 281. See also chapter 4 of this book by Trost and Billings.

11 See, notably, the "London Resolutions" approved in Nov./Dec. 1992 and subsequent Resolutions, Declarations and Joint Positions, as set out in *Compilation*

the 1990 Dublin Convention[12] and, in some cases, the 1990 Schengen Convention.[13] Increasingly, in each EU Member State, domestic legislation has been introduced, which has the effect of restricting asylum seekers' freedom of choice as to where they will make his claim, the idea, not unreasonably in itself, being that there should only be one asylum claim, at least within the EU. No doubt, this was one reason for the certification procedure introduced by the amendments in the Asylum and Immigration Act 1996 (AIA 1996).[14] Furthermore, the reason for some of the changes introduced by the Asylum and Immigration Act 1996, was at least in part that the immigration adjudicators and the courts frequently did not, on a review of all the evidence and independently of any policy considerations in the individual case, think that some of the EU countries were in practice safe.

There is a noticeable pattern in recent legislation, both in EU Member States and in Eastern and Central European countries, of restrictive approaches to the application of the obligation under Article 33. Despite assertions to the contrary, in many instances, the legislation has been, on the face of it at least, actually in breach of Article 33.[15]

It is against this background that the 1996 Act has introduced significant extensions to what has come to be known as "fast-track" appeals. The first change is a partial return to the pre-1993 position, where there was no in-country right of appeal for those who arrived via certain designated countries.[16]

---

of Texts on European Practice with respect to Asylum, 4464/1/95 REV 1, Brussels, 25 April 1996, and in Plender R., (ed.), *Basic Documents on International Migration Law* (2nd edn, Kluwer, 1997).

12 *Supra* n. 6.

13 1990 Schengen Convention applying the Schengen Agreement of 14 June 1985, 30 I.L.M. 84 (1991).

14 AIAA 1993, Schedule 2, para. 5, as amended by AIA 1996 S.2.

15 Russian Law on Refugees of 19 Feb. 1993, as amended in 1997 and Law on Forced Migrants (Involuntarily Relocating Persons) 1993 as amended in Dec. 1995. Art. 1 of the former appeared to exclude the possibility of a *sur place* claim and apparently may require actual violence to the person to satisfy a definition of persecution. However, the amended Federal Law on Refugees published in Rossiyskaya Gazeta on 3 July 1997, which entered into force on the same day, does now admit *sur place* claims.

16 See SS. 2(3) and 3(2) of AIA 1996 and countries designated as safe countries of origin under the Asylum (Designated Countries of Destination and Designated Safe Third Countries) Order 1996, SI 2671/1996 of 19 Oct. 1996, *viz.* EU member states and Canada, Norway, Switzerland and USA.

However, the current position differs in that, although there will not have been any consideration of the substantive claim to asylum, there will still be a certificate under Section 2(1) of the 1996 Act.

The provisions and preconditions to the issue of such a certificate are:

2(a) he is not a national of the country which he is to be returned;
(b) the threat is not from that country;
(c) the country of immediate destination would not send him on to the country where he fears persecution; and
2(1)(b) the certificate has not been set aside (on an appeal to a special adjudicator under Section 3).

Thus, the only in-country remedy where an applicant faces removal to a country designated as safe by the Secretary of State, is by way of judicial review. The certificate can still be challenged, albeit only from abroad, before an adjudicator. It is only if the certificate is set aside that there can be an appeal against the substantive claim (Section 3(1)(b)).

The catchment area in Paragraph 5 of Schedule 2 to the 1993 Act is dramatically extended under the 1996 Act. Sub-paragraph (5) is retained so there is still no further appeal to the Immigration Appeal Tribunal in respect of an appeal which has been successfully certified under Section 1 of the 1996 Act. There is no similar provision repeated in Section 2. Presumably therefore, certificates made by virtue of powers conferred by Sections 2 and 3 of the 1996 Act are appealable to the Immigration Appeal Tribunal. The burden of proving that a claim may be certified rests upon the Secretary of State for the Home Department on the balance of probabilities.[17]

Returning to Section 1 of the 1996 Act, which, as has been noted, extends the special ("fast-track") procedures. Broadly, the changes incorporate the "manifestly unfounded" claims approach in the EU Ministers' Resolutions together with the "safe country of origin" principle. Wherever an appeal lies to a special adjudicator on, or after, entry and the Secretary of State issues a certificate on the grounds that the country of origin where the applicant claims to fear persecution is one which parliament has deemed by Statutory Instrument to be a country (or territory, whatever that distinction may mean) "in which it appears to [the Secretary of State] that there is in general no serious risk of persecution",[18] he must first be satisfied that no "evidence adduced in support

17 *Ziar*, *supra* n.8, although as a preliminary issue the question as to whether a ruling requires evidence and findings of credibility has to be answered.

18 AIA 1996 S.1(2). See also SI 2671/1996 *supra* n.16.

[of the claim to asylum] *establishes a reasonable likelihood* that the appellant has been tortured in the country to which he is to be sent".[19] Torture is not defined in the Act and there is some suspicion that an over-exposure of decision makers to tales of indescribable horror can induce a heightening of the threshold of criteria for what injurious action does amount to torture.[20]

The power to certify an appeal, which curtails an asylum seeker's appeal rights where it is applied to the facts considered to indicate that the claim is manifestly unfounded for one reason or another under the Act, involves the exercise of judgment more appropriate to a trained and experienced judicial officer. For example, what is a "reasonable explanation" for failing to produce a passport? Is it sufficient to give an explanation which is reasonably likely to be true and which explains the absence of a document, such as, "I handed it back to my agent", or must the nature of the explanation be one which the asylum seeker can reasonably be allowed to have accepted.

It is interesting to compare approaches by different countries to identifying safe countries of origin or so-called "white" countries. In Germany, for example, before a country is placed on the "white list", extensive consultation has taken place with judges, organs of government, and other bodies which have access to material information. So far as I am aware, the UK government undertook no consultation outside itself before deciding which countries should be so designated. It remains to be seen whether the manner whereby a country is included on the list affects the burden or the standard of proof in individual cases.

The next group to which Section 1 applies, the "manifestly unfounded" group, contains those claims which are expressly so defined; some overlapping is apparent. For example, what is the difference between a "frivolous or vexatious" claim (sub-paragraph 5(4)(e)), one which "does not show a fear of persecution for a Convention reason" (sub-paragraph 5(4)(a)), and one which "shows a fear of such persecution, but the fear is manifestly unfounded" (sub-paragraph 5(4)(b))? This latter sub-paragraph introduces a possible

19 AIA 1996 S.1(5) (emphasis added).

20 The reference to torture is not unique to the 1996 Act. It is defined in S.134 of the Criminal Justice Act 1988 as "intentionally inflicting pain or suffering on another". With respect to the Police and Criminal Justice Act 1984, the Court of Appeal, in *R. v. Fulling* [1987] 2 All E.R. 65, applied S.76(2)(a) of the Act and, in the context of obtaining confession evidence by "oppression", chose to ignore the vast body of jurisprudence on the concept in favour of the ordinary dictionary definition of "oppression", which S.76(8) of the Act defines as including "torture, inhuman and degrading treatment".

complication, also to be found in Canadian legislation,[21] in that sub-paragraph 5(4)(b) also applies if "the circumstances which gave rise to the fear no longer subsist". The question as to what the circumstances were on a particular date that gave rise to the claim and whether they still exist or not is difficult. Decisions must be made upon the decision taker's view of the facts existing at that date and one may gauge the range of views from decisions on whether a "safe third country" is likely to be safe.[22] For the original decision to attempt to pre-empt any opportunity for an independent review of such facts is alarming, given the time constraints. Specific reference to change of circumstances (at least where it leads to potentially draconian results) would be best left to the context from which it has no doubt been borrowed, that is, Article 1C (5) and (6) of the 1951 Refugee Convention.

It is clear that a certificate issued without a statement that the Secretary of State is satisfied paragraph 5(5) is not applicable is flawed and cannot be corrected retrospectively.[23] The writer considers all certificates which are challenged or which on their face may be flawed must be the subject of a ruling before entering upon the substantive hearing. If not upheld it may be necessary to adjourn if a fair disposal of the appeal so requires.

Paragraphs 340 and 341 of the 1994 Statement of Changes in Immigration Rules[24] provided guidance to the case officers considering applications but have now in some respects been elevated to directions.[25] Decisions on issues which formerly fell to the adjudicator to assess can now result in a certificate, which "fast-tracks" the appeal and may preclude any independent assessment by the adjudicator. Professor Martin captured the importance – and difficulties – of reaching justifiable conclusions in many aspects of an asylum claim, when he said:

> Indeed the factual enquiry required [in asylum cases] is difficult in ways not found in most other adjudications known to our administrative law. Not only does the crucial determination require prediction – prediction based on political, not scientific judgments – but also the basic factual materials on which to base

---

21 See Bryne and Shacknove, *op. cit supra* n. 6; Hailbronner, K., "The Concept of 'Safe Country' and Expeditious Asylum Procedures: A Western European Perspective" (1993) 5 I.J.Ref.L. 31; Goodwin-Gill, G., "Safe Country? Says Who?" (1992) 4 I.J.Ref.L. 248.

22 See e.g. the decisions cited *supra* n. 10.

23 *Ziar, supra* n. 8.

24 Statement of Changes in Immigration Rules, 1993–94, HC 395.

25 AIA 1996, Section 2, paras (5)(3) and (5)(4d).

such a prediction are notably elusive.[26]

We will see in due course what, if any, interaction there is between the new sub-paragraph (4)(c)(i) and Schedule 2 of the 1996 Act. It is rare that a court exercising criminal jurisdiction will be in possession of sufficient facts or indeed knowledge of the Convention to be able to reach any conclusion upon risk following deportation, even if this is relevant to any decision by the judge to recommend deportation.

The powers of curtailment of leave to enter or remain contained in Section 7 of the 1993 Act have now been extended explicitly to dependents.[27] Further, the limitations on the right of appeal which can lead to a certificate under the new paragraph 5 to Schedule 2 of the 1993 Act have been extended in sub-paragraphs (4) (c)(ii), (iii) and (iv) of the 1996 Act. The power to issue a certificate, if a court has recommended deportation under sub-paragraph 4(c)(ii) of the 1996 Act, could, I would have thought, cause considerable difficulty.

The opportunities for the accumulation of vast wealth through "people smuggling" are now well known. Generous social security benefits paid to asylum seekers in Germany have provided strong incentives for those organising entry into the country, with the result that attempts to investigate where entrants have come from and how they reached Germany have resulted in the criminalisation of significant numbers of those who claim asylum. The way in which asylum seekers are treated in a country can have significant effects in the country where a claim is being considered. Access to asylum claim procedures, the effectiveness of those procedures, the availability of accommodation, social welfare and access to the labour market will all affect the decision makers when they consider whether an asylum seeker's claim is genuine "because he should have claimed asylum in a country through which he passed". There may be very good reason for "going to ground" or not making a claim and the frequency with which asylum seekers are arrested, detained, charged and sometimes arbitrarily expelled in some countries is one such factor.[28] The need for both knowledge of systems and practices in other countries and generous cooperation both at government and judicial

26 Martin, D., "Due Process and Membership in the National Community: Political Asylum and Beyond" (1983) 44 U.Pitt.L.Rev. 165 at 184.

27 AIA 1996, Schedule 2, para. 2.

28 Interview with two refugees in Kiev, Ukraine, in Feb. 1996, one from Ethiopia and one from Afghanistan.

level is readily apparent.[29]

It is not surprising therefore to see the extension of both crimes and penalties for assisting the entry or stay of asylum seekers contained in Sections 5, 6 and 7 of the 1996 Act. The German experience no doubt contributed to the decision in the UK to remove rights to social security payments (Section 11), housing accommodation or assistance (Section 9), and even child benefit (Section 10 (2)). In contrast to the situation in most of the East and Central European countries, an asylum seeker in the UK is also deprived of any right to earn whilst waiting for an appeal to be heard (Section 8), although in practice there may be little employment available in other countries which do not deny such a right. Schedule 2 of the 1996 Act contains significant provisions which, in general, may be seen as intended to discourage the would-be asylum seeker from coming to the UK.

The Procedure Rules

The rules of procedure applied are sometimes as important to the outcome of an asylum claim or to a fair determination of an appeal as the substantive law itself. Procedure and substance become blurred in refugee claims. The legislation itself obscures the demarcation by tying the hands of the decision maker, including the judicial one. Appeals are "fast-tracked", a certificate can deny an effective appeal altogether, and the opportunity to prepare an appeal, or even to obtain representation, is interfered with. For example, the Secretary

---

29 Examples of European-level government cooperation in this field include (i) the 1993 Council of Europe Parliamentary Assembly Recommendation 1211 on Clandestine Migration: Traffickers and Employers of Clandestine Migrants; (ii) the EU Council of Justice and Home Affairs (JHA) Ministers' Joint Action of 29 Nov. 1996 establishing an incentive and exchange programme for persons responsible for combating trade in human beings and the sexual exploitation of children, and (iii) the JHA Council Decision of 15 Dec. 1996 on monitoring the implementation of instruments adopted by the Council concerning illegal immigration, readmission, the unlawful employment of third country nationals and cooperation in the implementation of expulsion orders. An example of emerging cooperation at judicial level is the International Association of Refugee/Asylum Law Judges. See Care, G., and Storey, H., (eds) *Asylum Law: Report and Papers delivered at the First International Judicial Conference held at the Inner Temple, London, 1 and 2 Dec. 1995*, Conference Papers Series No. 1, Steering Committee of the Conference on Asylum Law (London, 1996).

of State is not obliged to disclose the information upon which he relied to reach a decision.[30]

This has nowhere been more in evidence than in the determinations of "safe third country" appeals under the 1993 Act. Time and again adjudicators and judges have opined that a signature to a treaty or seemingly fair and adequate procedural rules are not determinative. Also relevant are the implementation of these obligations and procedures; whether the claimant has a real opportunity to put his claim; whether, by reason of some other provision in a country's constitution,[31] or by reason of a bilateral readmission agreement, protection from *refoulement* may in fact be illusory.

It is unnecessary to dwell on the time limits introduced in the 1993 Asylum Appeals Procedure Rules[32] and perpetuated in the 1996 Rules,[33] except to point out that, whereas an overall time scale of 42 days (or 10 for certified claims)[34] has serious resource implications (as well as straining an appellant's capacity to prepare and present his or her case), an internal time limit, such as that contained in rule 6 (allowing five days to give notice of a hearing) or rule 13(4) (requiring the decision on an application for leave to appeal to the Tribunal to be given within 10 days) has dramatic adverse knock-on effects. The former has limited the opportunities to make a meaningful assessment of what directions can usefully be given, so as to obtain any useful estimate of how much time the appeal will occupy at any hearing, or, indeed, whether a hearing is required at all. By contrast, in Denmark the preparation for the hearing enables four or five appeals to be disposed of finally every day. The direct result of the imposition of strict time limits in the UK has been a high adjournment rate. This of course affects the listing of cases and has led to a current backlog of over 25,000 appeals. In turn, the appellant may have had to wait up to 15 months for the appeal to be heard. It is in this context that the removal of benefits and the denial of a right to work is of greatest concern.

The principal legislation, as we have seen, addresses the issues of delay, speed of disposal and cost to the public purse. What it does not do, of course, is recognise that the major problems lie in other directions. In so far as the

30 *R. v. Secretary of State for the Home Department and another ex p. Abdi* and *R. v. Secretary of State for the Home Department and another ex p. Gawe* [1996] 1 W.L.R. 298 (HL).

31 See *supra* n. 29 on the need to be aware of procedures, laws and practices in other countries.

32 The Asylum Appeals (Procedure) Rules 1993, SI 1661/1993 of 5 July 1993.

33 The Asylum Appeals (Procedure) Rules 1996, SI 2070/1996 of 6 Aug. 1996.

34 *Ibid.*, rule 9.

Procedure Rules address these issues, they purport to do so by the employment of four strategies.

Firstly, adjudicators, and the tribunal, may make their judgment in a concise manner, which decides the substantial issues raised in the appeal, contains the findings of material facts, and states reasons for the decision reached.[35] However, this change has had very little practical effect so far. It should be noted that rules 9(3) and 11 of the 1996 Rules, which *inter alia* set the 42-day and 10-day deadlines mentioned above, also encourage swifter determinations. Yet, rule 11 existed before. In any event, it is possibly over optimistic to expect large numbers of adjudicators to give satisfactory short, let alone short *ex-tempore* judgments, without adequate preparation of the appeal, an opportunity to read the papers properly in advance and to have a record taken by mechanical means.

Secondly, the new Rules positively discourage adjournments, requiring that they be only where "necessary for the just disposal of the appeal". Even then, this must be balanced with *"just, timely and effective conduct of the proceedings"*.[36] Furthermore, rule 41 alters the presumption against any extension of time, and rule 17(2) lends encouragement to the tribunal to dispose of the appeal itself, perhaps introducing a presumption against remittal. The rule contains some good advice, but it is seldom practical – or economic – for a three person tribunal to dispose of an appeal itself, except where there is no dispute upon fact. Sometimes it is advantageous, even then, for the Immigration Appeal Tribunal to hear evidence and dispose of an appeal, which has been heard more than once by an adjudicator.

Thirdly, new powers for the conduct of appeals are set out in rule 23. Some form of recognition of the need for a power to give directions has long been recognised in all immigration appeals. Some of the rules now spelt out in this rule were contained in the Practice Directions given in July 1993 and, following suggestions by practitioners at a Users' Meeting a few weeks earlier, published in the Law Society's Gazette.[37] They were more honoured in the breach than the observance and depended on cooperation between the Appellate Authority and the parties' representatives to supply time estimates, witness numbers, interpreter needs and so on. The ability to make directions, which can and will be complied with, is a real advantage but only where the representative is well versed in such matters. Where the appellant is

35 Rule 2(3)(b) of the 1996 Procedure Rules.

36 Rules 10 and 18 of the 1996 Procedure Rules (emphasis added).

37 Law Society Gazette, 28 July 1993, Vol. 90/29, p. 37.

unrepresented, or not represented by a competent and experienced person, directions are valueless.[38]

Sanctions for noncompliance with the Rules are limited, especially when it is the Secretary of State who is in default (rules 24, 33 and 35). A major defect in the rules will remain, so long as the Secretary of State is not obliged, under rule 5(8) or under any other rule, to make full disclosure. It has been shown that directions given in appeals to the Immigration Appeal Tribunal tend to be more readily welcomed and followed, with very appreciable savings of time, without sacrificing justice.

The short judgment has, as observed above,[39] not materialised, or at least, where it has, it tends to be inadequate to survive an, often rigorous, test on appeal. Whilst undue legalism should be eschewed in this jurisdiction, it is nevertheless necessary to write a decision which is supported by reasoning. The decision can decide the fate of appellants and their families, and influence the Secretary of State in the formulation of policy and future legislation. Without enough time or the right opportunity, it seems impossible to make useful directions, which are consistent with fair procedures, and give an opportunity to make sanctions effective. This may be why they appear to be more effective before the Immigration Appeal Tribunal.

Fourthly, a miscellany of "small hand tools" is also to be found, the main one being a power to correct accidental errors under rule 45.

Immigration Rules

The traditional design for the submission and consideration of, and for the approach to appeals remains. The *Statement of Changes in Immigration Rules*,[40] which for the first time comprehensively consolidated rules to be followed, both on entry and afterwards, has been amended on several occasions.[41] The significant provisions can be gathered into three groups.

38 There are current proposals to extend legal aid to representation before the Appellate Authority. This could be an advantage but greater powers to regulate representation have long been an aim; thus far it is one which has eluded our grasp.

39 *Supra* n. 35.

40 HC 395. *supra* n. 24.

41 Cm 2663 of 20 Sept. 1994; HC 797 of 6 Oct. 1995; Cm 3073 of 4 Jan. 1996; HC 274 of 7 March 1997; HC 329 of 2 April 1996, and, following entry into force of the Act, Cm 3365 which came into effect on 1 Sept. 1996.

These are (i) those which complement and parallel the Act; (ii) those which may independently affect a decision; and (iii) those containing "technical" changes.

An example of the first group are the rules dealing with curtailment of leave to remain and the effects upon dependents.[42] An example of the second group is provided by paragraph 346 of HC 395 concerning previously rejected applications, which gives directions with respect to alleged new facts as a "fresh application".[43]

There are a number of situations created by the Act and re-enforced by the Rules, which have substantially increased the likelihood of a decision being taken by a "faceless" administrative official on complex and substantive issues in the asylum claim, if not the actual decision itself. They include certification, which commits it to the special appeals procedure and very severely restricts the possibility for any "anxious scrutiny" by an independent judicial review.[44]

An example of this, and of what may lie hidden behind a certificate, is provided by the case of *Syeda Shah* which first came before Sedley J in 1996.[45] The issue of a certificate may itself require a much more stringent examination than hitherto, in the absence of any duty of disclosure on the part of the Secretary of State. Under the new legislation the officer faced with considering Mrs Shah's claim could conclude that her expressed fear of being stoned to death for perceived adultery in Pakistan, even if he believed it, was factually far-fetched even if authorised by the law. He may just find it manifestly unfounded, under S.1 5(4)(b) of the 1996 Act, either in law or because he does not find the story plausible (a definition invariably, but often inaccurately, covered by the use of the *credibility* label), or even if it is true, that it simply does not fall within the Convention. This is what the Secretary of State, the adjudicator and the Immigration Appeal Tribunal concluded.

Rule 341 of HC 395 (matters to which the initial decision-maker shall

---

42 HC 395, *supra* n. 24, paras 323, 339 as read with paras 349, 363 (iii), 365 (vii).

43 *Secretary of State for the Home Department v. Boybeyi*, CA, *Times Law Report*, 5 June 1997; [1997] Imm. A.R. 491.

44 *Bugdaycay v. Secretary of State for the Home Department* [1987] 1 A.C. 514 at 531; [1987] 1 All E.R. 940 at 952.

45 *R. v. Immigration Appeal Tribunal and Secretary of State for the Home Department ex p. Syeda Shah*, QBD, 25 Oct. 1996, *Times Law Report* 12 Dec. 1996, [1997] Imm. A.R. 145. In *IAT v. Secretary of State for the Home Department ex p. Syeda Khatoon Shah and Others*, CA, unreported, 23 July 1997, the court further defined what is a social group.

have regard) and rule 345 (i) and (ii) (evidence of admissibility to a third, safe country) are also relevant and one can well imagine the difficulties in the way of Mrs Shah putting her story across. In this case, it is fair to note that the basis for the grant of asylum was first noted as a result of the astuteness of our "faceless" ones.

Until *Ziar*,[46] it was a general practice of adjudicators in certified appeals cases to elide a decision on whether to uphold the certificate with a decision on the substantive appeal. This, of course, "put the cart before the horse". The appeal had been launched into the fast-track and remained there, even though the adjudicator might, in the end, decline to uphold the certificate, perhaps because he found the failure to produce a passport[47] to be reasonable.

Rule 341(iv) of HC 395 is an example of the group of rules which independently affect a decision. This sets out "matters which may damage an asylum applicant's credibility if no reasonable explanation is given" and includes under (iv) the fact that

> the applicant has undertaken any activities in the United Kingdom before or after lodging his application which are inconsistent with his previous beliefs and behaviour and calculated to create or substantially enhance his claim to refugee status.

If, for example, the Secretary of State concluded that for *such a reason* the claim was not credible, the application *would be* refused. The entire jurisprudential question, which has been debated since Simon Brown J's decision in *Re B.*,[48] may as well not exist.

With regard to fresh applications without changed circumstances (rule 346) and claims made in another country (rules 347 and 341(v)), if a claim has been lodged in another country, usually a safe third country, but has not been decided, the applicant's credibility may be affected. What if the claim has been considered and rejected as not admissible, for instance, because "out of time" under Belgium's "eight-day rule"? Will the claim in the UK be rejected and the applicant returned to try again if he so wishes?

46 *Supra* n. 8.

47 Under para. 5(3)(a) Schedule 2 of the amended 1996 Act.

48 *R. v. Immigration Appeal Tribunal ex p. "B"* QBD [1989] Imm. A.R. 166. See also *Gilgham v. Immigration Appeal Tribunal* CA [1995] Imm. A.R. 129. Further appeals on these cases are pending at the time of going to press.

The Appeal

There are four issues which I wish to highlight with respect to the appeal process and have not been raised before. These are, firstly, the questions raised by the *Ravichandran* case;[49] secondly, the issue of asylum and terrorism, as set out in *Re T.*;[50] thirdly, the proposal to issue guidelines to decision makers and, finally, the question of the approach to a finding on the acceptance or rejection of testimony.

On the first question, until Laws J raised the point, decisions focused on the date of the original administrative decision. Using the 1993 Act as the basis for his decision, Laws J opined that, in asylum appeals, the material date should be that of adjudicator's hearing of the appeal. In *Ravichandran*, Simon Brown LJ said:

> [I]n asylum cases the appellate structure as applied by the 1993 Act is to be regarded rather as an extension of the decision-making process. I am, I think, entitled to reach that conclusion as a matter of construction on the basis that the prospective nature of the question posed by section 8 of the 1993 Act overrides the retrospective approach ordinarily required (implicitly) on a section 19 appeal.[51]

Thus, at least up to the level of the Immigration Appeal Tribunal, it is upon current facts that the decision should be based. Whilst making good sense, this situation imposes an unusual obligation upon a judicial tribunal. For example, under these circumstances, it must second guess whether a Peace Treaty such as the 1995 Dayton Agreement on Bosnia-Herzegovina has, or has not, been effectively implemented, or decide on its view of the facts, as to the seriousness of the security situation in Sierra Leone, even if the Secretary of State says it is safe in Freetown. Given that Simon Brown LJ also said that decision-making on the basis of current facts is all part of the process, the confrontational approach of the Secretary of State, both in attempts to devise effective procedures and in the appeals themselves, by refusing to make full disclosure of information on which the decision is reached, is difficult to comprehend.

49 *Ravichandran v. Secretary of State for the Home Department* and *Rajendrakumar v. Immigration Appeal Tribunal and Secretary of State for the Home Department* CA [1996] Imm. A.R. 97.

50 *T. v. Secretary of State for the Home Department* [1996] 2 All E.R. 865; [1996] Imm. A.R. 443.

51 *Ibid.* pp. 112–3.

Secondly, the next decision, which developed jurisprudence in this jurisdiction, is the case of *T.,* where the House of Lords held, in considering Article 1 F of the 1951 Refugee Convention, that a crime was only a political crime when "it was committed for a political purpose" and "there was a sufficiently close and direct link between the crime and the alleged political purpose".[52] The "close and direct link" involves looking at the means used to achieve the political end, who, or what, was the target, and whether the crime involved indiscriminate harm to innocent people.

Thirdly, given the numbers of new adjudicators with little, if any, familiarity with this jurisdiction, let alone with judicial experience, the issue of guidelines, similar to those published in Canada, the USA, Australia, and most recently Switzerland, would ease the burden of the adjudicator, decrease the number of appeals remitted, expedite hearings, and generally improve the standard of the decision-making. Although it would assuredly help, there is no prior need for such guidelines to be in the form of legislation. In Canada, the initiation of the Guidelines preceded the enabling law. Statutory authority however lends greater weight to them and, in the end, is certainly desirable.

Finally, I turn to what is compendiously referred to as "credibility". This is not the place to address the general issue of assessing oral evidence or the weight of documentary evidence. There are, however, some aspects to the task in this jurisdiction which call for an awareness of a particular kind. The adjudicator is normally dealing with cultures, nationalities and complex situations of which he knows nothing, except what he has read about or heard in evidence. Given that the Secretary of State may not be disclosing all that it (speaking collectively as a government) knows, it is essential that an appellant is represented by someone familiar with the jurisdiction concerned, who has access to all necessary current information and background. It is important for the adjudicator to ensure that, where his accumulated knowledge affects the appeal, he apprises the parties of such knowledge and that he acquires the art of assessing the relative weight of documentary evidence. This is a matter, which has been little addressed in any court or any academic research.

As to the assessment of the worth of the testimony itself, Bingham J, as he then was, writing in the *Current Legal Problems*,[53] had this "advice" to give in what is altogether a most valuable piece of writing on the subject:

52 *Supra* n. 50, pp. 865 and 443–4 respectively.

53 Sir Thomas Bingham, "The Judge as Juror: the Judicial Determination of Factual Issues" (1985) 38 C.L.P. 1.

> In deciding the facts, the judge knows that no authority, no historical enquiry and (save on expert issues) no process of ratiocination will help him. He is dependent, for better or worse, on his own unaided judgment. And he is uneasily aware that his evaluation of the reliability and credibility of oral evidence may very well prove final. [And, I would add, fatal!].[54]

The Future

One of the main disadvantages of the UK system is that it is cumbersome, costly and inefficient. It is profligate in its use of resources and inordinately slow. The 1996 Act, far from being likely to expedite matters, is likely to entrench the aspects of the 1993 legislation which encourage bottlenecks. At best, it may speed the removal of claimants to other EU countries, leaving such countries to deal with the claims as best they can.

So far, the present Labour government has not indicated any intended legislation to make radical changes in asylum law. There is an Interdepartmental Committee, which was appointed by the former government, sitting to consider such changes. The danger of such an Interdepartmental Committee is that traditional approaches will remain and the changes will once more merely "tinker" with the entire problem.

The harmonisation of procedures is a more important task for government than attempts to make uniform interpretations of the law. For adjudicators, what must be important is to have a more effective, efficient and early first decision. The failure to remove an applicant whose claims have been rejected in all respects frequently leads to politicians deflecting blame onto the appellate system and "hyping" the public perception of numbers of so-called "bogus" refugees in the country.[55] The process in between needs to be freed of constrictions which lead to backlogs. For instance, the present system is based upon an adversarially oriented confrontation, which duplicates research into background material and induces a "win/lose" approach, with the result that both "sides" fight it out to the death, and it encourages legalism, which prolongs the process without any compensating guarantee of accuracy in identifying the refugee or transparent fairness towards doing so.

The increasing interchange of information and ideas among judges the world over, in my view, offers the best available option to discourage inadequate and unfair procedures and counter attempts to impose

54 *Ibid.*, at 1–2.

55 See also chapter 3 of this book by Richard Dunstan.

interpretations of the Convention, which may frequently be rejected by the courts in the domestic jurisdictions.[56] The perceived threat of an ever increasing flow of refugees which countries seem powerless to control, prevent or even deflect has led to calls for the abolition, modification or regionalisation of protective conventions. Before rejecting the 1951 Convention as outdated or returning to a regionalisation or geographical limitation of protection we should genuinely seek more harmonised, fair and efficient procedural remedies with a supranational body to coordinate the definitions within the Convention while also allowing for some national differences in culture.

---

56 See, e.g. Errera, R., "Recent Decisions of the French Conseil d'Etat, concerning the case of the *Ministre de l'Interieure c. M. Rogers*, decision of 18 Dec. 1996", (1997) Public Law 199.

Bibliography

Care, G., and Storey, H., (eds) *Asylum Law: Report and Papers delivered at the First International Judicial Conference held at the Inner Temple, London, 1 and 2 Dec. 1995*, Conference Papers Series No. 1, Steering Committee of the Conference on Asylum Law, London, 1996 (Thanet House, 231 Strand, London WC2R 1DA).

Dacyl, J.W., "Europe Needs a New Protection System for 'Non-Convention' Refugees" (1995) 7 I.J.Ref.L. 579.

Einarsen, T., "Mass Flight: The Case for International Asylum" (1995) 7 I.J.Ref.L. 551.

European Council on Refugees and Exiles (ECRE), *Asylum in Europe* Vol. II, p. 149 *et seq.* (London, 1994).

Gillespie, J., *Report on Immigration and Asylum Procedures and Appeal Rights in Member States of the EEC*, (Immigration Law Practitioners' Association, London, 1993).

Niessen, J., *The Making of European Immigration Policies*, Briefing Paper 15, p.12, Churches' Commission for Migrants in Europe, Brussels (1994).

Ogata, S., *Challenge to the United Nations: A Humanitarian Perspective*, public lecture given at Centre for the Study of Global Governance, London School of Economics, 4 May 1993.

Schermers, H.G. et al. (eds), *Free Movement of Persons in Europe* (Martinus Nijhoff, 1993).

Storey, H., "International Law and Human Rights Obligations" in *Strangers and Citizens: A Positive Approach to Migrants and Refugees*, Spencer, S. (ed.), (IPPR/Rivers Oram Press, London, 1994).

Wallace, R., *Refugees and Asylum: A Community Perspective* (Butterworths, 1996).

9 Researching "The Risks of Getting it Wrong"

ALISON HARVEY

In April 1996 the Asylum Rights Campaign (ARC) published a report entitled *"The Risks of Getting it Wrong": The Asylum and Immigration Bill Session 1995/96 and the Determinations of Special Adjudicators* (the Report).[1] ARC is an umbrella organisation of over 100 organisations members, all of which work on refugee and asylum issues. ARC commissioned the Report for use as a tool for lobbying on the Asylum and Immigration Bill (the Bill) and related measures, then going through parliament, and to contribute to its ongoing work in this field. The Report is a statistical and qualitative analysis of 622 determinations of Special Adjudicators of the Immigration Appellate Authority (IAA) promulgated in the second half of 1995. As such it is based upon empirical research and has been described as "the only detailed [analysis] of the way in which adjudicators ... reach their decisions".[2]

This chapter has been written to encourage further empirical research into the asylum determination procedure in particular and legal decision-making in general. It seeks to persuade the reader that such research is necessary and to show what it can achieve and how it can be undertaken. It examines practical constraints; the resistance of legal decisions and the asylum determination procedure to empirical analysis; and the implications of this for researchers seeking to overcome these problems and for readers seeking to assess whether they have done so.

---

1 Harvey, A.R., *"The Risks of Getting it Wrong": The Asylum and Immigration Bill Session 1995/96 and the Determinations of Special Adjudicators* (Asylum Rights Campaign, April 1996).

2 Henderson, M., *Best Practice Guide to Asylum Appeals* (Immigration Law Practitioners' Association (ILPA), the Law Society, Refugee Legal Group, London, May 1997) at 129.

The Project

Aims and Objectives

The Bill that became the Asylum and Immigration Act was predicated upon the assumption that the majority of asylum applications made in the United Kingdom were "bogus"[3] and was designed to deal with them accordingly. The then Secretary of State for the Home Department, Michael Howard, introducing the second reading of the Bill in the House of Commons, stated that "our procedures are being abused" and cited as evidence the fact that "[o]nly 4 per cent of those claiming asylum are deemed by the Home Office to be genuine refugees and just 4 per cent of appeals are upheld by independent adjudicators".[4] The value of the evidence depends upon the true value of two untested and unproven premises which the research project was designed to test and to challenge.

The first premise assumes that the existing determination procedures are infallible. It is presumed that the Home Office makes the wrong decision only in those cases in which Special Adjudicators allow appeals, while Special Adjudicators make no mistakes at all. The United Nations High Commissioner for Refugees (UNHCR) pointed to the dangers in "such a self-justificatory and circular analysis", stating: "In our opinion it is no satisfactory answer to argue that the vast majority of appellants are not successful on appeal. This is based on the unreliable assumption that the refugee determination procedures are reliable and effective in identifying all refugees."[5] The second premise is that all those who do not qualify as refugees under the 1951 Geneva Convention Relating to the Status of Refugees and the 1967 Optional Protocol thereto (the 1951 Convention) are abusing the asylum determination procedure by putting forward a claim to sanctuary here.

The method by which the research project set out to test and challenge those two premises was the examination of the determinations of Special Adjudicators for indices of error, and proof of error where this was available,

3 H.C. Hansard, Vol. 268, Col. 699, 11 Dec. 1995. See also chapters 2 and 3 of this book by Craig Young and Richard Dunstan respectively for discussion of these assumptions.

4 H.C. Hansard, Vol. 268, Col. 699, 11 Dec. 1995.

5 UNHCR, "Representations to the Social Security Advisory Committee from the Office of UNHCR", in *Benefits for Asylum Seekers: Minutes of Evidence taken before the Social Security Committee*, HC 17, (Jan. 1996), Appendix 25 at 92.

and the examination of the conclusions drawn in those determinations as to the *bona fides* of those whose claim to recognition as refugees was rejected.

Structure of the Report

The text of the Bill and related instruments provided a starting point for the framework of the Report. In what is now Section 1 of the Asylum and Immigration Act 1996 (the 1996 Act),[6] amending Paragraph 5 of Schedule 2 to the Asylum and Immigration Act 1993 (the 1993 Act), an attempt was made to codify the indices of a "bogus" claim. These were deemed to include the applicant's having come from a particular "white list" country;[7] having applied after refusal of leave to enter,[8] or notification of decisions pertaining to removal or deportation;[9] having made a manifestly-unfounded application or having produced manifestly fraudulent evidence in support of the application[10] and having failed to show a fear of persecution for a reason that would bring him/her within the 1951 Convention.[11] The Immigration Appeals Tribunal (IAT) has since characterised the Section 1 criteria as "the motley collection of grounds for certifying a claim".[12] These criteria covered most if not all of the areas in which one could search for indices or proof of error in determinations, with the added advantage of permitting examination of the weight given to each of these factors by Special Adjudicators in determining the appeals before them. Thus, the Special Adjudicators were under scrutiny but were also being used to scrutinise the proposed reforms.

Examples of Findings

Errors Detected

The Report presented evidence of errors in decision-making at the first

6 The Asylum and Immigration Act 1996, Chapter 49 of 1996.
7 1993 Act, Schedule 2, para. 5(2) as amended.
8 1993 Act, Schedule 2, para. 5(4)(c)(i) as amended.
9 1993 Act, Schedule 2, paras. 5(4)(c)(iii) and (iv) as amended.
10 1993 Act, Schedule 2, para. 5(4)(d).
11 1993 Act, Schedule 2, para. 5(4)(a) as amended.
12 *Secretary of State for the Home Department v. Salah Ziar* IAT [1997] Imm. A.R. 456 at 470.

appellate level. In some cases manifest errors of law were revealed. The first area in which problems were detected was that of the definition of persecution. Since the Report was written the leading IAT case of *Gashi and Nikshiqi*,[13] to which UNHCR was a party, has redefined the approach to this area of law, by requiring that Special Adjudicators start from a consideration of the fundamental human rights of the appellant, a similar approach to that advocated in the Report.

The second area in which errors of law were detected was that the definition of "agents of persecution". The government put on record during debates on the Bill its commitment to providing protection to those threatened by non-state agents, despite previous Home Office practice to the contrary.[14] The new approach has subsequently been upheld by the IAT, most notably in cases involving those persecuted in Algeria by non-state agents.[15] The treatment of Algerian draft evaders and deserters and failures to recognise the threats to them were made the subject of particular comment in the Report. The Home Office continued to express the view that a state was providing "effective" protection against non-state agents where it took all reasonable steps, having regard to its means and resources, to protect the applicant. The IAT in *Yousfi*,[16] to which UNHCR was a party, rejected this view and supported that advocated in the Report, declaring that effective protection meant protection which

13 *Gashi and Nikshiqi v. Secretary of State for the Home Department* IAT (13695) (22 July 1996) now reported [1997] I.N.L.P. 96.

14 See H.L. Hansard, Vol. 573, Cols 531–32, 20 June 1996, statement by the then Minister of State for the Home Office, the Baroness Blatch: "Persecution is normally related to action by the authorities of a country. However, we also accept that, in some circumstances, agents of persecution may be groups or elements within the applicant's country of nationality, other than the authorities. ... [A]n applicant may qualify for asylum if the persecution by those other elements is knowingly tolerated by the authorities or if the authorities refuse, or prove unable, to offer effective protection." She went on to refer to the definition of a "refugee" set out in the EU Joint Position of March 1996 [(1996) O.J. L63/2] which "acknowledge[s] persecution by third parties only if it is encouraged or permitted by the authorities", but reminded the House that the resolution was not binding on Member States and said: "I can assure the House that we have no plans to depart from our long held broader interpretation."

15 See *Rieda v. Secretary of State for the Home Department*, IAT (14359) (23 Dec. 1996) [1997] I.N.L.P. 72, and *Benmoussa*, IAT (14626) (10 March 1997, unreported). Leave to appeal to the Court of Appeal has been granted in *Benmoussa*, but refused in *Rieda*.

16 *Hocine Yousfi* IAT (14779) (unreported).

reduced the threat to the appellant until it was no longer a serious possibility.

A third area considered was that of those who suffer in civil wars. The judgment of the Court of Appeal in *Adan*[17] has revolutionised the approach to such cases by emphasising that the lack of any state protection will not necessarily mean that the applicants are excluded from protection under the 1951 Convention.

Evidence Strongly Suggestive of Error

The Report presented findings strongly suggestive of error and thus requiring further comment from those who suggested that the procedures were beyond reproach. One example was a lack of consensus in assessments of situations in particular countries. There was a marked divergence of views amongst Special Adjudicators as to whether young male Tamils from Sri Lanka could live free from persecution in Colombo and, if so, whether it was reasonable to expect them to go there rather than seek international protection.[18]

There was a similar lack of consensus as to the significance of the timing and circumstances of the asylum application or the use of false travel documents for the question of whether or not the appellant was to be believed. Willingness to believe the appellant varied greatly from Special Adjudicator to Special Adjudicator. The decision of the High Court in *Kingori*,[19] in which it was held that where a Special Adjudicator believes nothing that an appellant has said issues of the burden of proof do not arise, provided one example for study. One Special Adjudicator in the sample used *Kingori* in 90 per cent of his/her 29 determinations, although the IAT has specifically warned against "the over-zealous use of *Kingori*".[20] Two more used it in over 60 per cent of the appeals they determined and another in over 50 per cent, although the incidence of reliance upon the case in the sample as a whole was only 16 per cent. The case was misused where Special Adjudicators who stated that they did believe some of the appellant's evidence relied on *Kingori* to obviate either the need to engage with the evidence on the country of origin or to give

17 *Adan, Nooh, Lazarevic and Radivojevic v. Secretary of State for the Home Department* CA 13 Feb. 1997 [1997] 1 W.L.R. 1107; [1997] 2 All E.R. 723; [1997] Imm. A.R. 251.

18 *Anandanadarajah v. IAT* CA [1996] Imm. A.R. 514 at 515–17 and 519; *R. v. IAT ex p. Probakaran* QBD [1996] Imm. A.R. 603 at 605.

19 *Kingori v. Secretary of State for the Home Department* CA [1994] Imm. A.R. 539.

20 For example, *Alexandru Petre* IAT (13 Feb. 1996, unreported).

reasons for their disbelief of matters central to the asylum application.

Special Adjudicators who doubted any part of the appellant's account were extremely unlikely to believe the rest of it. In only six per cent of cases in the sample did the Special Adjudicator detect a lie on an issue considered material to the application but go on to believe the appellant on the other material issues. Yet in two out of three of the cases where the Special Adjudicator had done so the appellant was recognised as a refugee. The UNHCR Handbook on the Criteria and Procedures for Determining Refugee Status states that: "[u]ntrue statements by themselves are not a reason for refusal of refugee status and it is the examiner's responsibility to evaluate such statements in the light of all the circumstances of the case".[21] The IAT has endorsed this point in the case of *Chiver*,[22] which remained unreported until November 1997 although widely used by representatives. The figure of six per cent of appellants to which this rule had been applied raised questions about whether Special Adjudicators are correctly following this guidance.

Evidence strongly suggestive of error was also given by an examination of the way in which the system functions in practice. This also provided an opportunity to evaluate the 1996 Procedure Rules,[23] which provide for more active case management by Special Adjudicators.

There were examples of the lack of legal aid for asylum appeals functioning to deprive applicants of representation at their appeals. In the sample 31 per cent of appellants were without representation at the hearing, although only 4.5 per cent had no representatives on record at all. In several cases solicitors put on record that lack of funds, and specifically lack of legal aid, was the reason that they were not present at the hearing. 49 per cent of solicitors and 44 per cent of immigration consultants in the sample did not attend the oral hearing, for unpaid representatives from voluntary organisations the figure was only 20 per cent.

The House of Lords emphasised in *Bugdaycay*[24] the paramount importance of the issues at stake in an asylum appeal. The European Court of Human Rights made it clear in *Airey v. Ireland*[25] that where issues of gravity are at

21 UNHCR, *Handbook on the Criteria and Procedures for Determining Refugee Status* (Geneva, 1992 edn), para. 199.

22 *Secretary of State for the Home Department v. Adrian Gheorghe Chiver* [1997] I.N.L.P. 212.

23 The Asylum Appeals (Procedure) Rules 1996, S.I. 1996, No. 2070 (L.5).

24 *R v. Secretary of State for the Home Department* ex p. Bugdaycay HL [1987] 1A.C. 514; [1987] 1 All E.R. 940 and [1987] Imm. A.R. 250.

25 *Airey v. Ireland*, (1979) Series A, No. 32; 2 E.H.R.R. 305.

stake a legal system must either make provision for appellants/litigants to be represented, or ensure that the proceedings do not require this. Thus the debate on the provision of legal aid for asylum appeals is far from closed.

The issue of the competence of representatives was also addressed. Proposals for the licensing of immigration practitioners did not find their way into the 1996 Act. However, debate around the Bill drew attention to a multitude of concerns in this field and calls for some form of accreditation scheme continue to be made.[26]

The case for representation of appellants at asylum appeals was strengthened by the analysis of the role of Home Office Presenting Officers and the way in which Special Adjudicators dealt with them. The Report cites examples of Special Adjudicators allowing Presenting Officers to alter the case that the appellant had to meet; not by dealing with new issues raised at the hearing but by relying on matters known to the Secretary of State at the time of the refusal letter and not raised therein.[27] It also cites examples of Presenting Officers making, and adjudicators accepting, submissions based on clearly identifiable errors of law in the refusal letter, such as the assertion that the appellant was not a refugee because s/he had not been "singled out", an argument the Home Office must be aware has been rejected both in international refugee law and in the national courts.[28]

In none of the cases in the sample had the Home Office called for a medical report or called witnesses. No medical evidence was obtained by the Home Office in cases in which the appellant was alleged and/or accepted to have mental health problems, although the UNHCR *Handbook* states that "the examiner should, in such cases, wherever possible, obtain expert medical advice".[29]

Finally, useful insights were provided through the recording of all

26 See the Private Member's Bill, *Registration of Immigration Advice Practitioners"*, Bill 48, *"A Bill to establish a system of registration for approved immigration advice practitioners"* (HMSO, 24 Jan. 1996); see also chapter 10 of this book by Anne Owers and Madeline Garlick. For an overview of this issue see Harvey, A.R., *ARC discussion paper on the licensing of immigration practitioners* (ARC, 27 June 1996), Harvey A.R., Haywood, P. and Storey, E. *Reviewing the Asylum Determination Procedure: A Casework Study, Part One: Initial Decision Making* (Refugee Legal Centre, July 1997) and *Part Two: Challenge and Review* (Refugee Legal Centre, November 1997).

27 See the Report, Section 8.10 at 47–8.

28 See e.g. the robust rebuttal of this proposition by the then Taylor J in *R. v. Secretary of State for the Home Department ex p. Jeyakumaran* [1994] Imm. A.R. 45 at 48.

29 UNHCR *Handbook, supra* n. 21, para. 208.

authorities cited by Special Adjudicators, providing an overview of the extent to which legal issues are being tackled, of what those issues are, and of different approaches being taken by different adjudicators and/or representatives. The heavy reliance on *Kingori*[30] and the under-reporting of authorities widely used by representatives such as such as *Chiver,*[31] or *Latif Mohammed*[32] were described above. Such examples strengthen the case for making the IAT a court of record, while research into the citing of authority by representatives is of relevance to studies of the quality of representation.

Evidence that Unsuccessful Appellants are not Necessarily "Bogus" Appellants

The Report presented evidence that Special Adjudicators did not regard all those who lost their appeals as "bogus" applicants. Although only five per cent of appellants in the sample were recognised as refugees, in 35 per cent of the cases in which a finding on risk was made, the appellant was found to be at risk on return. Only 15 per cent of appellants were not believed at all by the Special Adjudicators hearing their cases.

The Section 1 Criteria

The Report challenged the presumption that the criteria set out in Section 1 of the 1996 Act represented the indices of a "bogus" claim. It revealed Special Adjudicators recognising refugees from the "white list" countries and assessing levels of risk in some of those countries as comparable to those in the sample as a whole. Special Adjudicators found risks of persecution for a 1951 Convention reason in 14 per cent of cases in the sample. For the "white list" country Pakistan the figure was 11.5 per cent, and for the Ahmadia in Pakistan, 36 per cent. Nor did Special Adjudicators regard failure to claim asylum on arrival as indicative of a "bogus" claim; 82 per cent of those whose appeals were allowed in the sample had failed to do so and there were refugees claiming after refusal of leave to enter, or after notification as liable to removal. The Report also presented evidence that the time limits imposed on cases coming under the special appeals procedures set out in Section 1 of the 1996 Act would increase the incidence of errors in decision making or in the ability of appellants to exercise meaningful rights of appeal.

30 *Supra* n. 19.

31 *Supra* n. 22.

32 *Latif Mohammed* IAT (7592) (1 Feb. 1991, unreported).

Obtaining the Results: Research Methodology

Data Collection: Purpose of Synchronic Study

The written determinations of Special Adjudicators formed the data for the study. Examination of one stage of the determination procedure yields a synchronic view of the asylum applications under consideration. Such synchronic studies, isolating the subject matter under analysis, are suited to challenging claims made about a particular stage of the procedures. Synchronic studies facilitate comparative analysis and examinations of consistency in decision-making, and thus provide opportunities for analysis of both the efficiency and fairness of the procedures. They could usefully be undertaken to examine Home Office refusal letters and decisions on applications for leave to the IAT. Current empirical research[33] has revealed widespread use of standard grounds in refusal letters, some containing erroneous statements of law, others taking issue with credibility without weighing the circumstances of the individual, for example in citing the applicant's failure to claim asylum on arrival as evidence that s/he does not truly believe him/herself to stand in need of international protection, without being able to cover within the standard format the reasons put forward for not doing so as required by the Immigration Rules.[34]

Applications for leave to appeal to the IAT present the very best opportunity for the IAT to monitor the way in which Special Adjudicators are dealing with the cases before them and to offer guidance. This is not happening and the same research has revealed widespread use of standard grounds by the IAT in refusing leave. The High Court has similarly been critical of the IAT's failure to give proper reasons in dealing with leave applications. In *Njie*,[35] Mr Justice Jowitt was critical of the use of standard words for refusing leave in a case where the grounds of appeal raise specific points, in this case the Special Adjudicator's failure to consider the relevance of two psychiatric reports. He stated: "[I]t does seem to me that when material like this is put before [the chair of the tribunal] that it really does deserve a sentence or two by way of reasoning and this is why I grant leave." Mr Justice Sedley, in the

---

33 Harvey, Haywood and Storey, *op. cit. supra* n. 22.

34 *Statement of Changes in Immigration Rules*, (1993–94) HC 395, as amended, Rule 341(i).

35 *R. v. Secretary of State for the Home Department ex p. Njie* (11 Oct. 1996, CO\3329\96).

case of *Shah*,[36] made it clear that he would look at whether or not what he identified as a standard form of refusal of leave[37] really applied to the refusal in question. The standard phrases "the adjudicator came to clear adverse findings of fact" and "the Tribunal has read all the papers on file" brought forth the retort: "It is frankly impossible, with respect, to accept this. The Adjudicator had come to entirely favourable findings of fact."[38]

In a synchronic study, the flawed determination which will be overturned on appeal enjoys the same status as the careful determination which is beyond criticism from the IAT and higher courts. The determination which accurately reflects the hearing cannot adequately be differentiated from one which does not. A diachronic study, following applications through the system, provides complimentary material. Tracking the results of decisions at each stage, as did KPMG Peat Marwick in their report for the IAA,[39] can provide evidence pertaining to the efficiency of the system. Qualitative diachronic studies, undertaking qualitative analysis of the applications tracked, can address the issue of the fairness of the asylum determination procedures as a whole. The Refugee Legal Centre has engaged in such research, tracking a random sample of four hundred of its own cases dating from July 1993 to January 1997.[40] Diachronic studies can also be used to look in detail at the treatment of specific groups by the asylum determination system, that is, those distinguished by their existing characteristics such as unrepresented appellants, minors or women, and groups distinguished by a shared history such as nationals of particular countries, and survivors of torture.

The comparison of determinations with the hearings they record is one example of a limited diachronic study. The IAA could undertake ongoing monitoring of the "fit" between the Special Adjudicator's notes and his/her determination. Comparison of the records of proceedings of the Special Adjudicator, representatives of the Home Office and Appellant and of independent observers, all submitted to a researcher, would reduce the risk of an attempt to second-guess the Special Adjudicator, providing controls for use in comparative studies of the hearing and the determination.

The limitations of concentrating on the first appellate tier in order to inform

36 *R. v. IAT and Secretary of State for the Home Department ex p. Syeda Khatoon Shah* [1997] Imm. A.R. 145.

37 *Ibid.* at 147: "the decision, in a form familiar to this court".

38 *Ibid.*

39 KPMG Peat Marwick for the Home Office/Lord Chancellor's Department, *Review of Asylum Appeals Procedure*, (Dec. 1994).

40 Harvey, Haywood and Storey, *op. cit. supra* n. 26.

other research, for example into the fate of nationals of particular countries, must also be recognised. Cases reaching this level are not necessarily representative of the body of applications from a particular country. In 1995 37 per cent, 38 per cent and 20 per cent respectively of applications from Bosnia-Herzegovina, Iran and Somalia were refused by the Home Office after substantive consideration of their merits.[41] Given that the majority of initial decisions on applications from these countries were favourable, it is probable that some of those reaching the first appellate level were in some way atypical. Once again, the practical problem for the researcher also alerts him/her to further areas of concern, such as whether the bias affecting a research sample also has an effect on Special Adjudicators and Home Office Presenting Officers. Special Adjudicators and Presenting Officers see only those appellants who have failed to convince the initial decision makers. The Report was strongly critical of Presenting Officers, identifying their perception of their role as being to defeat the appeal, rather than to present the case for the Secretary of State in an impartial and fair manner.[42] It is desirable for any training programme to expose Special Adjudicators and Presenting Officers to refugees whose initial applications have succeeded before the Home Office, in order that they form a balanced view of country situations and gain the widest possible insight into Home Office decision-making.[43]

Accessing the Determinations

The issue of access to the determinations of Special Adjudicators is not merely one of practical consequence for the researcher. It has implications for the openness and accountability of the whole asylum determination procedure, for the training and supervision of Special Adjudicators, and for the formulation of common standards by which cases can be determined. Such standards are not limited to the assessment of the risks to particular groups in particular countries, nor to the elucidation of difficult points of law, although there is marked lack of consensus on both issues;[44] they extend to the way in which

41 See *Home Office Statistics for 1995* (Immigration and General Unit, Research and Statistics Department, 8 Feb. 1996).

42 Harvey, *op. cit. supra* n. 1, part 8.10, at 47–50.

43 *Ibid.*, part 4.5.1.1. at 20: "It is recommended that ... resources and time be allocated to give adjudicators opportunities to receive in-depth training on countries from a plurality of sources, and for exchanges of views, particularly where lack of consensus is identified."

44 *Ibid.*, part 4.3, at 18–20, part 5.2.6, at 24–5.

Special Adjudicators approach issues of the appellant's credibility,[45] of evidence,[46] and of the conduct of the hearing itself. Random sampling was used in order to ensure adequate representation of all hearing centres in England and Scotland, of as many Special Adjudicators as possible, and of appellants from as many countries as possible.

I received every cooperation from the IAA in my research, and it was also gratifying to note that problems of access mentioned in my report had been addressed by the IAA by the time ARC first met with them following its publication. However, there can be no prospect of large scale or ongoing research on these determinations if each researcher, be s/he drawn from within the IAA or outside it, has to make the demands on IAA time and resources that I made. The determinations are matters of public record, yet nowhere are copies centrally held and different methods of filing are used in each centre. Determinations of Special Adjudicators, while not binding authorities, are useful for monitoring, training and research, and as persuasive authorities in other cases. They cannot be exploited to the full for any of these purposes until they are collected centrally, either in a library at one of the hearing centres or off-site, with comprehensive indexes being made available and detailing at least date of promulgation, reference number and country of origin.

The majority of the determinations not only of Special Adjudicators but also of the IAT remain lost to view. The Immigration Appeals Reports provide access to some, but by no means all, IAT determinations. Some of the authorities most frequently cited by representatives in the sample, remain unreported years after promulgation.[47] The provision of electronic access to determinations may go some way to resolving these problems, but it has been slow in coming and problems of anonymity and confidentiality in this most sensitive of areas have yet to be resolved. There are advocates for an independent Documentation and Research Centre to act as a resource for Special Adjudicators, and representatives.[48] The focus of discussion has been background country information and guidelines on interpretation of the 1951

45 *Ibid.*, part 7.3, at 33–7.

46 *Ibid.*, part 7.2, at 32–3.

47 For example, *Chiver*, *supra* n. 22, was promulgated 10 March 1994 and is still one of the most important determinations on the vexed issue of the judging of the credibility of the appellant. It is widely cited as such but was not reported until November 1997.

48 See chapter 10 of this book by Anne Owers and Madeline Garlick; JUSTICE, ILPA, ARC, *Providing Protection: Towards Fair and Effective Asylum Procedures* (July 1997), Recommendation 7, p. 30.

Convention, but a documentation centre has the potential to provide a full set of determinations which it would be possible to access and sort electronically, with restrictions on access to the centre providing safeguards for those whose appeals are being consulted. As matters stand it is impossible to be satisfied that adequate structures are in place for the training, monitoring and supervision of Special Adjudicators or for monitoring and control of uniformity in decision-making.

Lack of Hegemony in the Sample

Having collected the determinations, the problem was then to collect information from the determinations. Determinations of Special Adjudicators exhibit enormous variety, as do other legal judgments. In almost all cases it is impossible to use default values to fill in lacunae. Many potentially fruitful avenues of enquiry are thus closed where a random sample has been chosen. It proved impossible to correlate findings on credibility against the language of the hearing, or to study in depth the range of background evidence put forward by different representatives, because not all Special Adjudicators record whether an interpreter was used or list the evidence before them. While some Special Adjudicators use a standard format for their determinations, others use different styles for different cases.

Like the issue of access to determinations, this was not merely a methodological problem, but an area of study in itself. The 1996 Procedure Rules[49] address the content of determinations in rule 2(3)(b). This states that determinations "shall consist of a concise statement of (i) the decision on the substantial issues raised; (ii) any findings of fact material to the decision; (iii) the reasons for the decision".

Prior to 1996, the Procedure Rules were silent on the content of determinations. Rule 2(3)(b) is designed to ensure at least the minimum content necessary in determinations to ensure consistency in decision-making and the possibility of adequate review of the decision on appeal. This minimum content was not to be found in all the determinations in the sample.

There was no decision on the substantial issues raised in cases where the Special Adjudicator simply stated that the appellant had failed to discharge the burden of proof on him/her because s/he had failed to answer the points raised in the Home Office "reasons for refusal" letter. More attentive Special Adjudicators have drawn attention to what one characterised as the use of

---

49 The Asylum Appeals (Procedure) Rules 1996, S.I. 1996 No. 2070 (L.5).

"unsupported allegations in the explanatory letter".[50] As another observed: "In this case the Secretary of State "understands" that if an individual is not politically active and is only involved in trade unions, he has no reason to fear persecution. I have difficulty in following this argument and I do not know where he "understands" it from."[51]

A Home Office briefing in an Algerian case stated that deserters were punished with five to six months' imprisonment. UNHCR reports and the United States Department of State Country Report on Algeria were put in evidence, putting the period of imprisonment at 20 years. This evidence was preferred by the Special Adjudicator. Another Special Adjudicator, deciding an appeal on the papers, simply accepted the Home Office assertion (the Special Adjudicator's words) that punishment for failure to perform military service was not disproportionately harsh in Algeria because the appellant had put in no evidence to challenge this. Such a finding does not in practice meet the requirements of the new Rules, because the Special Adjudicator has given no reason for accepting the unsupported assertions of the Home Office.[52]

The Court of Appeal in the March 1997 case of *Drrias*[53] was very critical of determinations, in this case of the IAT, that merely reiterate the assertions of the Home Office. The IAT had found that there was "no concrete evidence that the Respondent would face interrogation and persecution if he returned to Sudan on the basis of his having stayed in the United Kingdom for over a year".[54] Lord Justice Thorpe, having considered the material before the IAT, including a UNHCR report to the Immigration and Nationality Department (IND) concluded:

> It, of course, was open to the tribunal to weigh all the evidence and to prefer the case presented by the Secretary of State but it would not possibly be a fair summary of the end position to say that there was no concrete evidence that the respondent would face interrogation and persecution.[55]

He continued:

50 Harvey A., *op. cit. supra* n. 1, part 8.10.1.5., at 49.

51 *Ibid.*

52 *Ibid.*, part 8.10.1.5.2, at 49.

53 *Atif Adli Drrias v. Secretary of State for the Home Department*, CA [1997] Imm. A.R. 346.

54 Cited in the Court of Appeal judgment at 9.

55 Judgment at 9 E–F.

> Equally defective, in my judgment, is the reasoning of the tribunal in relation to the question of religious persecution. Once again the approach of the tribunal seems to have been to rely upon a bland letter from the FCO [Foreign and Commonwealth Office] and to disregard all contrary evidence. ... There does not seem to be any attempt to note and balance the contrary evidence, for example, the evidence put before the special adjudicator by the Secretary of State in the form of the report of 1996 from the US State Department.[56]

The Report drew attention to several examples of this very practice by Special Adjudicators, but was also able to identify Special Adjudicators who had rejected Home Office assertions, just as the Court of Appeal did in *Drrias*, on the basis of background documents furnished to them by the Home Office Presenting Officers themselves.[57] The "findings of fact material to the decision" required by Rule 2(3)(b) were not being made in cases where Special Adjudicators misused the case of *Kingori*,[58] or were dismissive of original documents, as discussed above.

Analysis of the Determinations

Range and Potency of Variables in Legal Determinations

The number of variables in a legal determination limit the scope for meaningful statistical analysis. Moreover, these variables are very potent and can affect the whole result of the appeal. Statisticians must allow for the "null hypothesis", that is, the possibility that although a variable appears to affect a result the result would be the same with or without the presence of the variable. In some fields of statistical research attempts can be made to estimate how likely it is that the null hypothesis explains the result. For instance, in order to decide whether cigarette smoking affects lung cancer, the medical researcher must take account of the incidence of lung cancer among the population as a whole and attempt to come up with a value representing the margin for error in any given sample. It is not possible to ascribe such a value to issues such as credibility; we cannot discover incidence of truth-telling among the population as a whole and use this to cast doubt upon adjudicators' findings on credibility.

56 Judgment at 9 G–10 C.

57 Harvey, *op. cit. supra* n. 1, part 8.10, at 49–50.

58 *Supra* n. 19.

Other variables with explanatory force may not be known to the author of a determination, let alone the researcher. It tells us little merely to know that counsel was instructed, if we do not know whether or not counsel was a specialised immigration practitioner, whether or not he or she had been instructed by competent and experienced solicitors or other representatives, or whether he or she had received the file at the 11th hour without supporting medical and background evidence or the time to obtain this.

The difficulties of assessing the effects of given variables are increased by the small percentage of successful appeals and this remains a problem whatever size of sample is studied. The interest lies in discovering which factors affect an appellant's chances of success, be these the type of representative, the identity of the adjudicator, or the nature of the evidence submitted. But with a five per cent success rate across the sample as a whole, it would be unsurprising to learn that every type of representative loses more cases than s/he wins, that every Special Adjudicator dismisses more cases than s/he allows, and that detailed evidence is submitted in more unsuccessful than successful cases.

For these reasons, any statistical research in this field must largely be content with revealing trends and generating counter-examples, for which any hypothesis as to why, for example, so many asylum appeals fail, must be able to account if it is to gain credence. Any such hypothesis must be accompanied by qualitative analysis, detailed examination of sub-samples, and the subjecting of apparent statistical trends to close qualitative scrutiny. One example, discussed above, of this use of statistics is the reluctance of Special Adjudicators to give general credence to appellants in whom they believe they have detected in one untruth. Another possible example is that of gender. The sample contained 114 women and 508 men. Twice as many women as men succeeded in their appeals. Adjudicators made more recommendations for grants of exceptional leave to remain (ELR) to women than they did to men and refused to make a formal recommendation but asked the Secretary of State to consider granting ELR in 3.5 per cent of cases involving women and two per cent of all cases involving men. Whether such results are repeated over a larger sample, or when tested by the use of controls such as country of origin and age, awaits investigation.

The most obvious explanation for women's greater success rate from the data collected for this research is that while only 6.5 per cent of the men in the sample were found to be wholly credible by adjudicators, for women the figure was 15 per cent. It is not the case that women were consistently found more credible than men. When it came to those who were simply not believed at all by Special Adjudicators, the figures were 16 per cent of women and 15 per cent of men.

There may be other explanations for women's higher success rate. One Special Adjudicator observed, not once but in two determinations "the appellant fears rape and I accept that this may be a problem for someone as attractive as her". Both women, who came from former Yugoslavia were wholly believed by that Special Adjudicator and both appeals were allowed. As the debate rages over whether women constitute a "social group"[59] under Article 1 of the 1951 Convention, it is perhaps surprising to note that the ratio of both determinations would appear to entail accepting "attractive young women" as a social group.[60]

Devising Criteria for Comparison

Whether the method of analysis is statistical or qualitative it will always be necessary to undertake comparative investigation, and thus to create criteria for comparison which satisfy the requirements of objectivity and transparency and which also yield useful results. A fine example of how not to devise such criteria was provided by the Secretary of State himself in addressing the designation of countries for the "white list".[61] Two purely statistical criteria were put forward: that the country generated a large number of asylum applicants, and that a significant proportion of those applications were unsuccessful.[62] Once again, the asylum determination procedures were treated as beyond reproach. The third criterion was that there was, in the opinion of the Secretary of State, in general no serious risk of persecution in that country.[63]

59 For further details of Court of Appeal ruling in the case of *Shah*, *supra* n. 36. See also chapters 6 and 8 of this book by Simon Russell and Geoffrey Care respectively.

60 See *Secretary of State for the Home Department v. Sergei Vasilyevich Savchenkov* [1996] Imm. A.R. 28, at 35 where it is stated *inter alia* that a social group must possess immutable characteristics. Is attractiveness such a characteristic given the precondition of youth? Or does the characteristic of youth fail the test of immutability also?

61 A country designated in The Asylum (Designated Countries of Destination and Designated Safe Third Countries) Order 1996, S.I. 1996/2671 at para. 2 which states: "The following countries are designated as ones in which it appears to the Secretary of State that here is in general no serious risk of persecution: ..."

62 For more detailed discussion of "white list" and safe country of origin concept see chapter 4 of this book by Peter Billings and Rachel Trost.

63 H.C. Hansard, Vol. 268, Col. 703, 11 Dec. 1995.

This criterion was utterly subjective and thus quite opaque. Nor could it perform the task for which it was designed; the absence of a general risk, even if proven, could not be determinative of the risks to any individual coming from that country. This is demonstrated by the certification of applicants from "white list" countries since the coming into force of the 1996 Act. It is not merely individuals facing a special risk who have been certified, but also members of especially vulnerable groups such as Roma from Poland and Ahmadia from Pakistan.[64]

Devising Criteria in Straightforward Cases

In a limited number of instances the criteria were unproblematic, if they were recorded in the determination. Where they were not, it was necessary to determine whether or not a sub-sample of cases in which they were recorded provided material for an unbiased analysis. One example is that of time limits, for example from Home Office decision to date of hearing. After comparison of the mean, median and mode times taken for these steps, it was considered acceptable to rely on the sub-sample. However, reliance on maxima and minima was unacceptable when dealing with a sub-sample. Instead, attention was drawn to individual examples.

A Teleological Approach to Criteria for Comparison

Other criteria could be selected once the precise nature of the field of enquiry had been ascertained. If considering disposals of cases or the conduct of the hearing, for example, the researcher is interested in whether or not the appellant was a minor at the date of hearing; if considering issues such as credibility the interest may lie in the age of the appellant when persecuted or on arrival. Torture is another example. In examining the type of claims coming from a particular country, for example, it will be necessary to record all forms of physical ill-treatment or mental cruelty suffered by the appellant. If the concern is with whether medical reports are obtained for appeal hearings, it is necessary to account for those types of ill-treatment which may leave no scars.

Even where the appropriate teleological approach is apparent, it quickly becomes problematic. In some cases, a medical report was not or could not have been obtained in good time and physical scars have faded. In such cases, it is impossible to identify fault on the part of the representative without

64 Harvey, Haywood and Storey, *op. cit. supra* n. 26.

knowing when the appellant came to the representative. Nothing will reveal those cases in which representatives have taken all proper steps to obtain a medical report, but then decided not to disclose it because it is unfavourable to the appellant's case. As to psychological reports, the presence of psychological scars will depend on the individual concerned and upon their willingness to see a psychiatrist. Many advisors or researchers are ill-equipped to make judgments on what has left psychological scars. In these cases, all the researcher can do is be alive to, and make explicit, the limitations of the method by which the data is gathered in tackling these issues.

The issue of medical evidence in asylum appeals, and indeed in asylum applications to the Home Office, is a field worth of separate qualitative study, correlating the details of ill-treatment or mental anguish to which appellants were exposed and the types and sources of medical evidence produced, together with research into how representatives make decisions on the obtaining of medical evidence and the factors that influence them.[65] Such research is of particular importance given that under sub-paragraph 5(5) of Schedule 2 of the 1993 Act, as amended by Section 1 of the 1996 Act,[66] where there is a reasonable likelihood of past torture the application should not be certified for inclusion in the "fast-track" procedures. Torture is not defined in any of the relevant instruments, but it is accepted that mental anguish can amount to torture.[67]

65 For discussion of problems in medical report writing for asylum seekers see chapter 7 of this book by Michael Peel.

66 As introduced by a late amendment, see H.L. Hansard, Vol. 573, Col. 1322, 2 July 1996.

67 See e.g., H.L. Hansard. Vol. 573, Cols 494–95, 20 June 1996, statement by the then Minister of State for the Home Office, the Baroness Blatch: "I have made clear that the term "torture" can indeed apply to any severe form of physical and psychological abuse deliberately inflicted to cause suffering." The jurisprudence under the European Convention on Human Rights and under the United Nations International Covenant on Civil and Political Rights does not support the Baroness's qualification that the abuse must be deliberately inflicted to cause suffering, see *Pratt and Another v. The Attorney General for Jamaica and Another* [1994] 2 AC 1, Privy Council, and European Court of Human Rights ruling in *Soering v. U.K.*, (1989) Series A, No.161; [1989] 11 E.H.R.R. 439. See also chapter 8 of this book by Geoffrey Care.

Political Implications of Criteria Chosen

Other fields appear uncontentious at first sight, with difficulties emerging only when one seeks to devise the precise criteria for analysis. Whether or not one shares UNHCR's view that "a "bona fide" asylum seeker may have very good reason for not applying on arrival",[68] it is necessary to record the timing of an asylum application since many Special Adjudicators treat this as a matter going to credibility, just as the Home Office is enjoined to do by sub-paragraphs 341(i) and (ii) of the Immigration Rules.[69] Then the decision must be made as to whether or not to distinguish between those who apply soon after arrival and those who apply later, but still during the currency of their leave. To make such a distinction may be seen as reinforcing the perception that "genuine" refugees make applications at an early stage. However, not to make it is to deprive oneself of one means of identifying the significance of the length of any delay for Special Adjudicators, in the face of comments suggesting that it does have a significance for them.[70]

After consultation, I fixed the period for the purposes of the Report at a week. In the event, when the Bill was debated, one proposed amendment, which did not come become law, was that those who applied for asylum within *three* days of arrival should not lose their entitlement to benefits.[71] Reasons must be given for the unit selected, with the appropriate disclaimers and caveats, and the unit selected must be revisited in the light of data collected.

Complexity of Determinations

The preceding section dealt with the dangers of drawing up units of analysis based on what the researcher suspects may be false distinctions identified by the authors of the determinations. Different problems arise when the authors of the determinations are making distinctions in the course of their determinations, but not in an explicit fashion. For example, I wished to examine Special Adjudicators' findings on risks, either in a particular country, albeit that the appellant him/herself was not found to be at risk, or on risk to the

68 *The Position of UNHCR regarding the Asylum Bill and Draft Ancillary Instruments* (UNHCR London, 1993). The IAT shares this view as it made clear in *Latif Mohammed, supra* n. 32, and, more recently, in *Rieda, supra* n. 15, and *Juma* IAT (14583) (11 March 1997, unreported).

69 HC 395, *supra* n. 34, as amended.

70 Harvey A., *op. cit. supra* n. 1, part 6.2. at 30.

71 H.L. Hansard, Vol. 574, Col. 1184, 22 July 1996.

appellant where the risk was not found to amount to persecution. Special Adjudicators did find appellants to be at risk, while deciding that they did not fall within the 1951 Convention definition of a refugee. They went on to distinguish between, for example, risks to appellants from groups not considered to be agents of persecution; risks from civil wars or similar unrest, and risks for other than a "1951 Convention reason" (race, religion, nationality, ethnic origin, political opinion or social group), as set out in Article 1 of the 1951 Convention.

In these cases, the only way accurately to reflect the categories actually being used by adjudicators was to work through large numbers of determinations, refining and reworking the units of analysis before commencing data collection. In the case of risk, the final categories were based upon the Convention reasons with an extra category of non-Convention reasons. The findings on risk were categorised as follows: no finding; a finding of a risk of persecution; a finding of a risk of ill-treatment or discrimination not amounting to persecution; a finding that the risk came from other agents of persecution or from the background situation in the country such as a civil war, and finally a finding that the social group to which the appellant claimed to belong could not be recognised as a "social group" within the Convention definition. This gave a total of 27 units of analysis which could be further analysed by combining them with other fields of data, including the risks to the individual appellant, the ethnicity of the appellant, and whether the Special Adjudicator identified a particular group as agents of persecution protection from whom was not, in the circumstances of the appellant's case, within the scope of the 1951 Convention.

Avoiding Subjectivity in Appraisal of Determinations

Problems arise when the Special Adjudicator appears to have done one thing in the determination and claims to have done quite another. For example, it is an exceptional Special Adjudicator who does not in his/her determination correctly identify those cases setting out the burden of proof in asylum appeals. It may appear from the determination as a whole that the correct burden of proof has not been applied, but this is a matter for those drafting grounds of leave to appeal to the IAT and for the researcher in qualitative analysis subsequent to data collection, not for the data collection operation itself.

The distinction between the objective and subjective appraisal of the determination becomes blurred where the matters are less clear cut than that of the burden of proof. For example, the Special Adjudicator may state that s/he does not believe a word the appellant says, but the determination will reveal that this is not the case. Here the researcher must decide whether to follow consistently the Special Adjudicator's own assessment of his/her findings or whether to seek to devise objective criteria. Having experimented with both methods, I concluded that following the Special Adjudicator's own perception was preferable. That perception itself is an important part of the final decision, since the Special Adjudicator who does not think s/he believes a word the appellant says, is likely to decide the case on that basis. Following the decision-maker also has the advantage of giving clear-cut categories in a greater number of cases, although it does have the disadvantage that like is not being compared with like: where the Special Adjudicator has summarised his/her findings on credibility this is recorded, where s/he has not, it is necessary to evaluate the actual findings made in any event. One consequence is that it is impossible to use this approach this to compare and contrast the approaches of individual adjudicators. This must be left to a qualitative analysis.

It is a test of the categories used whether they can be consistently applied by different members of a team of researchers. Monitoring and checking of other researcher's findings, in a process resembling the marking of examination papers, is not only necessary to achieve consistency, it is a guide to whether the selected categories work.

Conclusion

The intensive lobbying during the passage of the 1996 Act was designed to influence its final form and content. In this respect it must largely be deemed a failure. The provisions fought against were for the most part enacted and many of the effects of 1996 Act, most notably the effect of Section 1 extending use of the accelerated and truncated appeals procedure, have been as unhappy as refugee advocates predicted. However, that intensive period of debate and research, sharing of expertise and information and of subjecting the asylum procedures to rigorous scrutiny, is arguably one of the causes of the bold developments in case-law during the year following the passage of the 1996 Act. It remains to be seen whether refugee advocates can continue this momentum. Empirical research has a role to play in enlarging and refining the terms of the debate. Close scrutiny of the inadequacies of a procedure, where the risks of getting it wrong are so very grave, can also act as a stimulus to both researcher and reader to maintain the pressure for reform.

Bibliography

Harvey, A.R., *"The Risks of Getting it Wrong": The Asylum and Immigration Bill Session 1995/96 and the Determination s of Special Adjudicators* (Asylum Rights Campaign, April 1996). Copies available from Research and Information Officer, Refugee Council, Bondway House 3–9, Bondway, London SW8 3SJ.

Harvey, A.R., *ARC Discussion Paper on the Licensing of Immigration Practitioners* (ARC, 27 June 1996).

Harvey, A.R., Haywood, P. and Storey, E., *Reviewing the Asylum Determination Procedure: A Casework Study*, Vol. 1 *Initial Decision Making* (1997), Vol. 2 *Challenge and Review* (forthcoming). Information from Refuge Legal Centre, Sussex House, 39–45 Bermondsey Street, London SE1 3XF.

Henderson, M., *Best Practice guide to Asylum Appeals* (Immigration Law Practitioner's Association, The Law Society, Refugee Legal Group, May 1997).

Home Office Statistics for 1995 (Immigration and General Unit, Research and Statistics Department, 8 Feb. 1996).

KPMG Peat Marwick, *Review of Asylum Appeals Procedure* for the Home Office/Lord Chancellor's Department (Dec. 1994).

Owers, A., and Garlick, M., *The Criteria and Procedures for a Fair and Effective Asylum Determination: Background Paper* (Justice, Jan. 1997).

Owers, A., and Garlick, M., *Summaries and Recommendations* (May 1997).

UNHCR, *The Position of UNHCR regarding the Asylum Bill and Draft Ancillary Instruments* (London, 1993).

10 Protection and Process: Towards Fair and Effective Asylum Determination Procedures

ANNE OWERS AND MADELINE GARLICK

When the Asylum and Immigration Bill was introduced into the UK parliament in November 1995, refugee and human rights groups criticised its provisions and mounted a vocal campaign against its passage.[1] After the Bill was passed despite their opposition, the challenge which faced those groups was clear: to come up with positive alternatives for asylum determination which would be both fair and workable in the prevailing domestic and international climate.

This chapter is based on a research project which came about in response to that challenge. It summarises the findings and recommendations from the project, which was conducted jointly by JUSTICE and the Immigration Law Practitioners' Association (ILPA), with support from the Asylum Rights Campaign (ARC).[2] The project examined refugee determination systems in

1 A key element in this campaign was the work of the Glidewell Panel and its *Report from an Independent Enquiry into the Implications and Effects of the Asylum and Immigration Bill 1995 and Related Social Security Measures* (April 1996).

2 This chapter is based on the report entitled *Providing Protection: Towards Fair and Effective Asylum Procedures* from the JUSTICE/ILPA/ARC asylum project, a 10-month research programme during 1996–97, which was supported by the Joseph Rowntree Charitable Trust, the Barrow Cadbury Trust and a private donor. Based on research visits and detailed analysis of alternative systems, the research critically assesses procedures used in other states, and analyses the practical operation of the existing UK system, including the problems which prevent it achieving its aims. Other asylum project documents are Country Reports on asylum determination in Canada, the Netherlands, Central Europe (Germany, Austria, Hungary, Poland, Switzerland) and Australia, and on Art. 3 of the European Convention on Human Rights and humanitarian protection in selected countries.

10 countries in Europe, Canada and Australia, and sought to identify successful elements which could be adapted for use in the UK system. The project's aim was to provide a starting point for a more constructive and positive debate about workable and fair asylum determination systems, which could address the concerns both of asylum-seekers and government. The resulting report is entitled *Providing Protection: Towards Fair and Effective Asylum Procedures*.

This chapter considers some of the basic principles which should underlie a fair process, based on international human rights standards and best practice in other states. It then identifies some concrete steps which states can, and should, take in moving towards better systems, which can operate in a more transparent and less adversarial culture, and focus on the obligation to provide protection to those who need it.

The Human Rights Context

The right to seek and enjoy asylum from persecution is guaranteed in one of the earliest international human rights instruments adopted by the UK: the 1948 Universal Declaration on Human Rights. It finds concrete expression in the 1951 UN Convention Relating to the Status of Refugees (the 1951 Convention) and its 1967 Protocol, which prohibit the return of those persecuted on grounds of race, religion, nationality or membership of a political or social group; as well as in Article 3 of the European Convention on Human Rights and Article 3(1) of the UN Convention against Torture, which prohibit the return of those facing torture and inhuman or degrading treatment.[3]

---

3 Art. 3 of the European Convention for the Protection of Human Rights and Fundamental Freedoms states: "No one shall be subjected to torture or to inhuman or degrading treatment or punishment." See, for instance, *Cruz Varas v. Sweden* (1991) Series A, No. 201; *Vilvarajah and others v. UK* (1991) Series A, No. 215; *Chahal v. UK* 15 Nov. 1996, (1996) Series B, No. 22; *Amuur v. France* (1996) Series B, No. 11. Art. 3(1) of the Convention against Torture and other Cruel, Inhuman or Degrading Treatment or Punishment states: "No State Party shall expel, return ('*refouler*') or extradite a person to another State where there are substantial grounds for believing that he would be in danger of being subjected to torture." See, for instance, *Mutombo v. Switzerland* Communication 13/1993; *Ismail Alan v. Switzerland* Communication 21/1995; *Pauline Muzonzo Paku Kisoki v. Sweden* Communication 41/1996.

In the immediate postwar years, this was seen as a positive responsibility. In most European countries, refugees were regarded much more favourably than other immigrants. Those fleeing the Hungarian uprising in 1956, defecting from the Soviet Union, and, at least initially, leaving Vietnam and Chile in the 1970s, were accepted, often on a group basis, with little question. Since the 1980s, however, two things have changed. There are more asylum-seekers, and most of them come from countries of the southern hemisphere. Group refugee programmes have been abandoned, complex and costly asylum determination systems have been set up to examine claims, and initial recognition rates in the UK have declined from 70 per cent in the 1970s to approximately five per cent now.

All countries in the northern and western hemispheres face the difficulty of determining, fairly, individually but swiftly, a large number of claims for asylum, many of them from people coming from situations of general political and social upheaval. They are only a small proportion of the world's asylum-seekers, most of whom are found in countries of the southern and eastern hemispheres. Asylum determination systems can only scratch the surface of the worldwide refugee problem, but they represent a very important scratch. First, the arrival of asylum-seekers requires host countries to put their theoretical obligations into action: for most of them, it is where human rights obligations begin to require financial commitment. Second, if states adopt systems which seek to circumvent those obligations, or undermine other standards of fairness, they not only fail those who seek protection; they also send signals to the main refugee-producing and refugee-receiving countries. If human rights are negotiable in countries with most resources and fewest refugees, they become unenforceable in poorer, more pressured states. Finally, systems which are inefficient send a different kind of signal: that an asylum application can secure a three- or four-year stay in a host country, with a decreasing likelihood of being removed at all, the longer the process lasts.

The Political Context

There are two important factors to consider which provide the political context within which determination systems in the UK and other countries operate.

The first is the regime of visas and carrier fines brought in by European, North American and Australasian countries in the 1980s. Mandatory visas have been imposed on refugee-producing countries.[4] Airlines and other carriers are fined (£2,000 per passenger in the UK) if they bring in people without those visas. This creates a classic "catch 22" situation. People cannot be refugees, or apply for visas to be refugees (if such visas exist), until they have left their own country; but they cannot leave their own country without visas. The regime is policed by airlines, which have no obligations under international human rights law, but which do have obligations towards their shareholders not to incur large fines.

UK and other countries' determination systems therefore rest on a policy of interdiction, operating to prevent refugee arrivals. As a result, sophisticated networks of agents have developed to provide false documents and routes to those seeking to leave. These escape routes are available only to those who can afford the huge four- and five- figure sums involved; and who may or may not be those most in need of protection. As a consequence, many asylum-seekers arrive on false documents, or having destroyed those documents *en route* on the instructions of the agent. This creates problems for the receiving country, both in terms of establishing identity and nationality, and, if the claim is rejected, in returning the asylum-seeker to the appropriate country. Such problems are the direct result of the carriers' liability regime; yet they are used, in legislation and in public debate, as grounds for casting doubt on the *bona fides* of those forced to use such means.

The UK, unlike some other countries, has no overseas acceptance or sponsorship programmes to assist asylum-seekers to enter legally. Some refugee community groups would strongly support such a programme; however, there are substantial difficulties in practice and in principle about making protection claims in the country of origin, for determination by immigration officers overseas.[5] Nevertheless, there are ways of mitigating the system: for example, by remitting fines in respect of those who are admitted

4 See, generally, Feller, E., "Carrier Sanctions and International Law" (1989) 1 I.J.Ref.L. 48; Cruz, A., *Shifting Responsibility: Carriers' Liability in the Member States of the European Union and North America* (Trentham Books, 1995); Nicholson, F., "The Immigration (Carriers' Liability) Act 1987: Privatising Immigration Functions at the Expense of International Obligations?" (1997) 46 I.C.L.Q. 586.

5 See also Randall, C., "An Asylum Policy for the UK" in *Strangers and Citizens, A Positive Approach to Migrants and Refugees*, Spencer, S. ed. (Institute for Public Policy Research and Rivers Oram Press, 1994) pp. 212–13; JUSTICE/ILPA/ARC *Asylum Determination in Australia*, Supplementary Report No. 5 (1997).

to the determination procedure. In the UK, fines may be waived for passengers who are ultimately granted refugee status; but not at present for the significant number who are given exceptional leave to remain on "compelling humanitarian grounds". The harsh effects of carrier liability regimes could be ameliorated by proactive programmes for family reunion or vulnerable groups, which are available in a few refugee-receiving countries, but not the UK. It is argued that though carrier sanctions are now firmly entrenched in states' law and policies, their consequences and operation at present raise serious questions of principle and practice.

The second important factor is the growing interest of Western states in temporary alternative forms of protection. The growth in the number of asylum-seekers, the generalised situations of civil war and state breakdown from which many may come, and the cost of asylum determination systems, mean that states are looking closely at alternative means of providing group protection on a strictly time-limited basis. This is being discussed at European Union level and may well result in a common policy. With the signing of the Amsterdam Treaty in October 1997, significant legislative and judicial powers over key areas of asylum law and policy, including temporary protection, have been transferred from Member States to Community competence. Among these, the European Council was given authority to adopt measures concerning "minimum standards for giving protection to displaced persons from third countries who cannot return to their country of origin".[6] A proposal has already been put forward by the European Commission for a Joint Action on the temporary protection of displaced persons,[7] designed to provide for a "coordinated response" to an actual or probable mass influx of displaced persons into a Member State. These initiatives highlight the degree of interest which exists at intergovernmental level in "burden-sharing" and "promoting a balance of effort between Member States in receiving and bearing the

6 Treaty of Amsterdam, Art. 2 (Amendments to the Treaty Establishing the European Community, Community Policies), Title IIIa, Art. 73k (2)(a). See (1997) O.J. C340/01 (10 Nov. 1997).

7 Brussels, 5 March 1997, COM(97)93 final: 97/0081 (CNS).

consequences" of refugee movements.[8]

There are some advantages to the temporary protection approach. It can be used swiftly and proactively to remove people from danger. It avoids the unnecessary cost of examining in detail the cases of people who clearly cannot safely be removed, and in fact are not removed. However, these new forms of protection may also be dangerous. They are offered outside the 1951 Convention and on criteria and terms defined by states. As such, they risk undermining the absolute protection against *refoulement*, and the effective status, which the Convention offers. They operate on the presumption that protection is like an umbrella, to be offered until the rain stops and then taken down and moved elsewhere. Reality is more complex, both in terms of the situations to which people may be returning, and the links they may have formed with the country of refuge. The temporary protection debate, and any new forms of protection proposed, should be very closely monitored by independent human rights organisations and should be subject to judicial supervision.

Fair and Effective Determination Systems

We begin with the proposition that the purpose of an asylum determination system is to allow claims for protection to be properly put, and to examine

---

8 There has been extensive discussion of the temporary protection concept, and the merits and dangers of its potential wider application in Europe and elsewhere. On the Joint Action proposal, see in particular *Comments from the European Council of Refugees and Exiles (ECRE) on the Proposal of the European Commission concerning Temporary Protection of Displaced Persons* (ECRE, London, April 1997); *Commission Proposal to the Council for a Joint Action concerning Temporary Protection of Displaced Persons: Briefing to the House of Lords* (JUSTICE, July 1997). On the temporary protection notion, see e.g., *Position of the European Council of Refugees and Exiles on Temporary Protection in the context of the Need for a Supplementary Refugee Definition* (ECRE, Feb. 1997); Marx, R., *Temporary Protection of Refugees from Former Yugoslavia: International Protection or Solution Oriented Approach?* (ECRE, June 1994); Kjaerum, M., "Temporary Protection in Europe in the 1990s" (1994) 6 I.J.Ref.L. 3; Kerber, K., "Temporary Protection: An Assessment of the Harmonisation Policies of European Union Member States" (1997) 9 I.J.Ref.L. 453; for UNHCR's position, see the High Commissioner, *Note on International Protection: International Protection in Mass Influx* (EXCOM, 46th session, Sept. 1995).

them fully. No country in our research had discovered a perfect means of doing so. Systems tend to become costly and sclerotic and were described by an official in one country as "expensive warehousing systems".[9] They often appear more concerned with the negative agenda of preventing abuse and deterring arrivals than with a positive desire to provide protection. However, it is possible to extract from experience in other countries some elements which offer possibilities, and warnings, for those seeking to create fair and effective determination systems.

First, such systems rely on good quality initial decision-making. Wherever processes are developed which allow space for the asylum claim to be presented and examined as fully as possible, this results in a greater number of positive decisions being made earlier in the process, and in negative decisions which are better-reasoned and more sustainable. This is true whether a decision-maker is independent (as in Canada)[10] or governmental (as in a recent experimental process in the Netherlands).[11]

This involves front-loading of resources. It also involves a reasonable allocation of time. Concentration on speed and cost-cutting at this stage will tend paradoxically to add to the length and expense of the system as a whole, because poor decisions will automatically, and often successfully, be challenged. Equally important is a culture of decision-making, the primary aim of which is to provide protection to those, and only those, who need it; rather than one which sees its role as the prevention of abuse and thus provides protection only to those whose applications can withstand early and vigorous

---

9 Researcher's conversation with official from the Department of Citizenship and Immigration, Canada (Oct. 1996).

10 The Canadian Immigration and Review Board is an independent tribunal, whose Convention Refugee Determination Division (CRDD) sits as a quasi-judicial body with jurisdiction to determine whether claimants fall within the 1951 Convention and are entitled to refugee status in Canada. For further discussion see *Asylum Determination in Canada*, Supplementary Report No. 2 (JUSTICE/ILPA/ARC, 1997).

11 The Dutch experiment involved a "consultation model" of decision-making, in which applicants were interviewed by Immigration and Nationality Service officials after receiving independent advice from Legal Aid lawyers. Where it was proposed to refuse the applicant, the lawyers were given an opportunity to discuss the provisional refusal, clarify points of fact or detail or put forward arguments in response to the decision-maker without being required first to lodge a formal appeal. For more detail, see Doornbos and Sellies, *Het overlegmodel in de asielprocedure* (1997).

challenge. This is one of the main distinguishing features between the UK system, which recognises around five per cent of applicants as refugees at first instance, and the Canadian system, which has never recognised fewer than 55 per cent.

Second, it is clear that the provision of accurate and up-to-date background documentation reduces the time and resources spent arguing factual issues in each case. Similarly, legal and decision-making systems which are able to clarify precedent and ensure its consistent application will reduce the need for each legal issue to be reargued case by case, and at each level of decision and review. This can be encouraged by effective training, which should aim to increase the decision-makers' awareness of recent significant developments in the law, and improve analytical and adjudication techniques. It may also be facilitated through decision-making guidelines, on the application of criteria or difficult or frequently-arising topics, similar to those used in Canada, Australia and the US for claims raising gender issues.

Third, the experience of the UK and other countries shows the danger of piecemeal and partial attempts to reform the system. These may take the form of grafting on new layers of process, without adequate resources or coordination (as happened in the introduction of the UK appellate process under the Asylum and Immigration Appeals Act 1993); or, more usually, restricting time scales and removing appeals or reviews.[12] The latter are usually counterproductive. In practice "fast-track" procedures have proved to be either too fast to be safe, or too safe to be fast. Often, they add another layer of process, while diverting resources which might better be employed to make the system as a whole more effective. In the same way, cutting down appeal rights may lead to overuse of the courts (as in the UK) or protracted administrative processes (as in Canada). In the case of Switzerland, by contrast, reform of the whole system resulted in a process capable of resolving claims within a year (and a 59 per cent reduction in the number of claims made annually, from almost 42,000 in 1991 to just over 17,000 in 1995).[13]

12 For a historical review of the development of UK asylum law and policy see chapter 1 of this book by Dallal Stevens.

13 "Asylum Applications in States Participating in the Intergovernmental Consultations, 1983–96" (1996) 8 I.J.Ref.L. 486.

The UK System

The UK has a three-tier determination system: initial decision (by the Home Office); an independent review of the facts and merits of the decision (by an adjudicator at appeal); and a second-stage appeal, to identify errors of law or interpretation (before the Immigration Appeal Tribunal). Yet in spite of its length and cost, it is not perceived to be fair by applicants and their representatives, or to be effective by government. It produces a high rate of refusal (over 75 per cent of applicants are refused any form of protection). Refugee advocacy groups claim that this reflects procedures and attitudes which are inimical to providing protection.[14] Government representatives disagree; yet the authorities in many cases are unable or in the end unwilling to remove most of those whose claims are rejected. This is partly because many decisions are badly made and poorly reasoned and cannot in the end by justified and partly because of the length of time it takes to resolve cases: an average of two years to resolve a substantive case if an appeal is lodged. The system carries a backlog of approximately 70,000 unresolved cases, many of which have been in the system for over four years. This disables it from dealing effectively with its current case load.

The most immediate impression is of a system which is uncoordinated, and one in which all the participants, decision-makers, judges and legal representatives, work under great pressure of time and resources. These two problems are not unconnected. Reducing costs and increasing speed are of course legitimate concerns of government. All our research, however, suggests that it is not only unfair, but also procedurally ineffective, to make those the primary aims in any single part of the system. Savings in the early stages can lead to badly-presented and poorly-decided cases which then fall to be reviewed

14 The so-called "culture of disbelief" which is perceived to influence Home Office decision-making in many cases is discussed, e.g., in the Glidewell Panel, *Report from an Independent Enquiry into the Implications and Effects of the Asylum and Immigration Bill 1995 and Related Social Security Measures* (April 1996), in section 4.2.1, pp. 5–8 and 39; evidence given to the Glidewell Panel by Asylum Aid, the Refugee Legal Centre and the Medical Foundation for the Care of Victims of Torture, as discussed in Glidewell Panel report; the apparent prejudgment of claims is discussed in section 7.1 of Jagmohan, J., *The Short Procedure: An Analysis of the Home Office Scheme for Rapid Initial Decisions in Asylum Cases* (ARC, April 1996); refusal decisions are considered in Asylum Aid, *"No reason at all": Home Office Decisions on Asylum Claims* (1995); JUSTICE/ILPA/ARC, *supra* n. 2, chs 3 and 4.

at higher, more expensive levels. Attempts to impose unrealistic time-frames in the early part of a procedure can mean that priorities are skewed to meet those time scales, or that the real decision is remitted elsewhere; so that the process as a whole is lengthened.

The system as it operates at present is not an effective mechanism for making decisions; rather, it is a series of processes to review other people's decisions. This is true even at first instance, where initial decision-makers now rely heavily on information taken at speed by front-line immigration officers, who will also have formed an implicit or explicit view about the strength of the claim and the credibility of the applicant. Issues are often unresolved at this stage, and there is little or no opportunity to clarify issues or correct matters of fact.

As a result, the whole case may be argued again before an adjudicator on appeal; but with the appellant now having to displace a negative decision. Adjudicators are under great pressure, their decisions may be inconsistent, and appellants in many cases are poorly represented or unrepresented. While the overall success rate is low (around four per cent), the most recent statistics for those people represented by the specialist Refugee Legal Centre show a 22 per cent success rate on appeal.[15] Over 50 per cent of unsuccessful applicants seek leave to go to the Tribunal. One in 10 of those decisions is overturned, and in most cases is sent back to be redetermined, thus adding to the pressure on adjudicators. The Tribunal itself is an inconsistent source of precedent and law.[16] Authoritative guidance is therefore increasingly sought from the courts. A case may thus go through four increasingly expensive layers of process before the real issues are identified or dealt with.

Such a process invites challenge and delay. A better system must be able to offer a higher quality, more informed and much more transparent primary decision-making process, supported by better information and training. Such an improved initial determination stage will allow the appellate system to perform its proper function of review. In the UK at present, procedural and structural reforms are needed to make that review process more effective; including the reconstitution of the second-tier Tribunal to make it a body capable of setting clear precedent. This solution would not remove any of the present tiers of review, but it would make their use less necessary and more

15 Statistics on outcomes of appeals to special adjudicators from Refugee Legal Centre *Annual Report* (1997).

16 See also chapters 8 and 9 of this book by Geoffrey Care and Alison Harvey respectively.

manageable by providing better decision-making at an earlier stage. Reform of this kind, and the introduction of certain framework elements which should apply at all stages of the process – central documentation, published guidelines, and criteria which can consider all protection needs concurrently – would reduce cost in the system as a whole.

There are two important underlying issues which must urgently be tackled if an effective and humane system is to be created. First, it will be impossible to create a leaner and more effective system within a reasonably short time-frame without clearing the historic backlog of undecided cases, and granting status to people who cannot in practice be removed because of the length of time they have been in the UK. Second, asylum-seekers must be able to pursue their claims in dignity and humanity. The use of extrajudicial detention,[17] and the removal of social support,[18] are measures of deterrence which are incompatible with proper access to protection procedures. Procedures which operate with reasonable speed and fairness should be able to deal effectively with unmeritorious claims.

The Decision-Making Culture

Initiatives to reform asylum determination must not only address process; they must also recognise the importance of the culture within which decisions are made. The overwhelming impression of the UK system is that there has been no sense of common purpose between those making asylum decisions, and those representing claimants. It has not been a process whereby accepted principles of protection are applied and implemented but rather a battleground. This is partly a result of the adversarial political and legal system in which it

---

17 For an analysis of the present use of detention for asylum seekers in the UK, see e.g. Amnesty International, *Cell Culture: The Detention and Imprisonment of Asylum Seekers in the United Kingdom* (1996); Amnesty International, *Prisoners without a Voice: Asylum Seekers Detained in the United Kingdom* (1994); Asylum Rights Campaign and Churches' Commission for Racial Justice, *Why Detention? Report of a Conference held 6 Nov. 1996* (1996); Joint Council for the Welfare of Immigrants, *Detained without Trial: A Survey of Immigration Act Detention* (1993); Pourgourides, Bracken and Sashidharan, *A Second Exile: The Mental Health Implications of Detention of Asylum Seekers in the United Kingdom* (North Birmingham Mental Health NHS Trust, 1996).

18 Asylum and Immigration Act 1996, SS.9–11 and Schedule 1; see also chapter 18 of this book by Caroline Hunter.

operates; but it is partly the strong cultures which have developed on both sides, and which have produced a fundamental absence of trust. Many decision-makers see lawyers, and the existence of appellate structures, as a problem; most asylum lawyers believe that decisions come out of a "culture of disbelief"[19] whose aim is to challenge, not facilitate, claims.

Constructive proposals must therefore be aimed at changing the culture in which asylum claims are considered. In many other systems, good practice results from formal and informal discussions and consultations between decision-makers, practitioners and refugee groups. In Australia, there is a regular forum of practitioners, government officials and non-governmental agencies to discuss issues of concern. In the Netherlands, new procedures were developed after discussion with lawyers, and reviewed by refugee law academics. Canada's procedures and new legislation are discussed in consultation with refugee advocates, with permanent working parties on particular aspects. There is no equivalent in the UK.

Yet, there are few bodies of lawyers or advocacy groups who have more commitment and experience than those who operate in asylum law. Ongoing discussion between the system's users and government can be a constructive means of identifying problems and possibilities in the process. Failure to engage with non-governmental agencies and individuals weakens the system enormously. First, it reinforces the adversarial model, since contact occurs only in the context of contesting a case, or criticising proposals or laws. Second, it fails to make use of a valuable source of expertise, as many asylum advocates have far more experience than decision-makers. Consultation in individual cases should be improved at the decision-making level. In addition, it is essential to have a forum where general procedural reforms and issues can be discussed between all participants in the system. Such a forum could address the need for and desirable form of reforms to the system. Following those reforms, it would then provide a continuing means of monitoring and improving the determination system.

More Fundamental Change

At this stage, the first, and most urgent, need is to seek to make the present determination structure work better. Much could be done, given the political will, without primary legislation, in the form of changes to regulation or

19 See references *supra* n. 14.

practice. There are, however, more fundamental changes which are suggested by some of the other systems examined. They would include, for example, giving the power to make initial decisions to a body independent of government, as happens in Canada.[20] Radical changes to the present appellate system have also been suggested: the adoption of an inquisitorial procedure (as in Australia);[21] or alternatively the institution of a different and less formal review process.

We consider, however, that it would be extremely dangerous, and on past experience ineffective, to undertake any radical change without a full, independent and costed review of the present legislative and procedural structure. There are strong arguments for undertaking such a review of UK asylum law and policy, in parallel with the immediate changes we suggest above. A review would be an opportunity to examine the whole legislative and procedural framework of immigration and asylum law, and to recommend a coherent and coordinated system. It should also examine immigration and asylum policy as a whole, including the impact (and any necessary mitigation) of the visa and carrier fines regime, and the arguments and scope of temporary forms of protection. Many other countries have found it necessary to undertake such reviews: one is taking place in Canada at present. No further major legislative change should take place without such a review, to avoid the piecemeal approach which, since the Immigration Act 1988, has created systemic problems, by offering only partial solutions.

---

20 *Supra* n. 10.

21 JUSTICE/ILPA/ARC, *Asylum Determination in Australia*, Supplementary Report No. 5 (1997).

Bibliography

Asylum Aid, *"No Reason at All": Home Office Decisions on Asylum Claims* (London, 1995).

Glidewell Panel, *The Asylum and Immigration Bill 1995: Report of the Glidewell Panel* (16 April 1996).

Harvey, A., *"The Risks of Getting it Wrong": The Asylum and Immigration Bill Session 1995–96 and the Determinations of Special Adjudicators* (ARC, 1996).

Henderson, M., *Best Practice Guide to Asylum Appeals* (ILPA, 1997).

Immigration Law Practitioners' Association, *Asylum Seekers: A Guide to Recent Legislation* (ILPA, 1996).

Jagmohan, J., *The Short Procedure: An Analysis of the Home Office Scheme for Rapid Initial Decisions in Asylum Cases* (ARC, 1996).

JUSTICE/ILPA/ARC, *Providing Protection: Towards Fair and Effective Asylum Procedures* (1997).

JUSTICE/ILPA/ARC, *Article 3 ECHR and UNCAT and Humanitarian Protection in Selected Countries*, Supplementary Report No. 1 (1997).

JUSTICE/ILPA/ARC, *Asylum Determination in Canada*, Supplementary Report No. 2 (1997).

JUSTICE/ILPA/ARC, *Asylum Determination in the Netherlands*, Supplementary Report No. 3 (1997).

JUSTICE/ILPA/ARC, *Asylum Determination in Selected European Countries: Germany, Austria, Hungary, Poland and Switzerland*, Supplementary Report No. 4 (1997).

JUSTICE/ILPA/ARC, *Asylum Determination in Australia*, Supplementary Report No. 5 (1997).

Lindsley, F., *Best Practice Guide to the Preparation of Asylum Applications from Arrival to First Substantive Decision* (ILPA, 1994, 2nd edn in preparation).

Refugee Council, *The State of Asylum: A Critique of Asylum Policy in the UK* (March 1996).

Refugee Legal Centre, *Reviewing the Asylum Determination Procedure: A Casework Study* (1997).

11 Taking Human Rights Seriously in the Asylum Context? A Perspective on the Development of Law and Policy

C.J. HARVEY

Introduction

The changes in asylum law and policy in the United Kingdom, as outlined in the preceding chapters and reflected in the provisions of the Asylum and Immigration Appeals Act 1993 (AIAA 1993), the Asylum and Immigration Act 1996 (AIA 1996)[1] and a number of other measures, have given rise to a general concern about the response of the UK to the increase in asylum applications. Western European states have shown that when confronted with the difficult issues raised by movements of refugees and asylum seekers, they are prepared to adopt exclusionary and restrictive policies, which displace the problem onto others. The UK is no exception to this trend. In the face of the "global migration crisis", the challenge for states is not to lose sight of the need for fairness and humanity in the treatment of refugees and asylum seekers, at a time when public policy imperatives are often pulling governments in the opposite direction.

It is important to remember, however, that this requirement is grounded in the legal guarantees which offer protection to the refugee and asylum seeker. The discretion which states possess in the areas of asylum and immigration is "bounded discretion", in the sense that international refugee and human rights

1 See also Statement of Changes in Immigration Rules HC 395 (1993–94), amended HC 797 (1994–95); Cm 3073 (1996); HC 274 (1995–96); HC 329 (1995–96); Cm 3365. (1996). See general bibliography for references to specific works on UK law and practice.

law combine to provide important legal standards which states are obliged to respect. The means adopted to address the increase in asylum claims has raised the question of whether the UK is acting in accordance with international refugee and human rights law and adhering to principles of basic fairness in this area of law and policy.

It is imperative to encourage the construction of a humane asylum determination system at a time when governments no longer view it as being in their interest to accept asylum seekers. As this suggests, developments have not been confined to the UK. In restructuring its asylum law and policy the UK is in line with trends established throughout the European Union (EU).[2] It has been faced with the challenge of trying to ensure the principled application of the 1951 Convention relating to the Status of Refugees,[3] while at the same time removing economic migrants from the refugee determination process. There is enough evidence now available to conclude that the UK has thus far failed to maintain a fair balance. The trend in the evolution of law and policy has been restrictive and focused on deterrence, inspired by the belief that the asylum determination system is under threat from economic migrants seeking to use the procedure for the purpose of entry.[4] The overall policy objective is stated to be the removal of economic migrants from the process without at the same time prejudicing the claims of "genuine" refugees.[5] A point worth making here is that, given the emphasis placed on this claim, the government has failed to provide convincing empirical evidence to support it. In fact, much of the reasoning adopted has been entirely circular. Simply referring to low refugee recognition rates is not enough, as this fact may be

---

2 For analysis of developments at EU level see chapter 3 of this book by Richard Dunstan; Wallace, R., *Refugees and Asylum: A Community Perspective* (1996); Joly, D., *Haven or Hell? Asylum Policies and Refugees in Europe* (1996); Guild, E., *The Developing Immigration and Asylum Policies of the European Union: Adopted Conventions, Resolutions, Recommendations, Decisions and Conclusions* (1996); Joly, D., "The Porous Dam: European Harmonisation on Asylum in the Nineties" (1994) 6 I.J.Ref.L. 159; Hathaway, J., "Harmonizing for Whom? The Devaluation of Refugee Protection in the Era of European Economic Co-operation" (1993) 26 Corn. Int. L.J. 719.

3 189 U.N.T.S. 137, entry into force 22 April 1954.

4 Ireland is the latest EU Member State to become embroiled in this debate, following an increase in applications from 39 in 1992 to 1,179 in 1996, see *Irish Times*, 19 April 1997. A new Refugee Act was adopted in 1996.

5 H.C. Hansard, Vol. 268, Col. 699–703, 11 Dec. 1995, (M. Howard, Secretary of State for the Home Department); H.C. Hansard, Vol. 213, Col. 22, 2 Nov. 1992, (K. Clarke, Secretary of State for the Home Department).

explained by a number of other variables, which have nothing to do with the merits of individual applications. In practice the ubiquitous logic of deterrence fuels the "culture of disbelief" surrounding applications, and undoubtedly impacts on how the 1951 Convention is interpreted and applied by administrative bodies. Considering the serious evidential difficulties involved in asylum cases, the attempt to divide applicants into formal (and simplistic) categories was bound to be problematic, and so it has proved in practice.

While it is important to map the latest legal developments, it also pays to reflect on the broader aspects of the asylum issue. As stated, legal discourse may function to break down a difficult international phenomenon, such as forced migration, into categories which fail to reflect the complexities of this all-too-human problem.[6] Restrictive interpretation of the 1951 Convention simply exacerbates this. Citizens of the 20th century have paid a high price for the dominance of instrumental forms of rationality. Whether it is in a more general context or in the attitude towards refugees and asylum seekers, the destruction wrought by treating everything and everyone purely as a means to satisfy narrowly defined policy objectives is now clear. The desire to reach the "view from nowhere", fostered by instrumental rationality, has had some appalling consequences for humanity. That we are all situated critics, engaged in rational discourse, should alert us to the need not to perpetuate approaches to asylum law and policy which mask the contextual nature of our analysis and practical reasoning. As stated, the result for the refugee of a failure to recognise this is that the complexity of his or her plight is often obscured by exclusionary legal discourses which neglect the purpose of refugee and asylum law.

When making this claim, however, it is also necessary to accept that refugee law is not blameless in this process. The inadequacies of the law are well documented. While law is thus implicated in the problems which the refugee faces, the constructive interpretation[7] and application of refugee and human rights law should negate pure utilitarian calculations, and give recognition to the deontological nature of basic human rights. In other words, by adopting this "internal" participant perspective (with all that this means in terms of interpretative strategies) it becomes clear that international refugee and human

6 For an interesting sociological analysis of the theories of migration, and the complexities of the problem see Richmond, A., *Global Apartheid: Refugees, Racism and the New World Order* (1994), 47–73.

7 For one particular definition of constructive interpretation see Dworkin, R., *Law's Empire,* (1986), at 52. See also Habermas, J., *Between Facts and Norms: Contributions to a Discourse Theory of Law and Democracy* (1996), 203–29.

rights law are areas where critical engagement will continue to yield progressive results. This critique of consequentialist reasoning is particularly important for those minority groups which are inadequately represented within the democratic process.

In this chapter the aim is to analyse some of the more recent changes in asylum law, which requires that the issue be placed in context. Therefore the international and European dimensions will be explored, followed by some consideration of the purpose and function of asylum law.

Paradigm Shifts, Interdependence and the Changing Face of Public Law: Recognising the Importance of the International and European Dimensions

As with public law generally, it is no longer adequate to ignore the international and European dimensions of the asylum issue.[8] This is especially true of asylum law where refugee movements must be viewed as an inherently "international" problem. The international dimension includes both the normative constraints upon state action contained in international human rights law, and insights derived from a knowledge of the practical reality of forced displacement. For example, in relation to international human rights law, there are a number of guarantees which are directly applicable to refugees and asylum seekers (even if at present they remain, in formal terms, unenforceable in UK courts).[9] When

8 See Morison, J., and Livingstone, S., *Reshaping Public Power: Northern Ireland and the British Constitutional Crisis* (1995) at 34, the authors argue that the orthodox approach to British constitutionalism is in serious trouble. This is traced to the failure to accommodate new forms of international and supranational order; Hunt, M., *Using Human Rights Law in English Courts* (1997), for an interesting critique of the "traditional account of the UK's constitutional arrangements", and its inadequacy in the light of international and other developments.

9 Although the orthodox position on incorporation retains its grip, it is deficient in many significant respects, and a strong case may be made for a rethink, see Hunt *op. cit. supra* n. 8. A good example of an international human rights instrument, of relevance here, is the UN Convention Against Torture and Other Cruel, Inhuman or Degrading Treatment or Punishment 1984 (UNGA Res. 39/46, 10 Dec. 1984, Art. 3. See *Ismail Alan v. Switzerland* Communication No. 21/1995 4 I.H.R.R. (1997) 66; *X. v. The Netherlands* Communication No. 36/1995 4 I.H.R.R. (1997) 73; *Pauline Muzonzo Paku Kisoki v. Sweden* Communication No. 41/1996 4 I.H.R.R. (1997) 78; *Mutombo v. Switzerland* Communication No. 13/1994, printed in (1995) 7 I.J.Ref.L. 322; *Khan v. Canada* Communication No. 15/1994 15

focusing on international refugee law (and its inherent limitations) it is essential not to neglect this body of law.[10] This is important at a time when a growing number of public lawyers are recognising the inadequacy of traditional conceptions of the subject.

In addition, there is the familiar problem of the way in which the law constructs "refugee identity".[11] Refugee law contains a limited conception of the refugee. It is a legal term of art designed for particular purposes.[12] The difficulty here is that, conceived from a needs-based perspective, it is inadequate as an inclusive legal tool for refugee protection (if this term is applied more holistically to include all those coerced into fleeing their place of residence).[13] A substantial number of individuals, who are forced to flee their homes, do not come within the 1951 Convention definition, yet remain in need of some form of protection.[14] This is reflected, for example, in the widespread application of a variety of "humanitarian" categories, which states employ in often ill-defined ways in domestic law.[15]

The centrality accorded to the concept of alienage is also problematic.[16] This continues to privilege boundaries in the classification of need at a time when some have noted a tendency to move "beyond borders" in the treatment

---

H.R.L.J. (1994) 426. In its Conclusions and Recommendations on the Report submitted to it in 1995 by the UK government, the Committee Against Torture expressed concern about the practice of *refouling* asylum seekers, and recommended a review of practices related to deportation and *refoulement*, 4 I.H.R.R. 493 (1997), paras. 7(e) and 8(b). See also UN Convention on the Rights of the Child 1989 (UNGA A/RES/44/25, 5 Dec. 1989 Annex, 28 I.L.M. 1448 (1989) Art. 22). See also Cohen, C., "The UN Convention on the Rights of the Child: Implications for Change in the Care and Protection of Refugee Children" (1991) 3 I.J.Ref.L. 675.

10 See Goodwin-Gill, G.S., "Who to Protect, How ..., and the Future?" (1997) 9 I.J.Ref.L 1, 2–3. See also n. 27.

11 For a critique of the way the law constructs the "refugee" see Tuitt, P., *False Images: The Law's Construction of the Refugee* (1996).

12 Goodwin-Gill, G.S., *The Refugee in International Law* (Clarendon, Oxford, 2nd edn, 1996) at 3.

13 Shacknove, A., "Who is a Refugee?" (1984–85) 95 Ethics 274.

14 Restrictive interpretation of the 1951 Convention has also contributed to this problem.

15 See Lambert, H., *Seeking Asylum: Comparative Law and Practice in Selected European Countries* (1995), 126–44; Dacyl, J., "Europe Needs a New Protection System for 'Non-Convention' Refugees" (1995) 7 I.J.Ref.L. 579.

16 See Hathaway, J., *The Law of Refugee Status* (1991) at 29.

of such international problems.[17] This has had a particularly damaging impact on gender issues in refugee law discourse, where the focus on exile, combined with the limited definition of refugee status, has resulted in the neglect of the plight of women refugees.[18]

With regard to the realities of forced displacement, there has been some new thinking in recent times, inspired by a willingness to view the problem within a more comprehensive framework.[19] Refugee law's focus on alienage and exile is criticised because of the resulting tendency to ignore the root causes of flight and more general issues surrounding prevention. It is a truism that migration and asylum are not the answers to the political, social and economic inequalities which fuel the policies of repressive governments, and which contribute towards the creation of refugee movements. With the ensuing turn to root causes and focus on prevention, there is now a willingness to develop new, more comprehensive strategies, and thus a number of the past problems and deficiencies are beginning to be addressed.[20] While this is a welcome development, an element of caution is required. The study of refugees and asylum seekers is not an either/or issue. A more inclusive approach which is alive to the problematic nature of partial perspectives demands genuine recognition of all aspects of the problem. What it should not do is allow states to evade responsibility for protecting refugees on the basis of highly abstract (and ultimately hollow) commitments to concepts such as prevention and the

17 See Ferris, E., *Beyond Borders: Refugees, Migrants and Human Rights in the Post Cold War Era* (World Council of Churches, Geneva, 1993); Collinson, S., *Beyond Borders: West European Migration Policy Towards the 21st Century* (Royal Institute of International Affairs, London, 1993).

18 The 1951 Convention does not, for example, include reference to persecution on grounds of gender. In recognition of the problems that may arise attempts have been made recently to draft guidelines on gender-based claims to asylum. The Canadian Immigration and Refugee Board published its *Guidelines on Women Refugee Claimants Fearing Gender-Related Persecution* in March 1993 and updated them in Nov. 1996. The US Immigration and Naturalisation Service issued gender guidelines, *Considerations for Asylum Officers Adjudicating Asylum Claims from Women*, in May 1995. In Oct. 1993 the UNHCR Executive Committee adopted Conclusion no. 73 on Refugee Protection and Sexual Violence. See also UNHCR, *Sexual Violence against Refugees: Guidelines on Prevention and Response* (extracts) (1995) 7 I.J.Ref.L. 720.

19 UNHCR, *The State of the World's Refugees: In Search of Solutions* (1995), ch. 1.

20 *Ibid.* at 19.

"right to remain".[21] In other words, the "turn to root causes" should not distract attention excessively from the fact that there is still a pressing need to ensure that asylum determination procedures within states are as fair and effective as possible. One must engage with a dual perspective in this area of social enquiry.

Analysis of the international dimension must be supplemented with consideration of the European aspects of the issue. Although progress has been sluggish,[22] it is apparent that there has been a steady "Europeanisation" of asylum and immigration law. EU Member States have adopted a number of measures in an attempt to secure common practice in this area.[23] The concepts which have been agreed upon are well known, and there is no need to examine them in detail here. The general trend is the adoption of what is best described as a "lowest common denominator" approach to asylum; a fact reflected in the disappointing scope of the minimum guarantees for asylum seekers adopted in a Council Resolution of June 1995[24] and the Joint Position on the definition of refugee status.[25] While the substance of the common policies adopted may be criticised, the overall process must also be questioned. The often secretive and unaccountable nature of policy development by EU States (exacerbated by the intergovernmental nature of the "third pillar" of the Treaty on European Union) is inappropriate at a time when minorities within the EU are recognised to be experiencing increasing harassment from racist and xenophobic elements in society. An open approach to policy development should therefore be the norm in this area and not the exception.

---

21 Goodwin-Gill, G.S., "The Right to Leave, the Right to Return and the Question of the Right to Remain", in *The Problem of Refugees in the Light of Contemporary International Law Issues* Gowlland-Debbas, V., ed. (Martinus Nijhoff, 1996); Hathaway, J., "New Directions to Avoid Hard Problems: The Distortion of the Palliative Role of Refugee Protection" (1995) 8 J.R.S. 288.

22 Giving rise to calls for reform of the present institutional arrangements.

23 See *Compilation of Texts on European Practice with Respect to Asylum*, General Secretariat of the Council, 4464/1/95 REV of 25 April 1996, and *Acts adopted under Title VI of the Treaty on European Union* (1996) O.J. C274, 19 Sept. 1996, for useful collections of some of the relevant texts.

24 5585/95, adopted 20 June 1995, (1996) O.J. C274/13. See also EP Resolution on the Council Resolution on minimum guarantees for asylum procedures, (1996) O.J. C362/270.

25 Joint Position on the Harmonised Application of the Definition of the term "refugee" (1996) O.J. L63/2. For a critical discussion of the general trends in policy-making see Ward, I., "Law and Other Europeans" (1997) 35 J.C.M.S. 79, 83–5.

The provisions of the Treaty of Amsterdam suggest that there is potential for more progressive legal regulation in the future.

There is little doubt that this evolving process is having an important impact on the nature of the legal changes in the UK. While it is possible to be highly critical of developments thus far at EU level, there is also room for more imaginative approaches in the future. Concepts such as burden-sharing and international solidarity are central to any defensible, and ethical, asylum regime.[26] By developing cooperation between Member States, the EU may help to avoid short-term reactions to refugee movements. While such an approach is eminently desirable in theory, it has proved rather harder to apply in practice. It appears that it will take some time before the requisite level of trust is established between Member States for them to explore more progressive joint policies in this area. In addition to the development of more inclusive concepts, the need for institutional reform, which increases both the judicial and democratic scrutiny of this area, must not be forgotten.

The European dimension is not exhausted simply by recognising the centrality of EU developments; the regional human rights mechanisms have also had an impact on this area of law and policy. Recent judgments of the European Court of Human Rights have, for example, demonstrated the relevance of the Convention to the asylum seeker and any individual facing extradition, expulsion, deportation, or removal.[27] It is now established that the guarantee under Article 3 of the European Convention for the Protection of Human Rights and Fundamental Freedoms 1950 (ECHR), which states that "no one shall be subjected to torture or to inhuman or degrading treatment or punishment", "enshrines one of the most fundamental values of democratic society".[28] It is thus of wider scope than both Articles 32 and 33 of the 1951 Refugee Convention.

The above is an attempt to demonstrate that it is no longer possible to view this area of public law separately from its international and European contexts. It is only when the wider dynamics of the issue are understood that more clarity may be gained in considering what the asylum determination system in a state may be expected to achieve, and how improvements may be

26 See EXCOM Conclusion No. 52 (XXXIX), *International Solidarity and Refugee Protection*; EU Council (JHA) Resolution on Burden-Sharing, Bull. EU 6–1995 132; Harvey, C., "Restructuring Asylum: Recent Trends in UK Asylum Law and Policy" (1997) 9 I.J.Ref.L. 60 at 70.

27 See chapter 12 of this book by Nicholas Blake.

28 *Soering v. United Kingdom* (1989) 11 E.H.R.R. 439, para. 88. See also *Chahal v. United Kingdom* (1997) 23 E.H.R.R. 413, para. 79.

made. Orthodox conceptions of sovereignty, which disguise this complexity, are now inadequate because of their failure to capture this process.

The Purpose and Function of Asylum Law

The protean nature of the concept of asylum may give rise to a number of problems. Its association with the lone political offender tends to highlight an individualistic bias, which may function at the expense of a neglect of the group nature of most refugee movements. Another related issue is the link made to permanent settlement in a state which, interestingly, has never been an explicit aspect of condified refugee law. Given that the substance of asylum is defined in the law and practice of individual states, it is arguable that there is nothing necessary about this conclusion. In the UK the term has been linked solely to the 1951 Convention, which is unfortunate in the light of other developments in human rights law relating to the prohibition on expulsion.[29]

There are, of course, reasons why refugee law contains an individualistic bias, and as the discussion below makes clear, the requirement of individual assessment is a definite advantage when criticising some of the recent excesses in state policy. Historical analysis reveals that the states which drafted the 1951 Convention were concerned not to grant a "blank cheque" and thus assume an unlimited future obligation.[30] The history of the various attempts to conclude an international instrument on asylum reveals a marked reluctance to commit to binding obligations in this area.[31] While Article 14 of the Universal Declaration on Human Rights refers to "the right to seek and enjoy asylum from persecution", it is well known that this is a non-binding instrument. The right to grant asylum remains a right of the state. It is nevertheless important to note that while the state is not obliged to grant *de jure* asylum, international law now contains specific prohibitions on return in

29 See *supra* n. 9 for developments concerning 1984 Convention against Torture and 1989 Convention on the Rights of the Child, and chapter 12 of this book by Nicholas Blake for developments concerning European Convention on Human Rights.

30 See e.g., Mr Rochefort (France) UN A/CONF.2/SR.22, 12–8.

31 See UN Declaration on Territorial Asylum, UNGA Res. 2312 (XXIX), 14 Dec. 1967; Report of the UN Conference on Territorial Asylum, UN Doc. A/CONF.78/12, 21 April 1977; Weis, P., "The Draft Convention on Territorial Asylum" (1979) 50 B.Y.I.L. 176; Plender, R., "Admission of Refugees: Draft Convention on Territorial Asylum" (1977) 15 *San Diego Law Review* 45.

a number of defined contexts. It is no longer appropriate to continue to refer exclusively to the absence of a duty upon the state to grant asylum when there is now such a strong and well-defined obligation of *non-refoulement*. The concepts are so intertwined that drawing rigid boundaries becomes rather artificial, although states continue to insist on making such distinctions in practice. The argument is reinforced if one considers that the prohibition on *refoulement* applies when the refugee presents herself at the frontier of the state. It is in fact the principle of *non-refoulement* which grounds the human rights orientation of refugee law and provides the link to the subsequent obligations of states to respect fundamental human rights.

It has been argued above that asylum law in the UK must be studied within its international and European contexts. However, this does not exhaust the demands of a contextual approach. Although rather artificial, a loose (and somewhat fluid) distinction between external and internal contexts may be drawn. The asylum process, as with any other social institution, serves certain purposes. When administering and/or adjudicating in the area it is possible to neglect the fact that purpose must be ascribed, in the sense that when we interpret we are all situated participants in the law and policy community. While historical analysis might reveal the limited original purposes of the drafters of the 1951 Convention, it is a document whose meaning is far from unambiguous. When imposing an interpretation upon the text it is important to view it purposively as a living body of law. In other words, if the 1951 Convention is not to become irrelevant to the world's refugees then it does need to be interpreted in the light of contemporary developments and trends. This requires that those entrusted with law application recognise and make explicit the paradigmatic understanding under which they are operating. This is not, however, to suggest the imposition of the values of the interpreter. The text of the Convention contains limitations which have to be recognised as such. The reason for the emphasis on purpose is the well-founded belief that policy factors may lead to a restrictive interpretation if due regard is not paid to the imperative of protection. Following this line of argument, asylum law must function in order to ensure the fair, effective and efficient assessment of asylum claims. The law should facilitate this process and not follow an exclusionary regulatory strategy.

Developments in Law and Policy

In the rest of this chapter some of the more recent legal developments will be examined, and their implications explored. When focusing on the changes in the UK it is again important to remember how many of these concepts and policies are now applied by other EU Member States.[32] Several of these developments are described in more detail elsewhere in this book, therefore the following is intended as an overview in support of the specific argument advanced in this chapter.

In response to the increase in applications, the UK has made a number of alterations to its system of refugee protection. The overriding policy objective has been control orientated, with the emphasis on the reduction of the number of those seeking asylum, and the acceleration of the asylum process. In 1996 there was a substantial reduction in asylum applications, leading the Conservative government to claim success for its policy of deterrence.[33] In seeking to achieve these aims, measures have been adopted which are not confined solely to the asylum determination system. The end result is that the case-by-case assessment of applications on their individual merits has been compromised in the drive to deal with the delays in the system. Efficiency in the administrative process is to be welcomed, but not if it is at the expense of fairness and effective assessment of applications.

"Safe Third Countries"

One of the most well-known aspects of recent law and policy is the "safe third country" concept.[34] The premise for its adoption and use is that the asylum seeker should be expected to claim refuge in the first safe country she reaches. Refugee law does not exclude the notion of individual choice,[35] but states use the safe third country concept to such an extent that it is now one of the most embedded concepts in the operation of the emerging EU asylum policy.

---

32 Care, G., ed., *A Guide to Asylum Law and Practice in the European Union,* (ILPA, Dec. 1995); UNHCR, *Legal Factsheets on Asylum Procedures in Western Europe,* July 1993.

33 H.C. Hansard, Vol. 290, Cols 1030–31, 20 Feb. 1997. The figure for 1996 was 27,930, a 36 per cent decrease. The same trend is also evident throughout the EU, see EUROSTAT, *Asylum Seekers,* 1996/2. In 1995 the number of applications in the EU, Norway and Switzerland decreased by almost 37,000 from approx. 325,000 in 1994 to 290,000, EUROSTAT, *Asylum Seekers,* 1996/1.

34 AIA 1996 s.2; Immigration Rules HC 395 para. 345 (amended Cm 3365 1996). For further details see chapter 4 of this book by Rachel Trost and Peter Billings.

35 Hathaway *op. cit. supra* n. 16 at 46.

Although it is now applied by a large number of states, it still gives rise to problems, and its basis in international law remains insecure.[36] In the absence of an effective international mechanism for cooperation in this area there is an inherent risk in the widespread application of the concept that in some cases *refoulement* will be the end result.[37] Returning an asylum seeker to another state on the basis of transitory contact with that state is a highly questionable practice, with potentially devastating implications for the individual involved.[38] Simply constructing a system within the EU which allocates responsibility is not enough, particularly as states retain the right to return an asylum seeker to a third state outside of the EU.[39] There must be concrete guarantees that the asylum seeker will be granted effective protection from *refoulement* in the third state, based upon clear evidence of admissibility. Effective protection refers not only to formal adherence to international obligations, but also to genuine access to procedures in the third state, and respect for the asylum seeker's basic human rights.[40] There are, for example, a number of practical reasons why an asylum seeker may be prevented from securing effective protection in the third state, indicating that any information upon which an assessment is based needs to focus on the practical application of the law in the third state.[41] Further to this, there is the protection afforded

36 For an impressive critique of UK policy see Amnesty International *Playing Human Pinball: Home Office Practice in "Safe Third Country" Cases* (1995). See also UNHCR Regional Bureau for Europe, *An Overview of Protection Issues in Western Europe: Legislative Trends and Positions Taken by UNHCR,* (1995) European Series, 18. UNHCR takes the view that application of the concept is legitimate but because of the extended scope given by some states to the basic concept it prefers not to refer to it as a "principle".

37 See Goodwin-Gill. *op. cit. supra* n. 12 at 341–42.

38 UNHCR *op. cit. supra* n. 36 at 20–1. Note that Conclusion No. 58 (XL) refers to an individual who has *already found protection* in a third state.

39 Dublin Convention 1990 Art. 3(5). Entered into force 1 Sept. 1997 (O.J. 1997 C254/1). See "Conclusion concerning the Practical Implementation of the Dublin Convention" (O.J. 1997 C191/27). Several decisions have been taken by the Executive Committee. See Decision No. 1 (O.J. 1997 L281/1), Decision No. 2 (O.J. 1997 L281/26).

40 The third state's procedures should ideally be in line with the recommendations of the Executive Committee of UNHCR, see e.g., Conclusion No. 8 (XXVIII), *Determination of Refugee Status,* Conclusion No. 30 (XXXIV), *The Problem of Manifestly Unfounded or Abusive Applications for Asylum.*

41 Goodwin-Gill *op. cit. supra* n. 12 at 343.

by Article 3 ECHR to be considered.[42] There is a need to ensure that the sending state respects the protections contained in both these instruments and, as stated, that the receiving state has a good record of general human rights observance and protection.

Finally, the morally questionable nature of the concept should not be ignored. Reflective reconstruction of basic intuitions about the concept suggests that there is a problem relating to the element of evasion on the part of affluent European states, which are no longer willing to welcome significant numbers of asylum seekers. Is it then ultimately just or fair for the asylum seeker to be returned to states which are not equipped to offer the same level of procedural fairness as may exist in Western Europe? This question of justice and fairness is now rather academic in the sense that the term is widely accepted and applied by states, but it is one that is still worth asking when considering the concept's legitimacy. If it continues to play such a major part in the law and practice of EU Member States, then before it can ever be accepted as a *principle*, it must include the various guarantees and protections discussed above.

"Safe Countries of Origin"

The AIA 1996 extends the "fast-track" appeals procedure, established in the AIAA 1993, to include a range of other concepts which will in future be applied to asylum applicants.[43] The concepts which have been adopted are viewed as being essential to the operation of accelerated procedures. The aims of the new procedure are to be achieved through the use of a certification process. The implication of certification is that the appellant is allowed to appeal to a Special Adjudicator (SA) who will deal initially with the certification issue, before being permitted to examine the substance of the application.[44] There are also a variety of procedural restrictions which are applicable to certified appeals.[45]

---

42 See EU Resolution on a Harmonised Approach to Questions concerning Host Third Countries, Nov./Dec. 1992, para. 2(b) which states that the asylum applicant must not be exposed to torture or inhuman or degrading treatment in the third country. Para. 2(d) provides that the asylum applicant must be afforded "effective protection" against *refoulement* in the third state.

43 AIA 1996 s.1.

44 AIA 1996 s.3.

45 The Asylum Appeals (Procedure) Rules 1996 S.I. 1996/2070.

One of the concepts which attracted a great deal of attention during the passage of the Bill through its parliamentary stages was that of safe country of origin.[46] While relatively novel in the UK context, it has been around for some time, and is part of the law and practice of a number of other Member States.[47] The concept springs primarily from the desire to accelerate procedures for some applicants, and from the belief that there are countries which may be regarded as safe for the purposes of assessing asylum applications.[48] It is part of a process of introducing aspects of "group determination"; the intention being to classify claims from listed states as initially unfounded.[49] The basic idea is that such claims may be dealt with more quickly. In theory this sounds straightforward, but as the practice has revealed, there are a number of serious difficulties which may compromise both the requirement of individual assessment and the prohibition on *refoulement.*

The willingness of the Conservative government to adopt and apply concepts developed at EU level has been noted above. This is no exception to the general rule. In 1992 the European Community Ministers responsible for immigration adopted a "Conclusion on countries in which there is generally no serious risk of persecution".[50] The Conclusion defines the concept as applying to countries which can clearly be shown, in an *objective and verifiable way*,[51] not normally to generate refugee flows, or where the circumstances which may have justified past recourse to the Convention have ceased to exist.

46 See H.C. Hansard, Vol. 268, Cols 699–711, 11 Dec. 1995; H.C. Hansard, Vol. 281, Cols 807–25, 15 July 1996. For general comment on the concept and problems that may arise see Winterbourne, W., Shah, P., and Doebbler, C., "Refugees and Safe Countries of Origin: Appeals, Judicial Review and Human Rights Law" (1996) 10 I.N.L.P. 123; Harvey, C., "The Right to Seek Asylum in the UK and 'Safe Countries'" [1996] P.L. 196. For further detailed discussion see chapter 4 of this book by Trost and Billings.

47 See Lambert *op. cit. supra* n. 15 at 88–91; Hailbronner, K., "The Concept of Safe Country and Expedient Asylum Procedures" CAHAR (91) 2.

48 H.C. Hansard, Vol. 268, Col.702, 11 Dec. 1995 (M. Howard, Secretary of State for the Home Department).

49 Another example of this is the "short procedure" introduced by the Home Office in May 1995, see Jagmohan, J., *The Short Procedure: An Analysis of the Home Office Scheme for Rapid Initial Decisions in Asylum Cases* (Asylum Rights Campaign, April 1996).

50 SN 4821/92 WGI 1281.

51 The use of "objective" and "verifiable" suggests that the information on which the assessment is based should be publicly available.

As to the countries which are designated as safe, the issue was debated in parliament on 15–16 October 1996.[52] Agreement was reached on the first list of safe countries which are Bulgaria, Cyprus, Ghana, India, Pakistan, Poland and Romania.[53] It is interesting to note the inclusion of India on this list in the light of the judgment of the European Court of Human Rights in *Chahal.*[54] When introducing the Asylum and Immigration Bill the Home Secretary listed three criteria to be adopted when applying the concept: there must be in general no serious risk of persecution; the country must generate large numbers of applications; and a large proportion of the applications must be unfounded.[55]

It is evident from the EU Conclusion that Member States are aware of their international legal obligations in this area. The UK government has also stressed that certification in this context will not lead to blanket refusals. In theory the commitment to case-by-case assessment remains. It is, however, difficult to see how such an initial presumption will not impact on assessment of the individual application. It is apparent that it will compromise the particularity of the "reasonable likelihood of persecution" test.[56] This is the end result of a process which is intent on privileging rapid decision-making over the need for fairness in the individual case. It is worth stressing again that the effective implementation of refugee law requires that general assessments of the safety of states of origin do not automatically lead to a negative decision.

Other Categories

The safe country concept is only one in a list of concepts which may give rise to the certification of an application.[57] It is apparent from the new legislation that there is a deep-seated official suspicion surrounding the stage at which

---

52 H.C. Hansard, Vol. 282, Col. 691, 15 Oct. 1996; H.L. Hansard, Vol. 574, Col. 1690, 16 Oct. 1996.

53 The Asylum (Designated Countries of Destination and Designated Safe Third Countries) Order 1996 S.I. No. 2671/1996.

54 *Chahal v. UK*, *supra* n. 28.

55 H.C. Hansard, Vol. 268, Col. 703, 11 Dec. 1995.

56 See *R. v. Secretary of State for the Home Department, ex p. Sivakumaran* [1988] A.C. 958. H.C. Hansard, Vol. 268, Col. 719, 11 Dec. 1995 (J. Straw); Goodwin-Gill *op. cit. supra* n. 12 at 348; Marx, R., "*Non-Refoulement,* Access to Procedures, and Responsibility for Determining Refugee Claims" (1995) 7 I.J.Ref.L. 383 at 402–3.

57 AIA 1996 s.1.

an application is made. Care is needed here, however, primarily because the focus of refugee law is on preventing *refoulement*, and not the stage at which an asylum application is made. There are good reasons why an asylum applicant may seek to delay making a claim. Attempts to divide applications on the basis of questionable, and ultimately flawed, assumptions need to be avoided.

The concepts which will now serve to trigger certification are potentially of wide scope, and they refer to a number of factors unconnected to the strict merits of the individual's case. As indicated, the measures are based on assumptions which may simply not be applicable in the highly specific asylum context.[58]

Discouraging Asylum Seeking?

The Conservative government was willing to secure the aims of its asylum policy by any means at its disposal. In other words, it was prepared to move beyond the asylum determination process in an attempt to enforce aspects of its punitive regulatory strategy. Given this major premise in the construction of law and policy, it was unsurprising that it sought to exclude a number of asylum applicants from social security and other welfare entitlements. It was against this aspect of policy that the courts displayed a willingness in intervene in an attempt to secure the protection of basic rights for asylum seekers.

The rather simplistic underlying idea upon which the policy was constructed (based on an inappropriate neoclassical economic theory of migration) was that the UK would become less attractive to economic migrants if the entitlements were removed from certain categories of asylum applicants.[59] The thinking is reflected in the much criticised[60] Social Security

58 See chapter 8 of this book by Geoffrey Care.

59 See H.C. Hansard, Vol. 281, Col. 845, 15 July 1996 (P. Lilley, Secretary of State for Social Security). In this statement he makes the assumption that the numbers will be small. *The 1951 Convention makes no reference to any such quantitative restrictions*. For analysis of the living conditions of refugees in Britain see *The Settlement of Refugees in Britain*, Home Office Research Study No. 141 (1995).

60 See Glidewell Panel, *The Report from an Independent Enquiry into the Implications and Effects of the Asylum and Immigration Bill 1995 and Related Social Security Measures* (16 April 1996), 37–8; *Report by the Social Security Advisory Committee under Section 174(1) of the Social Security Administration Act 1992*, Cm 3062, Jan. 1996; Amnesty International, *Slamming the Door: The Demolition of the Right to Asylum in the UK* (1996), 10–21.

(Persons from Abroad) Miscellaneous Amendment Regulations 1996,[61] implemented from 5 February 1996. The events which followed the adoption of the Regulations are now well known, and provide an example of what amounted to a bitter struggle between the government and the judges as to the final shape of asylum law.[62] The Regulations were challenged by the Joint Council for the Welfare of Immigrants (JCWI) and an asylum applicant, B. In *R. v. Security of State for Social Security, ex p. JCWI; ex p. B.*[63] the appellants argued that the Regulations were indeed *ultra vires* the Social Security Contributions and Benefits Act 1992 because parliament could not have intended to confer power to interfere in such a serious way with statutory rights protected in the AIAA 1993. The Court of Appeal held that the Regulations were *ultra vires*, and Simon Brown LJ made some strongly worded (and well-publicised) remarks about the nature of the changes and the impact on asylum applicants. He noted (as the Glidewell Panel among others had done) that the Regulations would affect all asylum applicants, genuine refugees included. The government reacted to the judgment by seeking to reinstate the Regulations, with a hurried amendment to the Asylum and Immigration Bill as it was going through its parliamentary stages in the House of Lords.[64] The amendments are now reflected in the AIA 1996.[65]

The story did not end there. In *R. v. Hammersmith and Fulham London Borough Council ex p. M.; R. v. Lambeth London Borough Council ex p. P.;*

61 S.I. No. 30/1996.

62 See Rozenberg, J., "Opposition Benches", *Guardian,* 6 May 1997.

63 [1996] 4 All E.R. 385; [1997] 1 W.L.R. 275 (C.A.).

64 H.L. Hansard, Vol. 573, Col. 596, 24 June 1996. For concern about the speed of this process see H.L. Hansard, Vol. 573, Cols 1016–27, 27 June 1996. The events which followed the judgment show that on this occasion the Court of Appeal was prepared to take fundamental human rights much more seriously than parliament.

65 AIA 1996 s.11, sch. 1. It is noteworthy that the new Home Secretary, Jack Straw, (possibly heralding a new era in this area of public law) made a declaration on 16 May 1997 with regard to applicants from Zaïre. This was the first time that the power had been used, see *Guardian,* 17 May 1997. A similar declaration with respect to Sierra Leone was made as of 1 July 1997. See also AIA 1996 s. 8. Immigration (Restrictions on Employment) Order S.I. No. 3225/1996; AIA 1996 s. 9. Homelessness Regulations S.I. No. 2754/1996; Housing Accommodation and Homelessness (Persons Subject to Immigration Control) S.I. No.1982/1996. See *R. v. Secretary of State for the Environment, ex p. Shelter and the Refugee Council,* 23 Aug. 1996 (unreported); AIA 1996 s.10. See also *R. v. Newham L.B.C., ex p. Gorenkin, Times Law Report* 9 June 1997. See chapter 18 of this book by Caroline Hunter.

R. v. Westminster City Council ex p. A.; R. v. Lambeth London Borough Council ex p. X.[66] the Court of Appeal held that the National Assistance Act 1948 s.21(1)(a) should be interpreted in the light of current developments, and it thus placed a responsibility on local authorities to provide assistance to asylum seekers who fulfilled the relevant criteria. The court held that parliament could not have intended that those in need be without recourse to assistance. The role of the courts in protecting vulnerable groups[67] (and the implications of a teleological approach to interpretation) were again demonstrated. The burden of provision therefore shifted from central government to local authorities.[68]

A point made consistently by those engaged in criticism of the above measures has been that the most appropriate place to deal with asylum claims which are said to lack merit is within the asylum determination process.[69] The fact is that the measures potentially affect "genuine refugees", and discourage applicants from making use of the determination system.[70] The need to ensure effective access must extend to providing basic entitlements to welfare benefits while this process is ongoing. If this is not the case then the refugee may be constructively *refouled*, in the indirect sense that she will be compelled to leave because of her economic circumstances.[71] It is also a basic

66 *Times Law Report,* 19 Feb. 1997.

67 Cf. *R. v. Secretary of State for the Home Department, ex p. Abdi and Gawe* HL [1996] 1 W.L.R. 298.

68 Some London authorities have been particularly displeased with this result. Westminster Council, for example, proposed to move hundreds of asylum seekers to Liverpool in order to cut costs, *Guardian,* 16 May 1997. See also H.C. Hansard, Vol. 291, Cols 837–58, 5 March 1997, a debate on the problems faced by a number of London boroughs; H.C. Hansard, Vol. 292, Cols 268–69, 12 March 1997, local authorities to be reimbursed for reasonable costs that have followed the judgments. For a description of the applicable housing law provisions see chapter 18 of this book by Hunter.

69 The main difficulty which this argument faces is the backlog in decision-making. At the end of Jan. 1997 there were 54,490 undecided applications, see H.C. Hansard, Vol. 292, Col. 835 (written answer), 21 March 1997. This contention is, however, easily defeated, as it is clearly inappropriate to penalise asylum seekers for this failure in public administration. It is for the state to ensure that its procedures are both efficient and fair.

70 It is noteworthy that the number of in-country asylum applications dropped by more than 70 per cent in the last quarter of 1996, H.C. Hansard, Vol. 291, Col. 138, 25 Feb. 1997.

71 Marx, *op. cit. supra* n. 56 at 403, argues that given the declaratory nature of refugee status claimants enjoy "presumptive refugee status" for procedural purposes.

requirement of fairness that those who seek asylum are not presented with such a stark choice.

Conclusion

The developments in asylum law and policy, sketched above, illustrate the problems which may arise when a state allows public policy imperatives to overwhelm legal protection of vulnerable groups. Constructed upon claims which were often not adequately proven, the government adopted measures which many correctly regard as highly questionable.

This chapter has sought to reject a purely instrumental view of refugee and asylum law, on the basis that such an approach may contribute to the neglect of consideration of the humanity of the "other", who comes to seek refuge in the UK. By focusing on the international and European dimensions, the purpose of refugee law and its prescriptive aspects, all participants in the debate should be encouraged to concentrate on the humanitarian imperative of protection in the interpretation and application of law and policy. Further to this, it is important to stress the need to explore the other aspects of international human rights law which are applicable to the plight of the refugee and asylum seeker. As the developing jurisprudence of the European Court of Human Rights shows, refugee law has limitations which human rights law does not possess. The proposed incorporation of the European Convention into domestic law is therefore a progressive development of the utmost importance for asylum seekers.

While in this chapter the willingness of the judiciary to intervene in defence of the basic rights of asylum seekers has been cautiously welcomed, it is also important to look beyond the courts. A comprehensive human rights-based approach should place equal weight on ensuring that a participatory process is constructed which is responsive to the expressed needs of minority groups. This is because too often in these debates the voices of refugees and asylum seekers are silenced. "Taking human rights seriously" in this sense also means attempting to secure rights to meaningful participation in processes of opinion and will-formation within the state. This involves institutionalising procedures for securing the uncoerced input of social groups affected by the legal regulation. One must acknowledge the practical obstacles to this critical project.

The functional and enabling aspects of asylum law are necessarily linked to the humanitarian purpose ascribed to the law in the above analysis. Asylum law must primarily facilitate the fair, efficacious and efficient consideration of the claims of those who seek protection. Asylum seekers must be guaranteed *effective access* to a proper decision-making process which is sensitive to the asylum context. The serious error in recent law and policy changes has been to target the act of asylum seeking itself by adopting restrictive measures unconnected to the asylum determination process. This has lead many to conclude that deterrence has been at the heart of UK asylum law and policy for at least the last decade. The challenge for the EU and the UK, in the next decade, is to construct a principled approach to refugee and asylum law which pays rather more attention to the needs of the forcibly displaced and to the advances made in other areas of human rights law, than has been the case in the past.

Bibliography

Achermann, A. and Gattiker, M., "Safe Third Countries: European Developments" (1995) 7 I.J.Ref.L. 19.

Amnesty International, *Slamming the Door: The Demolition of the Right to Asylum in the UK* (1996).

Amnesty International, *Playing Human Pinball: Home Office Practice in "Safe Third Country" Asylum Cases* (1995).

Cohen, C., "The UN Convention on the Rights of the Child: Implications for Change in the Care and Protection of Refugee Children" (1991) 3 I.J.Ref.L. 675.

Collinson, S., *Beyond Borders: West European Migration Policy Towards the Twenty First Century* (Royal Institute of International Affairs, 1993).

Dacyl, J., "Europe Needs a New Protection System for 'Non-Convention' Refugees" (1995) 7 I.J.Ref.L. 579.

Daoust, I., and Folkelius, K., "UNHCR Symposium on Gender-Related Persecution" (1996) 8 I.J.Ref.L. 180.

Einarsen, T., "The European Convention on Human Rights and the Notion of an Implied Right to *de Facto* Asylum" (1993) 2 I.J.Ref.L. 362.

Glidewell Panel, *The Report from an Independent Enquiry into the Implications and Effects of the Asylum and Immigration Bill 1995 and Related Social Security Measures* (16 April 1996).

Goodwin-Gill, G.S., "Who to Protect, How ..., and the Future?" (1997) 9 I.J.Ref.L. 1

Goodwin-Gill, G.S., *The Refugee in International Law* (Clarendon, Oxford, 2nd edn, 1996).

Gowlland-Debbas, V., ed., *The Problem of Refugees in the Light of Contemporary International Law Issues* (Martinus Nijhoff, 1996).

Greatbatch, J., "The Gender Difference: Feminist Critiques of Refugee Discourse" (1989) 4 I.J.Ref.L. 518.

Hailbronner, K., "Visa Regulations and Third Country Nationals in EC law" (1994) 31 C.M.L. Rev. 969.

Harvey, C.J., "Restructuring Asylum: Recent Trends in UK Asylum Law and Policy" (1997) 9 I.J.Ref.L. 60.

Harvey, C.J., *An Analysis of Refugee and Asylum Law with Special Reference to the Law and Practice of the UK and the EU* (University of Nottingham, unpublished PhD thesis, 1996).

Harvey, C.J., "The Right to Seek Asylum in the UK and 'Safe Countries'" [1996] P.L. 196.
Harvey, C.J., "The UK's New Asylum and Immigration Bill" (1996) 8 I.J.Ref.L. 184.
Harvey, C.J., "The Boundaries of Refugee Status" (1996) 146 N.L.J. 836.
Hathaway, J., "New Directions to Avoid Hard Problems: The Distortion of the Palliative Role of Refugee Protection" (1995) 8 J.R.S. 288.
Hathaway, J., "Harmonizing for Whom? The Devaluation of Refugee Protection in the Era of European Economic Co-operation" (1993) 26 Corn. Int. L.J. 719.
Hathaway, J., *The Law of Refugee Status,* (Butterworths, 1991).
Johnsson, A., "The International Protection of Women Refugees: A Summary of Principal Problems and Issues" (1989) 1 I.J.Ref.L. 221.
Kjaerum, M., "The Concept of the Country of First Asylum" (1992) 4 I.J.Ref.L. 514.
Joly, D., *Haven or Hell? Asylum Policies and Refugees in Europe* (Macmillan, 1996).
Joly, D., "The Porous Dam: European Harmonisation on Asylum in the Nineties" (1994) 6 I.J.Ref.L. 159.
Kelly, N., "Guidelines for Women's Asylum Claims" (1994) 6 I.J.Ref.L. 517.
Kelly, N., "Gender-Related Persecution: Assessing the Asylum Claims of Women" (1993) 26 Corn.Int.L.J. 625.
Lambert, H., *Seeking Asylum: Comparative Law and Practice in Selected European Countries* (Martinus Nijhoff, 1995).
Loescher, G., *Beyond Charity: International Co-operation and the Global Refugee Crisis* (Oxford University Press, 1993).
Marx, R., and Lumpp, K., "The German Constitutional Court's Decision of 14 May 1996 on the Concept of 'Safe Third Countries'– A Basis for Burden-Sharing in Europe?" (1996) 8 I.J.Ref.L. 419.
Marx, R., and Lumpp, K., "*Non-Refoulement,* Access to Procedures, and Responsibility for Determining Refugee Claims" (1995) 7 I.J.Ref.L. 383.
Massey, D.S., and Espinosa, K.E., "What's Driving Mexico-US Migration? A Theoretical, Empirical and Policy Analysis" (1997) 102 American Journal of Sociology 939.
Neal, D., "Women as a Social Group: Recognizing Sex-Based Persecution as Grounds for Asylum" (1988) 20 Columbia H.R.L.R. 203.
Oosterveld, V., "The Canadian Guidelines on Gender-Related Persecution: An Evaluation" (1996) 8 I.J.Ref.L. 567.
Richmond, A., *Global Apartheid: Refugees, Racism and the New World Order* (Oxford University Press, 1994).
Tuitt, P., *False Images: The Law's Construction of the Refugee* (Pluto Press, London, 1996).
Shah, P., "Safe Third Countries: European and International Aspects" (1995) 1 Eur.P.L. 259
Shah, P., "Refugees and Safe Third Countries" (1995) 9 I.N.L.P. 3.
UNHCR, "The Concept of 'Protection Elsewhere'" (1995) 7 I.J.Ref.L. 123.
Wallace, R., *Refugees and Asylum: A Community Perspective* (Butterworths, London, 1996).
Wallace, R., "Making the Refugee Convention Gender Sensitive: The Canadian Guidelines" (1996) 45 I.C.L.Q. 702.
Wallace, R., "Considerations for Asylum Officers Adjudicating Asylum Claims from Women: American Guidelines" (1996) 9 I.N.L.P. 116.
Weiner, M., *The Global Migration Crisis: Challenge to States and to Human Rights* (Harper Collins College Publishers, 1995).
Winterbourne, W., Shah, P., and Doebbler, C., "Refugees and Safe Countries of Origin: Appeals, Judicial Review and Human Rights Law" (1996) 10 I.N.L.P. 123.

12 Entitlement to Protection: A Human Rights-based Approach to Refugee Protection in the United Kingdom

NICHOLAS BLAKE QC

National Restrictions and International Obligations

In 1948 the United Nations Universal Declaration of Human Rights, proclaimed in Article 14 that "everyone has the right to seek and enjoy asylum from persecution". Despite the subsequent enactment of the 1951 Geneva Convention Relating to the Status of Refugees (the Refugee Convention), the 1966 International Covenant on Civil and Political Rights, regional human rights instruments taking their inspiration from the UN, and the activities of the United Nations High Commissioner for Refugees (UNHCR), the extent to which national law and practice gives effect to the promise of protection indicated by this founding document of the contemporary human rights programme, remains debatable.

It is to be noted that the right to seek asylum in the Declaration, is not matched by a duty imposed on states to grant it or even to grant access to procedures whereby asylum may be sought and enjoyed.[1] International law moved cautiously with respect to positive duties on states to admit aliens to their territory. The absence of an express duty to admit refugees and determine

1 The 1980 American Convention on Human Rights by contrast refers in Art. 22(9) to the right "to seek and be granted asylum in a foreign country". Similarly, Art. 12.3 of the 1981 African Charter on Human and People's Rights states: "Every individual shall have the right when persecuted to seek and obtain asylum in other countries in accordance with laws of those countries and international conventions."

their claims is also a notable feature of the 1951 Refugee Convention, which was designed to identify who should be recognised as a refugee and what rights followed recognition. It is this absence of a duty to admit for the purposes of protection that has permitted many states in the developed world to respond to the rising number of claims in the past 20 years with policies designed to deter asylum seekers from ever arriving in their territories in the first place.

In the United States, the coastguard service sought to intercept boatloads fleeing from the repression in Haiti.[2] Airlines and international carriers are fined if they bring in asylum seekers without appropriate documents and visas, even though there are no visas capable of being granted to refugees in their countries of persecution and most such countries are designated visa countries in the Western states. Consequently their nationals face enormous difficulties in travelling to seek the asylum their circumstances may merit. This inevitably requires either a forged visa or passport, or a false claim to a visa and usually an expensive outlay to an agent to arrange a circuitous route to avoid detection. Refugees are not unnaturally distressed at having to part with large sums of cash to frequently unscrupulous agents in order to exercise their right to asylum. However, given that carrier sanctions are likely to remain in place for the future, alternatives are hard to find. An in-country assessment for the grant of status is too subjective in scope and application to be satisfactory. Immigration officials are not equipped for determining admissibility for protection at an interview in an overseas post. Diplomatic, trading, or even personal connections with the persecuting agents of the state may well render a fair approach unattainable.

European states have exploited their geographical distance from contemporary zones of conflict and have sought to supplement the regime of carrier sanctions with a doctrine of safe third country[3] whereby refugees are returned down the line to the first country they entered where they might have sought protection, although access to such protection is not ensured and the absence of harmonisation for asylum criteria has meant that some claims are treated with significant differences in different European countries.[4] As a

2 See *Sale v. Haitian Centers Council* 113 S Ct 2549 (1993).

3 See also chapters 3, 4 and 8 of this book by Richard Dunstan, Rachel Trost and Peter Billings, and Geoffrey Care for current operation of the doctrine in the UK.

4 The Dublin Convention determining the state responsible for examining applications of asylum lodged in one of the Member States of the European Communities (30 I.L.M. 425 (1991) and O.J. 1997 C254/1) was signed in 1990 as a European Union Convention, but only came into force on 1 Sept. 1997. It remains to be seen whether the UK will send Somali cases to France and Germany

result, these states enjoy advantages over those of Africa or South America where social and political upheavals lead to mass exoduses of a substantial proportion of the population into the territory of neighbouring states. The disproportionate burden placed on developing counties in accommodating the bulk of the world's refugees is thus not merely a reflection of the fact that, for example, the 1969 OAU Refugee Convention[5] employs a wider definition of refugee than that of the 1951 Convention, but also that these countries generally afford greater access to the available protection. Access to protection in a contiguous state does not generally involve false visas, and complicated journeys round the world to find a chink in the fortress wall.

For the asylum seeker who overcomes these hurdles and reaches the United Kingdom, other techniques of deterrence have now been put in place. These can encompass insidious methods of restriction and control at the heart of the process of refugee recognition itself. In the UK, the introduction of a comprehensive system of asylum appeals[6] has led to a tendency to characterise claims as not credible even when they emanate from countries with notorious human rights records.[7] Most recently, these deterrents have included harsh provision for housing and social security assistance pending determinations of claims and restrictions on the exercise of rights of appeal.[8]

Many other countries have adopted a narrow definition of the criteria for protection, where a broad approach is seen as likely to lead to significant numbers arriving from neighbouring states. For instance, the US Board of Immigration Appeals has traditionally adopted a very strict approach to the

---

where there is a requirement of an effective state before refugee status can be granted, and claims likely to have merited status here will be rejected there.

5 Art. 1.2 of the Organisation of African Unity's 1969 Convention governing the specific aspects of refugee problems in Africa extends the definition to "every person who, owing to external aggression, occupation, foreign domination or events seriously disturbing public order in either part or the whole of his country ... is compelled to leave his place of habitual residence in order to seek refuge in another place outside his country".

6 See Asylum and Immigration Appeals Act 1993.

7 For the "culture of disbelief" see Glidewell Panel, *Report from an independent enquiry into the implications and effects of the Asylum and Immigration Bill 1995 and related social security measures* (April 1996), 5–8 and 39; Justice/ Immigration Law Practitioners' Association/Asylum Rights Campaign, *Providing Protection: Towards Fair and Effective Asylum Procedures* (London, July 1997), 38 *et seq.* See also chapter 10 this book by Anne Owers and Madeline Garlick.

8 As introduced in the Asylum and Immigration Act 1996.

victims of right-wing repression and guerrilla activities in Central America;[9] Germany has sought to limit claims from the former Yugoslavia by an illogical insistence that only a state can be the agent of persecution[10] and the High Court of Australia has recently adopted a definition of "social group" that would deny status to women or families fleeing the brutal enforcement of China's one child policy.[11]

This chapter is concerned with the scope of the international obligations of protection. No satisfactory answer can be given to the question of how protection is granted, to whom and for how long, until there is clarity as to who needs and is entitled to it. The rhetoric of "bogus" asylum seekers that surrounded the passage of the Asylum and Immigration Act 1996 and the litany of statistics suggesting low recognition rates and success on appeal belies a more complex reality. It is meaningless to equate unsuccessful applicants for refugee status with bogus claimants.

Firstly, the considerably higher numbers who are now afforded exceptional leave to remain must be included in the camp of the genuine asylum seeker. The criterion for the grant of exceptional leave was considerably tightened after the passage of the Asylum and Immigration Appeals Act 1993 when some 70 per cent of all claimants were granted some form of protection. Many of those granted exceptional leave should have been granted refugee status.[12] Others only fail to acquire refugee status because of a narrow interpretation of the terms of the Convention, but are clearly irremovable under other instruments of international law.[13] Many refused exceptional leave would have obtained it, if our appellate procedures permitted broader human rights

9 *Sanchez Trujillo v. Immigration and Nationality Service* (1986) 801 F 2d 1571.

10 See Marx, R., "The Criteria for the Determination of Refugee Status in the Federal Republic of Germany" (1992) 4 I.J.Ref.L. 151.

11 *A. v. Minister for Immigration and Ethnic Affairs* High Court of Australia (24 Feb. 1997) [1997] 142 A.L.R. 331. *Infra* notes 36 and 49 for further references to this case.

12 Until 1992 some 90 per cent of Somali asylum seekers were granted refugee status and the rest ELR; since then the proportion has been reversed, although the Court of Appeal decision in *Adan and Nooh v. Secretary of State for the Home Department* [1997] 1 W.L.R. 1107; [1997] 2 All E.R. 723; [1997] Imm. A.R. 251 suggests that many cases should be reclassified as refugees. For the general decline of ELR see *Providing Protection, supra* n.7 at 20 and 25.

13 See, e.g., *Chahal v. UK* (70/1995/576/662) European Court of Human Rights (ECtHR) judgment of 15 Nov. 1996; *Times* Law Report 30 Nov. 1996, (1997) 23 E.H.R.R. 413.

obligations to be taken into account, and if the requirements of public law obliged the Home Office normally to follow recommendations of adjudicators who were satisfied that *bona fide* claims had been made, even though appeals had to be dismissed.[14]

Secondly, the statistics for success on appeal can be misleading.[15] Cases where poor decision making at first instance has been remitted for reconsideration were not included as successes in the Home Office statistics, despite being so regarded by the asylum seeker and his or her representatives. An overall success rate of five per cent is to be contrasted with rates of between 25 and 40 per cent when the appellant has competent legal representation from specialised lawyers or advisory and representative bodies such as the Refugee Legal Centre and Asylum Aid.[16] The invaluable information base of the former organisation is not matched by a Home Office documentation centre that would provide appellants with all relevant material on the law, practice, history and human rights records of particular countries.

Finally, there is the revealing statistic that only a small percentage of those refused protection whose appeals were dismissed were actually removed by the Home Office in 1996 or the preceding years. The previous government could hardly be said to have had insufficient resolve to do this. Many such people were effectively irremovable because their countries of origin would not or could not receive them back. Others were engaged in costly and time consuming legal challenges to harsh expulsion decisions, particularly where strong family connections had developed over the extensive period when the asylum claim was being considered.

In the absence of a fair and effective procedure based on human criteria, at the very least complying with our minimum international obligations, the hue and cry over "bogus" asylum seekers can be said to be full of sound and fury but signifying little. Doubtless, a significant number of those seeking protection in the UK do not deserve to obtain it, but statistics will not identify these numbers. This chapter does not seek to expose the procedural defects of

14 See *R. v. Secretary of State for the Home Department ex p. Gardian* [1996] Imm. A.R. 6, *Times Law Report* 1 April 1996; *R. v. Secretary of State for the Home Department ex p. Khadka* [1997] Imm. A.R. 124.

15 At the time that benefit changes for asylum seekers were being introduced, the Home Office made great play of the fact that only four per cent of asylum appeals were successful.

16 See *Providing Protection, supra* n. 7, and statistics provided by the Refugee Legal Centre (July 1997).

our decision making and appellate system,[17] but focuses instead on the narrow criteria for protection by which asylum applications are judged.

The Refugee Convention and the Dynamics of Interpretation

Despite its manifest limitations, the 1951 Refugee Convention remains the centrepiece for the foundation of refugee protection law and policy in the developed world. It has a venerated status amongst governments, promoted by its able and active custodian, the UNHCR. Following recognition, a refugee is afforded a status including a right to an internationally recognised travel document, equality with own nationals in matters relating to housing, social security and employment. Subject to the application of the cessation clauses, protection is seen as a durable solution with the promise of integration into the host country and opportunities to acquire the nationality of that country.

If the fruits of Convention refugee status are clear, its scope is less so. Veneration can lead to ossification and diminishing relevance in a world of contemporary protection needs. There is no international judicial body charged with its development, interpretation and ultimate application in individual cases. The UNHCR can issue its *Handbook*[18] in response to a request by states participating in the programme of the Executive Committee of the High Commissioner, but this guidance is not part of the *travaux préparatoires* of the Convention or of authoritative force binding national governments.[19] National governments are free to adopt their own approach to the topics addressed in the *Handbook* and can pursue a more restrictive approach, for which they are merely accountable to their national courts.[20] Perhaps it is this very amenability of the Convention to national sovereignty that explains the willingness of governments to proclaim continued protection for those they consider "genuine" refugees while denouncing others as "bogus"; refugees remain a class apart only so long as the state retains the prerogative of Humpty

17 For an adjudicator's view of these procedural issues see chapter 8 of this book by Geoffrey Care.

18 UNHCR, *Handbook on Procedures and Criteria for Determining Refuge Status* (Geneva, re-edited 1992).

19 *R. v. Secretary of State for the Home Department ex p. Sivakumaran* [1988] AC 958.

20 See the comments of Staughton LJ in *R. v. Immigration Appeal Tribunal and Another ex p. Shah, Islam and Others* CA 23 July 1997 *Times* Law Report 13 Oct. 1997; [1997] 2 B.H.R.C. 590.

Dumpty: a word means what it wants it to mean.

The record of national courts and their interpretation of the Convention, remains uneven, depending on the type of judicial process available to challenge decisions, the quality of the legal argument, the availability of comparative jurisprudence, the status of international treaties in the particular constitutional regime, and the economic and political exigencies that have lead national administrations to regard asylum applicants as problems to be controlled. National judges have demonstrated that they are no less adept than politicians at acknowledging the sensitivity to popular opinion of decisions that appear to open the floodgates to hoards of foreigners.[21]

By contrast, there is the alternative model of treaties which have their own adjudicating body following individual complaints or references by national courts or others. At one end of the scale, there is the European Court of Justice charged with the interpretation of European Community law. European Community law demonstrates that aliens can have rights afforded in international law to enter and remain in the territories of neighbouring states and that such rights are capable of binding international interpretation which in turn becomes part of the national law of Member States.[22] At the other, there are bodies such as the UN Human Rights Committee,[23] which can review periodically the practices of participating states, and if the Optional Protocol granting an individual right of petition has been ratified, can make decisions on particular complaints. Whatever the identity of the body or its jurisdiction, an international body dedicated to the interpretation and application of an instrument free of the political restraints of national governments, enables a dynamic interpretation to be given to the international instrument in question.

One of the more remarkable products of the dynamic process of interpretation has been the development of a parallel right to asylum in the

---

21 See *Sandralingham and Ravichandran v. Secretary of State for the Home Department* CA [1996] Imm. A.R. 97; and most recently *ex p. Shah and Islam, supra* n. 20.

22 For a review of the case law holding free movement of persons to be one of the fundamental terms of the Community see Macdonald, I.A. and Blake, N., *Immigration Law and Practice in the United Kingdom* (4th edn, Butterworths, 1995) ch. 8; Martin, D. and Guild, E., *Free Movement of Persons in the European Union* (Butterworths, 1996).

23 See McGoldrick, D., *The Human Rights Committee: Its Role in the Development of the International Covenant on Civil and Political Rights* (Clarendon, Oxford, 1991).

construction of those instruments which forbid torture or inhuman or degrading treatment. Although such a prohibition appears to have been drafted primarily with regard for the responsibility of the contracting state for the acts of its own agents or those it is able to control, a simple focus on the logic of causal nexus has led to a prohibition on states expelling anyone to face such prohibited treatment anywhere in the world, whoever inflicts the treatment and whether the state concerned adheres to the particular instrument precluding such ill treatment or not.[24] It is surely a more logical starting point for discussion of refugee protection issues to identify the kind of harm that a person should be protected from, rather than examine the separate requirements for the qualification of refugee status as if they were clauses in a banking contract, unrelated to the basic premise of protection.

A technical consideration of the elements of the Convention definition of refugee, can rapidly turn an examination of a living instrument into an anatomical dissection of a dead one. There is no warrant for the suggestion that the drafters of the Refugee Convention intended a narrow definition, although plainly they did not adopt an unrestricted one.[25] The point is, to join the elements together to achieve the purposes envisaged by the Convention's drafters; not to find technical reasons for refusal. No response to an asylum claim is more calculated to induce rage and despair and uneconomic litigation than for an applicant to be informed that, although they have been ill-treated and face a repetition of such behaviour, it is ill treatment for the wrong reason and therefore outside the scope of the 1951 Convention.[26] For an understanding of how the competing arguments as to its scope have come about, it is necessary to briefly examine the terms of the Convention.

Development of the Definition of the Convention Refugee

Article 1 (A) of the Refugee Convention was intended to address the situation

24 The development can be identified in the decisions of the ECtHR in *Soering v. UK* (Series A, No. 161), *Cruz Varas v. Sweden* (Series A, No. 201), *Vilvarajah and Others v. UK* (Series A, No. 215), and most recently *Chahal* (*supra* n. 13), *Ahmed v. Austria* 17 Dec. 1996 (71/1995/577/663) and *D. v. UK* 2 May 1997 (Series B, No. 37). *Infra* for further details.

25 See Staughton LJ in *ex p. Shah and Islam*, *supra* n. 20, and the same judge's comments in *Sandralingham and Ravichandran*, *supra* n. 21.

26 For examples of this approach see cases cited in Macdonald and Blake, *op. cit. supra* n. 22, ch. 12, and supplement (1997).

of those recognised as refugees under previous instruments and those who had fled events in Europe before 1951 and were entitled to a status that had not yet been drafted. In 1967 the geographical and chronological restrictions on those who could come within the definition were removed,[27] leaving unresolved an important question as to whether past fear alone could satisfy the status or whether a continued well-founded fear of future persecution was always necessary. Since 1967 therefore, Article 1(A)(2) defines a refugee as someone who "owing to well-founded fear of being persecuted for reasons of race, religion, nationality, membership of a particular social group or political opinion, is outside the country of his nationality [or if stateless of habitual residence] and is unable or, owing to such fear, is unwilling to avail himself of the protection of that country of nationality [or if stateless is unable or unwilling to return to that country]". The dominant theme of the definition is thus that of being outside a country for a particular reason and being either unable to return to it or obtain the protection of one's country or nationality, or if such protection is available, being unwilling to seek it for the same reason that causes the person to be outside it in the first place.[28]

With this dominant reading in mind, it is possible to see that the heart of the definition is the absence of an available national protection for those who are outside their country owing to a well-founded fear of persecution. What Hathaway[29] had called the "surrogate" protection offered by the substantive provisions of the 1951 Convention is thus only available to those who have left their country and cannot be expected to return there. Effective protection cannot ever be available from a regime that would itself persecute the asylum seeker, but there is no reason to confine protection to "protection from persecution" or confine persecution to state-inspired harm. Otherwise the important two limbs of "unable" or "unwilling" become otiose and lacking in substance.[30]

The requirement to be "outside" the country, of course gives rise to the problems of access to surrogate protection. Refugee status cannot be equated with a general scheme of immigration admission where increasingly visas

27 By the 1967 New York Protocol, the text of the Convention considered in this chapter is the text as amplified by the Protocol.

28 *Adan and Nooh* CA, *supra* n. 12.

29 Hathaway, J., *The Law of Refugee Status* (Butterworths, 1991). This work has had significant influence on the Canadian Supreme Court in *Canada (Attorney-General) v. Ward* [1993] 2 R.C.S. 689 and [1993] 4 D.L.R. 103 and has been cited on many occasions in the UK.

30 *Adan and Nooh*, *supra* n. 12.

are required in advance from qualifying persons. Here, the essential first qualification is the fact of having departed the territory. Visas are neither possible nor appropriate,[31] and a national definition that in practice penalises the asylum seeker for having arrived in the first place, is inconsistent with the requirement of the international definition that the asylum seeker must have arranged his or her own departure from the territory whether regularly or otherwise. The definition is not confined only to those who have fled because of a fear of persecution. Those who have left for other reasons and subsequently make a claim can also be refugees, as long as they can demonstrate a causal connection with their being "outside" and the fear.[32]

The fear is usually identified as the subjective element of the claim, and this will normally always be the case: a person who has no genuinely-held fear at the time the request for recognition as a refugee is made will normally not have a claim to protection. However, there is no reason why a young child or person of diminished mental capacity could not be a refugee, merely because they are unaware of the fate that their persecutors may have in store for them. It is sufficient if their claim to protection is by reason of an objective threat of persecution. Nevertheless, it is with the qualifications to the fear which are imposed by the Article that domestic case law on the scope of protection has been largely been concerned. It is clear that (i) the fear must be well founded, that is, there has to be some objective reason for concluding that the person is at risk,[33] and (ii) it has to relate to *persecution* rather than economic hardship, natural disaster or the ordinary application of national law.[34]

Identification of refugees by the existence of a well-founded fear of persecution, might well have been sufficient to reflect the intentions of the drafters of Article 14 of the UN Declaration, leaving debate in borderline cases to an examination of whether the harm feared was in truth "persecution" of the kind envisaged by the drafters. However, the Convention refers to

---

31 This does not mean that a scheme of providing visas to travel to the UK to make an asylum claim could not be brought into effect for those who have arguable claims to protection and have a close qualifying connection with the UK to make this the most appropriate country of asylum. For the UK policy on admission to claim asylum see the report of *Conteh v. Secretary of State for the Home Department* [1992] Imm. A.R. 594.

32 The term favoured by the drafting committee was "has had to leave, shall leave or remains outside" and the eventual wording was intended to reflect all these limbs: see Grahl-Madsen cited in *Adan and Nooh*, *supra* n. 12 at 114G.

33 *Sivakumaran*, *supra* n. 19.

34 *Sandralingham and Ravichandran*, *supra* n. 21.

persecution for reasons of race etc., the so called Convention reasons, and it is necessary to give some effect to these words, particularly as they are repeated in the prohibition on *refoulement* in Article 33(1). The project of the drafters was to move away from previous definitions of refugee which responded to specific instances of persecution of ethnic, religious or political groups, and to formulate a general definition encompassing both past and future claims for protection.

It is unlikely that the promoters of the Convention intended the requirement of "Convention reasons" to be narrowly and restrictively interpreted as an additional hurdle to be faced by those who had demonstrated a risk of persecution. Rather, it is probable that a single composite test was being developed, where focus on either the motives of the persons carrying out the acts complained of, or the common characteristics of those who were the victims of those acts was relevant to an overall conclusion of whether it constituted persecution.[35] If there is ill treatment of such unambiguous severity to constitute persecution in the forms of threats to life or liberty, or of torture or inhuman or degrading treatment, there is little point in a national system of protection investing time and energy in determining further questions of the reasons for the treatment. We now know such people are irremovable in international law in any event. Nevertheless, in the light of national and international case law focusing on "Convention reasons", and in the absence of authoritative support for a broader approach, the theoretical possibility of persecution for the "wrong reason" must be admitted, although this gap in Refugee Convention protection weakens its universal applicability as an appropriate standard for asylum policies.

There is no reason to widen this theoretical possibility so that it substantially diminishes the scope of protection provided by the Convention. The preamble to the Convention, suggests that the concerns of the General Assembly in promulgating its terms were that those who were discriminated against in the enjoyment of their human rights were the protected class to be

35 It may be that the problem of Convention reason arises most acutely in terms of acts of non-state agents. The UK and Canada recognise that such acts may amount to persecution but shift the emphasis on to the question of Convention reason. In *Secretary of State for the Home Department v. Savchenkov* CA [1996] Imm. A.R. 28 the question was whether the intimidation of the appellant by the Russian mafia for refusal to cooperate with them was persecution for reasons of membership of a particular social group. In many countries the real question would be whether the harm complained of was persecution.

identified as refugees.[36] True, the preamble also indicated the concerns of governments that unmanageably large numbers might seek refugee status, but the elimination of unfounded claims is largely achieved by the focus on the need for a well-founded fear of persecution rather than by an unnatural restriction of the scope of Convention reason.[37] The circumstances when people are discriminated against in the enjoyment of their fundamental rights, can now be seen to extend beyond the Convention reasons enumerated in Article 1(A)(2), and to modern eyes the absence of express reference to gender or sexual orientation seems striking. There is no reason to believe that women or children who were murdered and abused because of their sex or age, were considered to be unworthy of protection in 1951, and they have certainly been the subject of specific international concern subsequently.[38] The "protection gap" in the definition of refugee can be narrowed by a purposive approach to construction taking discriminatory denial of human rights as a good indicator of the purpose of the treaty, to which regard shall be had in cases of ambiguity.[39] A number of pointers from academic writing and

---

36 The preamble was cited by the Canadian Supreme Court in *Ward*, *supra* n. 29 at 733, as evidence of the human rights approach to questions of construction. The Australian High Court in *A v. MIEA*, *supra* n. 11, has subsequently suggested that this approach was also unduly influenced by the Canadian Charter of Fundamental Rights. *Infra* for discussion of this case.

37 The first four indents of the preamble read:

> *Considering* that the Charter of the United Nations and the Universal Declaration of Human Rights ... have affirmed the principle that human beings shall enjoy *fundamental human rights and freedoms without discrimination*,
> *Considering* that the United Nations has on various occasions manifested its profoundest concern for refugees and endeavoured to assure refugees the widest possible exercise of these fundamental rights and freedoms,
> *Considering* that it is desirable to revise and consolidate previous international agreements relating to the status of refugee and *to extend the scope of and the protection accorded by such instruments* by means of a new agreement,
> *Considering* that the grant of asylum may place unduly heavy burdens on certain countries, and that a satisfactory solution of a problem of which the United Nations has recognised the international scope and nature cannot therefore be achieved without international co-operation (author's emphasis).

38 See, e.g., the 1979 Convention on the Elimination of All Forms of Discrimination Against Women and the 1989 Convention on the Rights of the Child.

39 Vienna Convention on the Interpretation of Treaties 1969 Arts 31–33; see also *R. v. Secretary of State for the Home Department ex p. Robinson* CA, 11 July 1997, [1997] 3 W.L.R. 1162; [1997] 4 All E.R. 210; *Times* Law Report 1 Aug. 1997.

Canadian jurisprudence in particular demonstrate the issues whereby this can be achieved

Firstly, a decision maker should not approach the term "for reasons of" as indicating that further proof is needed of the subjective motivation of the persecutor. A police officer who tortures a politically active member of an opposing ethnic minority may do so to extract information on others, but that does not preclude the activity being persecution for reasons of race etc.[40] Most persecutors claim a veneer of public order justification for their activities. If the search for guerrilla suspects took the form of wholesale internment, massacre or other ill treatment of civilians of the appropriate race, nationality, religion, political persuasion or other defining social characteristics, the persecution can be said to be for those reasons even though there is some ulterior motivation for the actions. In discrimination law, problems of relevant causation are now judged by the "but for" test, namely, whether the applicant can show that the proscribed activities have resulted because of a distinguishing characteristic that makes the applicant more vulnerable than the general population to this treatment.[41] Hathaway has suggested that Canadian law applies a similar test to the causal nexus between persecution and a Convention reason.[42] It is to be hoped this point will be followed in the UK when it is finally called on for determination. The application of such an approach to the question of civil war refugees will be considered below.

Secondly, the causal connection between persecution and the Convention ground can exist where the persecutor imputes the relevant characteristic to the victim.[43] Race, religion and political opinion are all factors that may exist in the mind of the persecutor rather than the conscious awareness of the victim. A victim of persecution on ethnic lines may be mistaken as belonging to the persecuted minority; a person with distant Jewish ancestry might well have considered themselves a German whilst the persecutors thought otherwise. Members of the security forces might well consider themselves to be politically neutral whilst their opponents might ascribe political motivation to their decision to belong to and carry out politically sensitive functions. This is not to pay undue emphasis on the motive of the persecutor but to identify the

40 See observations of Simon Brown LJ in *Sandralingam and Ravichandran*, *supra* n. 21.

41 *James v. Eastleigh Borough Council* [1990] 2 AC 751 at 760 *et seq.*, especially 765 *per* Lord Bridge.

42 Hathaway, *op. cit. supra* n. 29 at 141.

43 See dictum of Collins J in *R. v. Secretary of State for the Home Department ex p. Stefan, Chiper and Ionel* [1995] Imm. A.R. 410 at 413.

reason for the discriminatory treatment in question. As we will note below there is greater controversy as to whether a social group can exist in the perceptions of the persecutor, but if the causal link can be established there is no reason why this should not be the case.

Thirdly, the relevant reason may be found in a combination of different circumstances: considerations of race, nationality, religion, political opinion and social group may overlap to expose a particular individual to ill treatment, to which they would not otherwise be vulnerable. It is not a case of seeing whether each reason stands up in turn but whether the combination of circumstances does. If there is differential ill treatment because of who a person is, it does not matter that the identity is composed of fragments none of which might have made him or her a victim if they stood alone.

Fourthly, the scope of reasons themselves should be construed broadly. Political opinion cannot be restricted to formal party politics in the mode of nineteenth century discourse on the state.[44] The expression or even the suspected holding of views on free speech, natural justice, censorship, sexual identity and other more individual concerns might all invite persecution for reasons of a political opinion. Equally, religious persecution is not confined to persecuting those who seek to express their religious belief, but may include those whose way of life is said to infringe the religious customs of others. A person whipped for failing to conform with the dress code required by a fundamentalist Islamic regime, or other perceived slight to the tenets of the Koran may be said to face religious and political persecution. It has been pointed out that most gender-related persecution has some connection to acts or opinions by the victim that are objected to by the persecutor as a bid for independence or a threat to male control whether in the domestic or public arena.[45] In an era where the international community is determined to redress the historic invisibility of women's protection concerns in their own right, it is not possible to deny the political nature of such opinions, perceived or

44 For the broadening of political opinion in the context of extradition proceedings see *R. v. Governor of Brixton Prison ex p. Schtraks* [1964] AC 556 *per* Lord Reid; *R. v. Governor of Pentonville Prison ex p. Cheng* [1973] AC 931 *per* Lord Diplock.

45 Crawley, H., *Women as Asylum Seekers: a Legal Handbook* (Refugee Women's Legal Group, Refugee Action, ILPA, June 1997). See also the illuminating opinion of the New Zealand Refugee Status Appeals Authority in case no. 2039/93 *Re: MN* (12 Feb. 1996).

expressed, well articulated or not.[46]

All these considerations come to the fore in the extensive international case law on the most contentious Convention reason, that is, "membership of a particular social group". Decisions in the USA, Canada, Australia and the UK have all emphasised that the words cannot be equated with "or any other reason" so as to make any requirement of reasons for the persecution irrelevant. Beyond that its scope is far from certain. Those favouring a restrictive interpretation emphasise "membership" and "particular" as being indicative of the need for some measure of cohesiveness to the group in question, although the suggestion in *Savchenkov*[47] that the members of the group must have actually met and physically associated is unfounded.[48] The *travaux préparatoires* are not informative as to how such groups are to be defined other than to suggest that the term was inserted late in the drafting process and intended to cover economic and social classes persecuted in Stalin's Russia, such as *kulaks*, former merchants, and industrialists.

The most authoritative recent exposure of the international case law and the problems to which it gives rise is to be found in the Australian High Court decision in *A v. MIEA*[49] where the court was divided three to two in rejecting the applicability of the term to Chinese parents of more than one child who faced compulsory sterilisation or abortion for violation of the Chinese government's population control policy. The majority concluded that a social group had to possess a distinguishing characteristic which set them apart from society as a whole but was independent from the fact of persecution. The minority considered that persecution for a common distinguishing characteristic was sufficient, albeit that it was the persecution that gave the

46 Causation may still be a problem. In *Shah and Islam* Henry LJ was minded to accept that both appellants could only show persecution because they had violent husbands and not a connection with marginalised group; all the judges rejected Ms Islam's claim to persecution on the grounds of political opinion, because although her students regarded her as "politically attainted" to their movement this was because of her obstruction of their criminal rather than political activities.

47 *Savchenkov, supra* n. 35.

48 McGowan LJ appears to have based his comments on the reference in *Ward* to "association", which both sides considered helpful. La Forest J subsequently explained in *Chan v. Canada (Minister of Employment and Immigration)* [1995] 128 D.L.R. (4th) 213 at 248–50 that association meant a quality that associates rather than physical meeting. The UK government did not contend that the members of the group must have met in *Shah and Islam*.

49 *A. v. MIEA, supra* n. 11, extensively summarised in *Shah and Islam, supra* n. 20.

common characteristic its particular distinction in society. Neither the majority nor the minority were content to follow the US Court of Appeals 9th Division in *Sanchez-Trujillo*,[50] were it was said that the distinguishing characteristic had to create a cohesive homogenous group, nor the opinion of La Forest in *Ward*[51] subsequently explained in *Chan*,[52] that exercise of fundamental human rights could be a characteristic that associated people so as to form a particular social group. McHugh J's judgment with the majority recognised that whilst the group had to have an identity independent of the persecution complained of, the acts of the persecutor could over time give social significance to a characteristic that might not otherwise have been thought to have been significant. Thus, left-handed men are not a social group but would rapidly become so if they were persecuted for that characteristic. Such an approach reflects the last paragraph of the guidance given in the Joint Position of the countries of the European Union (EU) which is discussed below.[53]

Unconvincingly, the Australian High Court concluded that, whereas the parents could have claimed to have been the victims of political persecution if they had protested against the one-child policy and had been ill-treated for that protest, the mere fact of rendering themselves liable for prosecution and compulsory abortion and sterilisation was not sufficient to make them refugees on the grounds of political opinion. People express themselves politically by their deeds as much as by formal protest and organisation.

The case of *A. v. MIEA* proved influential in the decision of the English Court of Appeal in *ex parte Shah and Islam*.[54] In the *Shah* case, Sedley J[55] had at first instance quashed a refusal of leave to appeal by the Immigration Appeal Tribunal on the basis that a Pakistani woman who had been beaten and rejected by her husband might establish that she was a member of a social group in respect of ill treatment she might face as a suspected adulteress. Whilst recognising the limitations on social group played by the earlier decision of the Court of Appeal in *Savchenkov*, he observed that "unless [the 1951 Convention] is seen as a living thing, adopted by civilised countries for a humanitarian end which is constant in motive but mutable in form, the

50 *Sanchez-Trujillo, supra* n. 9.
51 *Ward, supra* n. 29.
52 *Chan, supra* n. 48.
53 *Infra* n. 59.
54 *Shah and Islam, supra* n. 20.
55 *R. v. Immigration Appeal Tribunal and Secretary of State for the Home Department ex p. Shah* [1997] Imm. A.R. 145.

Convention will eventually become an anachronism".[56]

Whilst not expressly disapproving this approach, the Court of Appeal held that Pakistani women, who faced persecution at the hands of their husbands, the broader community and even state-supported *sharia* laws for suspected sexual misdemeanour, could not establish that they were a social group, because the defining characteristics of the group as abandoned and ostracised women were themselves part of the persecution feared. The judges appeared to have been agreed that the relevant characteristics must be wholly independent of the persecution feared. Beyond this, the judges differed in their conclusions as to the dimensions of the term "social group". Waite LJ was willing to adopt the principle supported by the Australian High Court, which he summarised as "the members of the group must share something which unites them and which sets them apart from the rest of society" and must be recognised as such by society generally. Staughton LJ was inclined to agree with counsel for the Secretary of State that the expression involves "a number of people being joined together in a group with some degree of cohesiveness, cooperation or interdependence; the members must not be solitary individuals".[57] Henry LJ considered that most particular social groups will have a cohesive element involving ordinary social concepts associated with membership such as organisation, strength through association, fund raising, publicity or protest. He recognised, however, that cohesion is not necessary in every case, for instance, where the particular social group is recognised by the public as such though it is not organised. He nevertheless emphasised that the requirement that the persecution must be for reasons of membership of a social group, which will make it easier for the active supporter of a group to establish refugee status on the basis of persecution for belonging to the group. On such a view, it is difficult to see what social group would add to persecution on account of political opinion since persecution for conscious adherence to an organisation can always be said to be persecution for the expression of an opinion.

In the joined case of *Islam*, the false denunciation of adultery had arisen because politically active pupils considered that the appellant (their school teacher) had obstructed their activities at school. The claim to persecution on the grounds of political opinion was dismissed:

56 *Ibid.* at 152.

57 Even "cohesiveness" will not be enough according to the Court of Appeal in the unfortunate decision of *Secretary of State for the Home Department v. Ouanes* (7 Nov. 1997, Independent Law Report 12 Nov. 1997) which renders the social group virtually nugatory.

> Although she thus became politically attainted in the eyes of a body of her pupils which saw any obstruction of their wishes (whether it be to fight other pupils or to cheat in exams) as an affront to their MQM allegiance, it was held by both the Adjudicator and the appeal tribunal that there was no evidence of any independent political opinion formed on her own part, and that it was not possible in the circumstances to impute a political opinion of her own from the fact that she had been branded as a political enemy by others.

Like the Australian case, this appears to be an unnecessarily narrow view of political opinion and the causal nexus between politics and persecution required to establish refugee status.

Certainly the judgment in *Shah and Islam* has done little to narrow the protection gap. Waite and Henry LJ considered that the appellants had a good case for sympathetic consideration for exceptional leave to remain outside the Convention. Lord Staughton suggested that the restriction of refugee status to those who feared persecution for a Convention reason must have been the deliberate choice of states and the will of the people in democratic systems of government:

> The tension between humanitarian concern on the one hand and self interest on the other has produced in this country the whole elaborate apparatus of immigration control ... and a greater burden on the Civil Division of the Court of Appeal than any other single topic.

Henry LJ had earlier concluded that an application of the definition threw up hard cases and that children under two in Bethlehem murdered by King Herod would not form a social group, although an organisation of their supporters might.

In contrast to the decision of the Court of Appeal in *Adan*[58] and *Robinson*,[59] the Court did not draw any support for its conclusions from the EU Council's Joint Position,[60] which are instructive as to the considerations to which decision makers should have regard. Under the heading social group they provide:

58 *Adan and Nooh*, *supra* n. 12.

59 *Robinson*, *supra* n. 39.

60 Joint Position of 4 March 1996 defined by the Council on the Basis of Article K.3 of the Treaty on European Union on the Harmonised Application of the Definition of the Term "Refugee" in Article 1 of the Geneva Convention (1996) O.J. L63/2.

> 7.5 A specific social group normally comprises persons from the same background, with the same customs or the same social status etc.
>
> Fear of persecution cited under this heading may frequently overlap with fear of persecution on other grounds ...
>
> Membership of a social group may simply be attributed to the victimised person or the group by the persecutor.
>
> In some cases, the social group may not have existed previously but may be determined by the common characteristics of the victimised persons because the persecutor sees them as an obstacle to achieving his aims.

Women in an Islamic society clearly share a common inferior social status, and the recognition that the social group may be constituted by the persecutor's identification of a common social characteristic as the basis for persecution sits uncomfortably with the Court of Appeal's requirement of separation of these issues. It is worthy of note that in its asylum legislation the Republic of Ireland has specifically made provision for gender and sexual orientation as forming the basis of a social group, and for persecution as including serious assault of a sexual nature.[61] In addition, Canada, Australia and the USA have issued guidelines on gender-related persecution which have led appellate bodies there to grant refugee protection to women facing serious ill-treatment because of their gender, or the expression of their personality.[62] The complete separation of the social group and the persecution complained of is impractical, is unsupported by state practice or the terms of the Convention and is not necessary to give "social group" a meaning narrower than "any other reason".

Human Rights and a Broader Basis for Asylum

In dismissing the *Shah and Islam* appeal, Staughton LJ sympathised with the aspirations of the UNHCR that the words of the Refugee Convention be given the widest possible application, whilst concluding that the prospect of states agreeing a new and wider Convention was remote. However, the case law on Article 3 of the European Convention on Human Rights demonstrates that the UK is bound by international treaty to afford protection to a wider group of people who face ill treatment of sufficient severity irrespective of the reasons. It could be argued that there is little need of a new Refugee Convention, only sensible interpretation of the existing terms in the light of human rights

61 Asylum and Immigration Act 1996 s.5.

62 For review of the literature see *Women as Asylum Seekers*, *supra* n. 45.

developments.

The contrast between the two international instruments is most clearly demonstrated in the case of *Chahal*.[63] In this case the Secretary of State for the Home Department proposed to deport a well known Sikh activist to India for reasons of national security arising out of his political activities in the UK, and despite the fact that he had been tortured in India during his previous visit there and many family members had been killed or ill-treated at the hands of the security forces in Punjab. As this was a national security case, he had no right of appeal against deportation or the refusal of asylum and in the unsuccessful judicial review proceedings he was limited to a challenge based on irrationality grounds. The Home Office justified refusal of asylum because torture at the hands of police was not the policy of the Indian government, was not condoned by them and could be seen as an excess in the course of legitimate operations against terrorists, rather than Convention persecution. Further, even if he had a well-founded fear of persecution, the Home Office decided that the national security grounds for his deportation meant that the proviso to Article 33 of the Refugee Convention applied and he could not therefore claim the benefit of the prohibition on return to a place where his life and freedom would be threatened for Convention reasons.

By contrast, the European Court of Human Rights held firstly that expulsion was prohibited where there were substantial grounds for believing that there was a real likelihood of torture or inhuman or degrading treatment. Secondly, it found that the prohibition on expulsion was absolute and could not be balanced against a risk to risk security, and that, in this context, the European Convention on Human Rights offered greater protection than the Refugee Convention. Thirdly, it held that, having regard to the importance of the issues and the absolute nature of the obligation, the domestic court should itself ascertain whether the evidence demonstrated the existence of substantial grounds, and that that task should be evaluated without regard to the grounds for the expulsion.

Following *Chahal*, the government released several asylum seekers who had been detained on national security grounds, and whom the government had alleged were excluded from protection under the Refugee Convention, either subject to the proviso to Article 33 or the exclusion clause under Article

63 *Chahal*, *supra* n. 13. Subsequently, in *Ahmed*, *supra* n. 24, a Somali refugee in Austria was deprived of the protection of Art. 33 of the Refugee Convention because of a conviction for street robbery, but he was nevertheless protected by Art. 3 of the European Convention on Human Rights.

1(F).[64] Thus, the greater protection afforded by the European Convention on Human Rights extends to (i) the absence of the requirement of Refugee Convention reasons for persecution; (ii) a procedural requirement for assessment of the risk of ill-treatment, and (iii) a prohibition on dilution of the protection by exclusion or derogation. A reasonable observer might conclude that the tension between humanity and self interest and the administrative burden on the courts in resolving asylum appeals, might be considerably eased if the Refugee Convention were interpreted as far as possible in conformity with the European Convention on Human Rights and if, at the least, one set of appellate procedures dealt with all protection issues. However, a series of apparently disconnected questions is currently determined in different jurisdictions, with further tensions arising as to whether the facts found in one appeal should bind the decision-taker in considering other protection issues.[65]

Refugee lawyers might be concerned that the European Convention on Human Rights imposes disadvantageous difference compared with the definition of refugee, since, in theory at least, persecution under the Refugee Convention might encompass a greater range of ill-treatment than torture or inhuman or degrading treatment. However, this is unlikely to be so in the light of the subsequent decision of the European Court Human Rights in the case of *D. v. UK*,[66] where a similar absolute prohibition on expulsion was held to exist in the case of the proposed deportation of a convicted drugs smuggler who was suffering the terminal stages of AIDS and the medical and social facilities to maintain his life and to permit him to die with dignity were unavailable in his homeland. The recognition that interference with human dignity is the touchstone of the conduct prohibited by Article 3 of the European

64 These included the appellant in *T. v. Secretary of State for the Home Department* [1996] AC 742. T. was an Algerian asylum seeker whose participation in a terrorist bomb outrage had been held by the House of Lords to be a non-political crime that excluded him from protection.

65 For instance, in *Shah*, the case was remitted to the High Court for further consideration of the question whether the Minister was bound by the adjudicator's findings of fact in refusing to grant exceptional leave to remain. The Minister has now granted both ELR. In the case of *R. v. Secretary of State for the Home Department ex p. Danaei*, QBD [1997] Imm. A.R. p.366, *Times Law Report*, 28 March 1997, the High Court concluded that the Secretary of State was so bound when considering a case of ill-treatment outside the Refugee Convention, and the Court of Appeal agreed, *Times Law Report*, 3 Jan. 1998.

66 *D. v. UK*, *supra* n. 24.

Convention on Human Rights, is likely to supplement a reading of persecution that embraces severe discrimination as well as threats to life, liberty and bodily integrity. A similar approach to torture or inhuman or degrading treatment has been taken by the UN Human Rights Committee and the Committee against Torture,[67] suggesting that these provisions are now part of customary international law rather than some standard peculiar to the European Convention.

In summary, where there is a real risk of ill-treatment of a minimum level of severity, the international community has already agreed to broader criteria of protection. There is no balance to be performed between self interest and humanity but merely a duty to ensure that protection is provided to those who need it. Whilst the European Convention on Human Rights says little about the grant of a positive status and access to employment and housing benefits, there is every reason to believe that states which refuse humanitarian relief to those who they could not expel, or fail to fulfil the requirements of dignity as propounded by the European Court of Human Rights will fall foul of their national courts.[68] This is so, even assuming EU Member States fail to act on the proposals of the European Commission in Brussels for common standards of humanitarian assistance to asylum seekers and those in need of temporary protection.[69]

Refugee status will remain the more desirable option, whilst temporary protection under other instruments gives rise to an uncertain status with no expectation of regularisation or indefinite leave. The Court of Appeal has noted in the case of *Adan and Nooh*,[70] that the Refugee Convention neither requires residence for a particular period nor gives a right to settlement forthwith. Refugee status can be revoked under the cessation clause of Article 1(C) if the circumstances in connection with which it was granted have ceased

---

67 See e.g. Committee against Torture, *Mutombo v. Switzerland* (Communication No. 13/1993); *Ismail Alan v. Switzerland* (Communication No. 21/1995); *Tapia Paez v. Sweden* (Communication No. 39/1996); *Pauline Muzonzo Paku Kisoki v. Sweden* (Communication No. 41/10996); *Kaveh Yaragh Tala v. Sweden* (Communication No. 43/1996).

68 See, e.g., *R. v. Secretary of State for Social Security ex p. Joint Council for the Welfare of Immigrants* [1997] 1 W.L.R. 275.

69 See European Commission proposals for a Joint Action on temporary protection of displaced persons 1997, Arts 6–9 (published in ILPA European Update June 1997). For the potential applicability of Art. 3 see the opinion of the European Commission of Human Rights in *Ahmed v. Austria*.

70 *Adan and Nooh, supra* n. 12.

to exist. This possibility was an important consideration for the Court's conclusion that Article 1 could be given a broad humanitarian interpretation which includes firstly, all those who have fled because of a well-founded fear of persecution and could not now avail themselves of protection because of a state of civil war and, secondly, all persons targeted in the inter-clan ethnic fighting in Somalia, whether combatants or otherwise.

There is thus a potential dilemma for refugee organisations: in seeking to broaden the scope of protection, are the expectation of long-term protection and integration of Convention refugees diminished? In the author's opinion, temporary protection and review of the refugee status by application of the cessation clauses are consistent with the requirements of international law, as long as the protected persons are not kept in a state of indefinite uncertainty and proper provision is made for family reunion within the period that protection is granted.

The Court of Appeal has concluded that the reference to family reunion in the Final Act of the delegates who drafted the Refugee Convention was not a Convention obligation and is not a requirement of the Immigration Rules. Policies as to family reunion for refugees are thus questions for national consideration and determination[71] and present policies in the UK distinguish firmly between refugee status and exceptional leave.[72] Although there is room for debate as to the content of particular policies, there are minimum standards which must be respected which are again found in other human rights instruments. The special importance of the welfare of the child is recognised in the UN Convention on the Rights of the Child, and a prohibition on expulsion to a country would certainly amount to an obstacle to family life being enjoyed there within the meaning of Article 8 of the European Convention on Human Rights. In those circumstances, a refusal to admit close and dependent family members of a person entitled to protection in the UK is likely to be an unnecessary and disproportionate interference with the right to respect for family life. Admittedly the Strasbourg jurisprudence on this topic has been disappointing but it is likely that the key factor in the surprising decision in

71 *Secretary of State for the Home Department v. D.S. Abdi* CA [1996] Imm. A.R. 148.

72 *Hersi and Others v. Secretary of State for the Home Department* [1996] Imm. A.R. 569. Refugees are normally granted family reunion for spouses and minor children forthwith on recognition and the requirements of ability to maintain and support without recourse to public funds are disapplied. Those with exceptional leave normally have to wait four years with no such disapplication, but speedier consideration can be given in special circumstances.

Gül v. Switzerland,[73] was that the sponsor with exceptional leave had subsequently returned to Turkey, suggesting that there was no obstacle to family life being conducted there.

Even if there was no private and family life claims when a person was first afforded protection, it is likely that such factors will arise after a number of years residence. If the circumstances requiring temporary protection last for more than five years, it is inappropriate that a subsequent change of circumstances could justify a forced expulsion to the country of origin. The purpose of international protection is that people should be able to get on with their lives in dignity and tranquillity, and not face an institutionalisation of insecurity.

Conclusion

The authors of the report *Providing Protection*[74] suggest that the government should provide enforceable guidelines for the grant of protection that address the major issues of the day, such as gender persecution, objections to military service in internationally condemned conflicts, and civil war refugees. The policy for protection should primarily be based on the Refugee Convention, liberally construed in accordance with its human rights origins, but should certainly embrace all other international obligations that would require the UK either to admit or to refrain from expelling those at risk from harm. There should be a single assessment of all protection issues, with a right of appeal competent to address those issues and review the factual foundations of adverse decisions.

With the present government committed both to incorporation of the European Convention on Human Rights into domestic law and a thorough review of asylum policies and procedures, there is a great opportunity for the UK to address principle and then identify the practice to give effect to it. It is only when the criteria for protection are firmly and fairly identified, that it will be possible to identify claims which raise no genuine protection issue and can be expedited through the system without disproportionate public expenditure. The narrow emphasis on the Refugee Convention in both the 1993 and 1996 Asylum Acts, renders a good case for protection on either criteria liable to be certified and "fast-tracked" through the system without

73 *Gül v. Switzerland* (1997) 22 E.H.R.R. 93.

74 Justice, ILPA, ARC, *supra* n. 7.

any resolution of the issues which will haunt subsequent proceedings.

The protection afforded need not be permanent in the first instance, but should not lead to frequent reviews or prolonged insecurity. There must be humane provision for family reunion, particularly if part of the policy for a single protection consideration is to avoid applications and appeals to improve status merely for the purpose of being joined by a close family member. Temporary protection is not in fact particularly favoured by government, because it is feared that once an asylum seeker is here, it will in practice be impossible to remove him or her.

Abusive claims are certainly a problem which requires serious consideration because, unless they are resolved, they will continue to distort asylum practice and criteria. If governments conclude that they cannot get rid of anybody they will exclude access to everybody: the good, the bad and the arguable. It may therefore be that governments and refugee organisations have a common interest in identifying fair and effective procedures for eliminating claims which have no prospect of raising a *bona fide* protection issue and for speedy removal from the jurisdiction of such cases. However, until there is agreement on who is entitled to protection, consensus as to a fair and effective system to identify them is likely to be missing. A human-rights-based approach saves the 1951 Convention from desiccation and irrelevance as a means of protection in the contemporary world. It provides the basis for a fair and effective regime of protection within the context of immigration policy, and provides the essential foundations of a necessary common European policy, where mutually binding obligations rather than quixotic national deviations must be the basis of harmonised action and measures to identify the appropriate country to determine asylum applications.

Bibliography

Crawley, H., *Women as Asylum Seekers: a Legal Handbook* (Refugee Women's Legal Group, Refugee Action, ILPA, June 1997).

Glidewell Panel, *Report from an independent enquiry into the implications and effects of the Asylum and Immigration Bill 1995 and related social security measures* (April 1996).

Hathaway, J., *The Law of Refugee Status* (Butterworths, 1991).

Justice/Immigration Law Practitioners' Association/Asylum Rights Campaign, *Providing Protection: Towards Fair and Effective Asylum Procedures* (London, July 1997).

Macdonald, I.A. and Blake, N., *Immigration Law and Practice in the United Kingdom* (4th edn, Butterworths, 1995).

Martin, D. and Guild, E., *Free Movement of Persons in the European Union* (Butterworths, 1996).

Marx, R., "The Criteria for the Determination of Refugee Status in the Federal Republic of Germany" (1992) 4 I.J.Ref.L. 151.

McGoldrick, D., *The Human Rights Committee: Its Role in the Development of the International Covenant on Civil and Political Rights* (Clarendon, Oxford, 1991).

UNHCR, *Handbook on Procedures and Criteria for Determining Refuge Status* (Geneva, re-edited 1992).

SECTION II
BEYOND THE DETERMINATION PROCESS

13 Health Screening for Newly-arrived Asylum Seekers and their Access to NHS Provision

DAVID JOBBINS

In the United Kingdom there is no reception programme for asylum seekers and new arrivals generally find out about services and entitlements in an *ad hoc* fashion. This is very much the case with health services and in most cases new arrivals regard access to health care as less of a priority than their asylum status and getting accommodation and money. It means that many asylum seekers do not consider how they can access the National Health Service (NHS) until they become ill. This is borne out by the fact that many organisations offering advice to new arrivals find that very few queries are made about health services. While this is not surprising, it is essential that the importance of the health service is emphasised, so that asylum seekers can access and use the appropriate services when they do need them.

The majority of people who apply for asylum at the port through which they have entered the country (the port of entry) will be referred to the Port Health Control Unit by the immigration officials. This is certainly the case at major ports such as Heathrow and Gatwick airports, although at smaller ports, such as the sea ports, the Port Health Control Units are only open for limited hours and a doctor may not be available for anything other than emergency call-out.

In August 1996 the Refugee Council obtained funding from the Communicable Disease Branch of the Department of Health for a two-year project to improve the provision at Port Health Control Units of information about the health screening asylum which seekers receive there and rights of access to the National Health Service. The project is also looking at ways in which Health Authorities in specific areas can address some of the issues and problems of initial access to health services. This chapter assesses the need for this project, how it has been established, its findings at the end of the first year, and the issues the project has raised about the current system and about refugee access to and usage of the NHS.

Background

The Department of Health has been concerned that the existing arrangements for health screening at ports of entry are insufficient, particularly with regard to the provision of translated information about the process of screening new arrivals for tuberculosis (TB). As a result, a health screening project has been put together which will not only provide translated information on health screening, but also simple and succinct information on the rights of asylum seekers and refugees to use the NHS without charge. This information has been translated into 10 languages, corresponding to the largest language groups currently claiming asylum in the UK, that is, Arabic, Farsi, French, Kurdish (Sorani), Polish, Portuguese, Somali, Spanish, Tamil and Turkish. By helping to establish appropriate systems which ensure that appropriate follow-up arrangements are established in, initially, three and later six Health Authorities, it is hoped that working relations between Health Authorities and refugee community organisations can be improved and that an effective "reception" arrangement can be set in place to ensure that all new arrivals are registered with a general medical practitioner (GP) as a matter of course.

It is the case that TB is now regarded as one of the world's most virulent diseases and it is endemic in many countries in sub-Saharan Africa, South-East Asia and Eastern Europe. It is estimated that there are 2,900,000 deaths each year from what is the world's largest single infectious cause of death amongst adults.[1] It is also the case that the majority of refugees in the world come from these countries.

The other cause for Department of Health concern is that there has also been a significant rise in the prevalence of TB among the homeless and the poor in Western Europe and particularly in the United States. Concerns about this rise in TB led the homelessness charity Crisis to produce a report, which showed that, in 1992–94, two per cent of the single homeless in London had TB, a figure 200 times the current notification rate in England and Wales.[2]

1 Kessler, C., Connolly, M., Levy, M. and Chaulet, P., "Tuberculosis Control in Refugees and Displaced Persons" (WHO, Geneva, 1996).

2 Citron, K.M., Southern, A. and Dixon, M., *Out of the Shadow* (Crisis, London, 1995).

The combined threat of the rise of TB from both refugees and the homeless has resulted in the present concern shown by the Department of Health which also supported a project addressing issues relating to TB among the homeless, which is being carried out at the same time as the refugee project.

The Current System of New Arrival Health Screening

When a person applies for asylum at the port of entry they are interviewed by immigration officials who then refer them to the Port Health Control Unit. By this time it is quite likely that the asylum seeker will be tired, disoriented and confused, all the more so if the individual does not speak English well. The Port Health Control Units at Heathrow and Gatwick are located adjacent to the Immigration Control offices and it is easy to make the mistake that the two are part of the same department. There are no posters and leaflets available in the Units to explain the procedure and it is thus unlikely that this misconception will be rectified, unless the individual speaks good English and has the confidence to question what is happening to him/her. It is not simply a matter of there being a dearth of information on health screening; there is nothing available in English or in translation on any subject.

Having said this, it would be wrong to give the impression that the staff in the Units are unhelpful or unfriendly. However, it is often the case that asylum seekers arrive at the Unit in groups which can mean that it can be quite hectic so that explanations are often overlooked. Access to interpreters is provided by the immigration officers which can add to an individual's concerns about confidentiality. Many asylum seekers are concerned that their asylum applications will be looked upon badly if they are not in good health and fear that health issues can be grounds for refusing asylum. Whilst most other immigrant groups can be turned away on health grounds, this is most certainly not the case with asylum seekers, whatever their condition. This is a message that is most important to get across and is a key element of the information this project has produced and is working to encourage Health Authorities to produce.

Health screening is generally restricted to those people coming from countries in those regions described earlier where there are high levels of TB and where there is therefore a high risk that people coming from those countries will be carrying the disease, at least in a latent form. It is also relevant for all asylum seekers although, if the immigration officials are busy, they may not have the time to take people to the Port Health Control Unit.

Once an asylum seeker is in the Unit they are asked for the address where they are going to live. However, it has been found that the majority of new arrivals have no clear idea where they are going, unless they have come for family reunion with relatives who have been granted refugee status or "exceptional leave to remain".[3] Even if there is a particular area they want to go to, they often do not have an address. They are then seen by a doctor who asks them a short series of questions about their health and probably sends them to be X-rayed at the Unit to identify any TB scarring on the lungs. Once screening has been done, a form is completed which is sent to the District Health Authority where the individual intends to live after leaving the port. However, at this time many asylum seekers do not know where they are going, which leads to long delays in notifying the District Health Authority, sometimes as long as several weeks. In the event of a person needing urgent treatment they are sent immediately to a local hospital.

When the initial asylum application interview and Port Health Control Unit screening have been completed the asylum seeker may be given "temporary admission", which means that they are free to go to their intended destination and must register their address with the Immigration and Nationality Department (IND) or the police and return when recalled for their asylum application to be assessed. If they are regarded as being someone likely to abscond and not return for their interview, they are put into detention for an unspecified period of time.[4] Detention Centres no longer use the NHS for anything other than emergency and inpatient referrals and services are provided by private health providers, often on a quite minimal basis, with privately-purchased GP cover.

Asylum seekers are often a mobile population, particularly during the initial period in this country, and are likely to live in some form of temporary accommodation whether it be in a hostel or with others from their community.[5] They are likely to move on, often several times, which means that asylum seekers may "disappear" and, even if these changes are recorded with the Immigration and Nationality Department, it is much less likely that this will be the case with the NHS. This situation becomes more understandable when

3 "Exceptional leave to remain" (ELR) is granted when the asylum seeker does not meet the criteria of the 1951 Geneva Refugee Convention but for humanitarian reasons is granted leave to remain in the UK.

4 For further details see Amnesty International, *Cell Culture: the Detention and Imprisonment of Asylum-seekers in the United Kingdom* (London, Dec. 1996) and the up-date report entitled *Dead Starlings* (April 1997).

5 See also chapter 18 of this book by Caroline Hunter.

one takes into account the method of "reception" into the local health services.

As has been stated earlier, the provision of information at Port Health Control Units is very limited, to say the least, and there is certainly nothing about the rights of asylum seekers to use the NHS once they have entered the country. There is also nothing to explain what the NHS is and that whilst it is part of the government-run public sector infrastructure, it is completely separate from the IND. There is also no reference to the concept of patient confidentiality which means that the IND has no right to demand information on an individual and that even if such information did reach the hands of immigration officials that it cannot be used as part of the asylum determination process. This does not apply to any medical reports that have been submitted in evidence as proof of torture or physical or mental abuse in support of an asylum application.[6]

Of course, there has to be a balance between providing the necessary information and overloading asylum seekers with data at a time of considerable distress and disorientation. However, the information currently available is plainly insufficient for the needs of the clients. People are often told that they will receive a notification from the Health Authority in the area where they are going to live and, if appropriate, that they should visit a doctor or a local hospital as early as possible. However, this information is generally provided verbally and in English, meaning that the message can easily be partly or wholly misunderstood. There is also likely to be suspicion about what will be done with this information and about what might happen when they present themselves at the GP surgery, clinic or hospital.

When the Port form is received by the District Health Authority it should be the case that a letter is sent out to the new arrival, generally by the Public Health Department, requesting they attend a health check. This task is a clear Health Authority responsibility which is often acted upon inadequately. The system and its implementation vary between districts and it is also the case that, due to the large numbers arriving in certain areas, particularly the inner London Health Authorities, little or no follow up occurs.

There is also the issue of the nature of the initial contact which the Health Authority has with the new arrival. This contact often varies in quality, depending on how great a priority newly arrived immigrants (of any description) are for that Health Authority. The minimum responsibility is to send a notification letter which will be sent in a standard envelope giving it an official and quite intimidating appearance which may deter some people from

6 See chapter 7 of this book by Michael Peel.

opening it or responding to the request. This deterrent effect is further heightened by the fact that the letter is, in most if not all cases, only in English thus making it meaningless to a sizeable proportion of recipients.

Already it can be seen that many new arrivals are either never contacted or, for various reasons, do not respond to contact. In some parts of London the district nurse, health visitor or community thoracic teams make direct physical contact with new arrivals, although often this is the type of service either under threat or already discontinued due to funding pressures. A partial reversal in this trend is the appointment, in recent years, of TB nurses in certain areas who work closely with refugee community organisations and new arrivals. However, because they are generally health visitors, they work only with pregnant women and young children. Where there are instances of young children among new arrivals, Health Authorities make particular efforts to contact them.

If the Health Authority is one which does not follow up on non-responses, and this is probably the situation in most Health Authorities, no further action will be taken and the individual is likely to "disappear" and be unlikely to have any dealings with the NHS until there is an urgent or emergency condition.

Even if a new arrival does receive a notification and does attend for a health check (if this is available) or treatment, there is no guarantee that they will be given all the information that they need about their health rights and how to access services, or even that they will be advised and supported in registering with a GP. Indeed, unless the nature and the reason for the contact is explained, it is likely that there will be misunderstanding about what the responses should be and whether there is a likelihood of being charged for whatever service is provided.

There are issues which follow from this, such as whether GPs feel prepared to treat refugees and asylum seekers, or if they want them on their lists. This means that even if refugees and asylum seekers do get registered, they may not feel happy with the service they receive and may not use the NHS. They may get a poor quality service which does not adequately address their needs or they may only be registered as temporary patients.[7] It is true that as "ordinary

7 These issues have been widely researched and the issues raised are often similar whichever community is being discussed. See National Development Team, *The Health of Refugees* (Refugee Council, London, 1994) and Olatunbosun, T. and Hirst, M., *National Conference on the Health and Social Welfare of Refugees* (Healthy Islington 2000, London, 1992) for a discussion of the main issues and the Croydon and Ealing, Hammersmith and Hounslow reports to gain an understanding of what happens in particular areas, although the Health Authority

residents" refugees and asylum seekers are entitled to a GP and if they fail to find one, the Health Authority can assign them to a practice. However, they are still likely to experience the same problems and will probably face worse, in that they are at risk of being labelled problem patients that the GP does not want because they have been assigned to them.[8]

It can therefore be seen that, for many reasons, it is difficult for a sizeable proportion of newly arrived asylum seekers to find out about, access and use the health services to which they are entitled. With regard to the issue of TB transmission, accessing health services is particularly important when the standard of living of many asylum seekers (whether or not in receipt of welfare benefits) is taken into account. Indeed, it is clear to many of those concerned with TB transmission that "living in poor conditions ... raises the risk of communicable diseases such as tuberculosis which is a growing risk among the homeless".[9] It is the premise of this project that by explaining what is happening to them in an understandable form and by providing information and support from a joint "community organisation-NHS" base, rather than the standard NHS notification, newly arrived asylum seekers will have more information, more confidence in that information and be more likely to present themselves for any necessary treatment or consultations. Thus, they will be able to access and use the NHS more effectively.

From what has already been said, it can be seen that people claiming asylum after entry into the country are unlikely to receive a health screening, meaning that there is no record sent to the Health Authority and thus a reduced chance of linking into the NHS. The Asylum and Immigration Act 1996 has meant that the numbers claiming asylum at the port of entry are now rising from the previous norm of approximately one third to over half of all applications.[10] This figure is likely to continue to rise, although there will still be a high number of people claiming asylum after they have entered the country and thus not receiving information on the NHS from statutory sources.

reports may be difficult to obtain and the other two reports out of print. A more recent report on access to health services is Bariso, E.U., *The Horn of Africa Health Research Project* (Healthy Islington 2000, London, 1997) which assesses the situation in Camden and Islington and may be more readily available.

8 See Jobbins, D., *The Health Concerns of Asylum Seekers and Refugees – Factfiles Nos 1 and 2* (Refugee Council, London, 1997) which examine access issues.

9 See Jobbins, D., *op. cit. supra* n. 8, Factfile No. 1, p. 2.

10 The number of port applications for asylum rose from 32 per cent of all applications in Jan. 1996, before benefits were withdrawn, to 64 per cent by Dec. 1996 and an average of 50 per cent in the five months to May 1997. H.C. Hansard, Vol. 298, Col. 263 W.A., 17 July 1997.

Health Screening for Newly-arrived Asylum Seekers in Belgium

The system for the reception of asylum seekers in the rest of Europe is often very different from that in operation in the UK. Taking Belgium as an example, useful conclusions can be drawn by looking at that country's experience of addressing the issue of TB among asylum seekers.[11] In Belgium there is no system for the medical examination or TB screening of asylum seekers on arrival, as there is in the UK. However, whilst awaiting a decision on their application, they are accommodated in transit or reception centres. Medical care is available in these centres and those given refugee status can access all health services.

In 1993 the Flemish Lung and Tuberculosis Association (VRGT) began to visit the Central Transit Centre in Brussels, which accommodates a third of all Belgium's asylum seekers, on a weekly basis with mobile X-ray equipment and invited all asylum seekers to attend for a chest X-ray. Those found to have active TB were then referred for treatment. To date this is the extent of new arrival screening and there appears to be little evidence of later preventive work with refugee communities, despite the commonly held belief that poor diet and malnutrition are likely to suppress the immune system, thus raising the risk of the development of the disease.

The article in the *European Respiratory Journal*[12] recommends that the Belgian Government introduce a systematic screening process, on the grounds that nearly half of those screened who had suspect chest X-rays disappeared before further medical investigation could take place. It also appears to be the case that the Health Authorities in Belgium have no system for the registration of addresses of refugees which means that unless individuals come forward there is no structure for any follow up. It can be seen from this example that although the Belgian Government has a much more closely regulated system for the reception of asylum seekers and the processing of their asylum applications the provision of health-care and the prevention of infection is much less systematised and is less likely to provide health screening and treatment when people need it.

It is worth noting that despite the various barriers to accessing health care in the UK the example of Belgium shows that the UK compares favourably and indeed no other European country offers a universal right to access its

11 Van den Brande, P., Vydebrouck, M., Vermcire, P. and Demedts, M., "Tuberculosis in Asylum Seekers in Belgium", (1997) 10 *European Respiratory Journal.*

12 *Ibid.*

health service (even though there are often many problems in exercising this right in the UK). There is no reason for complacency in the NHS, as this project is seeking to show in the area of new arrivals, but the implication is that harmonisation of European policy on this issue may not actually enhance refugee access to health provision.[13]

The Health Screening Project for Newly-arrived Asylum Seekers

The project was carried out in the first year by David Jobbins, then Health Access Adviser at the Refugee Council, with the close support of Vivien Hughes, the project support worker, who undertook most of the liaison, monitoring and support work. The project can be divided into four sections:

(a) Initial screening at the Port Health Control Unit
(b) Follow up and linkage with Health Authority in district of residence
(c) Registration with a GP
(d) Developing working relationships between refugee community organisations (RCOs) and Health Authorities

Initial screening at the Port Health Control Unit

When the project began, the responsible Communicable Disease Consultant and the staff at the Port Health Control Units at Heathrow and Gatwick airports were briefed about the issues causing refugees to flee to the UK and about the resulting likely range of health implications. They were also given a briefing paper about the project, what it aimed to achieve and what the role of the Units would be. These meetings were a key component in the development of the project because it gave the staff the opportunity to air their concerns and discuss any potential problems that could arise. It also provided the opportunity to dispel a few myths about refugees and asylum seekers and to present the work as something which would not only improve the provision of information for new arrivals and strengthen their ability to access services but would help port health staff to do their work more effectively by improving information and communication and the quality of the service being provided. It was explained that provision of translated information would also reduce the stress

13 For more general discussion of harmonisation of European policy on asylum see chapter 3 of this book by Richard Dunstan.

which often results from not being able to communicate properly. Staff at the Port Health Control Units were regarded as important in promoting the project and avoiding any risk of hostility from staff who might otherwise have seen the project as inherently critical of the way that they did their jobs. It was also explained that there would not be any significant rise in their workload.

Although crucial to the success of the project, the process of screening at the Port Health Control Unit is very straightforward. Posters in English and 10 of the most commonly-spoken languages among refugees currently coming to the UK are on show in the Unit. These posters make three points which are (i) that a new arrival's health will be checked and they may be X-rayed for TB, which is a treatable condition; (ii) that asylum seekers and refugees have full free access to the NHS in most cases, and (iii) that health checks are not connected to the asylum application process.

Asylum seekers are asked for their contact address so that the Health Authority where they will live can contact them. If the asylum seeker says that they are going to one of the three pilot districts, namely Bromley, Hackney or Lambeth, they are given an information leaflet which is translated into the same languages as the poster. The leaflet gives brief information covering the health check in the Unit, entitlement to use NHS services and the sort of follow up that may occur in the area they are going to live. One of the most important parts of the leaflet is on the back page where the name, address and telephone number of a link refugee organisation has been stamped. This is an organisation which has agreed to be involved in the project and will give support and advice about health services in their area. Equally important is the fact that they are not part of the government system and so it is hoped that new arrivals will not feel intimidated and suspicious about what information will be believed and what they will have to reveal about themselves. People going to the three pilot districts are given a unique numerical identifier so that they can be traced through the system to see whether the provision of this information when they first enter the country improves their overall ability to access and use health services. This number is recorded on the Port form which is sent to the Health Authority.

The new arrivals are then seen by the doctor and are probably X-rayed. If they have not already been interviewed by the immigration officers they go to see them. Unless they are going to be detained, they are then given temporary admission and allowed into the country. If they do not have an address to go to, they are sent to the Refugee Arrivals Project (RAP) at Heathrow (this also applies to those arriving at Gatwick who go by shuttle to Heathrow). Those going into detention lie outside the remit of this project and, whilst it is important to identify this group, as work needs to be done to ensure that appropriate health services are accessible, they are not discussed further in this chapter.[14]

The Refugee Arrivals Project provides a service for new arrivals which consists of two nights' accommodation at a hostel in Hounslow, followed by the provision of an address and support in going to the Benefits Agency, the Homeless Persons Unit, social services and, if time allows, registration with a GP. Unfortunately the Refugee Arrivals Project can only spend one day with each client and this means that there is often not enough time to go to the doctor, so health access is not covered.

The Refugee Arrivals Project clearly plays an important role in access to services for new arrivals and so it was important to involve them as a partner in this project. When new arrivals go to RAP without an address they allocate them one. They are thus in a position to identify those going to the three pilot districts and can give them a leaflet. This address can then be notified to the Port Health Control Unit who can allocate a numerical identifier and give this information to the Health Authority of residence. The only major problem that has emerged so far is the fact that a large number of new arrivals do not receive an initial address until they go to RAP. This means that they do not receive a leaflet until after they have been screened. This is an issue which the project will need to examine to see if it can be resolved. It should be pointed out that this would not be a problem if all new arrivals were in the scheme because everyone would get a leaflet and initial address would be irrelevant. Another problem has been the time it has taken to translate and publish materials which has delayed the commencement of the project. However, now that all materials have either been produced or are in the process of production, this issue has been resolved.

Once asylum seekers have left the Port Health Control Unit their notification forms should be processed as soon as possible and sent on to the respective Health Authorities. This is generally done within two days although, as described earlier, delays sometimes occur. Inevitably, a number of people will not go to the address at all. Thus, it is important to note that parts of the sample groups will disappear throughout the system, although it may be the case that, if asylum seekers develop greater trust in the NHS and become less suspicious of dealing with the NHS, as a result of improved provision of information, this percentage will drop.

---

14 See *supra* n. 4 and chapter 14 of this book by Charles Watters.

Follow Up and Linkage with Health Authority in District of Residence

The rest of the project takes place at the pilot sites and concerns the building of links between involved parties and the provision of information about local services which enable access when it is needed. The project builds on the local structures and systems in each district which means that models have developed differently in each area. Having said this there are some guiding principles which the various NHS structures should be aiming to achieve. These principles are that

- translations and interpreters should be used to improve the quality of communication,
- contact should be sought as soon as possible, and
- lack of response should be followed up.

The involvement of refugee community organisations is a crucial element of this project and, whilst the project staff have actively canvassed and encouraged refugee community organisations to participate, it can only work if they are keen and supportive of the aims of the project. However, since many umbrella RCOs are not staffed, liaison has actually had to be with the individual member organisations. These are under-resourced and have a high demand for their services, and are largely dependent on volunteers, so contact and liaison is quite difficult. It is also the case that resources are not available to put new arrivals in touch with an RCO representing their own community in the first instance, so it is likely that people may need to be referred on from their initial point of contact.

Given that it has only proved feasible to work with a small number of community organisations (where possible with umbrella organisations), the project has meant that contact RCOs have had to take on extra work. This has been an issue which the project has had to take into consideration in assessing what is achievable. An important principle in linking new arrivals with RCOs is that contact must be at the instigation of the new arrivals and their right to confidentiality and privacy is paramount. This means that the RCOs are not given new arrival data and contact is at the instigation of individual new arrivals. Another relevant issue is that the human and financial resources of RCOs are very limited, making it quite difficult for them to be involved in meetings, even if they are providing help and advice to new arrivals. It is hoped that Health Authorities will see that resource availability is a key issue if communities are to play a major role in their own health.

Registration with a GP

The successful registration of the new arrival is being used as an indicative outcome to assess the success of the project in improving access to health services. Therefore, this is an issue which is being discussed with the pilot districts. Systems have been put in place to collect this information. Clearly access in itself does not prove that the system fully meets the health needs of newly arrived asylum seekers, but it is a crucial first step, particularly given the structure of the NHS. It is a building block on which to develop and improve the quality of the services provided.

Developing Working Relationships Between RCOs and Health Authorities

The development of working relationships between RCOs and Health Authorities is a by-product of the project but it is essential to the improvement of health service access. The aim is that the different organisations involved in the project will have a shared purpose and that by remaining in contact they can develop the debate and discussion about health service access beyond the parameters of the project itself.

In each pilot district a "district team" has been formed, with representation from involved organisations. This team assesses the progress of the project and any issues which arise, enabling all parties to "put faces to names" and thus making future debate and discussion more effective and, perhaps, less formal. The district team is thus central to the effectiveness of the project. Initially, there was a level of opposition to the project from some community organisations which felt that it contributed to the impression that refugees were to blame for TB and that the work would further stigmatise them as a group. This is a valid point and clearly the issue has to be presented carefully so as to emphasise that the work benefits asylum seekers when they arrive by linking them to health services, rather than the process being perceived as an adjunct to the work of the immigration service.

The Project Team

A "project team" has also been established for the project as a whole to provide a forum for monitoring progress and addressing problems which arise. This comprises representatives from the RCOs and Health Authority in each pilot district, the two Port Health Control Units, the Refugee Arrivals Project and the Refugee Council. The project team meets quarterly, allowing members to see the merits of the various systems employed in each district. In order to allow an independent perspective, the project team is chaired by the medical adviser from a major international charity who has been involved in TB programmes in developing countries.[15] This has the advantage of providing impartial input into the project from an informed source who is directly involved.

Findings of the Project

As of late 1997 the project was moving towards the halfway stage in its two-year life and the pilot sites had been active since 1 April 1997. This chapter outlines some of the initial findings and developments achieved thus far, although it is still too early to undertake any meaningful analysis of the figures. This will clearly form an important element of the final report. It is hoped that by the end of the project the pilot sites will have developed beyond their status in June 1997 and that some of the problems will be resolved by the end of 1998. However, this midpoint is a useful point at which to assess the interim findings.

The Port Health Control Units and Refugee Arrivals Project

Leaflets are now available at the Port Health Control Units but, as described earlier, the number being distributed is limited because many new arrivals do not have an address. At present the poster is only in English because changes in the text have delayed the translation and production timescale but the translated posters are expected to be ready by late 1997. In both Units the general impression of staff is that the project adds very little extra work to their day and they have no misgivings about involvement because they see the advantage of providing translated information. Having said this, they see little apparent advantage in this pilot stage because they are not able to distribute many leaflets due to the lack of addresses.

Consideration of what further information new arrivals may need resulted in a decision to produce a translated card giving further information about the X-ray process. This is to be given only to those who specifically ask, because it was thought that this information could worry people unnecessarily. It was also decided that the information provided should be kept to a minimum

15 Save the Children Fund.

because this was not the right time to give a lot of information when new arrivals undoubtedly had other, greater concerns. It is for this reason that the emphasis on information giving is placed on the pilot site where they are going to live. The staff in the Units have also been considering what other changes could be made to improve the service, such as the translation of some of the forms. Work in these other areas has not yet begun but it can be regarded as a positive sign that the project appears to be acting as a catalyst for other improvements being generated by the staff themselves. The final report will include the results of a qualitative survey which will look at the impression of the Units formed by new arrivals, both before and after the commencement of the project, to assess whether the project improves the experience of undergoing health screening. Unfortunately this study has not yet been completed so no analysis is yet available.

At this time the majority of leaflets are being given out by the staff at RAP, who see their input as adding to the value of their existing role. However, they are wary of the potential impact it might have on their team which is already very busy due to the rise in the numbers claiming asylum at the port of entry. It is also clear that they do not want to do the statutory authorities' work for them, which, while not the case at the moment, will need to be closely monitored. One outcome noticeable already is that the project has helped forge links between the Port Health Control Units and RAP, and there is now a more rapid flow of addresses from RAP to the Units, thus allowing the Port forms to be sent out more quickly.

The Pilot Sites

Research at the start of the project showed that different systems were in place in each of the three pilot sites and the project has aimed to build on the strengths within each. A team has been formed in each site which meets approximately every two months and has proved a useful forum for bringing people together locally, although it has often proved difficult to get attendance from community organisations because of resource issues.

All three Health Authorities have been enthusiastic about their involvement. This is likely to be due to a combination of concerns about the undoubted rise of TB in the UK and also a recognition of the problems that are likely to arise if newly-arrived asylum seekers as well as other refugees cannot access health services effectively. This even seems to be the case in Bromley, which has comparatively low numbers but has a weaker infrastructure, with poor access to interpreting, a small voluntary and RCO sector and a general lack of familiarity with refugee issues among the statutory authorities. In Hackney, funding problems have put the large array of projects and services aimed at improving access and quality of service for ethnic minorities at risk, and have also led to a deterioration in relations between the Health Authority and community organisations which, as yet, has not affected this project. In Lambeth, the large numbers of new arrivals has led the Health Authority to reduce the amount of follow-up since the inception of the project, with the result that follow-up only takes place with those displaying signs of TB and where there are young children and babies involved. The project is looking for ways to work around this problem by developing information and awareness raising through services such as the Lambeth, Southwark and Lewisham Refugee Outreach Team

An unexpected outcome has been the interest shown in the project by clinicians involved in the treatment of TB. The District Team meetings in both Hackney and Lambeth now involve practitioners which makes them a useful vehicle for raising issues and discussing problems which arise. It has also been the case that clinicians in Lambeth have offered to provide information for refugees on TB and health, and an article has already appeared in the Refugee Council's Community Development Newsletter, which is widely distributed to many RCOs. It is hoped that similar work will be undertaken in other areas and that districts will share each other's work.

The Other Port Health Control Unit Pilot Project

At the same time that this project has been running, the Department of Health has been piloting another project in the Port Health Control Unit at Terminal Three, Heathrow, which has streamlined and computerised the work they do. One element of this is that at Terminal Three the screening of most new arrivals has now stopped and responsibility for this has been passed to Health Authorities. In inner London this has serious resource implications due to the large numbers of arrivals and the failure to make extra money available to do this screening work. This means that in some areas new arrivals are not being screened, or their health checked, at any stage when they first arrive in the UK, unless there is a recognisable illness apparent at the Port Health Control Unit or there are young children involved. This other pilot is currently being evaluated and it is to be hoped that this serious flaw can be noted and remedied.

Impact of the Asylum and Immigration Act 1996 on Access to Health Services

It is important to note a key area which this chapter has not discussed, that is, the Asylum and Immigration Act 1996. Clearly this piece of legislation (together with the Housing Act 1996) has had a significant impact on all refugee communities, not least in the area of the provision of fixed accommodation.[16] In theory at least, there has been no change in the right to access health services. Despite this, the legislation was successful in raising the spectre of the "bogus" asylum seeker in the popular psyche[17] and this has undoubtedly led to a hardening of attitudes towards asylum seekers and refugees in some quarters. This change in attitude is likely to have had an impact on the experience of refugees in the UK, even though this is difficult to quantify. It should also be said that the election of a Labour Government in May 1997 has seen a softening of attitudes in the way that refugees are portrayed and the Act implemented.

The main group of asylum seekers affected directly by the Act are those who apply for asylum after entering the country and those who are on appeal following a negative decision on their initial application. The former of these two groups have probably not had the same experience as a port application asylum seeker at the Port Health Control Units, if they were referred there at all. They thus fall outside the scope of the project under discussion. The latter would have had the same experience as port asylum seekers and the point at which the impact of losing welfare benefits and having to rely on local authority support under the National Assistance Act 1948 was, at the very least, a number of months after arrival. It is important to note the impact of the Act on the health and social wellbeing of refugees in the UK which is discussed elsewhere in this publication.[18]

Conclusion

A report by the Joint Tuberculosis Committee of the British Thoracic Society in 1994[19] discussed what systems should be put in place to prevent and control

16 See chapter 18 of this book by Caroline Hunter.

17 See also chapter 2 of this book by Craig Young.

18 See e.g. chapter 14 of this book by Charles Watters.

19 See Joint Tuberculosis Committee of the British Thoracic Society, *Control and Prevention of Tuberculosis in the United Kingdom: Code of Practice* 49 (1994) Thorax 1198.

TB. They noted that there was at that time a high prevalence of TB among immigrants from Asia, Africa and South and Central America and that these were groups which should be targeted by the NHS. It was clear then that the structures in place were not robust enough to address the situation. It found:

> Most tuberculosis disease in immigrants develops after arrival in the UK and is not evident on admission. Whilst some initial screening occurs, it is neither comprehensive nor very effective in informing districts. It is vital that information on all new immigrants is passed to the Consultant in Communicable Disease Control, or equivalent in the district of intended residence, so that comprehensive screening can be arranged.[20]

This rather dry statement very much sums up the current situation. However, whilst there is much to do in improving the effectiveness of systems, care must be taken to ensure that other European models, such as that in Belgium, are not adopted as a way of saving money or streamlining the service.

The project has also given individuals working in the same field in different organisations the opportunity (their first in some cases) to discuss issues about how new arrivals access health services. It has allowed them to consider how the services they provide can be improved within the parameters of their local situations. The enthusiasm shown has proved that this is an area where work is needed. The value of the project has been as much in the opportunity it has provided for organisations which are directly involved to improve cooperation, as in the specific results achieved. The project has also raised questions about issues outside its core agenda, such as how the Port Health Control Units liaise with immigration staff and the limited input possible from RCOs, given the current low levels of funding they receive.

The final report of the project will be distributed to all Health Authorities and Port Health Control Units in the country. It will recommend good practice and encourage all areas to consider how best to address the issues concerning newly arrived asylum seekers in their own areas. It is also hoped that the Department of Health will give serious consideration to what it expects from Port Health Control Units and will fund them appropriately, so that, for example, all necessary information is translated and available as a matter of course. It will be the decision of each individual Health Authority as to how they respond to the work of this project but it is hoped that they will at least give serious thought as to whether they are really meeting their responsibilities towards this often vulnerable section of the community.

---

20 *Ibid.*

Bibliography

Bariso, E.U., *The Horn of Africa Health Research Project: An Assessment of the Accessibility and Appropriateness of Health Care Services to the Horn of Africa (Eritrean, Ethiopian Oromo and Somali) Communities in Camden and Islington* (Healthy Islington, London, 1997).

Citron, K.M., Southern, A. and Dixon, M., *Out of the Shadow* (Crisis, London, 1995).

Jobbins, D., *The Health Concerns of Asylum Seekers and Refugees*, Factfiles Nos 1–6, (Refugee Council, London, 1997).

Joint Tuberculosis Committee of the British Thoracic Society, *Control and Prevention of tuberculosis in the United Kingdom: Code of Practice* 49 (1994) Thorax 1198.

Kessler, C., Connolly, M., Levy, M. and Chaulet, P., *Tuberculosis Control in Refugees and Displaced Persons* (WHO, Geneva, 1996).

National Development Team, *The Health of Refugees* (Refugee Council, London, 1994).

Olatunbosun, T. and Hirst, M., *National Conference on the Health and Social Welfare of Refugees*, (Healthy Islington 2000, London, 1992).

Owens, B. and Redding, D., *Poor in Health* (Save the Children, London, 1996).

Palmer, C., *Health Provision to Refugees in Ealing, Hammersmith and Hounslow* (Ealing, Hammersmith and Hounslow Health Authority, London, 1994).

Refugee Health Team, *Specialist Team for Refugees and Recent Arrivals Report* (Croydon Health Authority, London, unpublished, 1994).

Van den Brande, P., Vydebrouck, M., Vermeire, P. and Demedts, M., "Tuberculosis in Asylum Seekers in Belgium", 10 (1997) *European Respiratory Journal*.

14 The Mental Health Needs of Refugees and Asylum Seekers: Key Issues in Research and Service Development

CHARLES WATTERS

This chapter focuses on three areas. Firstly, on the implications of recent legal and policy changes on the mental health of refugees and asylum seekers, highlighting, in particular, the response of local authorities. It then identifies key issues in the mental health care of refugees and asylum seekers in the United Kingdom, drawing attention to the needs of particular groups and deficiencies in service provision. Finally, it considers some theoretical and methodological issues in undertaking research on refugees and suggests that there may be lessons to be learnt from studies of settled minority communities.

Mental Health Implications of the Asylum and Immigration Act 1996

Among the measures introduced by the Asylum and Immigration Act 1996 were severe restrictions on asylum seekers' entitlement to welfare benefits and social housing. As a result only those claiming asylum at the port of entry are now allowed access to benefits. Asylum seekers who apply for asylum once inside the UK are not entitled to claim income support, housing and council tax benefits. All asylum seekers are no longer entitled to a wider range of benefits including child benefit, disability living allowance and family credit.

The effects of these changes were that many asylum seekers were faced with destitution having access neither to money nor accommodation. When the changes were introduced around two-thirds of all asylum claims were made once inside the UK.[1] Asylum seekers may well not apply for asylum at the port of entry for a variety of reasons. Arrival in the UK is, for many, the final stage of a very long and arduous journey during which they have faced great danger both within their own country and during flight.[2] Escape has often only been achieved through obtaining false documents. Use of false documents has been exacerbated owing to the fact that by 1995 the UK had introduced visa requirements for nationals from 85 countries, including all but two of the countries producing significant numbers of asylum applications to the UK.[3] Asylum seekers often fear that applying for asylum at this stage will result in them being removed from the country and there is ample evidence of asylum seekers being sent back and forth between countries. Furthermore, many asylum seekers have been severely traumatised by their experiences and are in no fit state to make an application on arrival.[4]

In response to the crisis faced by many asylum seekers, a broad coalition of voluntary agencies and other groups attempted to provide some basic necessities to asylum seekers. The Refugee Council opened a day centre for destitute asylum seekers in London during May 1996, called the Karibu Centre, and a night-shelter was opened in September 1996.[5]

The Response of Local Authorities

Some asylum seekers still had a right to access local authority services. Those with children under 18 were entitled to services under the Children Act 1989.

---

1 The 1996 removal of entitlement to benefits from all asylum seekers except those claiming asylum at the border, meant that the number of port applications increased from 32 per cent of all applications in Jan. 1996, before benefits were withdrawn, to 64 per cent by Dec. 1996 and an average of 50 per cent in the five months to May 1997. H.C. Hansard, Vol. 298, Col. 263 W.A., 17 July 1997.

2 Ager, A., *Mental Health Issues in Refugee Populations: A Review*, Working paper for Harvard Center for the study of Culture and Medicine, Harvard Medical School, Department of Social Medicine (1994).

3 Joly, D., Kelly, L. and Nettleton, C., *Refugees in Europe: the Hostile New Agenda* (Minority Rights Group International, London, 1997) p. 19. Visa restrictions continue to be used as a deterrent measure. See most recently, *Statement of Changes in Immigration Rules*, HC 161, 30 July 1997.

4 Ager, *op. cit. supra* n. 2, p. 10.

5 Refugee Council, *Just Existence: A Report on the Lives of Asylum Seekers who have Lost Entitlements to Benefits in the UK* (Feb. 1997).

This could include payments for accommodation, food and other living expenses. Unaccompanied children had a right to be "looked after" by local authorities under the Children Act.

A legal challenge against several London boroughs was initiated by the Refugee Council in 1996 to clarify the extent to which local authorities were required to offer assistance to asylum seekers under the National Assistance Act 1948. The resulting judgment confirmed that local authorities had a duty to provide assistance under the Act to any asylum seeker who could prove that s/he had "no other means of support". The services had to include provision for "food, shelter and warmth".[6] Despite an appeal by local authorities the judgment was conclusively upheld in February 1997 and local authorities were refused leave to appeal to the House of Lords.[7]

The effect of this judgment is that any asylum seeker without access to benefits is entitled to be referred to their local authority social services department where their needs will be assessed under the terms of the National Assistance Act and the National Health Service and Community Care Act 1990. The local authority then has a duty to provide services for the asylum seeker which ensures that s/he is adequately accommodated and has access to food.

As a result of these rulings, £40,000,000 has been transferred from the Department of Health to help compensate local authorities for the increase in expenditure. However, local authorities are concerned that the money they are receiving is not enough to meet asylum seekers needs. One London authority unsuccessfully challenged restrictions which prohibited it from passing on cash payments to asylum seekers.[8] Another, the London Borough of Westminster, reportedly sought to move hundreds of asylum seekers to Liverpool in an attempt to cut costs.[9] The borough estimated that the cost to the authority of feeding and housing an asylum seeker in Liverpool was £126 per week as compared with £175 per week in London.[10]

---

6 *R. v. Hammersmith and Fulham London Borough Council, ex p. M. (and other cases), Times Law Report,* 10 Oct. 1996. See also chapters 11 and 18 of this book by C.J. Harvey and Caroline Hunter respectively.

7 *R. v. Hammersmith and Fulham L.B.C., ex p. M. (and other cases), Times Law Report,* 19 Feb. 1997.

8 A view that was subsequently upheld in the courts: *R. v. Secretary of State for Health, ex p. Hammersmith and Fulham L.B.C., Independent,* 15 July 1997.

9 Travis, A., "Asylum Seekers Sent from Capital", *Guardian,* 16 May 1997.

10 *Ibid.*

While these judgments have prevented many asylum seekers from becoming totally destitute, the effect of the 1996 Act has been to remove any measure of autonomy which asylum seekers may have had. Local authorities often perceive asylum seekers as an unwelcome additional burden on already overstretched budgets. Their needs are neither known nor planned for and there are rarely facilities which are appropriate to them. Some of the problems local authorities face in relation to refugees and asylum seekers are summarised below. Many are shared with health services and other agencies.

- Very poor knowledge of the mental health needs of refugees and asylum seekers within the locality. Existing mechanisms for "ethnic monitoring" may be not provide any information about refugee populations as the categories used are too broad.

- Few, if any, mechanisms for consulting with local refugee communities.

- The exclusion of explicit consideration of the needs of refugees and asylum seekers in community care plans and in District Health Authority purchaser specifications.

- An absence of inter-agency collaboration and coordination in meeting the needs of refugees and asylum seekers.

- Insufficient knowledge of the cultures of refugee groups and of culturally-specific ways of addressing mental health and social care needs.

- A response to the needs of refugees and asylum seekers which consists solely in the funding of short term projects with little consideration of how these relate to mainstream health and social services.

Asylum seekers, in turn, are placed in a position of total dependency on the local authority with no money of their own and very little choice in any matters affecting their daily lives. It is a position of passivity which provides refugees with little or no opportunity to take an active role in seeking to address the problems they face or to contribute to wider society. In this way the organisation of services colludes with a wider perception of refugees and asylum seekers as "problems" or "victims" and ignores their resourcefulness and potential to benefit society. One leading authority on refugees has called for health and social care agencies to focus on the resilience of refugees and develop services which respond positively to, and reinforce the strengths of, refugee communities. Instead of being constantly characterised as "problems", agencies involved in the development of programmes for refugees should recognise that "refugees present perhaps the maximum example of the human capacity to survive despite the greatest of losses and assaults on human identity and dignity".[11] This view is echoed in the guidelines issued by the World Health Organisation (WHO) on responding to the mental health needs of refugees. These state:

> People who provide help to refugees or other displaced persons should look for the capacity to survive and cope and try to help build up this positive element. In this way refugees and other displaced persons will be encouraged to use their own abilities to help themselves.[12]

Key Issues in the Mental Health of Refugees and Asylum Seekers

The difficulties faced by refugees and asylum seekers are very wide ranging and relate to a variety of agencies. Key issues are highlighted below.

Post Traumatic Stress Disorder

Traumatic experiences and the shattering of values and beliefs regarding self, world and future can lead to severe psychological and psychiatric problems for refugees and asylum seekers. The most commonly diagnosed severe psychological problem is "post traumatic stress disorder" which is an intense and usually prolonged reaction to intense stressors such as war or persecution. However, this category has been criticised on the grounds that it is applied too loosely to be of value in describing the experience of refugees.[13] It also may be criticised for consigning traumatic experience to the past, thus implying that refugee trauma was something experienced preflight or during flight and not in the country of resettlement.

---

11 Muecke, M., "New Paradigms for Refugee Health Problems" (1992) 35(4) *Social Science and Medicine* at 520.

12 World Health Organisation (WHO), *Mental Health of Refugees* (World Health Organisation in collaboration with the Office of the United Nations High Commissioner for Refugees (UNHCR), Geneva, 1996) p. 1.

13 Muecke, *op. cit. supra* n. 11, p. 520.

Communication Problems and the Use of Interpreters

Many refugee groups consider the use of interpreters to be unsatisfactory for counselling work and for welfare advice. Concerns include trust and confidentiality, shame, and problems with objectivity, accuracy and technical knowledge. It is important that those employing interpreters take into account, as far as possible, the potential differences which may exist between the refugee and the interpreter in terms of ethnic or political affiliation.

Refugee Women

Refugee women are often isolated at home with young children in inadequate housing and with little money. They are likely to have received less education than men and are less likely to have the opportunity to learn English. They are therefore restricted in their movements and in their potential for employment. Many refugee women with children in the UK are single parents, as their partners may have been killed, detained or have stayed behind to fight. Many women may have experienced rape in their country of origin and/or in the process of flight.[14]

Children

As in the case of adults, refugee children may have witnessed death and destruction during civil wars or political repression prior to coming to the UK. Many experience constant nightmares, depression, anxiety and at times violent behaviour which may be easily provoked by their friends who are unaware of their inner feelings. Many refugee children appear lonely and do not interact with their schoolmates.

Counselling

Counselling is an alien concept for most refugee communities who are not used to discussing their most intimate feelings with a stranger. For counselling to work, a trust-building and befriending relationship must be developed first. It is important that those working with refugees initially demonstrate an ability to help with pressing practical matters. It is also important to recognise the potential for training members of refugee communities in counselling skills

14 WHO, *op. cit. supra* n. 12, p. 123.

and schemes have been established in the UK to achieve this.[15]

Social Support

Refugees may be extremely isolated. Often families and friends have been left behind and there is a very high level of anxiety regarding their well-being. Studies of the mental health needs of refugees confirm the importance of social support. Social links outside the family are seen as functioning to ameliorate the effects of psychological stressors.[16] It may be tentatively suggested from current research evidence that the best mental health outcomes are achieved when, in addition to refugees having close links with people from their own country of origin, they also have good ongoing links with the host community.

Socioeconomic Factors

The relationship between social deprivation and mental health has been widely demonstrated by several studies.[17] Recent debate about the provision of benefits to asylum seekers has highlighted the destitution faced by many.

Distress and Mental Illness

It is necessary to distinguish between distress and clinically defined mental illness. Mental health professionals need to be very careful about labelling distress caused by dislocation as mental illness. It may not always be appropriate or helpful for refugees to have their distress articulated through conventional Western definitions of psychological ill-health. In addition to a lack of understanding of their experiences by others, refugees also suffer language and communication difficulties, a lack of understanding of the culture, religious beliefs and attitudes of the host country, giving rise to misunderstandings which can lead to a misdiagnosis of mental illness.

15 Evelyn Oldfield Unit, *Refugee Mental Health Forum: Guidelines for Providers of Counselling Training to Refugees and Guidelines for Refugee Community Organisations Providing Counselling Services* (London, 1997).

16 Ager, *op. cit. supra* n. 2, p. 12. See also problems of isolation experienced by young, male refugees in London, discussed in chapter 15 of this book by Alison Harker and Dr Maknun Gamaledin-Ashami.

17 For a summary of the literature in this area see Pilgrim, O. and Rogers, A., *A Sociology of Mental Health and Illness* (Open University Press, 1993).

Key Issues in Service Development

While there have been a wide range of service developments directed towards establishing innovative services for settled migrant communities, there have been very few programmes specifically aimed at refugees. Many service providers have pointed both to a serious lack of resources to develop services to meet the needs of refugees and asylum seekers and to a very high level of ignorance regarding what these needs may be. Some of the key areas of concern regarding current services are outlined below.

Reception

When an asylum seeker arrives at the port of entry it is unlikely that there will be any opportunity for her/him to receive legal advice, nor will there be access to an advocate. Refugee organisations have expressed concern regarding the attitudes of some immigration officers and have pointed to the need for advocacy services to be available at ports of entry. It is suggested that there should be a review of the instructions to which immigration officers work. In many European countries legal assistance and help from independent organisations is available at ports of entry.[18]

Detention

The approach towards detention in the UK has been described in a recent Minority Rights Group report as being the worst in Europe.[19] As at 31 May 1997, 733 were detained of whom approximately 300 were held in Prison Service establishments.[20] Asylum seekers can be detained for an indefinite period of time and do not initially receive a written explanation of the reason for their detention. The detrimental mental health implications of detention

---

18 Justice, Immigration Law Practitioners' Association and Asylum Rights Campaign, *Providing Protection: Towards Fair and Effective Asylum Procedures* (1997) pp. 30–2. See also chapter 10 of this book by Anne Owens and Madeline Garlick.

19 Joly, *op. cit. supra* n. 3, p. 20. See also chapter 15 of this book by Alison Harker and Dr Maknun Gamaledin-Ashami.

20 Author's correspondence with Social Services Advisor, Refugee Council, London.

has been examined in a recent report.[21] Detention centres are normally run by private contractors who buy in professional health and social care services. The knowledge and training of those working in these centres may be minimal.

Access

While some services have been developed with a specific aim of addressing refugees social care and/or mental health needs, these have tended to be based in large urban centres, particularly London. This is obviously of limited use to a traumatised asylum seeker arriving in the port of Dover or in Gatwick airport. The services which are available in these areas may lack specific expertise in dealing with refugees and it may be impractical to transport people to more appropriate services. Geographical problems are, however, but one dimension of the problem of access. A further problem is that refugees and asylum seekers face a multiplicity of disadvantages. Lack of money and shelter will exacerbate mental health problems as will the experience of hostility from members of the host community.

Consequently, a service which focuses exclusively on treating mental or emotional problems without reference to their wider social context will be of very limited help. An effective response requires close coordination between a number of agencies including welfare benefits agencies, housing, social and health care. The relatively low priority given to asylum seekers and refugees can lead to a situation where the multiplicity of problems they face results in individual agencies being unable or unwilling to take responsibility.

Given the plurality of services and the relatively complex division of responsibilities between them, refugees are unlikely to be able to access appropriate care without the help of an advocate with knowledge of the refugee's culture and some appropriate language skills.

The only practical way of achieving this is through training members of the refugee communities themselves in giving advice, advocacy and counselling skills. This approach also has the merit of recognising the skills and potential that exists within refugee communities rather than simply regarding refugees as passive recipients of services provided by the host community. There are initiatives which are orientated in this way, for example, the Evelyn Oldfield Unit has pioneered the training of refugees in the

21 Pourgourides, C.K., Sashidharan, S.P. and Bracken, P.J., *A Second Exile: The Mental Health Implications of Detention of Asylum Seekers in the United Kingdom* (North Birmingham Mental Health NHS Trust, 1997).

development of counselling skills.[22] Nafsiyat, a London-based, inter-cultural therapy centre, has established a refugee service which aims to train refugees in advocacy and counselling skills.[23] There have also been attempts to develop similar initiatives by local refugee councils and support networks around the country.

Theoretical and Methodological Issues

Drawing on Ager's helpful review,[24] studies of the social care and mental health of refugees may be categorised as being of three types. First, there are epidemiological studies conducted in the main shortly after the Second World War. These focused primarily on trying to determine the extent to which refugee status correlated with a vulnerability towards mental health problems. These studies indicated a significantly increased risk of psychotic illness among refugees, while severe war experiences were found to predict psychiatric illness. These studies have been commended for their empirical rigour. However, assessment tools were used in an uncritical way with little consideration of the impact of cultural factors.

This deficiency was at least partly addressed in the second group of studies. These were primarily of South-East Asian refugees conducted after the Vietnam War. They were more clinically oriented but "acknowledged the role of culture in defining and shaping the experience of mental ill-health".[25] They also looked more specifically at the interaction between refugees and the "host" society.

The third and final group of studies is linked mainly to the "developing world" and focuses primarily on research arising from programmes initiated by international agencies such as WHO and UNHCR. Ager commends the work of these agencies in developing mental health and social care programmes but argues that this activity is not matched by the development of a coherent research literature which could guide such programmes.

While this typology is useful, it should not be concluded that there is a chronological development of studies in this area. Epidemiological studies using standardised instruments to measure psychiatric morbidity among refugees are currently very common. A wide range of studies using standardised

22 Evelyn Oldfield Unit, *op. cit. supra* n. 15.

23 This service is run by Gita Patel, Counselling Co-ordinator, Nafsiyat Intercultural Therapy Centre, 278 Seven Sisters Road, London N4 2HY.

24 Ager, *op. cit.supra* n. 2.

25 *Ibid.* p. 3.

instruments to identify levels of social support have also been undertaken in recent years.[26]

Studies of Refugees and Settled Communities

It is interesting to note parallels that exist between the ways in which studies of refugees have been approached and those of settled migrant communities. In respect of the latter a similarly crude chronology may be suggested.

Studies undertaken in the 1960s may be characterised as having an integrationalist or assimilationist agenda. The assumption underpinning studies tended to be that it was both likely and desirable that migrant groups become integrated into British society and studies were preoccupied with examining the ways in which this could be achieved and the intergenerational problems and conflicts which might arise from this process. A second group of studies in the 1970s reflected a growth of anthropological research into migrant groups in the UK, particularly those of South Asian origin. Here the focus was on the perceived distinctive features of South Asian cultures in the UK with a tendency to exoticise these while simultaneously presenting migrant groups as homogenous entities displaying high levels of "altruistic solidarity". This characterisation had the unfortunate consequence of being reflected in a response from health and social services to the effect that such communities could "look after their own".[27] The 1980s saw a growth in studies critical of the "multi-culturalism" underpinning these studies. Instead, it was argued that the focus should be on the manifestation and effects of racism on an institutional and individual level.[28] The focus thus shifted from the black and ethnic minority "communities" to the responses of institutions to them.

More recent studies have continued to explore the way in which institutions respond to black and ethnic minority people. Attention has been given to the particular ways in which these communities are represented in health and social services.[29] Misleading stereotypes have been shown to have a significant

---

26 See e.g. De Vries, J. and Van Heck, G., "Quality of Life and Refugees", (1994) 23:3 *International Journal of Mental Health* 57–75.

27 Ahmad, W. and Atkin, K., eds *"Race" and Community Care*, (Open University Press, 1996) p. 20.

28 See e.g. Lawrence, E., "Just Plain Common Sense: The 'Roots' of Racism" in *The Empire Strikes Back: Race and Racism in 70s Britain*, Centre for Contemporary Cultural Studies ed. (Hutchinson, 1982).

29 Watters, C., "Black People, Community Care and Mental Illness" in *"Race" and Community Care*, Ahmad, W. and Atkin, K., eds, (Open University Press, 1996).

influence on the type of services black and ethnic minority people receive and on the marginalised position these services occupy in relation to mainstream mental health services. Services for black and ethnic minorities frequently take the form of "special projects" which are usually funded by central government, are of very limited duration (raising significant problems in terms of the recruitment and retention of staff) and have little influence over the agendas of mainstream health and social services.[30]

While anti-racist writers in the early 1980s paid little attention to culture, beyond launching a broad critique of multi-cultural approaches, the 1990s have seen a renewed interest in the role of culture employed in attempts to address the particularistic manifestation of different "racisms". The term "cultural racism" has been used increasingly to attempt to come to grips with the ways in which racism may assume different characteristics and foci in different historical and geographical contexts.[31] Explorations of culture have focused on its complex and evolving nature, moving away from essentialist notions generated by some anthropological and sociological writing.[32]

The above brief review suggests that four approaches may be identified in writing about migrant groups. First, the *assimilationist approach* is concerned with identifying the ways in which groups are assimilating or integrating into "mainstream" society. This approach is underpinned by a somewhat simplistic duality, which presumes that, on the one hand there is a relatively fixed and stable mainstream society, while on the other there is a marginal group to be assimilated. It is assumed that it is the task of this latter group to incorporate norms and values which are acceptable to wider society.

Second, the *multi-culturalist approach* emphasises the identification of the characteristics of the cultures of minority groups. An underlying assumption is that knowledge and appreciation of different cultures will lead to more sensitive treatment of minority groups. The emphasis is on exploring the particular features of minority group cultures and in establishing programmes aimed at educating service providers in these cultural characteristics. The view is that the more service providers understand "other" cultures, the more likely they are to intervene in appropriate ways.

Third, is the *anti-racist approach*, as a result of which a crucial shift in focus takes place from investigating "other" cultures to examining at an

30 Watters. C., "Inequalities in Mental Health: The Inner City Mental Health Project" (1996) 6 Journal of Community and Applied Social Psychology 383.

31 Hall, S., "New Ethnicities" in *"Race", Culture and Difference*, Donald, J. and Rattansi, A. eds (Sage Publications, 1992) p. 153.

32 Clifford, J., *The Predicament of Culture*, (Harvard University Press, 1992).

individual and institutional level the practices which result in the structural inequalities faced by black and ethnic minority people. The "problem" is not other peoples' cultures but the racism of the indigenous white population.

The fourth approach addresses *"cultural racism"* and derives from critiques of the anti-racist approach, namely that the latter tends to homogenise black and ethnic minority populations and assume that experiences and manifestations of racism are uniform. Research indicates that, far from being uniform, racism manifests in ways that are particular to different groups and thus that the forms which racism assumes differ in terms of geographical locality and in relation to particular groups.

Studies of refugees have tended only to incorporate the first two approaches identified above. There are a number which have focused on the extent to which groups have assimilated into the "host" society with an assumption made that assimilation was indicative of, or a prerequisite for, improving mental health. Further studies of refugee communities have been multi-cultural in orientation but have tended towards descriptions of culture which have paid scant attention to the ways in which cultures change and evolve in different environments.[33]

Therapeutic Approaches

It has been pointed out by a number of clinicians that, in the main, refugees do not have a clinically identifiable mental health problem but are experiencing distress. Consequently, appropriate therapeutic interventions are often focused on the stress which refugees are facing. Refugees should be advised on ways of identifying stress and responding to it through a range of individual or group activities.[34]

Appropriate responses include creating opportunities for refugees to socialise with others from similar backgrounds who may share some of their experiences and the opportunity for communal activities, such as singing together. Relaxation techniques, such as breathing exercises, are recommended.[35] In many cultures similar techniques are well known and it may be possible to present these approaches within an identifiable cultural context.[36]

A further common problem is the presentation of "functional complaints"

33 As demonstrated e.g. in Clifford, *ibid.*

34 WHO, *op. cit. supra* n. 12, p. 16.

35 *Ibid.* p. 27.

36 Canda, E. and Phaobtong, T., "Buddhism as a Support System for Southeast Asian Refugees", (1992) 37:1 *Social Work* 61.

which may be closely related to psychological and emotional problems. Western psychiatry has coined the term "somatisation" to refer to a process whereby individuals present psychological problems through a medium of physical complaints. Those who present somatically are seen as attempting to repress or deny their psychological problem and causing health care professionals to undertake needless tests.[37] However, it is often more accurate to say that individuals are not denying the emotional or psychological dimensions of their problems but see the physical and the psychological issues as being interrelated.[38] When questioned about the causes of physical complaints many refugees will draw an explicit link between these and traumatic experiences. This suggests that an appropriate therapeutic response is to ask refugees themselves for their interpretation of their physical problems. A recent publication by the World Health Organisation on the mental health of refugees demonstrates ways in which the physical and psychological symptoms of distress are interrelated and describes therapeutic approaches which reflect this interrelationship.[39]

Those offering programmes of therapy to refugees have identified the importance of helping refugees to construct a narrative about their experience. Mollica has stressed the central importance of what he terms the "trauma story" as the "centrepiece of therapy".[40] According to Turner, "testimony" whereby the refugee gives a detailed description of the factors which led to his/her present situation now provides "the general basis for psychotherapy with survivors of torture and other forms of political violence".[41] A personal narrative is constructed which helps the refugee come to terms with his/her predicament and strengthens his/her own sense of identity. One note of caution regarding this approach is that it may be extremely disturbing for refugees to recall past events and great sensitivity is needed to ensure that any confidence the refugee has built up is not undermined.[42]

---

37 Rack, P., *Race Culture and Mental Disorder* (Tavistock, London, 1982).

38 Watters, C., "Representations of Asians' Mental Health in British Psychiatry" in *The Social Construction of Social Policy: Methodologies, Racism, Citizenship and the Environment,* Samson, C. and South, N., eds (Macmillan, 1996) p. 101.

39 WHO, *op. cit supra* n. 12, p. 19.

40 Mollica, R., "The Trauma Story: The Psychiatric Care of Refugee Survivors of Violence and Torture" in *Post Traumatic Therapy and the Victims of Violence*, Ochberg, F., ed., (Brunner-Mazel, New York, 1987).

41 Turner, S., "Therapeutic Approaches with Survivors of Torture" in *Intercultural Therapy*, Kareem, J. and Littlewood, R., eds, (Blackwell, Oxford, 1992).

42 For work of the Medical Foundation for the Care of Victims of Torture in this respect see chapter 7 of this book by Michael Peel.

Assimilation or Integration?

Drawing a distinction between "assimilation" and "integration" is one useful way of identifying shifts in policy towards the mental health and social care needs of refugees and asylum seekers. Berry suggests that a distinction should be made between "assimilation" and "integration", with the former indicating a policy of encouraging refugees to assume gradually the cultural characteristics of the majority.[43] "Integration", by contrast, refers to an approach to policy which stresses the importance of refugees valuing their own cultural identities as well as valuing the cultures of host communities. Berry suggests that there is a correlation between an "integration" strategy and good mental health and provides some evidence to support this.

This emphasis on integration indicates a shift towards a multi-cultural approach in which attention is directed to the ways in which the cultures of refugee groups may act as a resource for the promotion of mental health. An example of this approach is the work of Canda who has reported on the development of effective mental health programmes for South Asian refugees using traditional Buddhist meditation techniques. Woodcock has demonstrated ways in which rituals which are specific to the cultures of refugee groups can be integrated into therapeutic programmes.[44] Approaches which highlight the therapeutic potential of traditional practices in refugee communities are also outlined in a recent WHO report.[45]

To date there have been very few studies which, in parallel to the anti-racist approach outlined above, focus on studying the response of host institutions to refugees and asylum seekers and the impact these responses may have on mental health. While a number of writers have pointed to the ways in which migrant groups are represented as "problems" by health and social services,[46] few studies have focused specifically on the representation of refugees and the way in which such representations are "constitutive" in that they help to construct the response of services to these groups. This represents an important area for future investigation.

43 Berry, J., "Refugee Adaptation in Resettlement Countries" in *Refugee Children: Theory, Research and Services*, Ahearn, F. and Athey, J., eds, (John Hopkins University Press, Maryland, 1991).

44 Woodcock, J., "Healing Rituals with Families in Exile" (1995) 17(4) *Journal of Family Therapy* 397.

45 WHO, *op. cit. supra* n. 12, p. 89.

46 See e.g. Grillo, R., *Ideologies and Institutions in Urban France* (Cambridge University Press, 1985) on the way French social services have responded to migrants from North Africa.

Bibliography

Ager, A., *Mental Health Issues in Refugee Populations: A Review*, Working paper for Harvard Center for the study of Culture and Medicine, Harvard Medical School, Department of Social Medicine (1994).

Ahmad, W. and Atkin, K., eds *"Race" and Community Care*, (Open University Press, 1996).

Canda, E. and Phaobtong, T., "Buddhism as a Support System for Southeast Asian Refugees", (1992) 37 (1) *Social Work* 61–7.

Clifford, J., *The Predicament of Culture*, (Harvard University Press, 1992).

Daniel, E. and Knudsen, J., eds, *Mistrusting Refugees* (University of California Press, 1995).

De Vries, J. and Van Heck, G., "Quality of Life and Refugees", (1994) 23:3 *International Journal of Mental Health* 57–75.

Duke, K., (1996) "The Resettlement Experiences of Refugees in the UK: Main Findings from an Interview Study (1996) 22(3) *New Community* 461–78.

Evelyn Oldfield Unit, *Refugee Mental Health Forum: Guidelines for Providers of Counselling Training to Refugees and Guidelines for Refugee Community Organisations Providing Counselling Services* (356 Holloway Road, London, 1997).

Grillo, R., *Ideologies and Institutions in Urban France* (Cambridge University Press, 1985).

Hall, S., "New Ethnicities" in *"Race", Culture and Difference*, Donald, J. and Rattansi, A., eds (Sage Publications, 1992).

Joly, D., Kelly, L. and Nettleton, C., *Refugees in Europe: the Hostile New Agenda* (Minority Rights Group International, London, 1997).

Lawrence, E., "Just Plain Common Sense: The 'Roots' of Racism" in *The Empire Strikes Back: Race and Racism in 70's Britain*, Centre for Contemporary Cultural Studies, ed., (Hutchinson, 1982).

Muecke, M., "New Paradigms for Refugee Health Problems" (1992) 35:4 Social Science and Medicine 515–23.

Pourgourides, C.K., Sashidharan, S.P. and Bracken, P.J., *A Second Exile: The Mental Health Implications of Detention of Asylum Seekers in the United Kingdom* (North Birmingham Mental Health NHS Trust, 1997).

Rattansi, A., "Changing the Subject? Race, Culture and Education" in *"Race", Culture and Difference*, Donald, J. and Rattansi, A., eds (Open University Press, 1992).

Refugee Council, *Writing from Asylum Seekers and Volunteers at the Karibu Day Centre, Vauxhall* (Refugee Council report, Oct./Nov. 1996).

Refugee Council, *Just Existence: A Report on the Lives of Asylum Seekers who have Lost Entitlements to Benefits in the UK* (Refugee Council report, Feb. 1997).

Watters, C., "Inequalities in Mental Health: The Inner City Mental Health Project" (1996) 6 Journal of Community and Applied Social Psychology 383–94.

Watters, C., "Representations of Asians' Mental Health in British Psychiatry" in *The Social Construction of Social Policy: Methodologies, Racism, Citizenship and the Environment*, Samson, C. and South, N., eds (Macmillan, 1996).

Woodcock, J., "Healing Rituals with Families in Exile" (1995) 17(4) *Journal of Family Therapy* 397–409.

World Health Organisation, *Mental Health of Refugees* (WHO in collaboration with the Office of the UNHCR, Geneva, 1996).

15 The Needs of Young Male Refugees in London with Particular Reference to Education and Training

ALISON HARKER AND MAKNUN GAMALEDIN–ASHAMI

This chapter draws on and updates a research project on the education and training needs of young single male refugees in London, which was carried out by staff of the City Parochial Foundation, a London-based grant-making charitable trust.[1] The project also examined the wider experience of flight as encountered by those interviewed. It found that the needs of young male refugees were neglected as services for refugees, such as the provision of advice or accommodation, tended to be targeted at families and single women, as the most vulnerable refugee groups.

As part of the project, interviews were carried out with 45 young men between the ages of 16 and 30 from a range of countries. The sample included new arrivals and some who had been in the United Kingdom for several years. The interview sample included two men who had full refugee status and several with "exceptional leave to remain" (ELR). However, the majority had, at the time of interview, not received any decision from the Home Office regarding their status. All of those interviewed wished to pursue their education. Even those who had good jobs at home wished to take every opportunity to resume their education. Given a choice of employment or education, all chose education.

The issues affecting the young men interviewed included language problems, inadequate accommodation, difficulty in obtaining information,

1 Alison Harker and Maknun Gamaledin-Ashami undertook their study for the City Parochial Foundation in April–June 1995. It investigated the needs of young male refugees in London with particular reference to their education and training needs and was completed in September 1995.

advice and guidance on educational opportunities, lack of financial support, emotional problems resulting from isolation and loneliness, psychological problems resulting from the trauma they had experienced, the effects of torture, and uncertainty about their refugee status.

The young men in the sample all experienced difficulty in accessing education. The barriers to be surmounted included accessing English language courses, securing finance for fees, travel costs, books and materials for courses of study (this was complicated by an individual's status as well as the rules on what constitutes full time or part time study and who qualifies for home-based or overseas student status). The report found that the lack of initial and reliable information about educational courses meant that young men sometimes ended up doing the wrong course, thereby losing precious time. Furthermore, the assessment of previous qualifications and experience was not always accurately carried out and the accreditation of prior learning did not always occur.

Once accepted on a course of study, further problems sometimes arose due to a lack of command of academic English, lack of guidance, support and "mentoring" and a lack of ability to concentrate and produce work due to the effects of earlier trauma. The needs and demands (often financial) of relatives abroad sometimes obliged young men to give up studying in order to work and earn money to send home.

Methodology of the Project

The focus of the research project was the educational and training needs of young male refugees. They found themselves in a variety of situations, depending in part upon when they arrived in the UK and the circumstances of their arrival. In view of these factors, and changes in education and immigration policies in recent years, it was decided to interview a sample of those who had arrived after 1994, but also to include some who were earlier arrivals for comparative purposes.

Interviews were held in June–September 1995 with young men between the ages of 16 and 30 from Afghanistan, Colombia, Côte d'Ivoire, Eritrea, Ethiopia, Ghana, Iran, Iraq, Kenya, Kurdistan (including Iraqi and Turkish Kurdistan), Nigeria, Sierra Leone, Somalia, Sri Lanka, Zaïre (renamed the People's Democratic Republic of Congo in 1997). Those who had arrived after 1994 came from Afghanistan, Colombia, Côte d'Ivoire, Ghana, Iraq, Kenya, Kurdistan, Nigeria, Sierra Leone, Somalia and Zaïre. Those interviewed from Eritrea, Ethiopia, Sri Lanka and Iran had all arrived before 1994 and had had time to take advantage of education and training opportunities.

In addition to these interviews, discussions took place with workers from the Refugee Council, the Africa Educational Trust and the World University Service to gather the views of these agencies on the educational needs of young male refugees. The project also undertook an extensive review of literature on refugees in general, on policies relating to refugees in countries around the world, and on the situation in refugees' countries of origin, including the human rights situation in each country from which the sample originated.

The young men who agreed to be interviewed were contacted in a variety of ways. Sometimes refugee community organisations were able to assist by contacting people on behalf of the interviewers, but frequently, meetings were arranged via personal contacts established over the eight years in which the Trust for London, a sister trust of the City Parochial Foundation had operated. Difficulties were encountered with only one group: young Nigerian men were extremely reluctant to take part. Venues for the interviews were determined by the interviewees. Most frequently this was a public place such as a fast food outlet but sometimes meetings were in the offices of refugee community organisations or in someone's flat. On several occasions those met had acute needs and the interviewers felt they had to respond immediately by mobilising the appropriate forms of assistance.

The interviews were conducted with the aid of a checklist, but for the most part took the form of conversations. Frequently it seemed that people were eager to recount their experiences and glad to have someone's undivided attention. Where an interpreter was involved, as was the case on several occasions, the discussion was less free flowing, but with only one individual was there any apparent reluctance to respond to questions. The discussions concentrated upon when the men had come to the UK, what had made them leave home, what were the circumstances of their departure, their situation at home, their reasons for coming to the UK, their expectations and subsequent experience, what they found most difficult, their wishes and how they saw themselves in five years' time. Questions were also asked about their educational achievements, unemployment experience and their ambitions in relation to education and career. Everyone spoken to received £10 for their interview, although they did not know this beforehand. All interviewees were assured of complete confidentiality. They could remain anonymous if they wished, indeed the interviewers preferred this and took no details of names or addresses.

Countries of Origin

The countries from which the greatest number of people had arrived in 1994 and from which young men were selected for interview were identified from the referral statistics of the Refugee Arrivals Project (RAP) at Heathrow airport, London, for the period January to December 1994 (see tables below). Those seeking the help of the Refugee Arrivals Project do not have contacts or friends already in the UK to help them, and they have generally applied for asylum at the port of entry, even though at that time the majority of asylum seekers applied from within the country.

It was therefore assumed that young men from the communities figuring prominently in the RAP statistics would have greater needs than those from communities which are substantial in size and well established in the UK. Interestingly, the number of referrals to RAP of Indians and Pakistanis is very small, despite the fact that these nationalities figure prominently in Home Office statistics of asylum applicants. It is assumed that those young Indians and Pakistanis who are allowed to stay in the UK are assisted by their communities rather than by outside agencies.

Annual statistics published by the Refugee Arrivals Project on referrals to RAP by Immigration Officers detail the countries from which asylum seekers have come, their gender and whether they are single or family households. The figures in Table 15.1, indicate the numbers of males and females and of "single households" referred to RAP in 1994 and 1995. In 1995 and 1996 over 8,000 asylum seekers were referred to RAP, of whom over two-thirds were male. In both these years 59 per cent of referrals were individuals rather than family households. However, only a small percentage of total arrivals into the country are assisted by RAP. The nationalities selected for interview in the study included those where more than 100 young men had been referred to RAP during 1994.

With the exception of Somalia, the figures from countries with established communities in London are low in comparison with the total numbers of principal applicants for asylum as recorded in the Home Office statistics set out in Table 15.2. This shows the total number of asylum applications received by the Home Office.

The figures given by the Home Office and the Refugee Arrivals Project differ, in part as a result of the fact that at that time approximately two-thirds of asylum seekers made their applications once inside the UK and only those without papers or contacts would apply at the port of entry. Since the 1996 withdrawal of welfare benefits from all asylum seekers except those applying

Table 15.1 Individuals from selected countries referred to Refugee Arrivals Project

	Females		Males		Single households	
	1994	**1995**	**1994**	**1995**	**1994**	**1995**
Afghanistan	159	262	194	392	83	158
Colombia	87	104	107	129	61	89
Côte d'Ivoire	41	4	263	21	269	25
Ghana	55	71	166	196	211	247
Iraq	66	135	106	148	53	75
Kenya	191	206	465	308	329	354
Nigeria	32	174	103	340	120	456
Sierra Leone	146	1	521	8	625	9
Zaïre*	134	102	216	210	180	202
(Countries with established communities in London)						
Eritrea	4	5	22	8	23	11
Ethiopia	29	22	55	39	68	55
Iran	24	86	61	128	55	73
Kurds/Iran	3	5	4	6	4	3
Kurds/Iraq	13	9	7	12	4	6
Kurds/Turkey	10	12	16	31	8	19
Somalia	246	270	393	412	227	303
Sri Lanka	14	22	63	70	70	72

* Renamed the People's Democratic Republic of Congo in 1997.

Source: Refugee Arrivals Project annual statistics.

immediately on entry, however, the proportion of port applications has increased significantly.[2]

Refugee Status

The study focused on the needs of young male refugees and thus raises the complex issue of who exactly is a refugee. Within the UK there are three broad categories: (i) those who have been granted full refugee status under

2 For further details see below and chapter 3 of this book by Richard Dunstan.

Table 15.2 Asylum applicants (excluding dependants) from selected countries, 1994–96

	1994	1995	1996
Colombia	405	525	1,005
Côte d'Ivoire	705	245	125
Ethiopia	730	585	205
Ghana	2,035	1,915	675
Iran	520	615	585
Iraq	550	930	965
Kenya	1,130	1,395	1,170
Nigeria	4,340	5,825	2,540
Pakistan	1,810	2,915	1,640
Sierra Leone	1,810	855	335
Somalia	1,840	3,465	1,780
Turkey	2,045	1,820	1,420
Sri Lanka	2,350	2,070	1,260
Zaïre	775	935	650
Other	11,735	19,870	13,575
Total	32,830	43,965	27,930

Source: Home Office, *Asylum Statistics United Kingdom 1996*, Home Office Statistical Bulletin, Issue 15/97, 22 May 1997, Table 2.1.

the Geneva Convention relating to the Status of Refugees, (ii) those who have been granted "exceptional leave to remain" (ELR) on humanitarian grounds and (iii) asylum seekers whose status has not yet been assessed. In common parlance the term refugee is often used loosely to describe people who may fall into any one of these categories.[3] Of those interviewed, most were awaiting a decision on their application for refugee status and, strictly speaking, were therefore asylum seekers. Others had ELR for up to three years. Only two young men from the sample had full refugee status. However, the agencies, the personal contacts and indeed the young men themselves did not differentiate between these different statuses. All saw themselves as refugees.

The result of this somewhat confused situation is that in London there

3 For a more detailed discussion of these issues see chapter 11 of this book by C.J. Harvey.

exists a category of young men who might loosely be referred to as refugees, although few have full refugee status. Some have "exceptional leave to remain" and some have no status at all.

The Situation of Refugees in Britain

The number of people seeking asylum in Britain has increased significantly over the last decade. Thus, the number of asylum applications increased more than tenfold from 4,266 to 44,840 between 1986 and 1991. Although this figure was halved in 1993, the year of the introduction of the Asylum and Immigration Appeals Act, it rose again to 43,965 in 1995 after which the restrictions introduced in the Asylum and Immigration Act 1996 reduced it to 27,930.

The Asylum and Immigration Appeals Act 1993 marked a watershed in the history of refugees in the UK. The Act was a response to the Home Office's concern at the time about multiple and fraudulent claims for asylum.[4] The restrictions which the Act imposed on entry to the UK brought about a reduction in the numbers granted permission to remain in one form or another. Thus, between 1986 and 1996 the numbers of asylum seekers recognised as refugees or granted the lesser status of "exceptional leave to remain" has registered an opposite trend to that of the number of asylum applications. Of the 2,983 decisions made in 1986, 82 per cent were granted either refugee status or ELR, while after the introduction of the 1993 Act only 21 per cent of decisions approved in 1994 granted either refugee status or ELR, a "recognition rate" which has been maintained in both 1995 and 1996, when the Asylum and Immigration Act 1996 sought to reinforce further the restrictions introduced in 1993. These trends are shown in Table 15.3.

Although the number of applications for asylum in the UK has increased significantly in the last 15 years, it should be remembered that this is within the context of a greatly increased number of refugees worldwide.[5] In fact most refugees flee to and remain in a country near their own. It is the poorest countries in the world which accommodate the largest number of refugees. Only a small proportion of refugees come to Europe (and even then approximately half of all asylum applications in Europe are made in Germany).

4 For further details see chapters 2 and 3 of this book by Craig Young and Richard Dunstan respectively.

5 See generally, UNHCR, *The State of the World's Refugees: A Humanitarian Agenda* (OUP, 1997).

Table 15.3 Asylum applications received in the United Kingdom, decisions and percentages, 1986 and 1990–96

	1986	1990	1991	1992	1993	1994	1995	1996
Applications received (excl. dependants)	4,266	26,205	44,840	24,605	22,370	32,830	43,965	27,930
Decisions	2,983	4,025	6,075	34,900	23,405	20,990	27,005	38,960
% of decisions granted:								
Refugee status	12	23	8	3	7	4	5	6
ELR	70	60	36	44	48	17	16	13
Refused	18	18	56	53	46	79	79	81

Source: Home Office, *Asylum Statistics United Kingdom 1996*, Home Office Statistical Bulletin, Issue 15/97, 22 May 1997, Table 1.2.

It was clear from the study that more and more new arrivals were not being awarded *any* status. Many of those interviewed were awaiting a decision. Some had been waiting for over 12 months, and others had waited several years. In July 1995 the average time for decisions taken in the previous six months on applications made after the Asylum and Immigration Appeals Act 1993 came into force was 7.8 months.[6] As of the end of June 1997, there were 53,025 asylum applicants awaiting an initial decision, of whom it was estimated 11,300 had made their applications before August 1993, while a further 24,000 asylum appeals had yet to be completed.[7]

It would appear that as a rough "rule of thumb", individuals arriving some time ago were more likely to have been granted full refugee status fairly quickly. Those arriving in 1989–92 were more likely to be given "exceptional leave to remain", initially renewable on a yearly basis. Those arriving after mid-1993, especially those from countries which the Home Office did not perceive as "refugee producing", tended not to receive any decision on status until some considerable time after arrival.

It should also be noted that many arriving after mid-1993 were also liable to be detained and deported. Those detained in 1995 numbered approximately 600–700.[8] This figure reached 864 in October 1996 before falling below 800

6 H.C. Hansard, Vol. 263, Part 2, Col. 26 W.A., 3 July 1995.

7 H.C. Hansard, Vol. 299, Col. 552 W.A., 31 July 1997.

8 On 23 Feb. 1995, 635 asylum seekers were detained, of whom 268 were in prison (H.C. Hansard, Vol. 255, Cols 657–59 W.A., 2 March 1995). On 29 March 1995, 619 asylum seekers were detained (H.C. Hansard, Vol. 257, Cols 854–55 W.A., 31 March 1995). On 3 July 1995, 690 asylum seekers were detained, of whom 323 were in prison (H.C. Hansard, Vol. 263, Part 2, Col. 287 W.A., 5 July 1995).

in 1997.[9] Amnesty International has described this policy of "arbitrary detention of many asylum seekers in immigration detention centres and criminal prisons pending the resolution of their asylum claim" as a "relatively constant" element of government policy, the "only notable change" being "a significant increase in the extent and duration of such incarceration".[10]

Finally, at the time of the study, around two thirds of all applications for asylum in the UK in 1994 were made in country, as opposed to at the point of entry. However, the removal of welfare benefits from all asylum seekers who fail to claim asylum at the border has meant that the number of port applications increased from 32 per cent of all applications in January 1996, before benefits were withdrawn, to 64 per cent by December 1996 and an average of 50 per cent in the five months to May 1997.[11]

Analysis of Study Findings

If, for the purposes of this chapter, the term refugee can retain a loose definition, then it would appear from the interviews conducted, that those who had fled their country and who sought to acquire formal refugee status were generally from one or more of the following categories:

- Those who were politically active in their country of origin.
- Those who had been arrested at least once and who feared what would happen next time.
- Those who had been tortured.
- Those who escaped while under arrest.

---

9 On 31 Jan. 1997, 768 asylum seekers were in detention, of whom 174 had been detained for less than one month, 141 for 1–2 months, 278 for 2–6 months, 152 for 6–12 months and 23 for over a year. See Table 9 of Home Office Statistical Bulletin cited *supra* at Tables Two and Three. For table showing numbers of asylum seekers detained at selected dates from Nov. 1994 to April 1997 see H.C. Hansard, Vol. 295, Cols 441–42 W.A., 11 June 1997.

10 Amnesty International, *Cell Culture: The Detention and Imprisonment of Asylum-Seekers in the United Kingdom*, (Dec. 1996), p. 3. See also update to the latter report entitled *Dead Starlings*, issued in April 1997, and Amnesty International, *Prisoners without a Voice: Asylum Seekers Detained in the United Kingdom*, (Oct. 1994).

11 H.C. Hansard, Vol. 298, Col. 263 W.A., 17 July 1997.

- Students, particularly those with political involvement, though sometimes innocent students were caught up in mass arrests.
- Professionals and less qualified young men who had been persecuted.
- Those from ethnic minorities.
- Those from religious minorities.
- Those from ethnic groups which had lost political power (when past scores began to be settled).
- Those whose continued presence in their home country (albeit in hiding) was leading to persecution of their families.

In addition, one person interviewed had been a student in the UK when his family in Sierra Leone was attacked. His father was killed, his mother, brothers and sisters all fled and at the time of the interview he had no idea of their whereabouts. He had remained in London and applied for refugee status. Another young man, whose father had worked for his national airline, had arrived with his younger sister in the UK as unaccompanied minors.[12] The father was fearful of the situation in the country deteriorating for members of the ethnic group to which he and his family belonged. He had managed in conjunction with a "friend" to secure seats for the children on a flight to the United States. The "friend" subsequently (for unknown reasons) took the children to London and left them at Heathrow. The young man had "exceptional leave to remain". His father was one of hundreds sacked by the government from the national airline shortly after the children left.

The study showed that there was no typical young man likely to become a refugee. Common characteristics among those interviewed were their youth, the fact that they were single, and the fact that they were all unhappy and completely unsure about their future. All were managing as best they could in what appeared to be very difficult circumstances. All wanted to study and the prospect of resuming a disrupted education appeared to be a driving force.

The young men came from remarkably different backgrounds. Some had been students. For instance, all the young men from Côte d'Ivoire had been students. Others had been in employment when they left home. Included amongst the other interviewees were an accountant, two economists, a teacher, a journalist, a taxi driver, several school students, a factory worker, a bus conductor, a soldier, and a priest. Some were from close-knit families, others

12 Home Office Statistical Bulletin cited *supra* at Tables 15.2 and 15.3. Table 2.3 of the Bulletin states that the numbers of unaccompanied children, aged 17 or under, applying for asylum at ports in the UK were 360 in 1994, 490 in 1995 and 477 in 1996.

had been separated for years from their nuclear family and had been brought up by extended families. Some clearly came from wealthier backgrounds than others, but on arrival in the UK all of those interviewed found themselves in remarkably similar situations.

The Choice of the United Kingdom for Settlement

The question as to why refugees come to the UK implies that refugees have a choice about their destination when they flee from their home country, but this is not often the case. Some people did actively choose to come to London because they had relations there. The Tamils we interviewed frequently spoke about coming to relatives in London who would "protect" them. Others came to the UK because of a former colonial connection. Thus, the young northern Somali men spoke of Britain as being the mother or the parent because of the former colonial administration there. Conversely, others came to the UK because it was not the coloniser of their country. Young Zaïrean men spoke about how life would have been easier in France or Belgium because the language would not have been a problem, but they avoided France and Belgium because of former colonial influences. The young men from Côte d'Ivoire saw the problems at home as being at least in part due to the former French colonial regime and so preferred to come to the UK where the relationships and atmosphere were different.

Yet the majority did not deliberately choose to come to Britain. Several pointed out that it would have been a luxury to have been able to decide upon their final destination. When they left their homes they had no idea where they would end their journey. Many fled initially to a neighbouring country from where the journey into exile was arranged for them. It was common to find that people set out believing they were going to the USA or Canada and eventually found themselves abandoned by an agent in Britain.

Others had endured the "seesaw" which comes into force when an asylum seeker arrives from what is considered by the Home Office to be a safe country.[13] For example, one young Iranian man had fled Iran after being arrested several times. He went to Turkey, from where his escape to the UK via France was arranged by an agent. When he arrived at Dover he was detained for two months and then deported to France. The French authorities immediately sent him back to the UK where he was again detained before

13 For further details see chapter 4 of this book by Rachel Trost and Peter Billings.

being allowed temporary admission, renewable every six months.

His experience was characteristic of those interviewed. It is hardly surprising that these experiences, along with poor physical health and severe accommodation problems, have led to deep depression. The last choice he freely made was to leave Iran and whether that was actually a free choice is highly questionable. Once he embarked on his flight he, like many others, entered an existence where the luxury of making choices, making decisions about his own life and future was forfeited or, at best, suspended.

The Journey and Arrival in the United Kingdom

It is clear that the use of agents in arranging an individual's escape from his or her home country and the journey to the UK was common place. All of those interviewed had come to the UK with the assistance of agents, sometimes referred to as "friends". All had paid money (often considerable sums) to agents for travel documents. They had sold belongings, used savings and been given money by relatives in order to pay the necessary sums.

The travel documents which were purchased this way rarely became the property of the refugees. The common scenario is that the agent travels with the individual (or a group) and never lets the documents leave his possession. On arrival at Heathrow or another port of entry, the agent either "guides" the refugee through the immigration procedures then disappears or, more often, disappears before reaching the start of the immigration process. The refugee will be told to claim asylum when he reaches the Immigration Officer. Occasionally, refugees will present false documentation but it is more usually the case that they have never held any documentation at all.

Those who had left families behind and had no relatives in Britain spoke of how they missed them. The Afghans, the Zaïreans, the Iranians and the Sierra Leoneans had no way of keeping in contact and had no idea what had befallen their families. The Iraqi Kurds are able to telephone home, thanks to sophisticated technology (i.e. satellite), but at a cost of £120 for a few minutes. The young men from the Horn of Africa were able to maintain better contact and were frequently in a position to send financial help to family at home or in neighbouring countries.

Flight from a home country automatically means leaving a job, studies, accommodation, friends, family, surroundings, and a way of life that is familiar and known. Of those spoken to, all were having problems in adjusting and on occasion these were severe. The exception was the young Ivorians. Those spoken to had all been students at the University in Abidjan, had all been politically active, and had all been arrested. None had lived with their families for years and all appeared to have been distanced from their families long before the troubles in Côte d'Ivoire began. They lived in London communally as a group, and were completely focused on Côte d'Ivoire and on returning to it as soon as the situation allowed. They did not seem to be bowed down by life in the UK as were other groups, but drew support from each other and from their commitment to the cause at home.

The decision to leave a home country is never taken lightly nor easily and the young men who formed this study made clear that their decision was forced upon them and was only made in the context of no other options being available.

Expectations, Ambitions and Realities

All the young men who took part in this study gave as their main reason for leaving their homes the need to escape fear and persecution. Some had had high hopes of a better life abroad and had looked forward to the opportunity of resuming a disrupted education. Others had no expectations and yet others were so traumatised by their experiences that they could not see a clear future for themselves.

All said that they wanted to study and, given a choice of a job or a chance to study, they would take the latter option. Even those who had left good jobs at home wished to improve their education. All but one expressed a wish to return home when they finished their education and as long as the political situation allowed. Only two of those interviewed had realised their expectations and then only partially. Significantly, they were the only two out of the whole sample who had been granted full refugee status. Yet they had not been able to find employment or pursue their chosen course of study.

All acknowledged that they were safer in the UK than if they had stayed in their home country. One young Iranian, who had experienced detention and torture at home, described his fear on arrival of being interrogated and tortured. His fear grew as he was taken to an interview room only to be dispelled when a young woman came to conduct the interview and was polite and courteous. He said that he had not felt fear in the UK since that point. For many who have not received a decision from the Home Office on their status, the threat of having to return home is very real.

Refugees face similar problems in transit between their home and final destination, on arrival in a host country and during the initial phase of settlement. However, discussions with young male refugees suggest that the various ethnic, linguistic and national groups respond differently to the same problems. The issues of concern to each of them are listed below.

- Uncertain refugee status and the length of time it takes to receive a decision from the Home Office.
- Accommodation which is often inadequate.
- Language problems, that is, learning English to a high enough standard to be able to manage daily life or to be able to pursue a course of study, especially when academic English is required.
- The difficulty in obtaining information, advice and guidance on educational opportunities.
- The lack of available financial support for study, particularly when refugee status is unclear.
- Emotional problems resulting from isolation, loneliness, the lack of social networks and close relationships, having to adapt to a changed environment.
- Psychological problems resulting from their traumatic experiences. These frequently result in concentration difficulties, an inability to maintain any kind of routine and acute distress. They are often compounded by refugees' concern about the families they have left behind. Such problems can be particularly acute when young men have been detained and/or tortured before escaping.

The young men interviewed experienced some if not all of these difficulties and responded in different ways. Some, including all the Tamils, were attending the Medical Foundation for the Victims of Torture.[14] Others, particularly Tamils and Afghans and those staying with relatives, rarely went out. Some continually struggled to keep going by staying busy, going to the library, playing football and going to the offices of community groups. They were seeking a routine and a purpose. Others could not do this and several of those interviewed were clearly severely traumatised and damaged though they did not attend the Medical Foundation. It was not unusual to hear of suicide attempts or to talk to young men who had attempted suicide.

The need to learn English is paramount and it appeared that everyone had

14 For further details about the Medical Foundation's work see chapter 7 of this book by Michael Peel.

set out with the firm intention of learning or improving their English. However, it had not always been possible to secure a place on a college-based course immediately, so people were learning at home or receiving limited language tuition at the offices of the various refugee community organisations. Some had completed English language courses and progressed to college to continue studies in a chosen subject. Many others had had to leave, while in one case a young Somali felt he would probably do so because of his inability to concentrate or function effectively in academic English.

Accommodation problems affected people's ability to continue studying; all the Kurds spoke of this. Moreover, the lack of supportive networks made it impossible to adjust to academic life. This was the experience of the Somalis, Sierra Leoneans, and Eritreans. Financial problems compounded the situation. The financial needs of family members abroad pressurised young men into leaving education and finding employment (usually in fast food outlets) in order to maintain their family at home or in refugee camps in neighbouring countries.

The problems associated with adjustment to a new, and sometimes hostile environment frequently led to young men losing confidence in their ability to do things they used to do at home. One young man used to make a living by driving a minibus as a taxi service but when interviewed felt completely unable to drive a car.[15] Clearly many of those spoken to were still traumatised by their experiences and the majority badly missed family, friends, and community support. Isolation and loneliness were acutely felt by all of the young men interviewed. One young Tamil man seemed to speak for many when he said that he needed his mental and physical condition to improve before he could go to college. He had been tortured and detained and he was aware that he could not cope with college in his present state. This particular young man could easily have been seen as representative of all the Tamil, Kurd and Iranian interviewees. They all needed considerable emotional support and would continue to need even more help if they re-entered education, as they hoped to do. The most significant people in the lives of these young men were their close relatives (particularly in the case of Tamils who find protection in their families) and the members of the refugee community organisations who provide social support and guidance.

Amongst those interviewed were two young Eritrean men, both of whom had been in the UK for some years and who had successfully completed degree courses. Both emphasised the extent to which they had had to rely on friends

15 See case study of Mr C below.

and compatriots for help. They spoke of their problems in coping with academic English, though both spoke excellent English. They also underlined the need for "mentoring" of young students to help them through the difficulties of a course of study. They saw themselves as having been extremely fortunate in having successfully completed a course of study, but neither felt that the courses they had undertaken equipped them to work at home. As they could not find employment in the UK they also faced uncertain futures.

Barriers to Education and Training

The desire to study was clearly strong but breaking into the educational system for young men between 16 and 30 years of age was problematic, as was being able to maintain a place on an educational course. This section outlines some of the problems the young men interviewed for the study had to overcome to enter and stay within tertiary education.

Mastering English is the first step for anyone wishing to study, but there can be difficulties in accessing English language courses. Students often have to wait lengthy periods before a place is free on a college course. Travel costs can be high so students try to learn English at home but this is far more difficult.

Lack of finance to buy books and materials and meet travel costs to and from college makes it difficult for students to follow courses of study. Young men of 19 and upwards who are studying frequently encounter financial problems. Only those who applied for asylum at the border and are studying part time can claim income support. Full time students cannot do so and must instead apply for education grants. A young person's eligibility for benefits while studying may be disputed by the Department of Social Security. At the time the study was undertaken, part time education was regarded as 21 hours, but some of the young men interviewed were being told that 16 hours learning was the definition of part time education. Those wishing to study full time were not eligible for benefits and were told to apply for local authority grants. However, these are becoming less readily available and to qualify for such a grant there is normally a requirement of three years' residence in a borough. Under such circumstances, paying fees and living expenses can present major problems for young men not satisfying the three-year residence rule. Since the funding system encourages some colleges to designate certain courses as full time in order to attract more funding, different interpretations and definitions of full and part time education are likely to persist.

Once a young refugee is ready to embark on full time study other problems arise. Up to 1996, asylum seekers and those with "exceptional leave to remain" were not entitled to mandatory education grants until they satisfied the three-year residence requirement but those with full refugee status were exempt from this requirement. From 1997, asylum seekers have not been eligible for mandatory grants no matter how long they have been resident in the UK. Those with exceptional leave to remain still have to fulfil the three-year residency requirement in order to be eligible to apply for a mandatory grant and indeed to be liable to pay tuition fees as home-based rather than overseas students.

There is also a discrepancy between the fees charged to young men who have full refugee status and those who are asylum seekers. Recognised refugees are eligible to pay the same level of tuition fees as home-based students. Asylum seekers who do not satisfy the three-year residence requirement have to pay overseas students' fees which are considerably higher.

Since the Asylum and Immigration Act 1996 came into force those who apply for asylum "in-country" are only eligible for assistance under the National Assistance Act 1948.[16] Their chances of accessing education with no form of financial support are therefore extremely limited.

The lack of initial information about appropriate courses and educational opportunities can mean that young refugees embark on the wrong course. Their insufficient command of English may influence them to do science or engineering in the belief that a command of the language is not so important. Inevitably they cannot cope. Alternatively they follow a course which is easy to access but which does not qualify them for employment afterwards and certainly does not equip them to go home, if and when the situation allows. The assessment of previous qualifications and learning is not always accurately carried out. As a result, an individual's placement within the system can be wrong and their learning potential limited. The accreditation of prior learning does not always take place.

The trauma which young men have experienced frequently prevents them being able to concentrate and produce the necessary course work. The urgency to study and resume some kind of a normal life can mean that young men start courses too soon, whilst they are still traumatised. The lack of tuition in the English needed for academic studies is a major drawback for many whose spoken English may be of a very high standard.

Young refugees who successfully gain places on a course of study spoke

16 See more generally, chapters 3 and 11 of this book by Richard Dunstan and C.J. Harvey respectively.

of the need for guidance and help with myriad problems throughout their course. There is a clear need for mentoring for young refugees entering education. The help currently provided by tutors and other staff is insufficient to meet this need. For instance, inadequate accommodation often leads to young men being unable to maintain their studies and progress. Living in a small room shared with others prohibits concentrated study. Finally, the needs and demands of family members abroad, especially the demand for financial help, can compel young men to forfeit their educational opportunities in favour of a low-paid job which allows them to send money to family members.

Case Studies

Mr B

Mr B arrived in London from Sri Lanka in March 1995 with an agent who had arranged his flight to London. He had had problems with the police in Colombo where he was detained. Upon arrival at Heathrow, the agent who arrived with him on the same flight directed him to the immigration officers and disappeared. Mr B was left without a passport, now a criminal offence, which could result in his being denied refugee status. He was detained and put in the Campsfield Detention Centre near Oxford for one and a half months. He was finger printed, as provided under the Asylum and Immigration Appeals Act 1993. At Campsfield he feared that they might send him back to his country of origin. Mr B was eventually released to his brother's home after the intervention of a solicitor.

Mr B had not applied for income support and was living with his brother who has "exceptional leave to remain". Mr B was constantly depressed because he missed his family, but he felt protected by his brother, although he had no friends. He had done "O" and "A" Levels in Sri Lanka and had no immediate plans to start an education, although he hoped to do so in the future. He felt that he was currently unable to make up his mind about going to college. As he was on temporary admission, his entitlement to education was limited.

Mr P

Mr P was 25 years of age and had been in London since July 1995. Mr P was clearly nervous and very depressed. He was living in a hostel in west London. Mr P came from Ghana where he was a bus conductor and lived with his father and sister in Ghana. His mother had died when he was born.

Very shortly before Mr P left Ghana, his father was shot and killed during a demonstration against the imposition of new taxes. When Mr P returned from work neighbours told him that security forces had been to the house and were looking for him and his sister. His sister had returned home earlier and had fled when neighbours informed her that the security forces were searching for her. Mr P did not know where his sister had gone and he had had no contact with her since.

He felt he had to leave Ghana and paid an agent for the necessary documentation. He had no idea he was going to the UK until the plane arrived at Heathrow airport. At the airport he encountered no problems with the Immigration Authorities but after that he had had no idea where to go. He followed other people and eventually reached the underground. He waited at the underground and eventually a Ghanaian woman bought him a ticket to central London. He spent the night sleeping in a railway station (he did not know which one) and the following morning approached someone he thought was Ghanaian and asked for help. She took him to the Centrepoint shelter for the homeless from where he was referred to the hostel where he lived. Since arriving in the hostel he had not gone out, as he had been frightened by all the murders he saw reported on television. Mr P hoped to be allowed to stay in London and to be able to study to be a motor mechanic. He was clearly badly traumatised and was certainly not yet ready to study. He was awaiting a decision from the Home Office on his status.

Mr C

Mr C was 22 years of age and had arrived in the UK from Ethiopia 21 months earlier. He came from a family which was politically active in Ethiopia. He was a taxi driver and the main source of income for his family. The 1991 change of government in Ethiopia brought harassment and intimidation to his family and to himself. His taxi was constantly being stopped by the security forces and he realised that the situation was becoming dangerous. He decided to leave and paid an agent for the necessary documentation. He arrived in London where he said he had found freedom and personal security, though financially he was much poorer than in Ethiopia. He did not have the friends or contacts he had in Ethiopia, did not have a good command of English, and felt that the language barrier was a major obstacle. Nevertheless he cherished his freedom.

He wished to resume his education in London. He was interested in biology and was studying both English and biology. His ambition was to study for a degree in microbiology and return home when the political situation allowed. He was living in short term accommodation and had no tenancy rights. He lived with others and the situation was difficult. In addition, he had been refused leave to remain in the UK and, though he had appealed for judicial review of his case, his overall situation was extremely insecure. Mr C was naturally quiet and shy. He missed his family and he was also very depressed. He was receiving medical treatment. He felt he had lost all his confidence and, despite having been a taxi driver, felt completely unable to drive a vehicle.

Mr E

Mr E was 29 years of age. He arrived in London from Colombia in February 1994. He chose to come to London because he had friends there. Mr E had been a member of the Communist Party in Colombia and had been very active in opposition politics for 11 years, although he had latterly become involved in the coordination of party activities rather than physical fighting. He left Colombia because of harassment by the secret police. When three of his colleagues were killed in suspicious circumstances, he found that his name was on a death list and he decided that he either had to return to the armed struggle or leave the country. The Communist Party secured all the necessary documentation to allow him to leave the country. He had held a passport for 12 months as the Party had felt he was in particular danger for some time. He had the opportunity to go to Cuba but decided to go to the UK.

In Colombia Mr E had done one year of a petroleum engineering degree. He was currently learning English and wished to do a degree in marine biology or political economy. Mr E had had problems adjusting to life in the UK. On arrival he was very depressed and lonely. He felt that 11 years fighting had been wasted; that he had lost. He had been unable to contact his family because their telephone was tapped. He found it difficult to manage a new language and a new "system". As time passed things had improved, he had made friends, was learning English and played various sports. He was a member of a prisoners' support group. He was happy to have freedom and security and to feel safe walking in the streets at night. Mr E lived in poor-standard bed and breakfast accommodation with his girlfriend who had adapted to life in the UK better than him. As yet Mr E had had no decision from the Home Office on his status.

Conclusion

Young male refugees in the UK are in an unenviable position. They come to the UK looking for safety and peace and hoping to continue their education. They have usually been helped to escape by their family, who have made significant financial sacrifices to ensure the safety of a son, brother, or cousin. They are aware that the expectation at home is that they are now living a good life and will support the family left behind who are unlikely ever to be able to leave.

These expectations are strongly felt and it is a matter of pride, not to mention necessity, that financial support is provided regularly for those family members who have remained at home or are in refugee camps in neighbouring countries. In order to fulfil these deeply felt obligations young men know that they have to be qualified for jobs and must therefore resume their education. All but one of the young men interviewed wished to return home when the political situation allowed, in order to contribute to their countries. However, they were acutely aware that they could not return "empty handed". Too many hopes, ambitions and expectations had been invested in them. To return home without the wherewithal to find employment and to be able to support their families was unthinkable.

In reaching London, young refugee men had shown initiative, stamina, commitment and they were highly motivated to study. Many were already qualified in their home countries but knew that their qualifications would not necessarily be accepted in the UK. They also knew that a degree from a UK university was almost as good as a passport in many parts of the world. Even if, they do not return home in the future, the authors maintain that they should be assisted to become an asset to any country in which they live. They are highly motivated and wish to contribute to the country which provides them with asylum.

Furthermore, education and learning provide more than just good prospects. The process of attending a course of study can reduce isolation, relieve some worries and provide some distraction from the day-to-day concerns which beset young refugees. The worrying increase in the incidence of mental illness and suicide amongst young male refugees[17] must be, in part,

17 This increase has been reported anecdotally by refugee community organisations. The Mental Health Foundation has also been seeking to compile a suicide register in recent years. For further information on the mental health needs of refugees and asylum seekers see also chapter 14 of this book by Charles Watters.

due to their isolation, the lack of purposeful activity in which they can engage and the frustration of having little control over their lives, their own future and the future of their families. The need for work in the field of refugee mental health is already widely recognised and is being addressed. However, it is acknowledged that preventing the onset of mental ill health is infinitely better than curing it.

The young men interviewed form a tiny proportion of the total in London who are in exactly the same position. They are at a stage in their lives where the provision of appropriate resources can help them to plan and achieve a positive future. Without this intervention, there is considerable risk of their frustration increasing and of them reaching a point where their potential for achievement is exhausted.

Bibliography

Home Office Research Study No. 141, *The Settlement of Refugees in Britain* (1995).

Home Office Statistical Bulletin, *Asylum Statistics United Kingdom 1996*, issue 15/97, 22 May 1997.

Joint Council for the Welfare of Immigrants (JCWI), *Bulletin*, Vol. 5. No. 9 (London, summer 1995).

Refugee Arrivals Project, Annual Statistics (London, 1994–96).

16 Parent-child Communication Barriers and Mother-tongue Education for Vietnamese Children in London

TOM LAM

This chapter looks at the case of the Vietnamese refugees who began to arrive in the United Kingdom some 20 years ago. Though the community has a distinct social and cultural background of its own, most adults continue to experience difficulties in adjusting to life in the UK, whereas young people are found to be increasingly westernised. A recent survey undertaken by the Centre for Chinese Studies at South Bank University shows that the mother-tongue competency among the younger generation is now diminishing with the result that many adults are now experiencing difficulties when communicating with their children and/or grandchildren. Elderly Vietnamese are thus alienated not just from the host population because of cultural and language barriers, but also from their younger relatives. The survey also shows, however, that mother-tongue education has been a major lifeline helping to maintain the refugees' linguistic legacy and to some extent, their traditional values. These findings are significant and are likely to have implications for refugee settlement policies. With the language and cultural gap becoming ever wider between young people and their immigrant parents, the need to adopt a more positive approach backed by solid policies in the provision of mother-tongue education in contemporary Britain is more obvious than ever before.

The first groups of Vietnamese refugees arrived in the UK as early as 1975. Their total number is now estimated to be around 25,000. In the early days they were dispersed across the country in towns and isolated suburban areas by the receiving agencies for resettlement. However, a wave of intra-UK migration has brought them together again and they now form clusters in inner urban areas.[1] After this re-grouping the majority now live in major cities; London alone accommodates well over a half of the total Vietnamese population this country has ever received.

However, apart from perhaps a small number of those working on, or with, them one way or another, the public has, in general, had very limited knowledge about the situation of the Vietnamese refugees.[2] Whilst most people may assume that they should by now have settled down properly, their journey in search of a settled destination is, in reality, far from over.[3] Several studies suggest that the Vietnamese continue to experience hardships of various kinds, ranging from high unemployment and poor housing, to poor health. Furthermore, these problems are likely to hamper their social integration for a long time to come.[4]

There are, nonetheless, differences in respect of social adaptation between different age groups within the population. In terms of language acquisition, for example, young people have made the greatest progress and are therefore increasingly westernised,[5] whilst people belonging to the older generation continue to encounter enormous problems.[6] It is suggested that most non-English speaking adults are now experiencing communication difficulties with their younger family members, who speak mainly English. These adults are, consequently, alienated from not just the wider society, but also from their own children or grandchildren.[7]

---

1 Robinson, V. and Hale, S., *The Geography of Vietnamese Secondary Migration in the UK* (Research Paper 10, Centre for Research in Ethnic Relations, University of Warwick, 1989).

2 See, e.g. Bell, J., and Clinton, L., *The Unheard Community: A Look at the Housing Conditions and Needs of Refugees from Vietnam Living in London* (Community Development Foundation, Refugee Action, London, 1992) pp. 1–15.

3 Lam T. and Martin, C., *Vietnamese in London: 15 Years of Settlement* (South Bank University, Occasional Paper 2, 1994) p. 22.

4 Lam, T., and Diep, M., *The Vietnamese and Primary Health Care in the London Borough of Greenwich* (Research Report, Greenwich Health Project, 1992).

5 Lam, T. and Martin, C., *The Settlement of the Vietnamese in London: Official Policy and Refugee Responses* (Social Science Research Papers, No. 6, School of Education, Politics and Social Science, South Bank University, London, 1997) pp. 16–22.

6 Jones, P., *Vietnamese Refugees: A Study of their Reception and Resettlement in the United Kingdom* (Research and Planning Unit, Paper 13, H.M.S.O., 1982); Edholm, F., Roberts, H. and Sayer, J., *Vietnamese Refugees in Britain* (Commission for Racial Equality, London, 1983) pp. 20–26.

7 Duke, K. and Marshall, T., *Vietnamese Refugees since 1982* (Home Office Research Study No. 142, 1995).

The problems faced by Vietnamese refugees in the UK, however, are by no means unique. In North America, for example, where the largest populations of Vietnamese refugees are found, communication and cultural gaps between parents and children have long been observed, prompting calls for appropriate solutions to be sought.[8] Similar problems have also been observed in other immigrant groups, with young children refusing to speak to their parents because, they claim, their parents "don't speak English".[9] This chapter analyses the results of independent, in-depth interviews with a small sample of Vietnamese refugees living in South London, including parents, the elderly and teenagers and several others who have frequent contact with them. It discusses the problem of communication and cultural gaps between adults and young people among the population in relation to their integration and cultural identity in the host society, and assesses the potential for mother-tongue education as a means to preserve their linguistic and cultural heritage.

Background Linguistic Features

In order to get to the root of the problem, it is first of all necessary to understand some background features of this group of refugees. The cause of their exodus from Vietnam has already been well documented elsewhere.[10] Whilst most Southerners escaped the country after the fall of Saigon at the end of the Vietnam War in 1975, the Northerners were forced to leave prior to the outbreak of the Sino-Vietnamese hostilities in the late 1970s. There were thus two distinguishable waves of refugees from Vietnam: that which started around April 1975, consisting of mainly Southerners and that which started roughly three years later, consisting of mostly ethnic Chinese from the North.

8 See, e.g., Nguyen, Q.B., *Education Difficulties Faced by Vietnamese Refugee Students in Canada* (Vietnamese-Canadian Federation 1982, National Conference on the Resettlement and Adaptation of Vietnamese Refugees in Canada, Ottawa, 9–11 April 1982) pp. 45–57.

9 Brown, D., *Mother-tongue to English: The Young Child in the Multicultural School* (CUP, 1979) pp. 34–36.

10 See, e.g. Edwards, R., *The Vietnam War* (Wayland Publishers, 1986); Engelmann, L., *Tears Before the Rain: An Oral History of the Fall of South Vietnam* (Oxford University Press, 1990); Chen, M., *The Strategic Triangle and Regional Conflicts: Lessons from the Indochina Wars* (Lynne Rienner Publishers, 1992); Hood, S.J., *Dragons Entangled: Indochina and the China-Vietnam War* (M.E. Sharpe Inc., 1992).

The history of Vietnam has for many centuries been influenced by that of its northern neighbour and consequently, the country's religious outlook, called Tam Giao, consisting of three faiths: Buddhism, Confucianism, and Taoism, is strongly influenced by Chinese civilization.[11] Central to this is the traditional emphasis on family values whereby parents and children honour a mutual, collective obligation to one another and to relatives.[12]

Vietnamese refugees in the UK may be grouped into four categories on the basis of their ethnic and geographical origins: geographically, there are the Northerners and the Southerners and ethnically, there are the ethnic Vietnamese (or *Kinhs*) and the ethnic Chinese (the *Hoas*). The latter were formerly immigrants from China, whether in their own lifetime or that of their forebears. Between 80 and 85 per cent of Vietnamese refugees in the UK are Northerners and 75–80 per cent are ethnic Chinese.[13] In other words, the population is not homogenous, as is also the case with Vietnamese refugee communities in other recipient countries.[14] In short, the majority are ethnic Chinese from North Vietnam, a socialist Third World economy. Most of the early Chinese immigrants were from the border provinces, especially Guangdong and Guangxi, where Cantonese is spoken. Many left China as a result of the Sino-Japanese War in the late 1930s; others arrived in Vietnam with Chiang Kai-shek's army in the 1940s. Thus, some elderly people among this population had already been refugees once before in their lifetime.

Because of this ethnic heterogeneity, two languages are spoken among the population. The ethnic Vietnamese speak Tieng Viet, or Vietnamese, and the Hoas speak both Vietnamese and Cantonese. However, this linguistic

11 Beresford, M., *Vietnam: Politics, Economics and Society* (Pinter, 1988) pp. 1–15.

12 See e.g. Nguyen, H., *Preservation of the Vietnamese Culture in Canada* pp. 109–14; Nguyen, N.N., *Preservation and Development of the Vietnamese Culture* pp. 102–08; Nguyen, H.B., *Overseas Vietnamese and the Development and Preservation of Vietnamese Culture* pp. 91–101, papers presented at Vietnamese-Canadian Federation 1982, National Conference on the Resettlement and Adaptation of Vietnamese Refugees in Canada, Ottawa, 9–11 April 1982. See also, Caplan, N., Choy, M.H., and Whitmore, J.K., "Indochinese Refugee Families and Academic Achievement" (Feb. 1992) Scientific American, pp. 36–92.

13 See e.g. Jones, P., *Vietnamese Refugees: A Study of their Reception and Resettlement in the United Kingdom* (Research and Planning Unit, Paper 13, H.M.S.O., 1982) p. 15–22; Lam, T. and Diep, M. *op. cit. supra* n. 4, pp. 3–4.

14 See e.g. Liebkind, K., "Self-reported Ethnic Identity, Suppression and Anxiety among Young Vietnamese Refugees and their Parents" (1993) 1 J.R.S. pp. 25–40.

division needs further explanation. Whilst it is stated that the ethnic Vietnamese speak only Vietnamese, many of those, especially younger refugees, who have worked or stayed in relocation camps in Hong Kong before arriving in the UK, have also acquired reasonable fluency in Cantonese. On the other hand, some ethnic Chinese people speak little or no Cantonese. In order to understand the problem, a further explanation of the situation of the Hoa people is necessary.

First, except for those from the South, who are only a minority and are better educated, the Hoa Vietnamese are mainly from the cities of Hanoi, Hai-phong and Quangninh Province, plus a small number from other Northern provinces such as Lang-son, Lao-cai, Nam-dinh, Thanh-hoa, Hai-duong, Bac-thai and so on. Of the places mentioned, Hanoi, Hai-phong and Quangninh each had a notable concentration of Hoa people. Until the late 1960s there used to be independent Chinese schools for Hoa children and Cantonese was spoken among children as well as adults. In Hanoi and Hai-phong, Cantonese was primarily the "language of the home" and Vietnamese was the chief means of communication with the outside world. In the case of Quangninh, however, because of the high concentration of Hoa people in the eastern part of the province in particular, business transactions in some rural areas were largely carried out among the Hoa themselves and the use of Vietnamese was therefore less common. Many Hoa Vietnamese from that part of the country therefore never learnt to speak Vietnamese.

From as early as the late 1960s, Vietnam began to be increasingly affected by the Sino-Soviet dispute. As relations between the two communist superpowers deteriorated, Hanoi gradually became one-sided, inclining heavily, in both political and military terms, towards the Soviet Union.[15] Policies designed to reduce China's influence included discouraging the teaching of Chinese among the Hoa population. This was first done by the removal of the Chinese language from the requirements of the General Education Examination and later from the curriculum altogether for Hoa schools. Thus, by 1975, only a handful of young Hoas in Hanoi and Hai-phong were still studying Chinese at secondary level, whilst in the provinces there were no longer any Chinese secondary schools. Consequently, the level of Chinese competence among young people declined and the use of Vietnamese in the family became increasingly popular, especially in Hanoi, where children, including teenagers and even adults, no longer spoke Cantonese. As a result of the reduction of mother-tongue teaching and use,

15 Chen, M., *op. cit. supra* n.10, pp. 128–32.

few Hoa teenagers could be described as competent in written Chinese upon their arrival in the UK.

By comparison, most ethnic Vietnamese teenagers were reasonably competent in written Vietnamese. This is particularly so with those from South Vietnam, where schools, especially those located in the cities, were less severely disrupted during the war years. However, for many Hoa people, the first language that they speak often determines their feeling of nationality. Thus, most of those from Hanoi would feel themselves more Vietnamese than Chinese, whereas those from Cholon and Quangninh, are more likely to claim their Chinese origin.

The Language Barrier and Signs of Cultural Divide

As discussed above, the refugees from Vietnam were originally primarily Vietnamese or Cantonese speaking on their arrival in the UK. However, this is no longer strictly speaking the case. Instead, most young Vietnamese in the UK, except for recent arrivals, now speak English as their first language and some can no longer communicate with their older family members in their mother tongue. This is a rather sensitive issue for immigrant groups in general, as well as for the Vietnamese who are now living in a social and cultural environment vastly different from the one from which they came, for it is not simply a question of communication, but also of cultural survival and ethnic identity. In this regard, the findings gathered in this study have provided some interesting clues, as will be discussed in detail below.

Table 16.1 shows a rough picture of the survey: 20 interviewees randomly selected from the population living in London boroughs south of the Thames, including both male and female; among whom 14 adults (nine parents and five grandparents) and six "young persons".[16] Apart from this small sample, views and comments given by five other people including community workers, weekend school teachers and interpreters were also collected on a qualitative basis. Of the six young persons interviewed, two were British born; and the

16 It should be noted that the term "young people" here refers to those roughly under the age of 24. This categorisation is based on the general education (i.e. primary and secondary education) that a young person has received in the UK. Since on average the Vietnamese have been in the UK for over 10 years, people aged 24 or under will be very likely to have had most of their general education here. The categorisation is generally adopted as a guideline by Vietnamese community offices in London.

Table 16.1 Communication difficulties experienced by Vietnamese refugees in London

	Number of interviewees	Yes	No
Grandparents	5	2	3
Parent	9	5	4
Young persons	6	2	4
Total	20	9	11

N.B. The difficulties are self-reported and not pre-defined.

youngest was 13 years old. On average, the young people had received a total of 8.5 years' education in the UK. Three spoke English as their first language, two Cantonese and one Vietnamese. On the other hand, two thirds of the adults had also attended English classes for periods ranging from a few weeks to several years part time. All adult interviewees among the 20-person sample said that their young family members now spoke mainly English. Seven of them (five parents and two grandparents) perceived difficulties when communicating with their children or grandchildren. In contrast to the adults, two young persons admitted experiencing similar problems. Thus, roughly 70 per cent of those who did not speak their mother tongue experienced communication problems with their older family members.

With regard to the nature of communication difficulties encountered, the interviews show that the problems are various. Whilst most adults said that difficulties tended to occur when their children were asked to explain a letter, or a leaflet written in English, or to convey a symptom to the doctor, minor problems also occurred in everyday life. A Hoa man, whose wife was ethnic Vietnamese, said that since his wife spoke Vietnamese and he spoke Cantonese with the children, the youngsters learned neither language properly, and often misunderstood instructions given in these languages. The man also said that he had often tried to speak English with the children, but it made things even worse due to his incorrect pronunciation. In another case, a woman said her children never spoke Cantonese, either among themselves or with their parents, even though neither she or her husband spoke English. According to the woman, oral messages between the parents and children were often simple and fragmentary, while the children, who were now in their late teens, never discussed matters with their parents as fully as most teenagers would.

Where adults often have to rely on their children to interpret for them, it is the latter's weakness in their mother tongue which makes communication difficulties particularly obvious.[17] For example, when interpreting a written text, such as a leaflet from the council or a health centre, the children usually understand it well but are not always able to explain it in their mother tongue correctly. Likewise, when describing a symptom they can often make themselves understood in English but cannot satisfy the Vietnamese-speaking patient. Although this may sometimes be explained as a problem of interpreting skills rather than of language skills, it does, to some extent, imply a problem of communication between people of the two generations. A 55 year-old man said he had three children, aged 24, 21 and 18 respectively, though only the daughter, the eldest of all, could speak Vietnamese fluently. Once when she was away on a working trip within the UK her mother was rushed to hospital for an urgent condition. Yet her younger brothers, one of whom was a graduate in computer studies, were unable to convey the doctor's medical advice to their father clearly and the doctor had to write down his words for the man to seek help from someone else the following morning.

The survey, on the other hand, also shows that all but one of the six young interviewees still speak in their mother tongue when talking with their parents, even though the subjects are seldom beyond the domestic domain. A 16 year-old student who claimed English was his first language said he still managed to speak his mother tongue well:

> I speak English a lot better than Cantonese but I have little problem when talking with my mum and dad. Anyway we hardly talk about things outside the kitchen or the dining room. ... You hear these things everyday and you know what they really mean. So you don't really have to be brilliant to communicate with your parents.

Meanwhile, two other youngsters said that the reason they were unable to interpret well was because they often had to use technical terms which they had seldom heard of in their mother tongue and it was not easy to explain medical jargon even with a dictionary. Overall, comments such as these highlight the problem of parent-child language barriers. They do exist, even not visibly in every case.

However, even if the problem may not seem significant across the board, its impact is nevertheless not merely superficial. Although seven adults felt that they had no communication problem with their young family members

17 Lam, T. and Diep, M., *op. cit. supra* n. 13, pp. 20–21.

(Table 16.1), most elderly people belonging to this category said that they communicated more with senior than junior members of the family anyway. They said that young people did not want to stay with their parents or grandparents any more, but preferred to move out when this became affordable. This is an interesting development in terms of family structure in that traditionally all generations within a family stayed together under the same roof. For those still living together, there is often a gulf between people of different cultural backgrounds, namely, traditional and westernised.

A grandmother said that although her grandchildren still spoke Cantonese when talking to her, they spoke English among themselves just like other Western children. She expressed concern about the declining use of Vietnamese among young people and said:

> I don't know if my grandchildren really understand to me. But I just feel that it's a bit strange. When we were young we used to spend lots of time with old people in the family. ... My grandparents used to tell us bedtime stories and so forth. We had to help out at a very young age. Most children these days may not have heard of this anyway. ... By the age of eight I already had to help out in the kitchen whilst my older brothers worked in the rice-fields. So you are always kept close with your relatives, really like a family. ... But it is so different now. Small children these days spend lots of time watching cartoons and films instead. I hear that some teenagers mess around here and there in the snooker rooms or game-machine shops. Their parents don't even know their whereabouts.

In another case, a respondent felt that language difficulties were not entirely to blame for the parent-child gap. He maintained, for example, that his children understood Cantonese well but the problem was that they hardly wanted to use it. He said that they were westernised and simply did not want to stay with old people, that his eldest daughter had moved out years ago and his son seldom came home after he had acquired a car. Apparently, many elderly people felt isolated not just from the outside world, but also from younger members of their family. The fact that they talked less with younger members of the family than with older ones reflected their isolation from the younger generation, because of the latter's increasing westernisation.

Overall, it may be concluded that whilst their mother tongue still appeared to be the language of the home for most Vietnamese children, few could speak it with native proficiency. This was particularly obvious in the case of those born or brought up in the UK. What was more worrying was that, as a group, mother-tongue competency among the younger generation was progressively declining. Even more worrying was that the gap between the younger and older generations was not just in language, but also in cultural orientation. Elderly people seemed to be locked in their own backyard because their traditional values were not being perpetuated, although isolation within the family caused as a result of young people being westernised appeared to have affected the elderly rather than young parents so far.

It is also interesting to note that the parent-child communication problem is not necessarily a result of the latter speaking English as their first language and their mother tongue second. More precisely, it is a result of mother-tongue retrogression rather than English progression among the younger generation. Indeed, children whose first language is English can still speak their mother tongue well, provided they are taught properly. As will be discussed later, children are often able to improve their mother-tongue competency after a period of study at weekend schools.

Roots of the Problem

Whilst adopting English as first language is a sign of the increasing westernisation of the younger generation, as suggested above, this may not be the sole reason for the parent-child communication problem. The causes of this problem need further examination. Table 16.2 shows the reasons given by the nine interviewees who reported having problems. Most believed insufficient mother-tongue education was a major cause. The domination of the mainstream culture and a lack of a strong ethnic-cultural environment ranked joint second and finally poor schooling history came last.

Table 16.2 Causes of communication difficulties experienced by Vietnamese refugees in London

Reason	Number of people
Insufficient mother-tongue education	3
Social and linguistic environment	2
Lack of mother-tongue environment	2
Disrupted schooling	1
Don't know	1
Total	9

NB. The causes are self-reported and not pre-defined.

Of the two young persons who admitted being unable to communicate well with their parents, neither spoke their mother tongue (one Cantonese and one Vietnamese) fluently. One said her family had lived in a Glasgow suburban area for some five years, during which period they seldom met Vietnamese-speaking children with whom they could socialise. However, since moving to London she had gained more confidence in Vietnamese because most of the family's visitors were Vietnamese speakers. In another case, a man said that had his family continued to stay in isolation in the small Tyneside town where they had been, his children would not have been able to speak Cantonese so fluently.

Apparently dispersed settlement offers little chance of preserving refugees' linguistic legacy. On the other hand, the findings also suggest that there is some degree of correlation between a child's age and his/her mother-tongue competency. For example, most parents who had brought up their children in the UK said that communication difficulties tended to be more obvious with children roughly between the ages of six and 14. Although preschool toddlers were more familiar with the mother tongue, they picked up English quickly once they went to primary school and soon adopted it as their first language. A 43 year-old man said his first child used to speak some Cantonese, but since he had begun school his younger brother had begun to speak English as well, and the boys seldom spoke Cantonese.

Despite the fading of their mother-tongue competency at the early age, most children would regain command of the language after a few years of mother-tongue education, even if English remained their first language. A teenage respondent said that, apart from Chinese textbooks she read at her mother-tongue school, cassettes and video tapes imported from the Far East had also been important means for her to improve her written and spoken Cantonese skills. Only through a process of frequent contact with materials of this kind, she claimed, could one attain good mother-tongue skills and a high level of cultural understanding. Thus, there appeared to be a distinguishable pattern of mother-tongue competency in relation to age, or more precisely, to mother-tongue education. The more children were influenced by their parental culture, the more competent they were in their mother tongue, and thus the fewer problems they encountered in communicating with their parents.

It is also possible that the decline of mother-tongue competency among Vietnamese children is due to the turbulence and uncertainty of their childhood which has resulted from their being uprooted from their homeland. A survey of Indo-Chinese refugee families and academic achievement conducted by Caplan, found that many young South-East Asian refugees settling in the USA lost months, even years, of formal schooling while living in relocation camps, during which time they had received no formal education.[18] A story recorded in the current survey, to some degree, substantiates this view in a UK context. A 50 year-old single parent whose family originally came from Sichuan Province in China said that in 1978 when many Hoa people were leaving Vietnam, she and her small children went to live in a village some 100 miles north of Hanoi where Meo (a minority) language was spoken. A few years later they were told to move again from that village to another one where Tay (another minority language) was the main means of communication. In 1987, the family left Vietnam for Hong Kong, where they stayed for three years before coming to settle in the UK. Because of these frequent upheavals her children had to learn to speak Hua, their original Chinese dialect in Sichuan, Vietnamese, Meo, Tay, Cantonese (in Hong Kong) and finally English. As a result of the confusion, none of her four children, now in their early and mid 20s, was able to speak any of these languages fluently. She admitted the family now spoke a "mixture of broken languages" and they often laughed at each other for making "funny" mistakes.

The findings also showed that children from large, extended families often spoke their mother tongue better than those from small or single-parent families. A father of four said that the total number of his extended family in southeast London was well over 50 and that they met regularly for festive or religious gatherings. As result, he claimed, the children had maintained their mother-tongue competence reasonably well. By contrast, a single parent with two toddlers said that the main reason her children spoke little Vietnamese was because her children seldom heard Vietnamese spoken in their immediate environment. Despite her efforts to teach them Vietnamese, they showed little interest in the language. Eventually she had to speak "broken" English with them instead. As a single parent, though, she was also less certain whether she would later be able to afford to send her children to weekend Vietnamese classes miles from her home.

Finally, it should be pointed out that whilst all four young people experiencing no communication problems with their parents had previously attended, or were attending, mother-tongue classes, only one of the two people who experienced difficulty in communicating with their parents, had attended mother-tongue education for a brief period. All these examples, as will be seen, point to the importance of mother-tongue education for the younger generation.

18 Caplan, N., *op. cit. supra* n. 12.

Mother-tongue Education and the Question of Cultural Preservation

The linguistic signals people unwittingly transmit about themselves every moment of their waking day are highly distinctive. The question of ethno-linguistic identity often arises in relation to the demands and needs of those who are in an ethnic minority within a community, such as the many groups of immigrants, exiles, and foreign workers in Europe and the USA, or the tribal divisions that characterise several African countries. More than anything else, language shows where people "belong" and provides the most natural symbol of public and private identity.[19] As mentioned earlier, many Hoas declare themselves to be "Vietnamese" simply because they speak Vietnamese as their first language, even though they are of Chinese ancestry.

In multiracial societies, particularly in Africa and Asia, survival often requires multi-linguistic abilities. Even in developed countries, monolingual communication is less and less adequate for contemporary economic transactions. Foreign languages have now become fashionable not just in higher education, but also at other levels of training and learning. In North America, for example, mother-tongue education for minority groups, or bilingualism for the population as a whole, has for a long time received attention from the authorities concerned. Governments have increasingly recognised the advantages of having citizens who are educated speakers of languages other than English, as a national resource.[20]

There are, however, also those advocating the establishment of a global *lingua franca*. They maintain that the only way to break the language barrier, especially for international business transactions, is to adopt a common linguistic medium mutually intelligible to all. English, they argue, has more or less become the main contender for such a position by virtue of the political and economic progress made by English-speaking nations in the past two centuries. Since the end of the Cold War, the number of people learning English has increased rapidly. English has become a prominent subject in schools and colleges in many former communist countries. In China, the most populous

19 Crystal, D., *The Cambridge Encyclopedia of Language* (CUP, 1987) pp. 17–66.

20 See e.g. Perren, G.E., "Languages and minority groups", *The Mother Tongue and other Languages in Education*, Perren G.E. ed. (National Congress on Languages in Education, Papers and Reports. Vol. 2, Working Parties for the First Assembly, Centre for Information on Language Teaching and Research, Durham, 1978) pp. 45–60; Cummins, J., *Bilingualism and Special Education: Issues in Assessment and Pedagogy* (Multilingual Matters Ltd., Clevedon, Avon, UK, 1984) pp. 1–17.

nation on earth, besides students, millions of amateur learners are now eager to study English, either as a hobby or to improve their career prospects.

Nevertheless the idea of a monolingual world is almost certainly unrealistic. Cultural and religious practices in a multiracial environment require the existence of language diversity. Furthermore, language is never static. It is a living instrument, changing and developing along with the advancement of human society. As pointed out by some leading linguists,[21] the main danger to the growth of a world language comes from within. As a language becomes used in all corners of the world, by people from all walks of life, so it begins to develop new spoken variants which will again be used by local people as symbols of their identity.

Although, it should be pointed out that language and culture are not necessarily synonymous, they both symbolise a particular identity.[22] Many distinctive cultural representations are communicated through a particular language, for instance, in songs, myths, poems, folk tales. Whilst it is true that customs of a certain culture may be practised without knowing the language, one can hardly claim a clear cultural identity without knowing the language. In a multiracial society individuals declare their ethnic identity by allegiance to a group which sustains their ancestral links. One such link is the parental language. Although it is recognised that British society now consists of a variety of ethnic groups with distinct lifestyles and value systems and that the teaching of minority languages should be enhanced, responsibility for mother-tongue education is still generally left to the minority communities.[23]

From as early as the 1980s, Vietnamese refugees in the UK have made tremendous efforts to promote mother-tongue education for their children. They have set up weekend schools on their own initiative, largely with their own resources. As always, the Vietnamese value the teaching of their mother tongue very highly indeed, whether it be Cantonese for Hoas or Vietnamese for Kinhs. This is reflected in the views of some parents who even regard their mother tongue as enhancing their children's employment prospects, whether this be manual or professional. None of the respondents interviewed

---

21 Crystal, *op. cit. supra* n. 19 pp. 357–58.

22 Davies, A., "The Interaction of Language and Culture" in *Education in Multicultural Societies*, Corner, T., ed. (Croom Helm, 1984) pp. 60–67.

23 Committee of Inquiry into the Education of Children from Ethnic Minority Groups, *Education for All* ("The Swann Report"), presented to Parliament by the Secretary of State for Education and Science (H.M.S.O., London, March 1985) pp. 315–429.

in this sample, including those with no children or relatives attending mother-tongue classes, denied the importance of mother-tongue education.

The praise for mother-tongue teaching came from virtually every corner of the community. A Cantonese-speaking respondent, for example, said that his children, who were now in their mid 20s, had actually acquired their Cantonese at a mother-tongue school in London. A worker at a Vietnamese community office also said that he had frequently been told by primary school teachers that they had often been astonished by the bilingual and artistic skills of some Vietnamese pupils. Similarly, an English teacher from an adult education centre, who had attended many cultural events organised by mother-tongue schools over the years, said that she was often so impressed by the pupils' performance which explained why these schools were so successful. The importance of weekend schools in promoting young Vietnamese refugees' use of their mother tongue is undeniable. A retired weekend teacher said that "even though what has been achieved is trivial, without these efforts small children would have continued to lose their mother-tongue competency and eventually probably their cultural identity altogether".

Mother-tongue education is thus vital for Vietnamese refugees, not only for removing communication barriers, but also for preserving the culture and identity of earlier generations. Although preserving mother-tongue skills does not necessarily mean preserving all traditional values, empowering younger people by enhancing their mother-tongue knowledge and skills, means that refugees can help strengthen the links between their past and the future, and thus become an a more securely established minority within the broader multicultural environment.

Mother-tongue education has on the whole proved popular with both children and parents. The latter's enthusiasm is well illustrated by their readiness to pay tuition fees and make donations to these schools. In east and southeast London there are now seven Vietnamese-run mother-tongue schools, with pupils ranging from several dozen in number to several hundred. It is understood that one such school has even been able to attract generous funds from abroad and has considered acquiring freehold premises to allow for long term development.

Conclusion

The central message of this chapter has been the danger of the increasing distance between two generations in a new refugee community in the UK and the importance of mother-tongue education for the younger generation. Although it may not be visible at first glance, the communication barrier between young people and their older relatives is alarming. It does not result only in further isolation for the elderly, but more importantly, in growing uncertainty for the community's cultural identity in the future. In the face of an ever-changing social and economic climate in multicultural Britain, a more affirmative attitude is required in the provision of mother-tongue education and the preservation of minority cultures.

Bibliography

Bell, J. and Clinton, L., *The Unheard Community: A Look at the Housing Conditions and Needs of Refugees from Vietnam Living in London* (Community Development Foundation, Refugee Action, London, 1992).

Beresford, M., *Vietnam: Politics, Economics and Society* (Pinter, 1988).

Brown, D., *Mother-tongue to English: The Young Child in the Multicultural School* (CUP, 1979).

Caplan, N., Choy, M.H. and Whitmore, J.K., "Indochinese Refugee Families and Academic Achievement" (Feb. 1992) *Scientific American* 36–40.

Chen, M., *The Strategic Triangle and Regional Conflicts: Lessons from the Indochina Wars* (Lynne Rienner Publishers, Boulder and London, 1992).

Committee of Inquiry into the Education of Children from Ethnic Minority Groups, *Education for All* ("The Swann Report"), presented to parliament by the Secretary of State for Education and Science (H.M.S.O., London, March 1985).

Corner, T., *Education in Multicultural Societies* (Croom Helm, Sydney, 1984).

Crystal, D., *The Cambridge Encyclopedia of Language* (Cambridge University Press, 1987).

Cummins, J., *Bilingualism and Special Education: Issues in Assessment and Pedagogy* (Multilingual Matters Ltd., Clevedon, Avon England, 1984).

Davies, A., "The Interaction of Language and Culture" in *Education in Multicultural Societies* Corner, T., ed. (Croom Helm, London, 1984).

Duke, K. and Marshall, T., *Vietnamese Refugees since 1982* (Home Office Research Study No. 159, 1995).

Edwards, R., *The Vietnam War* (Wayland Publishers Ltd., 61 Western Road, Hove, East Sussex BN3 1JD, UK, 1986).

Engelmann, L., *Tears Before the Rain: An Oral History of the Fall of South Vietnam* (Oxford University Press, 1990).

Hood, S.J., *Dragons Entangled: Indochina and the China-Vietnam War* (M.E. Sharpe Inc., Armonk, New York, 1992).

Jones, P., *Vietnamese Refugees: A Study of their Reception and Resettlement in the United Kingdom* (Research and Planning Unit, Paper 13, H.M.S.O., 1982).

Lam, T. and Diep, M., *The Vietnamese and Primary Health Care in Greenwich* (Research Report, Greenwich Health Project, 1992).

Lam T. and Martin, C., *Vietnamese in London: 15 Years of Settlement* (South Bank University, Occasional Paper 2, 1994).

Le, X.K., *The Role of Vietnamese Association in Community Development* (Vietnamese-Canadian Federation 1982, National Conference on the Resettlement and Adaptation of Vietnamese Refugees in Canada, Ottawa, pp. 126–36, 9–11 April 1982).

Levin, M., *What Welcome: Reception and Resettlement for Refugees in Britain* (Action Society Trust, London, 1981).

Liebkind, K., "Self-reported Ethnic Identity, Suppression and Anxiety among Young Vietnamese Refugees and their Parents", (1993) 1 J.R.S. 25–40.

Nguyen, H.B., *Overseas Vietnamese and the Development and Preservation of Vietnamese Culture* (Vietnamese-Canadian Federation 1982, National Conference on the Resettlement and Adaptation of Vietnamese Refugees in Canada, Ottawa, pp. 91–101, 9–11 April 1982).

Nguyen, H., *Preservation of the Vietnamese Culture in Canada* (Vietnamese-Canadian Federation 1982, National Conference on the Resettlement and Adaptation of Vietnamese Refugees in Canada, Ottawa, pp. 109-14, 9–11 April 1982).

Nguyen, N.N., *Preservation and Development of the Vietnamese Culture* (Vietnamese-Canadian Federation 1982, National Conference on the Resettlement and Adaptation of Vietnamese Refugees in Canada, Ottawa, pp. 102-8, 9–11 April 1982).

Nguyen, Q.B., *Education Difficulties Faced by Vietnamese Refugee Students in Canada* (Vietnamese-Canadian Federation 1982, National Conference on the Resettlement and Adaptation of Vietnamese Refugees in Canada, Ottawa, pp. 45–57, 9–11 April 1982).

Perren, G.E., "Languages and minority groups" in *The Mother Tongue and other Languages in Education*, Perren G.E., ed. (National Congress on Languages in Education, Papers and Reports. Vol. 2, Working Parties for the First Assembly, Centre for Information on Language Teaching and Research, Durham, 1978)

Robinson, V. and Hale, S., *The Geography of Vietnamese Secondary Migration in the UK* (Research Paper 10, Centre for Research in Ethnic Relations, University of Warwick, 1989).

17 Asylum, Employer Sanctions and Race

SELINA GOULBOURNE

The Asylum and Immigration Act 1996 introduced employer sanctions as part of a package of measures to deter illegal employment in the United Kingdom. Similar measures have been introduced in a number of industrialised states.[1] As such, neither the UK legislation nor the political sentiments which have driven its implementation are innovative.[2] What is significant is the linking of illegal working with asylum in legislation which at the same time introduces harsh measures to deter asylum claimants who are perceived as "bogus". The legislation was rushed through parliament after a short period of consultation following the publication of two Home Office papers.[3] The response to the papers was generally negative. Even the business community expressed grave reservations,[4] mostly in respect of the negative impact on race relations.

1 For overview of wider harmonisation process within European Union see chapter 3 of this book by Richard Dunstan.

2 In the parliamentary debates on the Bill, the then Shadow Home Secretary Jack Straw quoted the following passage from an article by Andrew Lansley, the Conservative candidate for South Cambridgeshire: "Immigration, an issue which we raised successfully in 1992 and again in the 1994 Euro-elections campaign, played particularly well in the tabloids and has more potential to hurt". H.C. Hansard, Vol. 272, Col. 547, 22 Feb. 1996. For analysis of "new right" ideology of the then Conservative government see chapter 2 of this book by Craig Young. See also Guild, E., *The Developing Immigration and Asylum Policies of the European Union* (Kluwer, 1996).

3 Home Office Consultation Documents *Prevention of Illegal Working* and *Compliance Cost Assessment*, Immigration and Nationality Department, Nov. 1995. These documents amply demonstrate the glib reference to the two categories in one breath in the statement: "[T]he UK is especially attractive to illegal immigrants and bogus asylum seekers." (para. 4).

4 The Confederation of British Industry (CBI) and the Institute of Directors expressed the view that the Bill had serious implications for race relations, see e.g., H.C. Hansard, Vol. 272, Cols 392 and 396, 21 Feb. 1996. The *Economist*

Yet the consultation papers justified the proposed curbs on illegal working as promoting good race relations. Similar references to the importance of good race relations have prefaced the debates on all the immigration legislation passed since the Commonwealth Immigrants Act 1962. There is ample evidence that the stream of legislation concerning immigration since then has invariably encouraged racism and xenophobia by the identification of non-patrial immigration with problems of unemployment, crime, dependency on welfare and, most importantly, a perceived threat to indigenous culture.[5] The 1996 Act goes further down this line, in that it encourages immigration officials, employers and individuals responsible for welfare decisions to be suspicious of all asylum seekers regardless of the status of their claims, thus perpetuating the "culture of disbelief"[6] fostered by the Asylum and Immigration Appeals Act 1993.

Furthermore, the creation of additional criminal offences, and in particular the power to impose criminal sanctions on employers under the 1996 Act, generate an atmosphere of mutual surveillance and distrust which will inevitably rebound on black and Asian workers. Similar criminal sanctions imposed by the Immigration Act 1971 led to passport raids by the police and encouraged greater scrutiny by education and social services employees anxious to avoid the risk of prosecution.[7] The difficulties in gaining employment will force those asylum seekers who are permitted to work to accept poor employment practices, low wages and oppressive working conditions.[8]

This chapter investigates the threat posed to race relations in the UK, in the context of the debates concerning employer sanctions during the

---

was quoted in Hansard the following day (Col. 547) as making the following comment: "[B]y promoting anti-immigration policies the government risks encouraging racism and undermining liberty. It deserves contempt, not votes, for proposing this nasty little bill."

5 See e.g., Fryer, P., *Staying Power: The History of Black People in Britain* (Pluto Press, 1984); Layton-Henry, Z., *The Politics of Immigration* (Blackwell, 1992); 1990 Trust, *Without Foundation: Investigating the Implications of the Asylum and Immigration Bill on Britain's Black Community*, (1996), section 3.

6 This phrase was used to describe the impact of the Asylum and Immigration (Appeals) Act 1993 in evidence presented to the Glidewell Panel by a number of organisations working with asylum seekers. The Glidewell Panel, *Report from an Independent Enquiry into the Implications and Effects of the Asylum and Immigration Bill 1995 and Related Social Security Measures*, 16 April 1996.

7 Gordon, P., *Policing Immigration: Britain's Internal Controls* (Pluto Press, 1985) ch. 4.

8 H.C. Hansard, Vol. 272, Col. 399, 21 Feb. 1996.

parliamentary consideration of the Bill. Through an analysis of the comparative experience of similar legislation in other jurisdictions, conclusions are drawn as to the potential threat to fundamental freedoms and civil liberties of the groups most likely to be affected by the racist underpinnings of the legislation.

Employer Sanctions: the Asylum and Immigration Act 1996

Despite the tightening of border controls and the harsh measures taken since the Immigration Act 1971 to strengthen internal controls, there is still an official perception that a great number of illegal entrants have slipped through the net, quite often in the guise of asylum seekers. This perception is clearly reflected in the Home Office consultation paper which stated:

> The Government is in no doubt that illegal working is common in the United Kingdom. Although any estimate of the full extent of illegal immigration, including people working in breach of their immigration conditions, can be no more than speculation, we do know that in 1994 over 10,000 people were detected by the Immigration Service working while either here illegally or while prohibited from working. ... The Government believes that these people represent only a small proportion of the total number working in the United Kingdom illegally.[9]

Accordingly, Section 8(1) of the 1996 Act makes it a criminal offence to employ an individual who has attained the age of 16 and is "subject to immigration control", if:

> (a) the employee has not been granted leave to enter or remain in the United Kingdom; or (b) the employee's leave is not valid and subsisting, or is subject to a condition precluding him from taking up employment and (in either case) the employee does not satisfy such conditions as may be specified in an order made by the Secretary of State.

The definition of "persons subject to immigration control" is problematic, since it includes all those caught by the complex provisions of the Immigration Act 1971, as amended by the British Nationality Act 1981 and the Immigration Act 1988.[10] In addition, the 1994 Immigration Rules detail the criteria and

9 *Op. cit. supra* n. 3, *Prevention of Illegal Working*, para. 3.

10 For a comprehensive discussion of the right of abode and settlement see MacDonald, I., and Blake, N., *Macdonald's Immigration Law and Practice* (Butterworths, 4th edn, 1995).

procedures for leave to enter, or remain, in the country and set out the limits on employment, including the requirement of work permits.[11]

The concession to employers is that they are not responsible for verifying the immigration status of a potential employee. The employer is exempt from liability if, before the commencement of the employment, the job applicant produces a document which appears to the employer to relate to the prospective employee and which is in the category specified by an order of the Secretary of State. In addition, the employer either has to retain the document or a copy of it. The employer will not be exempt from liability if he was aware that the employment would be in breach of Section 8. The maximum penalty for noncompliance is a fine of £5,000.[12]

The implementation of Section 8 raises a number of issues. Among these are the question of its likely effectiveness and the burdens it imposes on employers. Most importantly, it raises concerns about its impact on the employment prospects of ethnic minority job applicants in general and of asylum seekers in particular.

In view of the wide range of documentation,[13] which may be produced as evidence of entitlement to work, it is unlikely that Section 8 will be a major deterrent to illegal working. Additionally, possession of the documentation is not necessarily proof of entitlement to work. For example, the Home Office has conceded that there are at least two million defunct National Insurance cards in circulation.[14] Neither is production of a birth certificate conclusive, since illicit acquisition of a copy of a birth certificate is quite straightforward.[15] On the other hand, there are a significant number of individuals, mainly asylum seekers, who have leave to work but do not have a National Insurance number

11 *Statement of Changes in Immigration Rules* (1993–94) H.C. 395, paras 7–34 and 128–199.

12 Asylum and Immigration Act 1996 (AIA), SS. 8(2), 8(3), 8(4).

13 The number of documents which could evidence the legality of an individual's status has been estimated at over 40. See H.C. Hansard, Vol. 272, Col. 395, 21 Feb. 1996. The Immigration (Restrictions on Employment) Order 1996, SI 1996 No. 3225, Part II lists 13 categories of documents which qualify under Section 8(2)a of the 1996 Act. The number of documents in some of these categories is difficult to estimate in view of the generic definition of the qualifying documents.

14 Home Office Consultation Document, *op. cit. supra* n. 3, *Prevention of Illegal Working*, para. 31.

15 This became apparent in the parliamentary debates when members urged the government to introduce legislation to close the loopholes in the procedure for acquisition of birth certificates. H.C. Hansard, Vol. 272, Col. 525, 22 Feb. 1996.

and who would experience even greater difficulties securing employment than at present.

Research indicates that, even before the 1996 Act entered into force, racism and prejudice in recruitment meant that only a small proportion of asylum seekers were in regular employment, even though the majority is desperate to work and many are highly qualified.[16] The documentation required by Section 8 exacerbates the difficulties encountered by asylum seekers, since employers, even if willing, are unlikely to understand the terms on which refugees are allowed to remain and, in the case of asylum seekers, whether, and on what terms, they are permitted to work pending resolution of their claim.[17]

The Act can also be seen as encouraging the increased use of false documentation, since employers are not required to check the authenticity of documents.[18] Those seeking employment in breach of the Immigration Act 1971 are likely therefore to fall prey to racketeers who, no doubt, will seize on the opportunities offered by Section 8 to promote the trade in forged documents.[19] Unfortunately, asylum seekers may also be under pressure to get embroiled in these activities though the evidence to date is that because of their insecurity they are unlikely to be involved in any illegal activities.[20]

The 1996 Act has least impact on employers in the public sector and businesses which recruit staff on long term contracts. The practice of such employers is to include National Insurance details in the application form. However, since, according to the Home Office's own figures, there are approximately 2.5 million new employees below the PAYE/National Insurance Certificate threshold,[21] employers would in any event be required to investigate other evidence of entitlement to work. The difficulties are compounded for businesses with a high rate of turnover of unskilled or semiskilled workers. The main areas affected are catering, building and cleaning services. However, in view of the vast increase in service industry employment, for example

---

16 See e.g. Asylum Rights Campaign, Evidence to the Glidewell Panel, *op. cit. supra* n. 6, p.xvi and Home Office Research Study No. 141, *The Settlement of Refugees in Britain*, (1995), ch. 9, pp. 99–108.

17 Refugee Council, *Refugee Education, Training and Employment* (Factfile No. 7, Nov. 1996).

18 *Ibid.*

19 Institute for Public Policy Research (IPPR) in evidence to the Glidewell Panel, *op. cit. supra* n. 6, p. xxvi.

20 Refugee Council, *The State of Asylum: A Critique of Asylum Policy in the UK*, (London, March 1996), pp. 20–1.

21 *Op. cit. supra* n. 3, *Compliance Cost Assessment*, para. 21.

among express delivery firms and supermarkets, the problems identified could extend to a wide range of casual employment where employers depend on immediate availability and flexibility as to the length of employment. It is not, in such circumstances, feasible for employers to check documentation prior to employment.[22] Yet the employer could face criminal sanctions if it subsequently became apparent that the employee was subject to immigration control. Conversely, an employer who decides to conduct sporadic checks may be made liable for discrimination under the Race Relations Act 1976.[23]

In cases where the employee is unable to produce easily recognisable evidence, such as a National Insurance number, passport, tax or birth certificate, the employer may justifiably be unwilling to make the effort to investigate the applicant's employment status, particularly in a situation where there is no scarcity of applicants and the cost and delay may appear to be disproportionate in relation to the particular vacancy. It is also unlikely, in such circumstances, that an employer would consult the Home Office detailed written guidance or contact the help line. In any event neither the written guidance nor the help line are likely to clarify the status of any individual applicant. It is still up to the employer to investigate the documents available and, if there are none, to refuse to offer employment.[24]

The legislation poses particular problems for small businesses, that is, those with under 20 staff. The Federation of Small Businesses pointed out:

> These small businesses or small employers have no legal department, no personnel department and, in many respects, they may not even have a wages clerk or book keeper. The employer, the proprietor, will do the work, namely, the invoicing, the ordering, the employing, the firing and hiring.[25]

---

22 H.C. Hansard, Vol. 272, Col. 455, 21 Feb. 1996.

23 *Op. cit. supra* n. 3, *Compliance Cost Assessment*, para. 13 states: "It would be up to individual employers to decide whether to make checks. However, the Government anticipates that in most cases employers will choose to make checks on all new employees, to avoid any danger of discrimination in the recruitment process."

24 See e.g. Home Office, Immigration and Nationality Directorate, *Asylum and Immigration Act 1996 – Section 8: Prevention of Illegal Working – Guidance for Employers*, issued by to 1.1 million employers in Dec. 1996.

25 Evidence to the Glidewell Panel, *op. cit. supra* n.6, p.29, para. 8.2.5. This point was forcefully supported by Jack Straw in parliamentary debates, when he stated: "The Government and the Secretary of State never cease to complain about burdening small firms and the labour market 'with bureaucratic and inflexible rules, regulations and practices', but, ... against the wishes of many representative

It would not be surprising, therefore, if such businesses resorted to informal recruitment through personal contacts to avoid the legislation. Furthermore, it is also likely that those seeking employment will be encouraged to become self-employed, often working from home, since Section 8 only applies to employers. There is evidence that the earnings of individuals forced to undertake work on these terms are extremely low and that a large percentage of individuals in this position is black and Asian.[26] Commenting on similar legislation passed in the United States,[27] Calavita stated on the basis of experience in other countries that "[w]ork settings will become more clandestine. ... Production can be subcontracted. ... Piece-rate home work will become still more common".[28]

The costs to the employer and the public of implementing the employer sanctions imposed under the 1996 Act are unjustified because there is no official estimate of the size of the problem, particularly in view of the evidence of the operation of similar legislation in other countries that the provisions have minimal effect on those who are sufficiently determined to beat the system.[29] The Home Office has already spent significant funds on the dissemination of the guidelines and on setting up the hot line. It is unlikely that any further expenditure would be incurred in setting up a system to ensure compliance with Section 8 in view of the experience of enforcing similar provisions under the 1971 Act. For example, there were only 12 prosecutions in 1994 for breaches of Section 24 of the Immigration Act 1971.[30] The government would have to invest a vast amount in policing compliance without any greater guarantee of success than under the provisions of the 1971 Act. In the circumstances, the effectiveness of the legislation depends very much on the cooperation of employers and the deterrent effect of criminal sanctions. Experience in the USA of the employment practices of "immigrant dependent employers" prior to, and after, the implementation of employer sanctions indicates that the legislation had very little impact. The majority of such

business organisations, the Government are doing just that: regulating ineffectively where they should not, but refusing to regulate where they should." H.C. Hansard, Vol. 272, Col. 546, 22 Feb. 1996.

26 Asylum Rights Campaign, written evidence to the Glidewell Panel, *op. cit. supra* n. 6, p. 30, Para. 8.2.6.

27 Immigration and Reform Control Act 1986.

28 Calavita, K., "The Contradictions of Immigration Lawmaking: the Immigration Reform and Control Act of 1986", (1989) 11 *Law and Policy*, 17 at 28.

29 *Ibid.* p. 31.

30 H.C. Hansard, Vol. 272, Col. 453, 21 Feb. 1996.

employers had previously requested documentation from their workers but this had little impact on the kinds of workers they hired. A study of the same employers after the legislation came into force found:

> While the vast majority of these employers are requesting the specified documentation from their workers, and hence are complying with the letter of the law, these employers report that the law has neither affected their hiring practices nor the people they hire; most of the employers admit that they "probably" have undocumented workers in their workforce; and the overwhelming majority report that despite high compliance rates, they believe sanctions will have no deterrent effect.[31]

Similar patterns are likely to emerge in the UK. Public sector employers and large industries and businesses are likely to encounter relatively fewer problems in complying with the requirements of Section 8 in terms of record keeping, though they may well face hidden costs,[32] which go well beyond that of the non-recurrent cost of training managers identified by the Home Office.[33] On the other hand, as argued in the parliamentary debates, the cost of compliance for small business may well be prohibitive. The Home Office recognised that small businesses with a high staff turnover could face difficulties.[34] However, these estimates were based entirely on the cost of photocopying and did not take account of the difficulties of record keeping, the risks of loss of original documents and the loss of business resulting from inability to recruit at very short notice. From such an employer's point of view, the low wages, nonpayment of National Insurance contributions and the like, would more than compensate for the remote possibility of a fine.[35] Again, the experience of the USA suggests that service industries with a high turnover of labour have incurred disproportionate fines compared with large

---

31 Calavita, *op. cit. supra* n. 28, p. 28.

32 Although the burdens imposed by the Immigration (Carriers' Liability) Act 1987 are greater than those on employers under the present legislation, the staff training costs incurred to date may be indicative of the costs that may be incurred by employers. See also Nicholson F., "The Immigration (Carriers' Liability) Act 1987: Privatising Immigration Functions at the Expense of International Obligations" (1997) 46 I.C.L.Q. 592.

33 *Op. cit. supra* n. 3, *Cost of Compliance*, paras 35–37.

34 *Ibid.*, paras 42–5.

35 It is anticipated that prosecutions under this section will be rare. Supperstone, M. and O'Dempsey, D., *Immigration Law and Practice* (FT Law & Tax Practitioner Series, 4th edn 1996), p. 535.

industries, but that this has not been a deterrent since compliance with the legislation would involve a total restructuring of the service industry.[36]

Race Relations and Section 8 of the Act

Consistent opposition to the draft legislation was expressed by voluntary organisations, the Commission for Racial Equality (CRE) and in Parliament with regard to its racist underpinnings, as epitomised by the definition of "immigrant" in clause 12 of the Bill, which included all those who required leave to enter or remain under the terms of the 1971 Act. This definition includes a significant number of individuals legally settled in the country but who do not have an automatic right of abode. Consequently, the 1996 Act legitimises negative perceptions of ethnic minorities. Concern has been voiced by a number of organisations on this issue. For example, the CRE stated:

> Even after decades of being in Britain, black people are still defined as immigrants not settlers. Now our problem is that the Asylum and Immigration Bill will enshrine the status in legislation so that some black people will be termed as immigrants and not settlers and treated as such.[37]

Despite the Home Office's assertion that the 1996 Act was intended to preserve good "race relations", it was clearly aware of the risk that the proposed legislation might reinforce racism, particularly in employment. For example, in the consultation process it specifically asked employers whether they anticipated any difficulties in making checks on documentation, in view of the existing requirement on them to avoid racially discriminatory recruitment practices. Concern was expressed that employers should not pick out any group for discriminatory treatment on the basis of their colour, race or nationality. The consultation paper went on to state:

> Employers should not make assumptions about entitlement to work based on the personal characteristics of the job applicant. Where employers decide to make checks on entitlement to take work, the same checks will need to be applied to all applicants whatever their background. Only if those checks raise legitimate questions should there be any further investigation of the entitlement of

---

36 Calavita, *op. cit. supra* n. 28, pp. 29–30.

37 Purkiss, B., a CRE Commissioner and leading trade unionist, in oral evidence to the Glidewell Panel, *op. cit. supra* n. 6, p. 9, para. 5.1.3.

individuals to seek employment.[38]

Despite acknowledgement of the risk of discrimination inherent in the legislation, the Conservative government refused to accept amendments which would have ensured, both a period of consultation prior to the passing of any order under the Act, and a reasonable time for an assessment of the costs and benefits of the legislation two years after its implementation.[39] Instead, after the legislation was passed, the CRE issued guidance to employers as to the practices which should be adopted to avoid liability under the Race Relations Act 1976.[40] The guidance does not go much further than the exhortation in the Home Office consultation papers that all applicants should be required to produce documentation where entitlement to work was unclear.[41] This does not meet the concerns voiced in parliament and by pressure groups about the negative impact of the legislation. Despite the elimination of a reference to "immigrant" in the 1996 Act there is real concern that Section 8, as legislation which engenders suspicion of the legitimacy of migrants, will lead to discrimination in employment.[42]

Even where employers make an effort to follow what is considered to be best practice, there is a risk of discriminatory practices by staff. Comparisons can be drawn with the Immigration (Carriers' Liability) Act 1987, which has led to scrutiny not only of those requiring visas but also of British passport holders.[43] Despite the investment of significant sums of money in staff training,[44] airline staff routinely photocopy passports of passengers in cases where they suspect their authenticity, in order to avoid any liability under the 1987 Act.[45] This same dilemma is likely to be faced by employers as a result of the Asylum and Immigration Act 1996, particularly since the size of the fine under the latter is £5,000, as compared with £2,000 under the carriers'

38 *Prevention of Illegal Working, op. cit. supra*, n. 3, para. 22.

39 H.L. Hansard, Vol. 573, Cols 688–694, 24 June 1996.

40 Commission for Racial Equality, *The Asylum and Immigration Act 1996: Implications for Racial Equality*, (Oct. 1996).

41 See *supra* n. 25 for concerns expressed by Federation of Small Businesses about the difficulties small business might encounter in complying with the Section 8.

42 See e.g., Refugee Council, *op. cit. supra* n. 17.

43 H.L. Hansard, Vol. 571, Col. 1616, 30 April 1996.

44 It was estimated that British Airways spends £500,000 a year and nevertheless incurs fines of £2,500,000 per year, *ibid.* Cols 1617–18.

45 See e.g. Commission for Racial Equality, News Release No. 620, 23 Oct. 1996; Nicholson, *op. cit. supra* n. 32, p. 597.

liability legislation. Indeed, even before the 1996 Act became law, University College London Hospital Trust sent reminders to its 300 domestic workers and porters of the requirement to have a work permit. It is not coincidental that a significant number of staff employed in these posts are black and Asian workers.[46]

The alternative course for the employer is to ignore applications from individuals in the "suspect" category where there is competition for jobs or, in the case of employers who depend on a quick turnover of casual labour, to ignore the guidelines and take the risk of prosecution under the 1996 Act.[47] Such a risk will only materialise if an aggrieved employee alerts the authorities. This is unlikely given the insecurity of this type of employment. The more likely scenario is the recurrence of police immigration raids on businesses suspected of infringing the legislation.

MPs debating the Bill declared that it would have an immediate impact on the employment prospects of refugees and asylum seekers.[48] Although the government's declared intention was to deter "bogus asylum seekers", the employment prospects of asylum seekers and refugees are inevitably affected by the implementation of Section 8. The Immigration Rules do not provide for an automatic right of settlement for those recognised as refugees; this remains a matter of Home Office discretion.[49] Normally, the refugee will be granted four years' leave to stay and may then apply for indefinite leave to remain.[50] The position of those granted exceptional leave to remain is more tenuous as they are generally only granted leave to remain for a shorter period. Individuals granted refugee status or exceptional leave to remain are only given confirmation of their eligibility to work for this limited period, until indefinite leave is granted.

The position with asylum seekers is more complex in that those who have had to wait for more than six months for a decision on their application may apply, and are normally granted, permission to work. However, if an asylum

46 Travis, A., "Hospital in Row on Immigrant Checks", *Guardian*, 13 March 1996, p. 7.

47 Even the Secretary of State for Employment and Education expressed the view that "[t]here is a danger that employers will concentrate checks on prospective employees whom they see as a risk, if not simply exclude them from consideration for the job. Either way there shall be racial discrimination". H.C. Hansard, Vol. 268, Col. 767, 19 Feb. 1996.

48 H.C. Hansard, Vol. 272, Col. 545, 22 Feb. 1996.

49 Supperstone, *op. cit. supra* n. 35, p. 488.

50 *Ibid.*

seeker wishes to appeal against a negative decision, the Standard Acknowledgement Letter (SAL), which is evidence of the right to work, has to be returned. The Home Office has only granted permission to work in a single such case since 1986, although until 1996, asylum seekers were eligible for social security benefits.[51] Despite the removal in 1996 of the entitlement to benefits from all but port asylum seekers, the Home Office stated, in a policy statement issued in November 1996,[52] that permission to work would not normally be granted, even if an appeal against a negative decision was lodged before permission to work had been granted. This statement affected not only those who applied for permission to work before the expiry of six months from the date of their application for asylum, but also those who had not previously applied for permission to work since they were receiving welfare benefit. The Home Office position was thus that asylum seekers, who lost their entitlement to benefits as a result of the 1996 legislation, should not be given special consideration when it considered whether or not to grant permission to work. The policy of granting permission to work after six months was originally initiated to prevent hardship caused by delays in processing applications. Whilst the policy itself had not changed the Home Office letter stated:

> The situation since 1986 has, of course changed considerably and a substantial number of asylum applications are now being determined well within six months. The recent package of asylum measures is designed to ensure that the number of applications determined within six months continues to increase and that the incentive for failed asylum seekers to spin out the appeals process is removed. We regard it as inappropriate to grant permission to work to those whose asylum applications have been refused, solely to enable them to pursue, and possibly spin out, an appeal, particularly as so few will ultimately be recognised as refugees.[53]

However, this policy was recently declared unlawful by the High Court in *ex parte Jammeh* in an application on behalf of four asylum seekers who had been refused permission to work, while awaiting a hearing on their appeal against refusal of asylum. Owen J accepted the argument that the destitution which would result from denial of social security benefits and permission to

---

51 *R. v. Secretary of State for the Home Department ex p. Jammeh and Others*, judgment of 31 July 1997. See also *Times Law Report*, 11 Sept. 1997.

52 Referred to *ibid.*, p. 12 of the judgment.

53 *Ibid.*, p. 12.

work would inevitably interfere with an asylum seeker's right to pursue an appeal.[54] He declared that the Home Office policy meant that "each applicant was deprived of the chance of relieving his destitution and providing himself with the finances which would enable him properly to pursue his appeal with the result that thereby, indirectly, he would be driven out of the country". The difficulties for asylum seekers trying to find work are compounded since they may be refused permission to work for failure to attend an interview or if they are deemed to be "employing delaying tactics".[55]

Following this High Court judgment in July 1997, the Home Office has issued instructions to Asylum Division staff that permission to work should normally be granted to asylum appellants. However, this concession does not affect the six month rule and the Home Office has stressed that

> as with asylum applicants, the granting of permission to work to asylum appellants is a concession and not an automatic right. Permission to work may still be withheld where a person has access to funds that would enable them to pursue an appeal without the need to take employment.[56]

The Home Office has also confirmed that the concession does not apply to dependants of asylum seekers. Meanwhile, in view of the wide discretion vested in immigration officers under the Home Office guidelines and the inevitable delays in implementation of changes, asylum seekers may have to wait for a considerable time before they can obtain documentation which employers may rely on under the 1996 Act. The situation is not helped by the refusal of the Home Office to accept that its policy is unlawful[57] and this may cloud the judgment of officials when exercising discretion. Furthermore, the chances of gaining employment diminish the longer the asylum seeker remains unemployed because employers are unlikely to have confidence in the reliability of any individual who has no track record of employment.[58]

---

54 *Ibid.*, p. 15.

55 This expression was adopted from a KPMG Peat Marwick report, *Review of Asylum Appeal Procedure*, submitted to the Home Office in Dec. 1994. The relevant paragraphs of the report are quoted in *ex p. Jammeh, supra* n. 51, at p. 6.

56 Immigration and Nationality Directorate letter to Refugee Council, 28 Aug. 1997.

57 The Home Office has served notice of appeal against the judgment of Owen J on the issue of the lawfulness of the Secretary of State's 1996 policy.

58 This was recognised by Owen J, *ibid.*, p. 18.

Employer Sanctions and Civil Liberties

The threat to civil liberties inherent in the 1996 Act was highlighted on several occasions during the parliamentary debates of the Bill. The details of implementation of the legislation are left very much under the control of the Home Secretary. This tendency to leave immigration decisions in the hands of the executive has been the hallmark of immigration legislation since the 1971 Act.[59] The result has been a succession of Statements of Changes in Immigration Rules which impose tighter controls and vest immigration officials with ever greater discretion. The 1996 Act goes further still, as the then MP for Newcastle-upon-Tyne, Doug Henderson, pointed out:

> It is an enabling Bill that does not specify how it will impact on the manner in which applications for political asylum are dealt with and how employers' checks are made .... Three crucial parts of the Bill are left for the Secretary of State to introduce by order. The Bill empowers him to determine which categories of immigrant are covered by clause 8, to classify which documents may be used to check whether someone is legally able to work and to decide which category is excluded from housing entitlement.[60]

The 1996 Act imposes "immigration functions" on employers legitimately carrying out their business. There is a risk employers will become "yet another arm of the state, involving them in the policing of fellow members of the community and undermining the delicate balance between the freedom of the individual and the power of the big state".[61]

A further threat to civil liberties is that, whereas under the previous legislation employers could be prosecuted if they knowingly committed offences, such as harbouring a person whom they knew or believed was not entitled to work in the country because of their immigration status, under Section 8 an employer is criminally liable for entering unknowingly into a

59 Some lawyers have argued further that the foundations for extensive executive control were established with the first controls on immigration in the UK introduced under the Aliens Act 1905. See Evans, J.M., *Immigration Law* (Modern Legal Studies, Sweet and Maxwell, 2nd edn, 1983) p. 6; chapter 1 of this book by Dallal Stevens.

60 H.C. Hansard, Vol. 272, Col. 391, 21 Feb. 1996.

61 *Ibid.*, Col. 549, 22 Feb. 1996. Similar issues were raised by a number of groups in evidence to the Glidewell Panel, see e.g., Charter '88 *op. cit. supra* n. 6, pp. xix–xx.

contract with individuals who are not entitled to work in the country.[62]

So far, there has been no legal challenge to these aspects of the Act in the UK. The debate concerning Section 8 has tended to be a reaction to the then government's contention that controls are necessary to foster good race relations. In response to similar legislation in the USA, it has been argued, with some success, that the courts ought to consider the constitutionality of such legislation and weigh the right of the individual to work against the obligation of the State to preserve jobs for its citizens.[63] However, the absence in the UK of a Bill of Rights or constitutional right to work makes any similar challenge on these grounds impossible.

It has also been argued that employer sanctions are contrary to the terms of the 1990 International Convention on Migrant Workers.[64] Although the Convention, which has yet to enter into force and has not been signed by the UK, preserves the right of States to determine their immigration policies, it is argued that such sovereign power must be exercised in accordance with the spirit of the Convention which requires States to protect the rights of migrant workers.[65]

The haste with which the UK legislation was passed, in the face of opposition and the experience of operation of similar legislation in other jurisdictions, indicates the need for lawyers in the UK to consider seriously its implications with respect to obligations under the Race Relations Act 1976. A worker denied access to employment as a result of Section 8 has no recourse to damages unless he or she can prove an infringement of the Race Relations Act 1976. This is unlikely to be of much assistance because the refusal of employment may be due to the employer's misunderstanding of his immigration status rather than to direct or indirect discrimination.[66] Provided the employer requests documentation from all job applicants, refusal of an

62 *Ibid.*, Col. 457, 21 Feb. 1996.

63 Scarpalanda, M.A., "The Paradox of a Title: Discrimination within the Anti-discrimination Provisions of the Immigration Reform and Control Act of 1986", (1988) *Wisconsin Law Review*, at 1043.

64 International Convention on the Protection of the Rights of all Migrant Workers and Members of their Families, 1990, UN Doc. A/RES/45/158, adopted Dec. 1990. See also Plender, R., ed., *Basic Documemts on International Migration Law* (Kluwer, 2nd edn, 1997).

65 Kitamura, Y., "Recent developments in Japanese Immigration Policy and the United Nations Convention on Migrant Workers", (1990) 1 *University of British Columbia Law Review*, 113.

66 Race Relations Act 1976, S.1.

offer of employment on the grounds that the documentation does not clearly fall within the categories set out in the Home Office guidance[67] or that further investigation into an individual applicant's status would cause unnecessary delay would be justifiable under the Race Relation Act.[68] In such a situation an employee "whether seeking employment lawfully or not" is likely to drift into low paid employment where the employer asks no questions. An illegal worker is unlikely to declare himself or leave the country as a result of the legislation. He is more likely to arrange for false documentation and fall prey to immigration racketeers.[69]

It was conceded by the opposition in the parliamentary debates that immigration racketeering is a problem. However, the then Conservative government refused to accept amendments to the legislation intended to regulate the activities of immigration advisors. Instead, the imposition of employer sanctions under the 1996 Act means that asylum seekers who are already disadvantaged in the labour market by the rule which prohibits them from taking employment within six months of entry and by the fact that their qualifications are seldom recognised, face discrimination by even the most well-intentioned employers. Research by the CRE and the Refugee Council six months after implementation of the 1996 Act indicates that, although indigenous ethnic minority workers are not ostensibly suffering direct discrimination as a result of Section 8, asylum seekers are being denied employment, mainly because of their foreign accents.[70] The situation is exacerbated by the practice of a number of public sector employers of including a statement in their job descriptions which places the onus on the applicant to prove entitlement to work for the purposes of the 1996 Act.[71] Such practices

67 *Supra* n. 24.

68 *Ibid.*, S.1(b)3. See also Bourn, C. and Whitmore, J., *Anti-Discrimination Law in Britain* (Sweet and Maxwell, 1996) ch. 2.

69 Similar legislative efforts to contain and/or deter the perceived problems of illegal working have led to more oppressive working conditions and social conditions in the USA. See e.g. H.C. Hansard, Vol. 272, Cols 396–97, 21 Feb. 1996.

70 Commission for Racial Equality, Joint Council for the Welfare of Immigrants and Refugee Council, draft report (forthcoming).

71 The CRE research found, for example, that a BBC advertisement on the internet included a requirement of the production of appropriate proof of entitlement to work. York University in a recent job advertisement included a statement issued by the personnel department requiring new members of staff to produce evidence that they are legally entitled to work in the UK. This is despite the fact that universities often obtain work permits for staff recruited from outside the UK.

are likely to deter asylum seekers awaiting official confirmation of their right to work, which may take months to process due to the backlog of applications.

The Labour government which came to power in May 1997 has made some concessions, for example, by lifting the threat of deportation with which nearly 1,000 Zaïreans in London were faced.[72] However, it has resisted pressure to grant a general amnesty to asylum seekers who have been caught up in the backlog of 50,000 cases awaiting decisions.[73] Despite its post-election promises to repeal a number of immigration and asylum measures introduced by the previous government,[74] there was very little indication at the autumn Labour party conference that the present government will repeal this legislation. A number of committees has been set up to investigate various aspects of the legislation but the strategy for change appears to be long term.

Conclusion

Intrusion into a legitimate sphere of activity such as employment, and imposition of criminal sanctions to eliminate a perceived rather than real problem, provides a further model for encroachment on civil liberties. The combination of measures in the 1996 Act deprive one of the most vulnerable groups in society, that is asylum seekers, of opportunities to work and use their skills to better themselves and to contribute to the host society. This is indefensible in a democracy.

The government must act speedily to repeal Section 8 to remove the confusion which has arisen regarding its implementation by employers and any further long term impact on asylum seekers and ethnic minorities. Such a repeal must be seen as part of a package of reforms to reinstate income support for asylum seekers and to grant permission to work in all cases pending determination of the application, in order to dispel fears that asylum seekers are seeking to enter the UK to take advantage of social security provisions.

---

72 Travis, A., "Straw Changes Asylum Policy", *Guardian*, 17 May 1997, p. 18. A similar policy was adopted towards asylum seekers from Sierra Leone from 1 July 1997.

73 "Asylum Seekers' Amnesty Refused", News in Brief, *Times*, 27 Sept. 1997.

74 Bennetto, J., "Straw to Abandon Tory Asylum Laws", *Independent*, 29 May 1997.

Bibliography

1990 Trust, *Without Foundation: Investigating the Implications of the Asylum and Immigration Bill on Britain's Black Community* (1995).

Bourn, C. and Whitmore, J., *Anti-Discrimination Law in Britain* (Sweet and Maxwell, 1996).

Calavita, K., "The Contradictions of Immigration Lawmaking: The Immigration Reform and Control Act of 1986", (1989) 11 *Law and Policy*, pp. 18–47.

Carter, R. *et al.*, "The 1951–55 Conservative Government and the Racialisation of Black Immigration" in *Inside Babylon*, W. James and C. Harris, eds (Verso, 1993), pp. 55–72.

Cruz, A., *Shifting Responsibility: Carriers Liability in the Member States of the European Union and America* (Trentham Books, 1995).

Evans, J.M., *Immigration Law* (Modern Legal Studies, Sweet and Maxwell, 2nd edn, 1983).

Feller, E., "Carrier Sanctions and International Law", (1989) 1 I.J.Ref.L. 48–66.

Fryer, P., *Staying Power: The History of Black People in Britain* (Pluto Press, 1984).

Glidewell Panel, *Report from an Independent Enquiry into the Implications and Effects of the Asylum and Immigration Bill 1995 and Related Social Security Measures*, 16 April 1996.

Gordon, P., *Policing Immigration: Britain's Internal Controls* (Pluto Press, 1985).

Guild, E., *The Developing Immigration and Asylum Policies of the European Union* (Kluwer, 1996).

Guild, E., *Dublin Convention Comes of Age*, Justice in Europe, p. 3, issue 2, 1997.

Home Office Consultation Paper, *Compliance Cost Assessment*, Immigration and Nationality Department, Nov. 1995.

Home Office Consultation Paper, *Prevention of Illegal Working*, Immigration and Nationality Department, Nov. 1995.

Home Office, *Asylum and Immigration Act 1996 – Section 8: Prevention of Illegal Working – Guidance for Employers*, Immigration and Nationality Directorate, Dec. 1996.

Kitamura, Y., "Recent developments in Japanese Immigration Policy and the United Nations Convention on Migrant Workers", (1990) 1 *University of British Columbia Law Review*, 113.

MacDonald, I., and Blake, N., *Macdonald's Immigration Law and Practice* (Butterworths, 4th edn, 1995).

Mallet, N., "Deterring Asylum Seekers: German and Danish Law on Political Asylum, Parts I and II", *Immigration and Nationality Law and Practice*, Vol. 5, No. 4, 1991 and Vol. 6, No. 1, 1992.

Nicholson, F., "The Immigration (Carriers' Liability) Act 1987: Privatising Immigration Functions at the Expense of International Obligations" (1997) 46 I.C.L.Q. 592.

Refugee Council, *The State of Asylum: A Critique of Asylum Policy in the UK*, March 1996.

Refugee Council, *The Education, Training and Employment of Asylum Seekers and Refugees*, Factfiles Nos 1, 2, 3, 7 and 8, Nov. 1996.

Richmond, A.H., *Global Apartheid, Refugees, Racism, and the New World Order* (Oxford University Press, 1994).

Scarpalanda, M.A., "The Paradox of Title: Discrimination within the anti-discrimination provisions of the Immigration Reform and Control Act of 1986" (1988) Wisconsin Law Review, 1043.

Shah, P., "Access to Legal Assistance for Asylum-Seekers" (1995) 9 I.N.L.P. No. 2, 55.

Shah, R., "Border Controls Revisited" (1995) N.L.J. 283.

Supperstone, M., and O'Dempsey, D., *Immigration Law and Practice* (FT Law and Tax Practitioner Series, 4th edn, 1996).

18 Asylum Seekers' Rights to Housing: New Recipients of the Old Poor Law

CAROLINE HUNTER

Asylum seekers, almost by definition, arrive in this country without any means of support, so that they are unable to provide shelter for themselves. They may occasionally have friends or relatives who can provide shelter for a short period. Some asylum seekers have a small amount of money with which they can provide hotel accommodation for themselves, but again this is usually only a short term option. Accordingly many asylum seekers are reliant on state assistance to provide housing or the income with which to pay for housing immediately on arrival in the United Kingdom or soon thereafter. This reliance continues when and if the claim is accepted and the asylum seeker officially becomes a refugee.

This chapter examines the withdrawal of housing rights from asylum seekers over the last four years, the attitudes of the courts to this withdrawal and the practical consequences of Government policies. All this must be seen in the context of the clear need for those fleeing persecution abroad for a stable and secure home, a need which has increasingly been denied.[1]

Access to Housing in England and Wales[2]

Realistically, the options for asylum seekers in need of housing are few. Rented housing may be sought either from providers of "social housing", i.e. local authorities or housing associations, or in the private rented sector.

---

1 On this latter issue see, more generally, chapter 11 of this book by C.J. Harvey.

2 Although the law makes no geographical distinctions, it should be noted that the vast majority of asylum seekers are to be found in London, and that it is the London boroughs which have almost exclusively been concerned with the problems outlined in this chapter.

Social Housing

The biggest providers of social rented housing are local authorities. Access to their stock may be achieved either through allocation from a waiting list or as a homeless person. Given the urgency of their situation and inability to wait most asylum seekers have, in the past, sought assistance through the homeless persons legislation, rather than through the waiting list.

Access to housing associations may also be routed through local authorities, who may have nomination rights and agreements. Some associations also operate their own waiting lists, and a number have offered specific assistance to refugees. Most are not, however, equipped to deal with the immediate needs of asylum seekers.

Homeless Persons

Until amendment in 1993 and repeal in 1996 (see below) the legislative provisions for homeless persons[3] did not differentiate on the basis of an applicant's immigration status. Although the courts held that only those legally in the country could make an application under Part III of the 1985 Act,[4] this clearly did not affect those who had made asylum claims since they did have legal status in this country.

Under Part III of the Housing Act 1985 authorities had to decide if applicants were homeless, in priority need, and whether applicants were intentionally homeless. Asylum seekers would generally have no difficulty as to the first and third of these, since they had no accommodation in this country and thus were homeless.[5] Nor would it have been reasonable for them to continue to occupy accommodation in the country from which they had fled and thus they were not intentionally homeless.[6] All those with children or who were pregnant would fall within the definition of priority need, as would those single people who were "vulnerable" due to a physical illness or handicap or mental illness.[7] The duties to those who were not in priority need were limited simply to providing advice and assistance. For those who were

3 The Housing (Homeless Persons) Act 1977, and subsequently the Housing Act 1985, Part III.

4 *London Borough of Tower Hamlets v. Secretary of State for the Environment* [1993] Q.B.D. 632.

5 See Housing Act 1985, s. 58.

6 See Housing Act 1985, s. 60.

7 See Housing Act 1985, s. 59.

in priority need, however, the duties were much greater.

Once unintentional homelessness and priority need were established, the local authority would be under a duty to ensure that accommodation was made available to the applicant.[8] Authorities generally provided such accommodation from their own stock, although they were not legally required to do so, but often this would mean a period in less secure, temporary accommodation until a permanent offer was secured. The use of "staged" accommodation was recognised by the courts as lawful, and meant that in the case of asylum seekers an offer of permanent accommodation could await the outcome of the asylum claim.

Private Rented Accommodation

Access to private rented accommodation is clearly far less legally constrained, although the practicalities of finding accommodation and paying for it can represent difficult hurdles for an asylum seeker to surmount. Where asylum seekers have found private rented accommodation it has tended to be of a very low quality, often of the bed and breakfast variety.[9]

Asylum and Immigration Appeals Act 1993

The first inroads to be made into the rights of asylum seekers to local authority housing through the homelessness route came with the Asylum and Immigration Appeals Act 1993. The Act made two changes to the rights of asylum seekers. First, there was no duty under the Housing Act 1985, Part III, to secure accommodation for an asylum seeker if "he has or has available for his occupation any accommodation *however temporary*, which it would be reasonable for him to occupy".[10] The effect of this provision was to disapply earlier law which had suggested that even though an applicant literally had accommodation it should in any event be disregarded because of its temporary nature, for instance, in the case of women's refuges.[11] This distinction between "settled" and "temporary" accommodation was itself later undermined by the

8 See Housing Act 1985, s. 65.

9 See Carter, M., *Out of Sight: London's Continuing B & B Crisis* (South Bank University, 1995).

10 Asylum and Immigration Appeals Act 1993, s. 4(1)(b) (emphasis added).

11 *R. v. London Borough of Ealing, ex p. Sidhu* [1992] 2 H.L.R. 45.

House of Lords in *R. v. London Borough of Brent, ex parte Awua*,[12] so that the only difference between the position of asylum seekers and other homeless persons could be said to be that there was no duty towards asylum seekers when they were "threatened with homelessness" within the 28-day period set out in the Housing Act 1985, s. 58(4).[13] The accommodation did, however, have to be reasonable for the applicant to continue to occupy. This led to the Code of Guidance issued by the Department of the Environment suggesting[14] that where a family had been initially accommodated in emergency accommodation, such as a large single room or an assembly hall shared by a number of other families, this would not relieve an authority of its duty to secure accommodation.

Another new element in this provision was the reference to accommodation which the asylum seeker "has available". This imported for the first time consideration not just of the accommodation which the asylum seeker was actually occupying, but also that which he could occupy. Thus the revised Code of Guidance[15] stated at paragraph 16.11:

> If, for example, an applicant had been given notice to terminate the tenancy of a flat, but there were other similar flats vacant and to let in the area, that might constitute "accommodation available for his occupation".

The second change introduced by the 1993 Act went to the nature of the duty towards those who were homeless (as defined), in priority need and unintentionally homeless. The duty was reduced to one of provision of accommodation only while the asylum application was decided and the right was therefore only to "temporary" accommodation.[16] As has been pointed out above, this did not represent a great change in housing practice since many authorities would use their right to discharge their duty in stages to await the outcome of the asylum application. Furthermore, the decision of the House of Lords in the *Awua* case,[17] effectively put non-asylum seekers on the same footing, since the duty under the 1985 Act, Part III, was held to be satisfied in all cases by the provision of temporary accommodation, provided

12 *R. v. London Borough of Brent, ex parte Awua* [1996] 1 A.C. 55.

13 See *R. v. Kensington and Chelsea Royal Borough Council, ex p. Korneva* [1996] 29 H.L.R. 709 at 714.

14 At para. 16.14.

15 Under the Housing Act 1985, s. 71, local authorities must have regard to the Code.

16 Asylum and Immigration Appeals Act 1993, s.4(3).

17 *Supra*, n. 12.

it was of a duration of more than 28 days.

The 1993 Act did not, however, directly alter the requirement that in discharging their duty towards a homeless person an authority must secure "suitable accommodation".[18] Yet some authorities were of that view and sought to argue that the more limited duty to provide "temporary accommodation" under the 1993 Act no longer imported a duty that the accommodation was "suitable". This approach was roundly rejected by the Court of Appeal in *R. v. Kensington and Chelsea R.B.C., ex parte Korneva.*[19] The authority accepted a duty towards Ms Korneva, who was an asylum seeker, in August 1995. She was eventually placed in a damp flat with a single bedsitting room. Due to the health problems of both Ms Korneva and her son, it was conceded by the authority that the flat was not "suitable" for her. Nevertheless, they sought to maintain that the flat was an adequate discharge of their duty under the 1993 Act. However, as Simon Brown LJ concluded "the fact that [the accommodation] is temporary only does not mean that there is not a need for suitable accommodation ...".[20] The Court concluded therefore that asylum seekers were in all other ways to be dealt with in the same way as other homeless applicants.

Thus, on the implementation of the 1993 Act, the position is reached that asylum seekers will either have to fend for themselves in the private rented sector or may, if in priority need, obtain help from their local housing authority, but this can only secure the provision of temporary, albeit suitable, accommodation.

Paying for Housing

Any access to housing will generally be dependent on the ability to pay for it. This is true whether the applicant seeks social or private rented housing. Asylum seekers are not generally entitled to work at least for the first six months after their arrival, and are thus usually dependent on welfare benefits in order to pay for their accommodation. Until 1996, asylum seekers were not excluded from benefits but were dealt with under special provisions dealing with "urgent cases" which entitled them to income support at 90 per cent of the usual rate. They were also entitled to housing benefit to cover their rental payments.

18 See Housing Act 1985, s. 65(2).

19 *Supra* n. 13.

20 *ex p. Korneva, supra* n. 13 at p. 714.

In 1995, however, the Government announced that it intended to change the Regulations relating to social security payments to asylum seekers and effectively withdraw all benefits from in-country applicants for asylum. From the implementation of the Regulations only asylum seekers who made "port applications"[21] were eligible for income-related benefits. Furthermore, the Regulations withdrew benefits to all those whose asylum claims were rejected but who were pursuing an appeal. The Social Security (Persons from Abroad) Miscellaneous Amendment Regulations[22] (the Regulations) came into force on 5 February 1996. Thus:

> a significant number of genuine asylum seekers [found] themselves faced with a bleak choice; whether to remain here destitute and homeless until their claims [were] finally determined or whether instead to abandon their claims and return to face the very persecution they have fled.[23]

There were two responses to this. First, there was a charitable response which sought to provide immediate emergency accommodation through setting up hostels and using church halls and also to provide funds to asylum seekers.[24] Second, a legal challenge was mounted. This challenge, which was brought by the Joint Council for the Welfare of Immigrants (JCWI), was made to the lawfulness of the Regulations on behalf of an asylum seeker who was deprived of benefits by the legislation. The application was dismissed at first instance, but was heard by the Court of Appeal in May 1996. This was to be the first of a number of decisions in which the courts effectively struck down or undermined the government's policy towards asylum seekers.

The challenge which succeeded in the *JCWI* case[25] was based on the argument that the Regulations were in conflict with the Asylum and Immigration Appeals Act 1993, which while in some respects reducing the rights of asylum seekers (see above in relation to homelessness), did for the first time set out the rights of asylum seekers to remain in this country pending

21 On "port" and "in-country" applications see more generally chapter 3 of this book by Richard Dunstan.

22 S.I. 1996 No. 30.

23 *R. v. Secretary of State for Social Security, ex p. JCWI; R. v. Secretary of State for the Environment, ex p. B* [1996] 4 All E.R. 385, C.A., per Simon Brown LJ at p. 393a–b.

24 See Refugee Council, *Welcome to the UK: The Impact of the Removal of Benefits from Asylum Seekers*, (1996) ch. 4.

25 *Supra* n. 23.

the decision on their application and appeal. The majority of the Court of Appeal concluded that these rights were rendered nugatory by the Regulations; "[e]ither that or the Regulations necessarily contemplate for some a life so destitute that to my mind no civilised nation can tolerate it".[26] The Regulations altered the benefit system so drastically, so as not merely to prejudice but, on occasion, to defeat the statutory right of asylum seekers to claim refugee status.

In reaching this decision reference was made to a case which is now nearly 200 years old, and concerned access of foreigners to the then poor law. In *R. v. Inhabitants of Eastbourne*[27] Lord Ellenborough said:

> As to there being no obligation for maintaining poor foreigners before the statutes ascertaining the different methods of acquiring settlements, the law of humanity, which is anterior to all positive laws, obliges us to afford them relief, to save them from starving.

Thus, so basic were the human rights involved here, that it was not even necessary to refer to the 1950 European Convention on Human Rights; the common law principle of the "law of humanity" would suffice.

Priority Need of Destitute Asylum Seekers

An immediate question which arose out of the loss of benefits to asylum seekers was whether they were thereby rendered in priority need for the purposes of the Housing Act 1985, Part III, notwithstanding that they did not fall into the priority need categories on any other basis (see above), but simply due to their now destitute position. The attitude of local authorities, fearing an overwhelming flood of applicants, was to reject any such argument. Several challenges were mounted to the refusal of local authorities to accept that single destitute asylum seekers were in priority need. The applications were dismissed at first instance, but were considered by the same Court of Appeal which heard the *JCWI* case.

The Court, this time unanimously, allowed the appeals by the asylum seekers.[28] The cases turned on the interpretation of section 59(1)(c) of the Housing Act 1985 which provided that the definition of those in priority need includes:

---

26 *Ibid.* p.401e–f.

27 (1803) 4 East 103 at p. 107.

28 *R. v. Kensington and Chelsea Royal Borough Council, ex p. Kihara* [1996] 29 H.L.R. 147, C.A.

> a person who is vulnerable as a result of old age, mental illness or handicap or physical disability or other special reason or with whom such a person resides or might reasonably be expected to reside.

It was argued that the applicants should be considered vulnerable as a result of "other special reason" viz. their destitution. The Court of Appeal rejected a contention made by the local authorities that "other special reason" was limited to physical or mental characteristics of the applicant; it was more wide-ranging than that. The word "special" in the subsection "indicates that the difficulties faced by the applicant are of an unusual degree of gravity and are such as to differentiate the applicant from other homeless persons".[29]

Given this approach to the meaning of vulnerability, the Court then considered whether the particular applicants fell within this meaning.

> I can take the circumstances of Miss Araya as an example. She has no capital. She has no income. She is prohibited from obtaining employment and therefore has no opportunity of earning any money. She has no family or friends in this country. ... She has no knowledge of the English language. ... She is homeless. Her situation is certainly not unique, but her vulnerability results from circumstances which mark her out from the great majority of homeless people.[30]

Thus, destitute asylum seekers were owed a duty under the Housing Act 1985, Part III (as limited by the Asylum and Immigration Act 1993), and the authorities were bound to house such an asylum seeker, even though he or she had no means of paying for the accommodation.[31]

Yet what accommodation would be available? Even if provided free of charge, unfurnished accommodation has to be furnished, bedding and crockery need to be provided and utilities have to be paid for. The story of Fatna and Musa,[32] who were granted the tenancy of a two-bedroomed flat by a London Borough illustrates the difficulties:

> The flat was completely unfurnished, and did not possess any cooking facilities. The local authority refused further assistance providing these items. The couple had insufficient clothing or blankets, and Fatna was five months pregnant at the point of moving into the accommodation. The Karibu [Refugee] Centre supplied

29 *Ibid.*, per Neill LJ at p. 158.

30 *Ibid.*, at p. 159.

31 *Ex p. JCWI*, *supra* n. 23 per Simon Brown LJ at p. 395e.

32 Refugee Council, *Just Existence: A Report on the Lives of Asylum Seekers who have lost Entitlements to Benefits in the UK* (1997) at p. 34.

them with a small cooking stove, and they slept on blankets on the bare floor.

For those with no money, housing options are very limited. As pointed out by Mary Carter, "private landlords require deposits and rent in advance, housing associations and hostels are unlikely to accept anyone who is unable to pay the rent".[33] She continued by quoting a hostel manager who related the dilemma faced by an Ethiopian woman:

> This woman had received a negative decision on her asylum application in July 1985. Her appeal was heard in January but no decision had been made by 5 February so she was entitled to transitional protection when the benefit changes came into force.
>
> She was successfully resettled from the hostel into a housing association property on 26 February, but had to make a new claim for benefits in which she was asked when her appeal was heard. On 8 March she was told by social security that her appeal had failed in February and she was no longer entitled to benefits. She is now faced with the dilemma of informing her hew landlord that she is no longer entitled to housing benefit and may lose her accommodation as a result.

So even where the authority was under a duty to secure accommodation under the 1985 Act this led to very limited, insecure and poor quality housing. Although the outcome in the two Court of Appeal cases provided some respite for applicants, it was only temporary as the government sought to enforce the policy, through legislation.

Asylum and Immigration Act 1996

In the *JCWI* case Simon Brown LJ found that only primary legislation could

33 Carter, M., *Poverty and Prejudice: A preliminary report on the withdrawal of benefit entitlement and the impact of the Asylum and Immigration Bill* (Commission for Racial Equality and Refugee Council, 1996) at p. 18. See also the Housing Corporation Circular, "Lettings to Certain Persons from Abroad" (R3–04/97) issued in Jan. 1997, which states at para. 3.5: "Registered social landlords should carefully consider the effect on their financial position if they house applicants who do not have the means to pay their rent and service charges. In particular, they will wish to satisfy themselves that applicants from abroad, who are not eligible for housing benefit or other forms of income support, have adequate resources to pay the rent and service charges."

achieve the "sorry state of affairs" contemplated by the Regulations, and maintained that "Parliament cannot have intended a significant number of genuine asylum seekers to be impaled on the horns of so intolerable a dilemma: the need either to abandon their claims to refugee status or alternatively to maintain them as best they can but in a state of utter destitution". At the time of the defeat on the Regulations, the Asylum and Immigration Bill 1996 was already before parliament and the government was enabled to use this to enact the necessary primary legislation.

There are two relevant sections in the 1996 Act. Section 11 gave the Secretary of State power to exclude asylum seekers from income-related benefits, and also amended the Regulations accordingly. Thus, a month after being thwarted by the Court of Appeal,[34] the government achieved their primary aim of removing benefit rights to in-country asylum seekers. The second relevant section is Section 9 which deals with rights under the Housing Act 1985, Part III. The provision is very broadly drawn, effectively preventing access to local authority housing stock whether as a homeless person or under waiting list provisions to all persons subject to immigration control, unless they are reincluded by the Regulations. Under the relevant Regulations,[35] while port applicants were reincluded and thus permitted to make applications as homeless, in-country asylum applicants were not.

These Regulations came into force on 19 August 1996. They gave rise to a particular difficulty for applicants who had applied as homeless prior to that date, but in relation to whom the authority had not made a final decision. Were authorities entitled simply to say in relation to such applicants that, given the Regulations, there was no further duty towards them? This was certainly the view taken by some authorities, and they took steps immediately to evict some asylum seekers from the temporary accommodation in which they had been placed.

The housing charity, Shelter, and the British Refugee Council moved quickly and sought a ruling as to the proper interpretation of the Act in relation to those asylum seekers who had already made applications to local authorities as homeless. In a judgment given on 23 August, Mr Justice Carnwarth held that the effect of Section 9(2) of the 1996 Act was that

34 The Court of Appeal decision was given on 21 June, the Act came into force on 24 July.

35 Housing Accommodation and Homelessness (Persons subject to Immigration Control) Order 1996, S.I. 1996 No. 1982.

> those affected are not to be taken as having the qualifications necessary to entitle them to any form of assistance under the [1985] Act. That does not mean that whatever rights they might have acquired before 19 August are peremptorily and automatically removed on that day. Rather it affects the way the authority deal with that matter as and when it falls to be reconsidered by them.[36]

Thus, for those to whom the authority has already recognised a full duty, but for whom the duty had been discharged by finding accommodation in the private rented sector, the asylum seeker would have security of tenure, although this would be "obviously precarious if he cannot pay the rent".[37] However, should the accommodation be lost, and a further application made at that point, the asylum seeker would have no further rights under the 1985 Act.

For those whose applications had not been determined the situation was even more precarious. The authority was to apply the Regulations in making the decision, and the applicant was not eligible for any assistance. The judge did, however, comment that this did not give authorities carte blanche simply to terminate any temporary accommodation that was being provided while enquiries were being completed. Authorities were "under a public law duty to act reasonably, which is of particular importance when one is dealing with a need as basic as the need for a roof over one's head".[38] While the length of time to be given to each applicant was a matter for each authority, an analogy was drawn by the judge with those cases in which applicants were found to be intentionally homeless where applicants were given upwards of 14 days in temporary accommodation.

> In particular, given the extreme circumstances in which these asylum applicants now find themselves, one has to take into account the need for time for other potential routes of assistance to be examined. What I am quite clear about is that it cannot be reasonable for people to have been faced with immediate eviction on the first day of the Act, as appears to have happened in some cases here.[39]

36 *R. v. Secretary of State for the Environment, ex p. Shelter and the Refugee Council*, unreported, transcript p. 16F. The decision was later followed in *R. v. Southwark L.B.C., ex p. Bendiako, Times Law Report*, 27 March 1997 Q.B.D. In *R. v. Hacknew L.B.C., ex p. K, Times Law Report*, 17 Nov. 1997, the Court of Appeal, while broadly agreeing with Carnwath J's analysis, made it clear that the coming into force of the Act could not in itself be a ground for reconsideration once the full duty was accepted, even where the applicant was in temporary accommodation provided by the authority itself.

37 *Ibid.*, p. 17E.

38 *Ibid.*, p. 18A.

39 *Ibid.*, p. 18F–G.

Housing Act 1996

To complete the legislative picture, the Housing Act 1985, Part III and the housing provisions of the Asylum and Immigration Appeals Act 1993 were repealed and replaced by the Housing Act 1996, Part VII. Equivalent provisions are made for homeless asylum seekers in Sections 185 and 186 of the 1996 Act and the Regulations made under them.[40] The Act also made new provision in Part VI for the regulation of access to local authority housing through the waiting list. Asylum seekers are excluded altogether from access through this route.[41]

Continuing Duties Under Other Legislation

Thus, by August 1996 the government had reached the position that all direct state aid towards housing assistance, whether in the form of housing itself or in payment of rent had been withdrawn from in-country asylum seekers. By this stage also, the charitable efforts to provide practical help were drawing to an end.[42]

This did not mean, however, the withdrawal of the State entirely from any responsibility for in-country asylum seekers. The government recognised from the outset that those asylum seekers with children, or indeed children who arrived on their own and claimed asylum, would still be owed duties under the Children Act 1989.[43] Section 20 of this Act places duties on local social services authorities to

> provide accommodation for any child in need within their area as a result of –
> (a) there being no person who has parental responsibility for him;
> (b) his being lost or having been abandoned; or
> (c) the person who has been caring for him being prevented (whether or not permanently, and for whatever reason) from providing him with suitable accommodation or care.

40 See Homeless Regulations 1996, S.I. 1996 No. 2754. These came into force on 20 Jan. 1997.

41 See Housing Act 1996, s.161 and Allocation of Housing Regulations 1996, S.I. 1996 No. 2753. These provisions came into force on 1 April 1997.

42 Affidavit of Kate Smart of the Refugee Council to the Court in *R. v. Hammersmith and Fulham L.B.C., ex p. M (and other cases), Times Law Report*, 10 Oct. 1996, quoted in the judgment of Collins J.

43 See the Social Security Committee, First Report, Session 1995–96, para. 43.

A more general duty is imposed by Section 17 which requires authorities "to safeguard and promote the welfare of children within their area who are in need and so far as is consistent with that duty to promote the upbringing of such children by their families". While only a few asylum seekers have children (or are children themselves), providing for these children has placed a large burden of social services authorities which has only been partially offset by an increased grant from the government. In any event social services authorities are simply not geared up to provide either income maintenance or housing for families. Typically they seek to provide assistance for children through residential or foster homes. Where children arrive with their parents, it is particularly inappropriate to split the family and only provide assistance for the children. So, although the legislation provides some form of safety net where children are concerned, it is one which is heavily flawed.

The vast majority of asylum seekers falls outside this safety net, however, and for them a different line of legal attack was mounted. This was based on the National Assistance Act 1948, which replaced the existing poor law.[44] The 1996 Act did not mention these provisions, and did not seek to exclude asylum seekers from their benefits. The question, therefore, was whether, properly interpreted, the 1948 Act applied to asylum seekers. Section 21 of the 1948 Act (as amended) provides that:

> (1)Subject to … this part of this Act, a local authority may with the approval of the Secretary of State, and to such an extent as he may direct, shall make arrangements for providing:
> (a) residential accommodation for persons aged 18 or over who by reason of age, illness, disability or any other circumstances are in need of care and attention which is not otherwise available to them. …
> (5) Reference in this Act to accommodation provided under this part thereof shall be construed as … including references to board and other services, amenities and requisites provided in connection with the accommodation.

Generally this provision has been used to provide assistance for the elderly and the mentally and physically handicapped, rather than those whose handicap was purely lack of means of supporting themselves. Nonetheless, a challenge against four London authorities which refused to assist destitute asylum seekers under this provision was successful at first instance in October 1996.[45] Collins

44 See National Assistance Act 1948, s. 1.

45 *R. v. Hammersmith and Fulham L.B.C., ex p. M (and other cases)*, *Times Law Report*, 10 Oct. 1996.

J again drew attention to the dilemma that the applicants were faced with, that is, either starve without a roof over their head or return to the country from which they had fled.

The authorities sought to argue that destitute asylum seekers were not in need of "care and attention" but rather in need of money. The judge found that someone who is unable to provide for himself the basic necessities of life can properly be said to be in need of care and attention. These basic needs were at least shelter, warmth and food. He stated: "The point is that they cannot get money and without it they cannot fend for themselves."[46] Again, the case of *R. v. Inhabitants of Eastbourne*[47] was referred to along with the reference in that case to the "law of humanity". Although the judge recognised that such a law, which was interpreted as the protection of fundamental human rights which included the right to life, could not prevail against the clear words of the statute, and it was therefore to be presumed that parliament had legislated in accordance with it.

The local authorities immediately appealed and judgment was given by the Court of Appeal in February 1997. In a unanimous single judgment, the Court upheld the first instance decision.[48] The Court focused on the history of the 1948 provisions in replacing the Poor Law and accordingly its significance as a "prime example of an Act which is 'always speaking' and so should be construed 'on a construction that continuously updates its wording to allow for changes since the Act was initially framed'".[49] Again, the argument that asylum seekers were not in need of care and attention was rejected:

> The fact that asylum seekers have a need for food and accommodation which would but for the statutory prohibition contained in the 1996 Act be met under other statutory provisions does not mean that they cannot qualify as having a problem which results in their needing care and attention.[50]

The words "other special circumstances" in s.21(1)(a) were to be given a broad meaning:

46 *Ibid.*, Lexis transcript.

47 *Supra*, n. 27.

48 *R. v. Hammersmith and Fulham L.B.C., ex p. M. (and other cases)*, *Times Law Report*, 19 Feb. 1997.

49 *Ibid.*, Lexis transcript, quoting Bennion, F., *Statutory Interpretation*, 2nd edn, section 288, p. 617.

50 *Ibid.*

> The poor laws had provided, inter alia, for assisting by providing work for "poor persons" having no means to maintain themselves (Halsbury's Laws, 4th edn, Vol. 33, para. 701, footnote 2), and we accept Mr Pannick's [counsel for the applicants] submission that the general approach of Parliament was that those who were in need, should not be without all assistance.

The Court held that while Section 21 did not provide a general safety net for all those lacking money and accommodation, asylum seekers could claim that after they arrive in the UK they reach a state where they do qualify because of the effect upon them of the problems under which they are labouring.

> In addition to the lack of food and accommodation is to be added their inability to speak the language, their ignorance of this country and the fact they have been subject to the stress of coming to this country in circumstances which at least involve their contending to be refugees. Inevitably the combined effect of these factors with the passage of time will produce one or more of the conditions specifically referred to in section 21(1)(a). ... In particular authorities can anticipate the deterioration which would otherwise take place in the asylum seeker's condition by providing assistance under the section. They do not need to wait until the health of the asylum seeker has been damaged.[51]

At the time of the decision London boroughs were supporting over 3,200 refugees at an estimated cost of more than £200 each per week.[52] While the government again produced some funds for authorities in response to this decision, this has led to authorities providing "meals on wheels" services and food tokens to asylum seekers (particularly as some authorities have received advice that they cannot provide assistance by way of cash payments)[53] and also to one London Borough considering "shipping" asylum seekers to a private hostel in Liverpool.[54] Local authority social service departments (which are already generally overstretched) have struggled to provide a new service outside their usual areas of responsibility. Most accommodation has been found through hostels and bed and breakfast hotels, but this frequently turns out to be very short term, so that asylum seekers are often moved on.[55] The assistance provided covers only the most basic level of support and fails to address asylum

---

51 *Ibid.*

52 *Inside Housing*, 21 Feb. 1997.

53 A view that was subsequently upheld in the courts: *R. v. Secretary of State for Health, ex p. Hammersmith and Fulham L.B.C.*, *Independent*, 15 July 1997.

54 Travis, A., "Asylum seekers sent from capital", *Guardian*, 16 May 1997.

55 Refugee Council, *Just Existence ...*, *op. cit. supra* n. 32 at p. 34.

seekers' wider needs.[56] It has had a negative effect on the ability of asylum seekers to pursue their legitimate claims for asylum in the UK effectively.[57]

Furthermore, if the asylum seeker manages to house him or herself, so that his or her main need is for food it has now been held that the 1948 Act does not apply. The "care and attention" of the Act relates to those requiring residential accommodation. Thus, a decision by Newham London Borough Council to withdraw assistance to single destitute asylum seekers unless they were already homeless or in accommodation provided by the council was upheld in *R. v. Newham L.B.C. ex parte Gorenkin*.[58] Carnwarth J acknowledged a lacuna in the Act, one he found very difficult to resolve, "because I feel instinctively that the provisions of the 1948 Act were probably not designed to cover the situation".[59] He did acknowledge, however, that "where someone has accommodation of some sort, but is otherwise wholly destitute, it is certainly possible that he may reach a stage where he is in need of care and attention" as defined in Section 21 of the 1948 Act.[60] Where a person "who is starving in a garret" needs care and attention, the point may come where the authority must consider providing residential accommodation and the food that goes with it, even while the applicant has a roof over his head. However, as Carnwarth J acknowledged: "[I]t is unfortunate that [authorities'] powers in that sort of cast are limited. ... Maybe there should be such a power,[61] but as far as I can see there is not."[62] This was an occasion where judicial inventiveness had reached its limits.

Whatever assistance is provided, if any, it is clear that the plight of in-country asylum seekers is very bleak. As one of the asylum seekers expressed in the Refugee Council report:

> This is not a life for people, it's a life for animals. I can't believe that I have a future with this life. There's not one day that is good. I'm like a dead man, only my body is moving. Every day I ask God why hasn't He taken me. This life is only for a sick man.[63]

56 It does not stretch beyond shelter and food to cover e.g. hygiene needs, *ibid.* at p. 35.

57 *Ibid.*

58 *R. v. Newham L.B.C. ex p. Gorenkin*, *Times Law Report*, 9 June 1997, Q.B.D.

59 *Ibid.*, transcript, p. 8.

60 *Ibid.*, p. 9.

61 i.e. to take over payment of rent and provide food, to an applicant who already has a roof over his head.

62 *Ibid.*

63 Refugee Council, *Just Existence ...*, *op. cit supra* n. 32 at p. 38.

While the Courts have seemingly done all they can,[64] effectively reviving the poor law for asylum seekers, it must be remembered that the poor law was often punitive, particularly for the "undeserving poor".[65] The Conservative government clearly labelled asylum seekers as the most undeserving of the poor and they are suffering accordingly. At the time of writing it remained to be seen whether the change to a Labour government which took place in May 1997 will produce any significant change for asylum seekers.[66]

---

64 And perhaps can already be seen to be withdrawing from the high point of *ex p. M.* (*supra* n. 48), in the later cases of *Gorenkin* (*supra* n. 58) and *Hammersmith and Fulham L.B.C.* (*supra* n. 53).

65 See e.g. Thane, P., *Foundations of the Welfare State* (Longman, 2nd edn, 1996) p. 34.

66 The special grants being paid to authorities have been extended to March 1998 and the prohibition o local authorities housing asylum seekers has been lifted by the Housing Accommodation and Homelessness (Persons subject to Immigration Control) (Amendment) Order 1998 (S.I. 1998 No. 139), although it is by no means clear how asylym seekers would furnish accommodation or pay rent. In the meantime the numbers being assisted in London have risen to 458 unaccompanied children, 2,673 families, and 5,011 single adults, *Inside Housing*, 8 Aug. 1997, p.6.

Bibliography

Carter, M., *Poverty and Prejudice: A Preliminary Report on the Withdrawal of Benefit Entitlement and the Impact of the Asylum and Immigration Bill* (Commission for Racial Equality and Refugee Council, 1996).

Refugee Council, *Welcome to the UK: The Impact of the Removal of Benefits from Asylum Seekers* (1996).

Refugee Council, *Just Existence: A Report on the Lives of Asylum Seekers who have Lost Entitlements to Benefits in the UK* (1997).